From
Wulfstan
to
Colston

Severing the sinews of slavery in Bristol

Mark Steeds and Roger Ball

First published in Great Britain in 2020
by Bristol Radical History Group

c/o Dreadnought Books
125 St George's Rd
Bristol
BS1 5UW

brh.org.uk
brh@brh.org.uk

ISBN 978-1-911522-44-7

This book is dedicated to the memory of Caribbean historian Richard Hart (1917-2013) and Living Easton plaque designer Mike Baker (1961-2020).

Richard is shown here, on 1st May 2009, unveiling Mike's 3D plaque telling the story of the abolitionist Thomas Clarkson at the Seven Stars pub.

In 1787, at this pub that "changed the world", Clarkson received help and solace during his epic six-month investigation into the slave trade in Bristol.

The money for the plaque was raised by public subscription, including proceeds from the sale of BRHG's first ever pamphlet, *Cry Freedom, Cry Seven Stars*.

Contents

Acknowledgements

All history books are collective efforts to varying degree and this text is no exception.

Of primary importance was the research; the authors were aided by a number of people. In London, Maureen Ball, Dr Di Parkin and Hoare's bank archivist Pamela Hunter were essential in our investigations into Edward Colston and the Royal African and South Sea Companies. We also had help from Dr Helen Paul (University of Southampton), Dr Reg Murphy in Antigua and Harriet Pierce in Barbados. In Bristol, Prof Madge Dresser, social historian of slavery, provided useful advice and contacts throughout the project. Ruth Hecht was of great help to us in cross-checking our quantitative analysis of the emancipation compensation money and Jacqui Mayhew guided us though the connections with the slave trade in St Mary's Church in Henbury. Doyens of the museums and library service past and present Sue Giles, Karen Garvey, Jane Bradley and especially Dawn Dyer all helped with the research and encouraged us to look deeper. Thanks also to the staff at Bristol Archives who were as helpful and efficient as ever. Special regards go to those sources who we cannot name, we salute you.

Countering Colston activists Ros Martin, Christine Townsend, Jo Burch-Brown and Marti Burgess helped us research the history of contemporary movements in the city and, along with Cleo Lake, Michael Jenkins and Ben Prichard, provided critical perspectives. Members and friends of Bristol Radical History Group, Silu Pascoe, Rosemary Caldicott, Mike Richardson, Steve Mills, Theo Llewellyn, Geoff Woolfe, Jim McNeil, Ian Bone and Trish Mensah aided the research along with Bristol academics Peter Fleming and Steve Poole (both UWE), and Evan Jones, Mark Horton, George Davey Smith and Richard Stone (from the University of Bristol). Elizabeth Baird in Edinburgh, Elizabeth Jube in Nantes, Toni Reynolds in St Kitts and Gail Dore in Nevis opened up new perspectives on memorialisation. Authors Gary Best, Maurice Jackson, Marcus Rediker, Peter Linebaugh, Adam Hochschild, Laurence Fenton, Spencer Jordan, Derek Robinson, Richard Hart and activist Paul Stephenson provided us with both knowledge and inspiration.

Guidance and advice during the writing of this book was provided by a number of people including local writers/historians Richard 'get on with it' Jones, Mike Manson, James MacVeigh, Royston Griffey and Andrew Swift. Support also came from Koulla Pearce, Mike Baker, Roy Gallop, Tess Green, Ken Gabriel and Deborah Bidwell and in Hawkesbury from Bill Fairney, Andrew McLaughlin, Rick Deniff, Barrie Hope, Phil Dennett, Rich Shapcott, Jonathan Sandy, John Appleby and Pete Webb. In the media *Bristol Times* guru Eugene Byrne, ace *Bristol Post* reporter Tristan Cork, BBC Radio Bristol's Steve Yabsley, *The Bristolian* crew and Tony Gosling of community radio station BCFM have all played their part in publicising our findings.

We owe a great deal of thanks to our comrades in BRHG who gave their labour for free in putting this book together particularly Richard Grove (graphic design), Richard Musgrove (publishing) and the proofers and checkers Barbara Segal, Julie Roome and Maureen Ball.

Finally we give our special thanks to our families for putting up with us doing this book. Mark's long suffering family of Fiona, Vivi Gonzales and Maddy Waddy and Roger's nearest and dearest, Rachel, Alex and Francis. And, yes, it is finally finished....

Introduction

From Wulfstan to Colston

Any visitor coming to Bristol would think that the city only had three people to remember and celebrate: Cabot, Colston and Brunel. The truth is all three have been over-memorialised at the expense of others. This book hopes to present alternative Bristol people who are worthy of memorialisation, especially with respect to the slave trade, slavery and their abolition. One such public figure is St Wulfstan, one of the first abolitionists, who commands no memorial in central Bristol at all. It was recently suggested that the Colston Hall could be renamed the 'Wulfstan Hall'. Who was Wulfstan and why should this person be so remembered? More importantly, why don't we know about Wulfstan? Why has his history been obscured for so long?

It's an unseemly fact that at the start of the twenty-first century there are far more memorials and celebrations in Bristol to those that ran and profited from the nefarious slave trade than those who opposed it. Monuments include statues, portraits, stained-glass windows, buildings, schools, streets, public houses and until recently even the City's most prestigious concert hall (see Appendix 1). There's no balance and that's not surprising as most Bristolians never had a say in who should be memorialised. Instead those merchants and businessmen who organised and profited from slavery and the slave trade and their descendants and supporters largely made the decisions about who was to be remembered (and who was to be forgotten) on the streets of Bristol.

One man who stands out as being celebrated more than any other is Edward Colston, feted to this day as a 'great philanthropist' by church ceremonies and banquets. Eminent personages and bodies such as the Society of Merchant Venturers, the various Colston societies, Bristol Cathedral and St Mary Redcliffe

Church, some Bristol schools and Bristol University still do him honour—and (as we shall see) Colston not only profited from the slave trade but took a leading role in organising it!

In 2017 accusations flew that changing the name of the Colston Hall would be 're-writing history'. But is it re-writing history? And do people really know the actual history of the locale and the public figures involved?

Not many cities have such a unique history as Bristol. From early medieval times it encompassed monks, martyrs and merchants before culminating in the colonial period with traders, traffickers and tyrants. To help end slavery an epic battle ensued in the city between abolitionists and apologists, culminating in victory for those who wanted it eliminated.

With an undercurrent of tumultuous events and with a focus on slavery and emancipation, this book presents a brief thousand-year history to try and set the record straight. But first, here are some notes about the structure of the text and what we have left in and left out.

About this book

The reason for this book is that we felt that the Bristol story of slavery, the slave trade, abolition and emancipation was spread across a number of history books, pamphlets and online sources, many of which are out of print, obscure or difficult to obtain. We wanted to bring these sources together and add new research where it was relevant. We are thus indebted to a great many historians both living and dead who have researched, written and spoken about these subjects. We salute them all for their work.

The structure of this book returns to the style, popular in the Middle Ages, of the chronicle. These days it is better known by the trendier description of *timeline*. Amongst these pages you will find two timelines meshed together. We are thus grateful to printer and writer John Evans[1] and his 1824 book *The Chronological Outline of the History of Bristol*.[2] Key dates from this work have been used copiously and are marked by a single vertical ruled line throughout this book. Further entries have been added from the *Chronology of Slavery* by Madge Dresser and Sue Giles which appeared in their catalogue of the 'Respectable Trade' exhibition of 1999, entitled *Bristol and Transatlantic Slavery*.[3] A double vertical ruled line differentiates these items. We reproduce these entries as text accurate, that is, we go with the spelling and dates of the author(s) unless corrected, translated or explained by our contribution [in square brackets].

These timelines, which highlight historical events relating to slavery and its abolition, provide the skeleton upon which our pieces of history hang. We have fleshed out this narrative with research into both primary and secondary sources.[4] As historians operating in the twenty-first century we have the benefit of numerous online sources including huge databases of historical information gathered over many years of research. In particular two stand out, the *Trans-Atlantic Slave Trade Database* and the *Legacies of British Slave-ownership*, both of which allowed us to rapidly analyse large amounts of data pertaining to Bristol, something which would have been impossible several decades ago.[5] From the local perspective we have tried to isolate the social, political, religious and economic networks which united those who organised and profited from slavery as well as those who opposed it over many centuries. This includes those who have continued the struggle to expose the City's links with slavery, challenge the celebration of its leading figures and remember those who suffered under its horrors, right up to the publication of this book. Although the emphasis is on Bristol, the effect of national and international events on slavery, the slave trade and abolition are included where they impacted on the City.

The main thread of this book is chronological though there is also a spatial theme relating to the location of the present day 'Colston' Hall, previously the site of the 'Great House' and before that a Carmelite monastery. Our interest in this site relates to the many misconceptions around its history which came to the fore in 2017 during the debates concerning the renaming of Bristol's premier music venue. Through researching the history of the location we uncovered a fascinating history which had connections to the formation of the city's elite, their entry into the business of slavery and how they used the profits they made to propagate their memories.

Some limitations

The chronicles we have chosen to use in this book, along with the focus on Bristol, suited the lengthy swathe of history we wanted to analyse. As a consequence of considering such an extended historical period, and for reasons of time and space, we have been unable to consider in detail the social history of forced labourers in the Americas as either individuals or groups. Where we have turned to them it has generally been (all too briefly) to record some of their revolts, insurrections and revolutions, all of which, successful or unsuccessful, had a role in bringing slavery to its end. However, you will find many sources in the bibliography which do justice to the everyday lives and struggles of the bonded, indentured and enslaved. Similarly, our story of abolition and emancipation ends in the 1860s, so we do not cover the rapid colonisation and decolonisation of Africa in any detail. That is another important story, the effects of which are still being felt today.

A note on the transatlantic slave trade

The transatlantic slave trade was an historic event of great importance not only for Africa but also for the Americas and Europe. Lasting 350 years from 1516 to 1866, its legacy is still being felt today through the massive displacements of people, the devastating effects it had on Africa in particular, the stimulus it gave to European colonisation and economies and the effects of its ideological justification: racism. In order to measure its scale, it is useful to look at it from three perspectives: the overall European and American engagement, British involvement and Bristol's specific role.

As we have noted, historical researchers of slavery and the transatlantic slave trade have powerful tools available to them today through the use of computing power and the internet. These are also available to you the reader. One of the tools we have employed many times in our research is the *Trans-Atlantic Slave Trade Database.*[6] Turning to this huge source of information we are able to put some figures on the transatlantic slave trade.

Over that 350-year period (1516-1866) it is estimated that 36,000 slave-trading voyages took place, the majority of which were undertaken by Portuguese, British, French, United States and Spanish merchants. In all, it is estimated that 12.5 million African men, women and children were embarked on slave ships, with about 10.7 million surviving the crossing; a death toll of 1.8 million people. To put these huge figures in context, at the height of the slave trade, around 1800, the population of the whole of the African continent has been estimated at about 90 million people. The effect of the business of slavery, particularly on West Africa, was thus immense.

From 1676 to 1800 Britain was the leading transatlantic slave trading nation. In all, British ships undertook 12,000 voyages and transported 3.2 million enslaved Africans, with more than 500,000 men, women and children dying en route. From 1698 to 1807, 2,083 slave ships left Bristol, transporting 560,000 enslaved people from Africa to the Americas. Almost 100,000 Africans died as a result. These are conservative figures for a number of reasons. First they do not include 'illegal', clandestine voyages or where enslaved Africans were smuggled and not officially recorded. Second they only cover the transatlantic passage. Large numbers of enslaved people died on forced marches in Africa and after their arrival in the Americas.

A note on forced labour and the enslaved

In this book we make reference to 'forced labour'. We use this term as a category which includes several forms of coerced work, including chattel slavery,[7] penal labour and bonded labour such as serfdom, indenture and debt peonage. All of these types of forced labour have differences. They entail varying social relations between 'labourer' and 'master' (i.e. ownership in chattel slavery), conditions of work and relations of force. By using the definition 'forced labour' we are not conflating them or attempting to equalise the levels of human misery they entail. Far from it, instead we use the term to recognise the historical links between them and their changing use through the dynamics of feudalism and capitalism. However, neither are we naïve about the nature of so-called 'free labour' under capitalism which is coercive to varying degree based on a person's access to property and wealth.

We have also tried to avoid using the dehumanising term 'slave' wherever possible, employing the more appropriate term 'enslaved'. Though, if some of the former have slipped through, you know what we mean.

A note on measuring worth

In this book you will find references to sums of money. There are a number of methods for converting these into equivalent amounts today. We have employed the website *MeasuringWorth.com* to carry out these calculations, taking 2016 as 'today'. In general, the sums we deal with are the province of the wealthy, typically trading in commodities, capital investments such as stocks and shares, ship, land and building purchases, as well as interest, compensation payments and inheritances. In order to gauge the size of these relative to the amount of wealth today we have used two measures. The lower bound is the conversion *GDP per capita* and the upper, *share of GDP*. The former is a measure against the average standard of living, that is, the output of the economy divided by the population. It gives the "economic status or relative 'prestige value' of the owners of this income or wealth because of their rank in the income distribution". The latter is a comparison with the total output of the economy and demonstrates "the relative 'influence' of the owner of this income or wealth in controlling the composition or total-amount of production in the economy".[8] These measures should give you, the reader, a feel for the economic status and power a particular historic sum would give you if you were a rich merchant, businessperson or landowner in 2016.

A note on endnotes

This book is full of endnotes. They are in the text for two reasons. First they allow readers and future historians to find the sources we have used to collate this bit of history so they can follow our path and improve or criticise our analysis (or both). Second, the endnotes contain information, explanations and sources which we think are useful and interesting background material. However, as they might distract the more impatient reader from the flow of the narrative, feel free to ignore them if you want a racier read.

The triumvirate of the Bristol Nomenclature. Top, Edward Colston. Middle, Isambard Kingdom Brunel. Bottom, John Cabot.

Saint Wulfstan

Early life

We begin our story in the eleventh century, with excerpts of Wulfstan's life which come from *Vita Wulfstani* written by William of Malmesbury.[9] This was a later version of the *English Life* by the monk Coleman.[10]

Wulfstan,[11] the last ever Anglo-Saxon Bishop, was the first to get the slave trade in Bristol banned in 1090. Born in Warwickshire in 1008, son of Aethelstan and daughter of Wulfgifu "with happy omen the hopeful child borrowed from the name of either parent to draw holiness of each, and, methinks, marvellously to surpass it", his parents "of no mean birth or estate" sent their son away to Evesham (and later Peterborough) for his early education where he showed great promise.[12] By the time of his return home though, his father and mother:

> had both grown weary of the world, and began to long and sigh earnestly for another habit and another way of life. Indeed old age and poverty lay before them… His father took the monk's habit at Worcester, his mother the veil in the same city.

This change of events led to Wulfstan joining the household of Brihtheah,[13] Bishop of Worcester, where he became something of a protégé. In time he was offered several priesthoods and despite resistance—he really wanted to become a monk—was finally ordained as a priest at Hawkesbury, twenty miles north of Bristol and at that time the most impoverished parish in the See of Worcester. Here's Coleman's take on his early life:

Nor was it only upon the monks, but the common people also that Wulfstan scattered the seed of his loving kindness. For often in the morning, when the day's duties were done, he was to be seen standing before the doors of the Church that those who would speak with him might have easier access. Never weary in well-doing he would often prolong his day there till noon and even to evensong, if he could help those who had suffered violence, or baptize the children of the poor.

For already the love of money had crept up from the shades below, so that priests refused to administer that sacrament to infants unless the parents would fill their pockets. So Wulfstan, pitying the destitution of the parents, pitying also the avarice of priests in his heart while he scourged it by his act, busied himself with a task of exceeding loving-kindness in baptizing poor children.

Whilst proving very popular as a priest, it was at this time that he became a vegetarian:

Wulfstan was then barely come to manhood, yet he did not give thought to the pleasures of the world as a young man might. Meanwhile he did not altogether eschew savoury meats, and one day he ordered a goose to be roasted. The fowl was spitted and roasting, carefully tended by a scullion. In the heat of the fire the dripping began to run from it. Some of the servants were putting hot coals under. Some were making ready the sauce. The savoury smell made their mouths run with water; they could not refrain from saying how good it was.

Even Wulfstan was ensnared, and his soul melted in delight, as it were foretasting the goose. And now the table was all but laid, when he and his steward were called forth from the house on business which came untimely but could not be delayed. So he went empty away; and began to find a fault in his lust of a moment. How weak was the flesh that could so be tempted to evil. The pleasure passed quickly away: the sin remained. He exacted from himself this penalty that he should pay for the inordinate desire of one hour by perpetual abstinence.

He didn't only strive for abstinence from meat but he also made a vow of chastity and expected others in the house of God to follow suit; this was despite having temptation thrown his way on several occasions:

…She, nothing loth, began to dance before Wulfstan with lascivious movements apt to take the eyes of a lover. And he, whom touches and

2

glances had not moved, yielded to her seductive gestures, and panted with desire. But in a moment he came to a better mind, and burst into tears: and took flight into rough thickets and thorny places.

All the while he longed to become a monk and after only a few years as priest at Hawkesbury "Wulfstan became a monk at Worcester and Brihtheah gave him his blessing and a monk's habit". Here he quickly ascended the ranks, first as schoolmaster, then precentor, sacristan, prior and finally bishop.

Bishop Wulfstan

1042—June, Hardicanute died suddenly, at the nuptial feast of a great lord at Lambeth. Edward (the Confessor), only surviving son of king Ethelred, by Emma, his second wife, (afterward the wife of Canute) succeeded to the crown.

Five years before his death King Edward made Wulfstan Bishop of Worcester. Edward had consulted with his Cardinals and they had put forward Wulfstan's name, Coleman again:

He, they said, was worthy of a bishopric who had added more honour to the priestly office than he had received from it: whose nature answered to his diligence: in whom life squared with wisdom.

He then received his crozier (a bishop's badge of office similar to a shepherd's crook) directly from Edward.

His fame went abroad through England—so that the greatest nobles of the land eagerly sought his friendship, and held it fast. They looked to it as a safeguard in prosperity, a refuge in adversity, and a protection in all changes of fortune. Among them Harold, feeling himself capable of greater power, and already claiming the kingdom by his noble qualities, loved Wulfstan above all men… No less dearly did the Saint love the Earl. He received his confessions kindly, and was the faithful interpreter of his prayers to God.

1066—Jan. 5, Edward the Confessor died, aged 65. On the evening of his funeral, Harold assumed the crown, in opposition to the will of Edward in favour of William, duke of Normandy, a descendant of Canute, and who, in 1058, had betrothed his daughter to Harold.

Despite Wulfstan's prophesising that no good would come of Harold's quest for kingship, Harold declared himself king and soon faced an immediate revolt led by his estranged brother Tostig:

Harold, whether it was by goodwill or by force that he gained it, became master of almost the whole kingdom. Only the Northumbrians, a great and turbulent folk, were not ready to submit. They vowed that they would not suffer the proud North to yield to the feeble South.

Their lust for power and their fierce temper were inflamed by Tostig, the kings own brother, a man of unfailing courage if he had but chosen to turn his hot spirit to the pursuits of peace. Thereafter he was slain in that same land [Stamford Bridge] together with Harold [Harald] king of Norway, whom he had brought to his aid; and so paid the price of his rash daring.

1066—Sept. 5, William arrived at Pevensey, in Sussex. Oct. 14, he came to an engagement with Harold, and killed him at Battle Abbey. William hence assumed the title of Conqueror.

Renowned for his holiness and great piety, Wulfstan's fame grew, all the while preaching peace and reconciliation between Saxons and Normans. Wulfstan also had his own foibles; on one occasion he tried to discourage an amorous suitor by slapping her across the face and on other occasions he would hack at hirsute men's luscious locks in order for them to get their hair cut if he thought them too long.

The Conqueror's early reign saw him establishing complete control of England. After four years of purges against the leading Anglo-Saxon clergy there were only three bishops left, including Wulfstan, but this position looked tenuous. Lanfranc, Archbishop of Canterbury, accused him of 'illiteracy'— his biggest crime being that he couldn't speak the court language of French. To prove his position was merited, Wulfstan drove his crozier into the tomb of Edward the Confessor, the man who had given it to him, and challenged others to extract it. Wulfstan was the only one who could and he promptly kept his position. This event may have been the forerunner of the 'sword in the stone' legends. Thereafter King William thought highly of Wulfstan and even commanded that he have some of his own knights as armed retainers to look after him.

Bristol: 'Step-mother of all England'

| **1080**[14]—The survey recorded in 'Domesday-Boke' commenced.

Under orders from William, the Duke of Normandy, Wulfstan was responsible for the Domesday Book throughout the See of Worcester, from Bristol in the South to Birmingham in the North. It must have been while compiling this tome that he first encountered the slave pens beside the River Frome in Bristol (re-routed in the thirteenth century but sited now on modern day Baldwin Street). According to the Irish Chronicles a slave trade between Bristol and Dublin had existed for over 400 years. For example, it is claimed that the patron saint of Ireland, Saint Patrick, who was from North Somerset, was enslaved and shipped to Ireland in the fifth century. It is likely that he was dispatched from Bristol.[15] In the later Anglo-Saxon period it is estimated that approximately 10 per cent of the population of England were chattel slaves[16] with men employed as agricultural labourers whilst women "had the tedious task of grinding corn, or were serving maids, wet-nurses, dairy maids, weavers and seamstresses". Slaves were usually obtained from warfare:

> As invading Angles and Saxons swept across the country many native Britons were taken captive. These would often be women and children, since enemy warriors were more likely to be killed if caught. Yet it was not only the Celts who were enslaved. Far from it. The Anglo-Saxons were not at all averse to enslaving their own kind. The Germanic tribes fought each other until England was unified under Alfred the Great. This constant strife would have been a rich source of slaves.

Another supply of slaves came from poverty and associated crime:

> Bondage could also be a punishment for theft or other crimes. If the thief's wife and children were privy to the theft, the entire household could be enslaved. Sheer poverty drove some to sell themselves or their children into slavery.[17]

The establishment of settlements in Ireland in the ninth and tenth centuries by the Vikings, at the time the greatest slave traders in northern Europe, created the conditions for Bristol to expand and become a major slaving port. Many Bristol merchants were engaged in the trade, which was followed openly and shamelessly, and Bristol earned the unenviable name "Step-mother of all England". While compiling the Domesday Book for Worcester, Wulfstan managed to return some recently 'stolen' estates to the See, and even increase its size by encompassing three more Shires; Chester [Cheshire], Salop [Shropshire], and Stafford [Staffordshire].

1086—Domesday-Boke finished. In this the people of Bristol are styled burgesses: 'Bristow, with Barton, an adjoining farm, paid to the king 100 marks of silver (73*l*. 6*s*. 8*d*.) and the burgesses returned that bishop G. (the custos, keeper or propraetor of the Castle) had (received) 33 marks (28*l*.) and one of gold.

According to Coleman, there are twenty-one miracles attributed to Wulfstan, ranging from prophecies and punishments to saving and healing, but it was the saving of a Bristol ship in the Irish Sea that led to his greatest miracle, the ending of the Anglo-Irish slave trade. Even at the time Coleman had some trouble convincing his peers at Worcester that the miracle was genuine as it was exercised 'remotely':

Some Bristol men and other English were sailing to Ireland, as was their wont, with merchandise. And now they had put forth into the deep, when the face of the sky was changed, and the light of day gave place to the darkness of night. The tempest raged, the rain poured down; it was as though the world was being broken up. You might have thought the winds were fighting for the destruction of the unlucky sailors. The ropes parted, the mast broke, the oars were carried away; the ship was drifting unguided at the mercy of chance.

The sailors could only look for death, and for three days and nights dragged on a wretched existence, without food or sleep… methinks it is less hard to die swiftly like a man, than to wait for a craven's end. On the fourth day when all spirit was departing from them, God, who would not the death of the wretched but their life, put it into the heart of one of them to say, Ye that are of the bishopric of the right reverend Wulfstan, why do ye not pray the pity of God, by his intercession he may bring us out of this sore peril?

The others caught up the word from his mouth, and with one voice poured forth their hearts in prayer…showing to them not [the shadow of death, but] …Wulfstan, the present image and semblance of him. Marvellous it may be to relate, but what so many good men declare cannot but be true. He went about the ship, making fast the tackling, splicing the ropes; calling now on one man, now on the whole crew. Take heart, he said, hoist the yards, belay the halliards and sheets; and by God's good will and my aid you will soon reach land.

Coleman continues, "This miracle had such power with the men of Bristol that they were wholly minded to do whatsoever Wulfstan bade them", and he fully needed this support for the campaign that followed.

Putting down the slave trade

1090—The Life of Wulfstan… 'There is a sea-port town, called Bristol, opposite to Ireland, into which its inhabitants make frequent voyages on account of trade. Wulfstan cured the people of this town of a most odious and inveterate custom, which they derived from their ancestors, of buying men and women in all parts of England, and exporting them to Ireland for the sake of gain. The young women they commonly got with child, and carried them to market in their pregnancy, that they might bring a better price. You might have seen, with sorrow, long ranks of young persons of both sexes, and of the greatest beauty, tied together with ropes, and daily exposed to sale. Oh! horrid wickedness! To give up their nearest relations, nay, their own children, to slavery. Wulfstan, knowing the obstinacy of these people, sometimes stayed two months among them, preaching every Lord's Day; by which, in process of time, he made so great an impression on their minds, that they abandoned that wicked trade, and *set an example to all of the rest of England* to do the same.

Coleman then relates the first recorded rising of the Bristol mob:

One of them [a slave trader], who stubbornly transgressed the counsel of the Bishop, they cast out of the city and blinded his eyes. Therein I praise their goodwill, but blame there [sic] deed. But when the minds of rough men are once stirred, no force of reason can withstand them.

Archbishop Lanfranc, in one of his last acts (he died in 1089) must share some of Wulfstan's credit for this as it took the two of them to petition William II [Rufus] to finally end the trade.

Some modern-day historians have questioned Wulfstan's position on slavery. In her 2007 book, *Ireland, Slavery and Anti-Slavery: 1612–1865*, Nini Rodgers argues:

For Wulfstan, like [St] Patrick, it was the fate of the Christian slave, uprooted from his homeland, which the bishop unequivocally denounced. Wulfstan himself was rooted in this pervasive institution; on his ecclesiastical demesne in the West Midlands he possessed 472 slaves.[18]

Researching the word 'demesne' revealed that it was a feudal system of manorial land tenure, which was brought to England by the Normans after the Conquest. Initially the demesne lands were worked on by villeins or serfs, on the lord's or bishop's behalf; they had no right of tenure on it, in fulfilment of their feudal obligations. Neither villeins nor serfs were technically slaves but in the social hierarchy of the day, a serf's life was little better than that of a slave—the only real difference being that a serf couldn't be bought or sold like the enslaved. According to Pip Jones in *Satan's Kingdom*, 25,000 slaves were listed in the Domesday Book and these constituted about nine per cent of the entire population. Their use died out as Lords found it easier to pay a small wage rather than to look after their welfare.[19] The wider use of coinage also helped, making labour more "cost effective".

A great church and monastic builder, Wulfstan's feats include the re-building of Worcester Cathedral (started 1084) and the Benedictine monastery at Westbury-on-Trym which he re-established in 1093 (now Holy Trinity Church). According to Coleman, who became Prior at Westbury himself in 1095:

> …at Westbury an ancient church, half fallen, in sore need of repair. He rebuilt it from the foundation upward, mending the walls with hewn stone, the roof with lead. He endowed it with glebe and tithes and furnished it with Office books, and by a formal deed of gift presented it to the Church of Worcester.

> **1093**—Westbury Monastery re-edified, to the honour of the Blessed Virgin: the old lands were recovered, new added, and the monks restored by Bishop Wulfstan, who made it a cell to the Priory of Worcester; but his successor, Bishop Sampson, in the same reign, revoked the grant, and removed the monks.

Wulfstan never forgot people of humble means and when challenged on this he was reported to have said:

> They are rich who know the will of God and can do it. Them we must serve who have naught to repay us withal. God will repay since the needy cannot bid us in feasts. For me it is more joyful to hold this company than if I were, as I often have been, sitting down with the King of England.

In addition to the magnates of England others also venerated Wulfstan:

> The Kings of Ireland paid him many signs of reverence. Malcolm, King of Scotland, with his royal lady Margaret, commended himself to his prayers. The fame of his holiness had gone through all the land, and even

8

to the ends of the world. The Pope of Rome, the Archbishop of Bari, the Patriarch of Jerusalem, in letters which are extant, besought his advocacy with God. Indeed there was no earthly glory that did not pursue him while he shunned it and refused it.

Active until the end of his life, Wulfstan died on the 20th January 1095, undertaking his daily task of washing the feet of a dozen poor. He was buried at Worcester Cathedral and within a short space of time local people were visiting his tomb and recording yet more miracles. It's fair to say that during Wulfstan's long life he was held in great affection, but after his death affection turned to veneration.

Veneration

Between 1135 and 1154 Bristol was at the epicentre of the civil war (known as 'the Anarchy') between Queen Matilda—confusingly also called Empress Maud—and King Stephen. Matilda was the legitimate heir to the throne of her father Henry I, who wanted her to succeed him. In Bristol, Robert of Gloucester, builder of the city's castle keep and Matilda's illegitimate half-brother, sided with her giving her crucial support. Unfortunately, Matilda delayed too much on the continent and her cousin Stephen seized the crown. It was a devastating time for the country as war and famine ripped through the land, neither side being able to deliver a knockout blow. One sign of the intensity of the conflict was the fact that during Stephen's reign a staggering 1,150 castles were built. Stephen died "of the piles" at Dover in October 1154, aged 50. Matilda's son, the future Henry II, spent about four years of his childhood in Bristol.

> **1155**—A few weeks after Henry's accession, Nicholas Breakspear, an Englishman, was raised to the pontificate, under the title Adrian IV. The British monarch sent a formal embassy to congratulate the new pope on his elevation. A strict friendship arose between them. This encouraged the King to request a grant of the kingdom of Ireland from the Pope. Adrian, flattered at a circumstance that acknowledged in the See of Rome the power of disposing of kingdoms and empires, readily granted the request, by a special bull, dated December 1156; but various occurrences prevented Henry from profiting immediately by the noble donation.

During the Easter of 1158 King Henry II and his wife Eleanor of Aquitaine visited Worcester Cathedral and symbolically placed their crowns on the tomb of Wulfstan vowing to never wear them again.

Wulfstan's Worcester from Bishop Carpenter's tomb of 1476, the fresco fell to pieces after exposure to the air during restoration in 1851.

Bristol's Castle Keep, central to 'the Anarchy' between Matilda and Stephen.

Tomb of King John in Worcester Cathedral with St Wulfstan on John's nearside shoulder.

1172—The King [Henry II] visited Ireland, landing at Waterford on the 18th of October. At Cashel, Henry produced the bull of Adrian IV, confirmed by his successor Alexander III, which transferred the sovereignty of Ireland from its natural princes to himself. At Dublin, he executed the charter to his men of Bristow (Seyer's No. 2), 'giving and granting them this city of Dublin for them to inhabit, with all the liberties and free customs which the men of Bristow had at Bristow and through his whole land.'

Henry used the resumption of the slave trade between Bristol and Dublin as one of his pretexts for taking Ireland; the trade had become rampant again during the reign of King Stephen. It would not be the first time that English rulers would use slavery as a pretext for invasion and colonisation. According to Derek Robinson in *A Darker History of Bristol*:

These former owners of English slaves were not happy with the new arrangement. They raided the town vigorously and often, and when on Easter Monday in 1209 they caught the Bristol colonists holidaymaking at Killin Woods outside Dublin, the Irish had a bloody holiday of their own. Few of their enemies made it back through the gates of Dublin. The slaughter was so great that reinforcements had to be sent out from Bristol. Black Monday was commemorated for many years thereafter, with much parading of troops, waving of banners, and issuing of challenges—which the Irish took up, in their own sweet time, and finally won their Dublin back again.[20]

On 21st April 1203 Wulfstan was canonised as a saint by Pope Innocent III, thus becoming Patron Saint of Vegetarians and Peasants, his saint's day being 19th January. In celebration, a tremendous ceremony was held at Worcester Cathedral in June 1218. Saint Wulfstan's body and that of Saint Oswald, Worcester's other great Anglo-Saxon saint and co-patron, were transferred from their tombs to shrines. King John was then laid to rest between them. Throughout the Middle Ages pilgrims, including Kings Edward I and III—in addition to Kings Henry II and John—came to Worcester to pray before St Wulfstan's shrine.

The Carmelite Priory

The twin ruling elites at this time were the Church and the Crown and disaffection with the former would lead to seismic changes in the makeup of the country within a few short centuries. After the Reformation each reigning monarch would become head of the state church and merchants would fill much of the void left by the Catholic Church and its monastic orders. The location and prominence of the Carmelite Priory in Bristol would bring all of this into sharp focus. The Priory was subsequently given over to a succession of wealthy merchants in the guise of the Great House, which in turn would play host to the very kings and queens most culpable for inaugurating and promoting the transatlantic, or African, slave trade.

The 'White Friars'

1267—Edward, Prince of Wales, founded the Priory of the Carmelites in St Augustin[e]'s parish, 'on the right ripe of the Froom [the Trench], over against the Key.' –LELAND[21]. The Carmelite Friery, and Church on the south-west side of it, were dedicated to God and the Blessed Virgin Mary. Their boundary extended from Steep-street on the eastward, to Pipe-lane westward, and backward including the Red Lodge garden. Leland calls it 'the fairest of all the houses of Friers.' This Monastery was supplied with water from the spring rising at the top of Park-street, whence Pipe-lane; the same which supplies St. John's Pipe, within the Gate.

At the time, the Carmelites, or White Friars, were in the ascendancy. Founded in the late twelfth century and then spreading throughout Europe, they were a Roman Catholic Order that originated on Mount Carmel, their spiritual focus being contemplation. The area in which the Priory lay had undergone great change only twenty years previously when the Frome was rerouted from Quay Head (Colston Avenue) to what is now Narrow Quay with the creation of the 'Frome Trench'; doubling port capacity and ensuring growth throughout the medieval period.

The Carmelites had the largest and finest church in Bristol. It dominated the landscape with a steeple and spire 200 feet high and a nave 90 feet long. Bristol surveyor William Wyrecester (c. 1480) described a thin needle-like steeple, common in English Friaries but unique in Bristol, probably placed between choir and nave. By about 1300 the priory had a tiled pavement, of unusual charm, with some of the tiles showing tilting knights.[22] To supply the priory with water the Carmelites built arched subways from a reservoir under what is now Park Street. The reservoir was filled with water emanating from springs on Park Street and Brandon Hill.[23] After successive years building up the Priory, hard times followed with the advent of the Black Death.

> **1348**—Famine's sister, the Plague, 'passed into Devonshire, Somersetshire and Bristol, and raged so that the Gloucestershire men would not suffer the Bristol men to have access unto them… so wasted and spoyled the people, that scarce the tenth person of sorts was left alive…' The grass grew several inches high in High-street and Broad-street.

Staggeringly, an estimated 30 per cent of the entire working population of England died.[24] This huge loss of peasants left the survivors in a stronger bargaining position with their land-owning masters. The amount of labour they had to give to their overlords could now be reduced, and if they were treated badly they and their families could leave to work for a more accommodating master. These everyday disputes would culminate in major uprisings such as the Peasants' Revolt of 1381 and finally marked the beginning of the end of serfdom. Norman serfdom had replaced Anglo-Saxon chattel slavery; its demise would lead to other forms of forced labour, such as indenture, and ultimately the return of chattel slavery by the seventeenth century. Other social and religious changes were about to overtake the country; in the vanguard was John Wycliffe who, in 1377, wrote in opposition to the Pope's supremacy.[25] As a result the reputation of both monks and friars began to decline rapidly in the general estimation.

Within a century Bristol merchants would once again dabble in the slave trade. As Peter Fleming notes, during the period 1430–1480, the city was heavily involved in England's North Atlantic trade. This involved the export of the "necessities of life" to Iceland and the import of child labour to work primarily for Bristol's medieval weavers. Fleming continues:

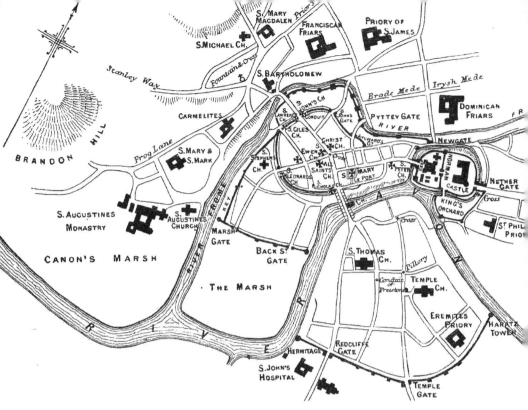

Map of the many medieval priories in Bristol (c. 1300).

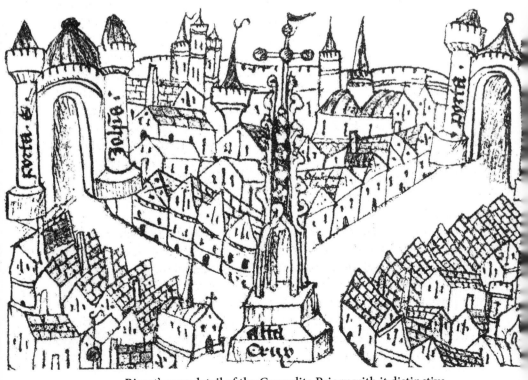

Ricart's map detail of the Carmelite Priory with it distinctive
central spire (upper centre right).

English merchants kidnapped Icelandic children, or persuaded their parents to sell them, to work as servants in English households and workshops, supposedly in virtual slave conditions.[26]

1479—Robert Ricart, a Kalendary, and one of the five chaplains or charity-priests, was elected Town-Clerk of Bristol. He commenced the Mayors' Kalendar or Register.

Famous Bristol Carmelites in this period included John Spine, a native of Bristol, who went on to become a Doctor of Divinity (DD) in Oxford, where he died in 1484, leaving "some books of his writing",[27] and Friar John Milverton who became a provincial of the order. In 1486, just after he was elected to the bishopric of St David's in Wales, Milverton preached against the office in favour of monks and friars. He was promptly imprisoned for three years in the Castle of St Angelo in Rome.[28] Unfortunately for the Carmelites, within 50 years they were going to be run out of town.

1497—John Cabot [Italian born explorer Giovanni Caboto] sails from Bristol to the North American mainland.

It is probable that Cabot was co-sponsored by Bristol merchants, an Italian banking house in London and King Henry VII. He used not only a Bristol ship, the *Matthew*, but also Bristol sailors as crew and it has been suggested that both Columbus, who had landed in the Bahamas just five years before, and Cabot, consulted Bristol fishermen prior to their own voyages of exploration. Cabot's transatlantic voyage took him to the edge of America and it's assumed he made landfall at Newfoundland. John Cabot and this voyage are a key element in the Bristol Story. In 1991 Bristol's fifteenth century mariners were memorialised with a sculpture in Redcliffe Quay Piazza. A sculpture of John Cabot had already been erected outside of the Arnolfini on Narrow Quay in 1986.[29] In 1897, on the 400th Anniversary of his voyage, Cabot Tower was erected on Brandon Hill in his honour,[30] and Bristol's newest shopping quarter was named Cabot Circus in 2008. The name 'Merchants Quarter' had originally been chosen for the shopping centre but this had to be dropped due to a public outcry concerning its associations with the slave trade.

After Bristol was banned from dealing in Icelandic cod by the Hanseatic League in 1475, customs officer Thomas Croft and merchant John Jay found their own source of cod, developing a lucrative trade not only in England but with Spain as well. The fishermen went further west than anybody else had at this time, into the 'wine dark sea' of the North Atlantic between Iceland and what is now Canada. The industry made fortunes for many and from the seventeenth century onwards it was found that salted cod was the perfect food for the slave-based economies of the West Indies.[31] Stockfish (air-dried cod) and saltfish, as salted cod was known in the British West Indies, became so important that tobacco, molasses and even the enslaved were exchanged for them, saltfish eventually becoming Jamaica's national dish. In Bristol it was also known as Tea Fish and was very popular amongst the 'lower orders'.

The fundamental reason for the European voyages of exploration towards the west at this time was the need for access to the riches of Cathay (China) and the Far East. After 1453 and the fall of Constantinople, the western end of the Silk Road was controlled by the Ottoman Empire, and this made goods from the east even more expensive. Initially Portuguese explorers sailed south around Africa to try to reach the Far East, but another option was a western sea route across the Atlantic. By the 1510s Portuguese merchants had established themselves in the East Indies while the Spanish had done the same in the West Indies. In the 1520s, Bristol merchants led by Robert Thorne (junior) canvassed Henry VIII to allow them to explore to the north-west in the path of Cabot. After encountering the land mass that would go on to be named the Americas, searches for the fabled North West Passage to reach the East went on to occupy the minds of backers and explorers for more than 400 years.

The Reformation

The English Reformation came about because of the political necessities of Henry VIII who clashed with the Catholic Church primarily over his obsession with producing a male heir. Starting in 1529 and ending in 1537, it effectively brought about a separation of the Church of England from that of Rome, culminating in England broadly becoming part of the continental Reformation movement. Reform in the Church of England, however, alternated for decades between ancient Catholic tradition and more radical Protestant principles, much to the cost of ordinary people. Anti-clericalism already existed in Bristol having been initiated by John Wycliffe and the Lollard movement which had called for reform of the Catholic Church.

> **1536**—This year William Tyndale was burnt at a town in Flanders, between Brussels and Mechlyn, called Villefort, for translating into English, the New Testament and divers parts of the Old; who, having been long imprisoned, was, upon the Lord Cromwell's writing for his deliverance, in all haste burnt. In 1520 he resided with Sir John Welsh, at Little Sodbury, as tutor to his children, and frequently preached on Sundays in Bristol. He had often debates with the abbots and clergy, who frequented the house of his patron, and with his approbation, but not entirely to the satisfaction of the lady his wife...

16

Six years earlier Tyndale's New Testament bible, which he had translated from the original Greek and Hebrew into English, was forbidden to be read. Copies of it were burnt in St Paul's churchyard and Tyndale became a wanted man.[32]

1538—Divers roods were taken down by command of the King; and all the notable images, objects of special pilgrimages and offerings, also taken down and burnt. All the orders of friers and nuns, with their cloisters and houses, were suppressed.

The house of the Carmelites was the first of four Catholic religious orders in Bristol (collectively known as the 'Mendicants') to be surrendered to the King in July 1538.[33] Prior to this the Carmelites had made the magnificent gesture of presenting the parishioners of St John's with the following:

To these Friars the parishioners of St John's parish were under deep obligation for the gift of a never ending supply of pure water... Let us pay 'the passing tribute of a sigh' to the memory of the good friars for the inestimable boon they conferred on the townsmen.[34]

The property of the Franciscans was (inter alia) conveyed to the Corporation of Bristol "in consideration for £1,000 cash and yearly fee farm rent of £20 to the King, by letters patent, dated 2nd May 1541". This granted to the Corporation certain properties including the site of the house of the Carmelites or White Friars.[35] In turn this was conveyed to the Mayor and Commonality of Bristol as "late house of the late Carmelite Brethren etc., Letters Patent 6th May 1541".[36] The Corporation then divided up the spoils, and the house and grounds of the Priory were sold on to merchant John Young (1519–1589), in all probability after securing the lead from the roofs and timber and stone from the buildings. Richard Bishop, the Government commissioner, in writing to Thomas Cromwell —Henry VIII's enforcer—reported:

Of the Whyte Fryeres in Brystow ... all that was in it little more than paid the debts. It is a goodly house in building, mete [meant] for a great man, no rents but their gardens. There is a chapel, and an aisle of the church, and divers gutters, spouts and conduit lead, the rest all tile and slate. A goodly laver and conduit coming to it [water supply]...

Also in writing to his "synguler Goode Lorde Crumwell," the same agent requests that the remaining Carmelite friars Thomas Wraxall, Thomas Clifton, Thomas Vaugan and John Ho[o]per have permission to "change their apparel," that is, pursue another course of life.[37] By this time the Friary was in a sorry state: the Sexton had fled before the royal commissioners reached the house having already stolen and sold off much of its wealth.[38] Few changes could have been more drastic than the swallowing up by "minters' furnaces" of the rich metalwork of the churches. The Corporation also helped itself to the plate and the proceeds went to fund the purchase of a mixed bag of "Churchspoil", chiefly the Carmelite and Franciscan buildings and most of the estates of St Mark's.[39]

> **1542**—The King having determined to establish six bishopricks, viz. Westminster, Oxford, Peterborough, Bristol, Chester and Gloucester, on the 4th of June Paul Bush, an Augustinian frier of Oxford, canon of Salisbury, and one of the King's chaplains, was appointed Bishop of Bristol; the Abbey hereafter to be called Trinity College of the City of Bristol. And so the church of the Abbey of St Augustine becomes the Cathedral of the City and Diocese of Bristol... one of the 'Cathedrals of the new foundation' for the nascent Anglican Church.

The Dissolution of the Monasteries during Henry VIII's Reformation saw Saint Wulfstan suffer the same fate as the Carmelites. His shrine and tomb along with that of Saint Oswald, the founder of Westbury, were destroyed at Worcester—their bones were covered in lead and then buried near the High Altar of the Cathedral. The transfer of power not only changed personnel but also attempted to physically remove icons of the previous religious and social order.

In February 1544 Westbury College with all its endowments was surrendered to Henry VIII by Dean Barlow. The following month the king granted "the whole site, foundation, border, compass and precincts of the...College of Westbury-on-Trym, in our County of Gloucester, now dissolved" to Sir Ralph Sadlier and his wife Ellen, for one thousand marks. Pleased with his acquisition Sadlier then "secured much of the surrounding church property".[40]

Sir Ralph Sadlier picked up much monastic wealth. He was a member of Thomas Cromwell's household and had married Cromwell's laundress; they later found, in all good faith, that her first husband was still alive and that Parliament "had to make it right for their children". In Latimer's *Annals* mention is made of Sadlier's "ever greedy hands"[41] Many forthcoming owners of Westbury College and its endowments would play a major part in the African slave trade.

The Society of Merchant Venturers

In the 'fallow' period between the demolition of the Carmelite Priory and the building of the Great House more religious ructions that would affect Bristol were taking place in the nation. Through this period the Society of Merchant Venturers would come to the fore and fill the power vacuum created by the Reformation.

> **1551**—Dec. 14, by letters patent the King [Edward VI] incorporated the Society of Merchant-Venturers, with four consuls and twenty-four assistants. Sebastian Cabot was the first Governor.

John Cabot's son, Bristol born and bred Sebastian, accompanied his father on his voyage in the *Matthew*, but was luckily absent when the follow up trip was made. It is claimed that when exploring along America's eastern seaboard Cabot senior encountered some over protective Spanish and 'disappeared'—no one will ever know exactly what happened to him. Sebastian had many other adventures, apparently more a talented cartographer than a leader of men; he entered the Spanish service, first exploring the River Plate for them (when he should have been following Magellan's route) and then leading an expedition to Brazil in 1526, both with mixed results. For the next 11 years, as Pilot-Major, he was an examiner of Spanish pilots and in 1544 drew a world map for Ortelius, the renowned cartographer from Antwerp. Dresser notes that Sebastian Cabot, while working for the Spanish government, travelled to the La Plata estuary in Latin America with a contingent of African slaves. He was also said to have enslaved a small party of Amerindians whom he kept with him at his house in Seville, prior to returning home to England.[42]

By 1548 he was invited back from Spain and granted a royal pension with the title 'Grand Pilot of England'. In 1551 he became a life governor of the Company of Merchant Venturers. When trade stagnated due to a war on the continent, he sent merchants Chancellor and Willoughby to open up new trade with Russia, where, under Ivan the Terrible, the Russians were happy to deal with the English as they saw it as a good way to break up the Hanseatic League's monopoly. Incidentally, Sebastian Cabot was the first Englishman to promote ships' sheathing for protection, his favoured material being lead! He died in 1565, after Queen Mary had his pension commuted.[43]

> **1555**—Oct. 7, William Shapton, weaver, was burnt for religion.

This period was marked by Queen Mary's attempt to restore the Catholic faith and undo the work of the two preceding reigns. Married bishops were now disapproved of, and Bristol's Bishop Bush had to retire in favour of Bishop

Sebastian Cabot showing the 'tools of his trade'—globe and dividers.

Holyman. The latter was, fortunately for Bristol, opposed to violent persecution and explains why only five persons suffered there. These unfortunate martyrs, all of them working men, were over a two-year period burned to death on St Michael's Hill on the site of Highbury Chapel.[44] A similar fate met the last of the order of the Bristol Carmelites, John Hooper. Hooper had travelled abroad after the dissolution of the monasteries and became acquainted with some of the reformers. In due course he converted to Protestantism. He was made Bishop of Gloucester but fell foul of Queen Mary's attempt to restore Catholicism to the country in the 1550s. Hooper was tried and burned at the stake before the west-end gate of his very own cathedral in 1555.[45]

1558—Nov. 17, the Queen [Mary] died of dropsy, in her 43rd year. She was buried in a chapel in the minster of St Peter's Church, Westminster, without any monument or other remembrance.

Bishop John Hooper, Bristol's last Carmelite, being burnt at the stake in Gloucester..

The Great House

In 1568 leading Bristol merchant John Young began the construction of the Great House on the site of the Carmelite Priory on St Augustine's Back. It immediately became Bristol's most high-status address, hosting the great and the good from around the country and beyond. One hundred and fifty years later one of its future owners, Edward Colston, would take the building from being a major home and place of commerce and turn it into a seat of education. He achieved this by using the proceeds of his involvement in the African slave trade which was about to take off.

> **1574**—Aug. 14, the Queen [Elizabeth I] to Bristol, in her progress to Wales, and remained till the 20th. She kept her court at the residence of Sir John Young (knighted to receive this visit), on St. Augustin[e]'s Back.

Befitting the most prestigious residence in Bristol, the Great House played host to the Queen on her seven day visit of 1574. She would lie here each night after feasting and merriment, costing the Corporation a staggering £1,053 14s 11d.[46] During her visit she managed to negotiate the 'Treaty of Bristol' with the Spanish ambassador, thus ensuring fourteen years of peace between England and Spain.

Origins of the African slave trade

Elizabeth's 'progress' heralded not only many royal visits to the Great House but also early associations with the African slave trade, for it was Elizabeth who became a sponsor of Tudor sea dog John Hawkins (later becoming Sir John during the battle with the Spanish Armada in 1588). On his second slaving

Left: Queen Elizabeth I on her progress through Bristol in 1574.
Right: The Red Lodge's heavily carved and ornate internal oak porch.

voyage of 1564 Elizabeth leased Hawkins her 700-ton ship *Jesus of Luebeck* which netted a handsome 60 per cent profit.

The originator of the 'triangular trade' between England, Africa and the Americas, Hawkins didn't bother with such niceties as commerce with the people on the African coast; he just went in attacking and kidnapping them. Thus was the start of English involvement in state sponsored transatlantic slavery. Elizabeth may have expressed the view that such activities would "call down the vengeance of Heaven", but she seemed to have contradictory attitudes to black people. Despite having a black handmaiden and musicians, by the end of her reign she wanted all black people expelled from the country. It's not known whether or not she met the guardian employed by Young to watch over his garden at the Great House in Bristol, the first black person to be recorded as living in the city.[47]

Young's time at the Great House wasn't without incident. He was one of the protagonists in a famous confrontation, the other being Hugh Smyth of Ashton Court, who appears to be the villain in the story. Smyth was apparently jealous of Young's success and encouraged his men to hurl insults at his rival's household and servants. On one such occasion they caught up with one another on College Green in front of Bristol Cathedral and had a massive set-to.[48] Toward the end of his life, to complement the Great House, Young commissioned the Red Lodge, now world famous because of its association with the nineteenth century social reformer and abolitionist Mary Carpenter. The building still contains cells belonging to the Carmelites as well as magnificent rooms in their original Tudor style. The Red Lodge was completed in 1580.

1582—wealthy merchant and mayor, Thomas Aldworth advised the Queen's right hand man, Walsingham, of his intention to invest 1000 marks and two ships, of 60 and 40 tons, for 'discoveries on the coast of America'.

The leader of the expedition was Sir Humphrey Gilbert who tried to colonise Newfoundland, arguably the beginning of the British Empire. Gilbert perished in the waters of the North Atlantic on his return home in the ship *Squirrel*, which went down with all hands. Around this time, Richard Hakluyt, Renaissance diplomat, sometime spy and famous geographer, settled into Bristol's new cathedral, the former Augustine abbey, as a prebendary.[49] He was in the process of gathering together all the known accounts of voyages of discovery to use in his seminal work *The Principle Navigations, Voyages, Traffiques and Discoveries of the English Nation*, "the prose epic of the English nation".[50] One such account was that of Anthony Parkhurst who, in 1578, had sent him his writings on the natural history of Newfoundland where he had lived for four years. Hakluyt was concerned about Gilbert's failure because he didn't want it to dampen the country's blossoming zeal for exploration. MacInnes outlines Hakluyt's obsession with colonisation:

In 1585, Hakluyt, whose qualities Walsingham had come to appreciate, was granted a prebend in Bristol. From then on to the end of his life, he was constantly in that city, and always, it would seem, concerned with plans for colonisation and the promotion of overseas expeditions. To the day of his death he never ceased in his labours to induce his country-men to establish permanent colonies, and the disappointing results of the various attempts made during the Elizabethan period served only to strengthen his determination. In his writings he tried to instruct the nation how best this great aim might be achieved.[51]

Hakluyt set the template for English colonial expansion for the next 200 years; he encouraged colonies in Ireland in 1594 and Virginia in 1612, and proposed that they be populated by the "rank multitude" from England's cities. The Elizabethan monarchy had passed the Beggars Act of 1597 and out of this Hakluyt suggested that England's rogues and vagrants be sentenced and transported to work on plantations in "prisons without walls". In addition he had campaigned for the new found colonies to provide an additional service by removing "swarmes of idle persons". He also shared Gilbert's view that England's late foray into colonisation could be turned to the country's advantage by redeploying her large and desperate population overseas.[52] In addition Hakluyt recorded all of the voyages of Elizabeth's 'sea-dogs', Hawkins, Drake and Raleigh; he even corresponded with Raleigh who was famously responsible

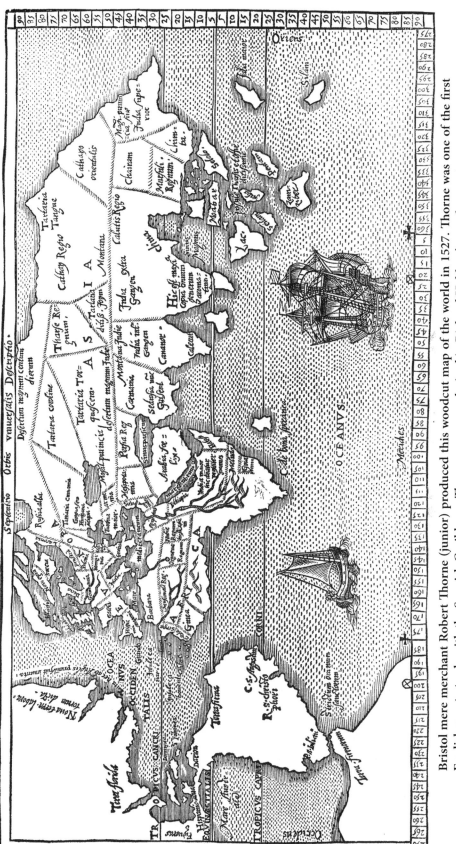

Bristol mere merchant Robert Thorne (junior) produced this woodcut map of the world in 1527. Thorne was one of the first Englishmen to trade with the Spanish Caribbean. The map was popularised in Richard Hakluyt's travel narratives.

for introducing tobacco into England. In a letter encouraging Raleigh to 'carry on colonising', historian Maurice Jackson believes Hakluyt helped to promote negative views of African people:

> …go on as you have begun, leave to prosperity an imperishable monument of your name and fame such as age will never obliterate. For to posterity no greater glory can be handed down than to conquer the barbarian, to recall the savage and the pagan to civility, to draw the ignorant with the orbit of reason.[53]

Hakluyt is memorialised twice in Bristol Cathedral with a fine marble tablet and a stained-glass window.

> **1598**—The Red Lodge, and Sir John Younge's lower house [Young's Great House], sold to Nicholas Strangeways [Strangways], of Bradley, in the county of Gloucester. Sir John Young's monument is in the south wall of the Cathedral-choir, in the place of the confessionary. His wife, Joan, died June 14, 1602, aged 70 years.

Young's magnificent memorial in Bristol Cathedral, which he shares with his wife Joan, has since been relocated. After his death his son and heir Robert turned out to be a bit of a ne'er do well, losing the family fortune and having to sell the Great House to his half-brother Nicholas Strangways. Then:

> Early in the seventeenth century, in a final twist to the rivalry between Hugh Smyth and Sir John Young, Nicholas Strangways sold the Great House to Hugh Smyth's nephew and heir, Sir Hugh Smyth of Ashton Court.[54]

Located right next to the river Frome on St Augustine's Parade, where he could keep an eye on his burgeoning trade, Sir Hugh preferred living here to his mansion at Ashton Court. Incidentally, the Smyth family motto is 'Qui Capit Capitur' which, according to the Malago Society, means literally 'He who captures is captured'.

C. Roy Hudleston gave this overview of Bristol's economy in the seventeenth century in his 'Historical and Prefatory Notes' in the 1931 edition of Arrowsmith's guide book *How to see Bristol*:

> The prosperity of Bristol had greatly declined during the reigns of the Tudors, and showed no evidence of a rebound until the conquest of Jamaica, the acquisition of other West India islands, and the growth of the American colonies. Commerce was then directed into new channels, and

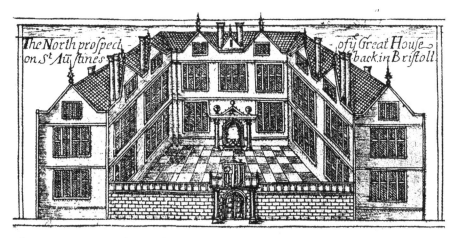

The Great House as depicted in the border of James Millerd's 1673 map of Bristol.

advanced with surprising strides in spite of the gradual decay of the cloth trade, for which the city had long been famous. The direct intercourse with the New World was lucrative, but its profits were not comparable with those arising from English goods to Africa for the purchase of slaves, the sale of the captives to the West India planters, and the freight homewards of rich cargoes of sugar and other tropical products. Such a triangular voyage occupied a twelvemonth.[55]

1603—March 24, the Queen died at Richmond, in the 70th year of her age, having appointed James VI, of Scotland, son of her unfortunate rival, to be her successor. James I, Aged 36 years, the first 'King of Great Britain'.

The tumultuous age of the Stuarts had begun.

In 1603, John Whitson, Mayor and founder of Red Maids School in Bristol, along with Robert Aldworth and others, sponsored a ship, under the command of Martin Prinne [Pring], in order to attempt to discover the North-West Passage. Pring was then just twenty-three years of age and afterwards showed his prowess as a seaman in the East-India voyages. Pring is buried in a massive memorial in St Stephen's church in central Bristol, on the north side of the chancel, surmounted by the arms of the Society of Merchant Venturers.

|| **1607**—English settlement of Jamestown, Virginia, founded.

Running parallel with Bristol merchants' efforts at colonisation, Jamestown was established by a London expedition and became England's first colony on the American mainland. Famously linked with Captain John Smith and the native-American Pocahontas, the colony came into conflict with the indigenous population and had to be rescued by Thomas de la Warr. John Rolfe introduced a sweeter strain of tobacco from Trinidad and saved the colony with the birth of 'Virginia tobacco'. The de la Warrs were a West Country family with land around Brislington and Wickwar; the Delaware tribe, river and state were later named in honour of Thomas.[56]

1608—The Society of Merchant-Venturers purchased the manor of Clifton.

The manor of Clifton formally belonged to the college of Westbury-on-Trym, in addition to: "the lordships, manors, rectories and lands of the college, the manor of Westbury, the rectory and church of Westbury and Henbury, including the tithes; also the tithes of Laurans Weston [Lawrence Weston], Aust, &c. and the site, manors, lands &c. of St Lawrence Hospital".[57]

1609—Mr. John Guy and his son went to Newfoundland to begin a plantation there.[58]

Bristol born John Guy was the son of shoemaker Thomas Guy; in early life he was an apprentice farmer[59] and went on to become a merchant and member of Bristol's wine importing cartel. Initially a member of Bristol's common council in 1603, he became Sherriff in 1605 and a Rear Admiral of the Royal Navy. Guy, along with members of the Society of Merchant Venturers took part in an attempt to colonise and exploit Newfoundland, becoming its Governor in 1610. On his return to Bristol he became a fully-fledged member of the Venturers and resumed his post in Newfoundland. After the failure of the colony he returned to politics, becoming Mayor again in 1618, alderman in 1619, and MP for Bristol from 1620–1621 and then from 1624 until his death in 1629; he was also master of the Society of Merchant Venturers in 1622.[60] The path taken by Guy illustrates the rising power of the merchant class. Although from a relatively humble background, the maritime and mercantile skills he obtained allowed him a level of social mobility. Others followed this route into the Merchant Venturers, which by fusing first economic and then political power ultimately formed a new ruling elite in Bristol.

1610—Over the course of the next 50 years, 110,000–135,000 white English go to the Caribbean, mainly as indentured labourers, some as transported prisoners.

In order to encourage colonists to travel to the new American possessions and to provide the labour required for the emerging plantation economy, a plan known as the 'headright' system was introduced. It first appeared in the new colony of Virginia in 1618 and was replicated in most of the British North American settlements. The plan granted plots of land (about 50 acres) to each colonist (including members of their families) who made the voyage to America and further plots if they paid for the transportation of indentured servants (or latterly enslaved Africans) to work their claim. It is clear that colonists with significant disposable wealth and connections could rapidly build up major land holdings and labour forces whilst at the same time depriving their new migrant workers of access to property. The headright land-grants also caused conflicts with the indigenous population as the new land-owners began to encroach on Native American territories. However, the system achieved its aims and encouraged, from 1610 to 1660, somewhere between 170,000 and 225,000 emigrants from the British Isles to travel to the Americas. More than half of these were indentured servants who often, due to poverty, had signed several years of their lives over to their new masters; others included penal labourers who were shipped to the plantations as punishment. The majority of these new emigrants, 110,000–135,000, went to the Caribbean, 50,000 to Virginia and 20,000–25,000 to New England.[61]

‖ **1619**—First recorded cargo of enslaved Africans in Virginia.

The first enslaved Africans to arrive in Virginia had been taken captive by Dutch and English privateers after a raid on a Portuguese slave ship, probably off the coast of Mexico. The privateers sailed to Jamestown, Virginia with the "20…and odd negroes" which they exchanged with the colonists for victuals.[62] This event is commonly regarded as marking the beginning of English chattel slavery on mainland North America. In fact, this was a process which took more than 50 years to develop and progressed at different rates in different locations. It wasn't until the 1640s that the first legal bases for chattel slavery were introduced in Virginia. Before that date, the few Africans who arrived as captured slaves were treated as indentured servants, alongside their counterparts from Britain and Ireland. In 1670, a Virginia law:

> defined as slaves-for-life all non-Christian servants brought to the colony 'by shipping'…The law already precluded freedom through conversion, and in 1682 it expanded its description of slaves-for-life to include all non-Christian servants (in other words, Virginia Indians, who were imported into the colony, in addition to Africans).[63]

‖ **1623**—Thomas Warner founds the first successful English settlement on St Kitts.

Initially shared with the French, by 1625 the St Kitts settlers had come into conflict with the indigenous Carib population. In a pre-emptive combined English and French attack, the colonists massacred more than 2,000 Caribs, most of the indigenous population, and gained full control of the island. The remaining Caribs were enslaved by the settlers. Warner then carried the first tobacco crop to London and eventually returned with more 'servants' from South West England and Ireland; by 1628 a number had travelled to nearby Nevis and settled there as well.[64]

‖ **1625**—First English settlement on Barbados.

Captain John Powell landed on Barbados in 1625 with his London backed expedition and immediately claimed it for King James I and England. Two years later his brother Henry returned and settled the island with 50 colonists and 10 enslaved Africans picked up en route. Amongst their number was 18-year-old colonist James Drax whose later actions would dramatically change the fortunes of the English in the Caribbean.[65] Soon after, England expanded her interests in the region by gaining control of Antigua, Barbuda and Montserrat in 1632.

The Guinea Company (GC) was initially formed in 1618 by James I to control and exploit trade between Africa and England. The company failed to flourish until it came under the control of London merchant and staunch royalist, Sir Nicholas Crispe, in 1625. Crispe came from the landed gentry of Gloucestershire and owned a number of estates in the county. When he gained control of the GC he was already an experienced investor and trader in London; he had shareholdings in the East India Company and used one of their commodities, shells, to trade for enslaved Africans. Although the GC initially had serious financial problems and was plagued by interloping merchants, Crispe, who had the majority shareholding, was able to implement two strategies which would lead to its rapid expansion into West African trade. First, he enforced the Company's monopoly and then promoted the idea that there should be permanent English 'factories' with resident merchants and agents on the West African seaboard. However, these factories were not undefended trading posts, they were actually forts. Crispe is credited with the establishment of England's first which began construction in 1638 on the Gold Coast. King Charles I backed Crispe's plan in 1631 by granting a further patent to the newly reorganised company which was renamed as "The Company of Merchants Trading to Guinea, or, significantly enough, Nicholas Crispe and Company".[66] Crispe's model of enforced monopoly with royal patronage and the development of a string of forts would be the pattern for expansion on the West African coast for the rest of the seventeenth century. His organisation would be a pre-cursor to the later Royal African Company.

Although Crispe originally traded in African redwood he soon developed an appetite for more lucrative commodities. Porter notes:

The chief article to be sought was of course gold…However, other commodities were not to be neglected; redwood remained a major objective, ivory could also, on occasions, be expected in large quantities, slaves (though not mentioned in the patents) were known to be becoming increasingly important, and there was also trade to be had in hides, wax, gum and pepper.[67]

As the demand for labour in the fledging American colonies grew, Crispe and his cohorts turned their attention to purchasing enslaved Africans. Crispe even took out a patent to manufacture glass beads to exchange for these captives and his ships traded directly with the Americas, notably Virginia. He became fabulously wealthy and built a 'Great House' in Hammersmith where he was MP until becoming a baronet.[68]

|| **1626**—First boatload of African slaves arrives on St Kitts.

The first enslaved Africans brought to St Kitts were a group of 40 purchased from Senegal by the Compagnie de Saint-Christophe, set up by Cardinal Richelieu to exploit the island's resources. Within ten years the number of enslaved labourers had increased to around 500. Having gained control of St Kitts the English and French invaders used the island as a staging post for further expansion across the Lesser Antilles. The English settled Nevis (1628) and then moved northward amongst the Leeward Islands capturing Antigua (1632), Montserrat (1632) and later Anguilla (1650) and Tortola (1672). The French colonised Martinique (1635), the Guadeloupe archipelago (1635), St Martin (1648), St Barths (1648), and Saint Croix (1650).

|| **1630s**—Bristol merchants give credit to early colonists in Caribbean in return for a share in their tobacco crops.

1630 also saw the founding of the first English settlement with predominantly slave-worked plantations established on Santa Catalina and other islands of the Providencia group off the coast of modern-day Nicaragua. In many ways the history, social hierarchy and pressures on this settlement were a microcosm for the English expansion into the Caribbean as a whole.

The settlement was founded by the Providence Island Company (PIC), with the Spanish remaining an ever-present threat. The PIC was formed from a select group of Puritan "aristocrats and great gentlemen", several of whom were in Parliament.[69] The islands' plantations produced tobacco, indigo, sugar and latterly cotton and were initially worked by indentured labourers transported by the Company from England. Most of the settlers were tenants with half of their profits going to the elite investors in the PIC.

The Company's plan for the island group wasn't just to grow cash crops but for it to operate as a forward base for raids on Spanish shipping. Dutch and English privateers connected to the PIC had used the islands for several years and offered to trade enslaved Africans they had captured from the Spanish with the settlers. Several took this opportunity, as their indentured labourers had reached the end of their four years of servitude and they required more workers. One of the senior colonists, Samuel Rishworth, publicly challenged the holding of African captives, effectively chattel slavery, and was removed from the island's council by the PIC. Despite this Rishworth explained his views to the Africans and encouraged them to escape, which some did, leading to early communities of 'runaways'. As a result of this challenge the PIC declared:

> That slavery was lawful for persons who were 'strangers to Christianity', but urged the colonists to abstain from further purchases, since a growth in slave numbers would pose a security threat and deprive free colonists of gainful employment.[70]

Many of the colonists ignored the Company's advice and continued to purchase slaves who by the mid-1630s probably made up half the islands' population. On May Day 1638, after the PIC threatened to execute runaways, the enslaved Africans revolted with many escaping to the interior. Despite numerous "hunting" trips by the colonists over the next year, it appears they were unable to recapture many of the rebels. After several attempts, in 1641 the islands were finally overrun by the Spanish, whose commander noted that the English colonists had "killed fifty [enslaved Africans] for conspiracy against them".[71]

In Barbados, early colonists were given or sold parcels of land that first had to be de-forested and then planted; cotton was initially fairly successful, but the tobacco grown was of an inferior quality and unpopular in England. In 1644 James Drax quietly introduced sugar cane from the Dutch in Brazil and, all of a sudden, a sugar revolution was underway. Drax's second son Henry would go on to write a hugely influential series of 'Instructions'—a book informing people on how to run a plantation using enslaved Africans, from growing and processing sugar cane to maintaining machinery—the model of which would be copied in Jamaica, South Carolina and beyond for the next 200 plus years.[72]

| **1632**—John Locke born at Wrington, Somersetshire.

Locke became the 'Father of Liberalism', one of the most influential philosophers of the Enlightenment, and, later on, a major shareholder in the

Royal African Company, the premier English slave trading organisation of the seventeenth century.[73] Locke would go on to provide theoretical opposition to slavery in his writings but as with many Enlightenment philosophers this was contradicted by his practice in government and finance.

Bristol merchant Robert Aldworth and his younger associate Giles Elbridge were in the vanguard of the English colonial expansion into the Americas. In 1632, they were given a patent of 12,000 acres of land in New England. Under the 'headright' system they benefited from an additional 100 acres for every extra person that they transported there. There was a three-year qualifying period and the scheme lasted until 1639.[74] This illustrates how those with access to wealth, contacts in England and access to shipping to move indentured servants, penal labour and other unfortunates across

Robert Aldworth's grand canopy tomb in St Peter's Church. Badly damaged in the Blitz, the highly decorated base denoted Aldworth's trades of shipping and sugar.

the Atlantic could grow their land holdings spectacularly, a pattern repeated through similar arrangements in other developing colonies in the New World.

1634—Nov. 6, died Robert Aldworth, without issue. He was buried in St Peter's Church, at the upper end of the south aisle. He bequeathed all of his estates to Giles Elbridge, merchant, who married his niece. Near the church-yard of St Peter was an alms-house, erected by Robert Aldworth, who also built the parsonage-house (now, 1824, occupied by a basket-maker, with the date 1613 on its front) opposite the well of St Edith. One MS. [manuscript] says, 'he built the faire house in St Peter's church-yard, with all the sellars and lofts for refineing of sugar. Another large building he raised in the Marsh; made two docks for shipping which came to nothing.'

London started sugar refining in 1544 and Bristol followed suit between 1612 and 1616. Robert Aldworth bought Norton's house in 1607 and converted it into his residence in 1612 when he then started 'sugar baking'. Subsequently and popularly known as St Peter's Hospital, the business relied upon foreign imports from Brazil, Madeira and Canary Islands. It was the sole sugar house in Bristol until 1654.[75]

An early colonist in Barbados was Christopher Codrington (I), from an old Gloucestershire family with local connections—one Francis Codrington had been sheriff of Bristol in 1543; the family seat being in south Gloucestershire. He arrived in the late 1630s and would go on to found one of the greatest dynasties in the West Indies, forged partly by his marrying into the Drax family. His first son, Christopher Codrington II, was "destined to be at one time the most important Englishman in the Americas".[76]

Colstons and Company

William Colston was born in 1608 and became an apprentice to Robert Aldworth, in the most exclusive set of Bristol's merchant aristocracy.[77] Aldworth and his contemporaries were known as 'mere [or meire] merchants'—traders that "lived exclusively by their large-scale dealings in foreign commerce". In sixteenth-century Bristol their operations were mainly located in the Iberian Peninsula and the Mediterranean. These traders had become Bristol's new mercantile elite after the 'old guard' of weavers trading to Gascony had been superseded.[78] In the late sixteenth century they numbered around 100 people[79] and it was some of this group that established the monopolistic role of the Society of Merchant Venturers. Key to the success of 'mere merchants' was to keep tight control over domestic and foreign markets by excluding smaller traders and retailers who might attempt to 'cut them out' by engaging in their own overseas trade. The 'closed shop' that the Society of Merchant Venturers operated not only protected the mercantile interests of the 'mere merchants' but also began to alter the class structure of the city. Sacks notes:

> As those Bristolians who engaged in overseas trade became an increasingly tight-knit community exclusively engaged in wholesale enterprise, separate from other crafts and trades in the city, a reorganisation of society occurred that touched nearly every aspect of social life in the city...[80]

As we shall see, in the following two centuries, the activities of this mercantile elite would not just impact on Bristol but on the peoples of the African and American continents.

The Colston family first came to Bristol in around 1400, attracted by the city's thriving wool trade in which they already had significant expertise. When Bristol merchants switched from being wool and wine traders with Western France, William and the family followed suit, becoming large scale merchants in Spain, Portugal, the Canaries, North Africa and the Levant.[81] Their expertise in the wool trade would help the family become pre-eminent in the burgeoning slave trade. By virtue of being apprenticed to Robert Aldworth, William Colston became a freeman of Bristol and one of its leading merchants. In 1634 he was admitted as a member of the Incorporated Society of Merchant Venturers and in 1643 became a Governor.[82] Also during the 1630s William Colston lived in Lisbon where he served the interests of his fellow Bristolians as a 'factor'. Sacks notes:

> These factors were servants to their native merchant community as much as they were agents for individual traders. Bristolians turned to them, not only for their familiarity with local market conditions, but because they were known and trusted.[83]

In 1635, after five 'Turkish' ships (probably Barbary pirates) wreaked havoc in the 'Severne', Giles Penn[84] petitioned King Charles I to raid the Moroccan base of Sallee. The following year the king dispatched Captain William Rainsborough with a fleet of four ships who then destroyed 28 ships hemmed into the port. The Governor sued for peace and hundreds of English and Irish slaves were freed and returned home. Some had been missing for 30 years. In celebration the former slaves were paraded at night through London dressed in white robes—there were so many it was said to be "like daylight". From the sixteenth century onwards these Turkish corsairs, as they were known at the time, were a persistent thorn in the side to all of the European powers, their favourite trick being to snatch people away and hold them for ransom. If this proved 'un-commercial', they used them as galley slaves or worse.[85]

1636—Nov. 13 [new style], Edward Colston born, son of William Colston [sheriff in 1643], by Sarah Bettins, daughter of Counsellor Bettins.

Sarah's father was a Barrister at Inner Temple, London and Edward, their oldest son, was born in Bristol in Temple Parish on November 2nd and baptised in the Weaver's Chapel in Temple Church, before moving back to the family home in Wine Street soon after. He was to be joined by another ten brothers and sisters.[86] Edward was assured of position and opportunity; his education and career were set, however, in London. He also preferred to make his massive fortune, preserved by simple habits and bachelordom, in the even greater trading centre of the capital. He was typical of many others of his century. The provincial would go to London, amass a fortune, and then return large sums, by way of charities, to his native place.[87]

Royal connections with the Great House continued throughout the seventeenth century; Anne, wife of James I, lodged there in 1612 and Henrietta Maria, wife of Charles I did the same in 1644 during the Royalist occupation of Bristol in the English Civil War. By this time though, the house was falling slowly into disuse and it was necessary to borrow beds from the *Red Lion Inn*. The following year when the Prince of Wales (the future Charles II) stayed, furnishings were even more of a problem and the Corporation had to promise to return them "undamaged". According to Brown and Harris's *Bristol, England*:

> Five councillors each undertook to send in a feather bed, mattress, bolster, two pillows with pillow bearers, a pair of sheets and a pair of blankets.[88]

1640s—Sugar cultivated in Barbados by mixed teams of white and black [forced] labourers.

Sugar production was labour intensive and highly dangerous[89] and within a short space of time James Drax decided enslaved Africans were more suited to the work than their impoverished white counterparts. Despite this, demand for labour was so great that many different groups of coerced people were brought to the island as Linebaugh and Rediker relate:

> The first cargo of convicts reaches Barbados in 1642. An act of 1652 permitted English magistrates summarily to seize vagrants or beggars and ship them to the plantations. A shipload of prostitutes from the jails of London was transported to Barbados as 'breeders'. Besides these the island was inhabited by all sorts: English, French, Dutch, Scots, Irish, Spanish Jews, Indians and Africans... The Native Americans were mostly Guianese Arawaks, who came to the island early on as free people but were enslaved by 1636. English servants and African slaves arrived in the first English ships in 1627, and the Irish in the 1630s; two thousand per year came from England in the 1640s and 3,000 in the 1650s. They were sometimes sold according to their weight.[90]

The English and Irish servants were unruly and were treated cruelly by their masters. In 1649, in response to this bad treatment, a large group of servants got together and planned to gain control of Barbados. The plot was discovered, hundreds of people were rounded up and 18 of the ringleaders were tortured and hanged.[91]

The transition from the primacy of indentured labourers from Britain and Ireland to chattel slaves from West Africa in the Caribbean plantations was for a number of reasons. These are outlined by Parker:

> With supply from the Dutch abundant, a Barbados planter could buy from a local trader an enslaved African for about £20—less for women and children.[92] This was in the region of twice the price of a five-year indentured servant, but it was for life, and the slave-owner also owned

any offspring the slave might have (as a contemporary put it: 'miserabell Negros borne to perpetual slavery they and Thayer seed'). Furthermore, the planters decided that the black man was the better worker; some said he did the work of three whites. A young George Downing[93] wrote to Governor Winthrop in August 1645 that the Barbados planters had bought that year as many as 'a thousand Negroes; and the more they buie [buy], the better able they are [to] buye [buy], for in a year and a halfe they will earne (with gods blessing) as much as they cost'.

The main suppliers were the Dutch, but English traders who had thrived in the servant trade, like William Vassall, Thomas Kendall and Martin Noell, simply switched their operations to dealing in slaves… By the early 1650s, the leading planters, including Drax and his neighbour Middleton, had shares themselves in slave trading vessels, if not outright ownership.[94]

By now, Barbados had become England's wealthiest colony and, according to George Downing again: "one of the richest Spots of earth under the Sun".[95]

The English Revolution

The English Revolution—or Civil War—finally broke out in 1640, initially seeming to be a conflict between the kingdoms of England, Scotland and Ireland; it soon became a struggle between the absolute rule of King Charles on the basis of 'divine right' and Parliament's assertion of its historic 'rights and powers', their slogan being "No taxation without representation". This was the very same cry taken up roughly 130 years later on by Americans in their revolutionary war against Britain.[96] The conflict split families and broke up cosy cartels.

1642—Oct. 23, the Battle of Edgehill, Warwickshire. By this time the Castle and walls of Bristol were repaired by the Magistrates, also a fort built on Brandon-Hill, with a communication to another on St Michael's Hill, where previously stood a wind-mill (which was afterward improved as a royal pentagonal fort), and to another, on the site of a garden behind the existing house erected by Mr William Racster, at Montague Parade, which, after the first siege was called Colston's Mount,[97] from the circumstance of William Colston (father of the benevolent Edward) having then the command of it, and being also, under the Duke of Beaufort, Deputy-Governor of the City and Castle. The Mayor, Richard Aldworth, refused Lord Paulet, who sent to him Sir Fernando Gorges[98] and Mr Smyth of Ashton to bring troops of horse into the city; he having received express orders from the King to admit no troops of either party, but to keep and defend the city for His Majesty's use.

During the Civil War William Colston was one of the "many malignants of the great ones" when Colonel Essex declared "Bristol's fidelity to parliament" on 10th December 1642. Colston was named as one of the leaders of a plot to let Prince Rupert's forces into the city and initiate a royalist uprising. The plan was discovered by the Parliamentarians "upon the information of some females" and consequently failed on the night of 8th March 1643. For their part in the plot, royalists George Boucher and Robert Yeamans were executed on 30th May 1643, whilst Colston (and others) were reprieved.[99]

On 23rd July 1643, Prince Rupert, who was on his way to Bristol, fixed his quarters at Westbury College. Before leaving he set fire to the buildings, in order to prevent their occupation by Parliamentary forces. These were the college buildings, erected by Bishop Carpenter in 1447 with the aid of William Canynges. They were splendid buildings, a worthy home for a society which, either in a monastic or collegiate form, had been in existence from about A.D. 715.[100]

Bristol finally fell to Rupert on 27th July 1643.[101] Many of the injured were treated in the Great House where the fight for the Frome Gate had been especially fierce.

Dissident non-conformist Dorothy Hazard had refused to surrender the city as Parliamentarian leaders vacillated. She and some 200 other women and girls had shored up the defences at the Frome Gate by using woolsacks and had offered to "march up to the cannons mouths and deaden the bullets" in order to rally the defending troops. After the fall of the city to the Royalists, Dorothy and a small group of her closest allies first escaped to Wales, then walked to London, where they continued their religious beliefs. Not yet Baptist, they called themselves the 'assembly' and it was as this gathering that they were joined by a black maid from the Backs, (nowadays Welsh Back) Bristol called Francis. Described as a 'servant, Blackymore, sister and Baptist', she remarkably went on to become one of the leaders of the sect. Hazard, formerly Mrs Kelly, had been a religious dissident since the 1630s and had endured much persecution. It's thought the assembly attended the 'Putney Debates', see 1647.[102]

> **1643**—Aug. 2, the King [Charles I] and his sons [the future Charles II and James II] entered the city, and were entertained at Mr [William] Colston's house in Small-street.

On 14th September, William Colston became a member of the Corporation of Bristol and was elected Sheriff the following day; he was also made Treasurer of Queen Elizabeth's Hospital. As an active member of the Church of England, he had already been a Churchwarden of Christ Church (Broad Street) since the previous year.[103] Charles I was in Bristol to settle the differences between Prince Rupert and the Marquis of Hertford about the Governorship of the city. As Sheriff, William led the King's procession to a Cathedral service.

Dorothy Hazard (Kelly) defending the Frome Gate during the English Revolution.

As we have seen, William was staunchly Royalist and so were other members of the family including his brother Thomas, Edward's uncle, who became Colonel of the Trained Bands of Charles I in Bristol. Thomas used a good deal of his own fortune strengthening the Kingsdown redoubt, known at the time as 'Colston's Fort or Mount'. A former Master of the Society of Merchant Venturers himself, the organisation had promised to repay Thomas for his expenditure on the Fort but seemingly failed to do so.[104]

Cromwell's New Model Army was formed in early 1645 and first unleashed on the Royalists at the battle of Naseby, where Charles suffered a crushing defeat. Fresh from that encounter the New Model Army marched straight to Bristol to take back England's second port. Leading the assault on Prior's Hill Fort, Bristol's most strategic northerly point—Colston's Fort was south west from here[105]—was Colonel Thomas Rainsborough's[106] regiment. The fighting was especially fierce in this location and neither side gave any quarter. Just after the bloody encounter, which lasted some three hours, New Model Army Commanders Fairfax and Cromwell were sitting on top of Prior's Hill Fort watching the continuation of the battle. Within moments a bullet from the Castle grazed within two hands breadth of them, without hurting either.[107]

Rupert surrendered Bristol to Parliament on 10th September 1645. William Colston and other pro-royalist councillors were immediately 'purged' of their positions.[108] In addition, both William Colston and his brother Col. Thomas Colston were dismissed from their roles in Bristol's governance by Order of the Lords and Commons as punishment for assisting the King.[109] It is supposed that during this tumultuous period of Bristol's history, the young Edward Colston and his siblings had been sent to "breathe the purer atmosphere of Winterbourne" in South Gloucestershire, where the family had more property.[110] After the fall of Bristol to the Parliamentarians, it's thought that William and the family left for London.[111]

The Putney Debates of 1647 are a little known but pivotal moment in English history where the victorious New Model Army discussed their, and the nation's, future. Representatives of the army proposed the *Agreement of the People*. Hunt described this as a:

> purposively radical text proposing a constitutional settlement that would be the envy of many post-conflict nations today. It urged religious toleration ("The ways of God's worship are not at all entrusted by us to any human power"); a general amnesty and an end to conscription; a system of laws that must be "no respecter of persons but apply equally to everyone: there must be no discrimination on grounds of tenure, estate, charter, degree, birth or place"; regular, two-yearly parliaments and an equal distribution of MPs' seats by number of inhabitants. At its heart was a profound belief in human liberty and a conviction that politicians were as dangerous as princes when it came to undermining personal freedom. It was the people who were sovereign.[112]

Prominent amongst the debaters was Thomas Rainsborough who, as well as being a great commander, was a leading Leveller—arguably England's first Democratic movement. Two other topics that defined the debates were the encroachment on the people's commons and slavery of every kind. Here's Linebaugh and Rediker's take on Rainsborough's contribution

> When Rainsborough inveighed against slavery, he included emancipation of several kinds: the practice of impressments, spiriting or kidnapping to the Americas, the capture for forced labour of English people in West and North Africa [for the actions of his father against 'Turkie and Argiere' see 1635], and the enslavement of Africans. Agitation against slavery was an essential element in the publications and practices of the Levellers. They fought to abolish slavery. What was at issue, then, was not a rhetorical abstraction of political propaganda, but something real, experienced, suffered and known. A rough definition of slavery at the time would include these features: it began in an act of expropriation and terror; it affected children and young people particularly; it compelled violent exploitation; and more often than not, it ended in death... The labouring subjects of the Atlantic economy met this definition an era well before race or ethnicity came to define slavery.[113]

Rainsborough was assassinated the following year by a group of Royalists.

| **1649**—Oct. 4, Col Scroop [Scrope] made Governor of Bristol Castle.

Colonel Adrian Scrope was governor until Bristol Castle was demolished on the orders of Oliver Cromwell in 1655. He was the 27th of 59 commissioners who signed King Charles I death warrant and, after the Restoration, was hanged, drawn and quartered on October 17 1660.[114]

One by-product of the English Civil War was a surfeit of prisoners whose only crime, in general, was to be on the losing side. The demand for labour in the plantations of the Americas provided a fortuitous 'solution' to the costly problem of incarceration and subsistence for these unfortunates. Bristol was at the forefront of the scheme to transport prisoners of war into forced labour on the plantations, as Robinson relates:

In August 1648—during the Civil War—Cromwell defeated the king's Scottish army in Lancashire and took thousands of prisoners. Promptly, 'the gentlemen of Bristol applied to have liberty to transport 500 of the prisoners to the plantations'. The request was granted, and 500 Scottish slaves were shipped from Bristol to live, work and die on the big estates in Jamaica or Virginia, many of them owned by Bristolians. After another royalist defeat at Worcester in 1651, more Scots prisoners went down the Avon to be transported into slavery. In July 1652 it was the turn of the Irish. The Council of State ordered the Governor of Waterford to deliver to three Bristol merchants as many Irish prisoners as they wanted for the West Indies; and three months later another merchant took collection of 200 Irishmen for sale in Barbados.[115]

After a stand-off between Parliamentarians and Royalists in Oistins, Barbados, a settlement was reached whereby the island accepted the rule of Parliament in exchange for "as great a freedom of trade as ever". It followed on from the First Navigation Act of 1651 which demanded that:

...no colonial produce be shipped to England except in vessels owned and for the most part manned by Englishmen or colonials, and that European goods could not be imported by the colonies except in English ships or those of the country where the goods were produced. It was a measure to ensure that the English colonies benefited no one but the English at home.[116]

This promotion of mercantilism through the control of shipping immediately led to the first Anglo-Dutch war, and then further acts such as the Molasses Act and the Sugar Act led to the American Revolution. Another act controlling flags of convenience inadvertently led to the abolition of the slave trade in 1807.

> **1653**—Dec. 16, Cromwell was declared Lord Protector of the Commonwealth of England, Scotland, and Ireland, and of all the dominions and territories thereunto belonging.

In 1654, Alderman John Knight Jr. bought the Great House, St Augustine's Back, to be used as Bristol's second sugar refinery, the first to use sugar from the Caribbean. It was purchased from Lady Gorges, the wife of the famous Sir Fernando Gorges who has been called 'The Father of American Colonisation' and who was amongst the original group of wealthy investors in the Royal African Company. Gorges was also a financial backer and patron of Knight's refinery in the Great House.[117] Lady Gorges was the fourth wife of Fernando and the widow of Sir Hugh Smyth. Her oldest son was Thomas 'Honest Tom' Smyth, father of Florence.

Part of the house was converted into the sugar refinery whilst the remainder was occupied as private apartments.[118] Knight soon got into trouble with the Corporation for using up the supply of water to St John's parish—the refining process needing an abundant supply. The dispute wasn't resolved until 1st March 1679 when the owners and occupiers of the Great House—Joseph Knight (son of John Knight Jr. who had died earlier that year) and lessee Sir Richard Lane—came to an agreement with George Dighton, brewer, and John Deane, ropemaker, of St John's. Sir Richard Lane had become the sugar baker the year before and occupied the Great House that year. It flourished under his stewardship right up until his death in 1704/5. Both Knight and Lane had remarkably similar careers; both were Freemen of Bristol, Common Councillors, Sherriff, Mayor (Knight once, Lane twice) and Masters of the Merchant Venturers.[119]

The Dissenters

Dissenters, or non-conformists, were people who split away from the established church in the 16th, 17th and 18th Centuries. They had been central to the English Revolution, fighting passionately against absolute monarchy and opposing state interference in religion. There were numerous organised groups of dissenters in this period as one critical commentator Thomas Hall pointed out in 1660:

> ...a numberless crew of locusts have sprung out of the bottomless pit, assuming to themselves the names of Arians, Arminians, Socinians, Antinomians, Anabaptists, Familists, Antiscripturists, Antisabbatarians, Antitrinitarians, Libertines, Erastians, Levellers, Mortalists, Millenaries,

Enthusiasts, Separatists, Semiseparatists, Quakers, and many more of the same brood ... No country from the foundation of the world hath brought forth and brought up, so many monstrous births as it [England] hath done.

These groups represented a major threat to the church and state leading to repression or 'Quaker-Bashing' as historian Derek Robinson succinctly put it in 1973. As we shall see this became particularly prevalent after the restoration of the monarchy in 1660.

> **1654**—This year the city was much troubled by a sort of people called Quakers, who interrupted the ministers in their pulpits. Therefore the *Apprentices* rose to turn them out of the city.

After an extensive research of school registers in London, Wilkins concludes that young Edward Colston was most probably educated at Christ's Hospital School in London. At midsummer 1654, according to the books of the Mercers Company (London), at the age of seventeen years and seven months Colston was apprenticed for a term of eight years to Humfray Aldington, mercer.[120] A mercer in layman's terms is a merchant in cloth; to this day the Worshipful Company of Mercers is the premier, and most influential, Livery Company of the City of London.

> **1655**—British [English] take Jamaica from the Spanish—Bristol Admiral Sir William Penn in command. Slaves on the island escape into the mountains and establish 'Maroon' settlements.

This mission was part of Cromwell's 'Western Design' with the aim to take the larger island of Hispaniola—today split between Haiti and the Dominican Republic. The Western Design was a shambles from beginning to end and set the template for further disastrous forays into the West Indies by first English and then British Armed Forces. The expedition was mismanaged and ill-equipped; delayed deployment of the soldiers led to disease and drunkenness that decimated the troops before a shot was even fired. Penn's land-based commander General Venables was so inept he was ambushed by the Spanish and their allies twice in the same place on Hispaniola.

En route to Hispaniola, Penn and Venables stopped off at the island of Barbados and, according to Linebaugh and Rediker "carried away some four thousand servants and former servants" to aid in the invasion. This severely depleted the island's workforce and encouraged the big planters to use yet more enslaved Africans.[121] One such 'carried away' man was Henry Morgan who had been shipped from Bristol to Barbados as an indentured apprentice. Having tired of working for a Bristol cutler, Morgan joined the 'Western Design' and ultimately became a notorious pirate and dodgy Deputy Governor of Jamaica. On their return to England, Penn and Venables were sent to the Tower of London for their "ill conduct" in losing the prize of Hispaniola. Cromwell was obviously not satisfied with the 'booby prize' of Jamaica, although it was nearly 30 times the size of Barbados. The forthcoming colonisation of Jamaica was, as Linebaugh and Rediker noted, "closely linked to England's greedy rush into the slave trade".[122]

> **1656**—Oct. 31, a Committee of Parliament appointed to examine into the blasphemy of James Naylor, the Quaker, who personated our Saviour at Bristol and other places. Nov. 10, the Protector sent for James Naylor, Dorcas Erbury, and other Quaker-preachers, to London. Dec. 8 the Committee resolved that Naylor was guilty. Dec. 17, the Speaker pronounced judgement,—whipping, the pillory, and boring his tongue with a hot iron. He stood once in the Palace-yard, and once at the Old Exchange—was whipped from Westminster to the Old Exchange by the common hangman, where his tongue was bored, and the letter B marked on his forehead—sent to Bristol, and conveyed through the city on a horse with his face backward—here publicly whipped on a market-day, and then committed close prisoner to Bridewell, London, during the pleasure of Parliament. (Naylor's extravagancies doubtless increased the public prejudice against the Quakers generally. He was discharged Sept. 8, 1559; when he came to Bristol, and made a public recantation in a meeting of his friends, in so affecting a manner, they were convinced of the sincerity of his repentance, and became reconciled to him. He died aged 44.)

Naylor's severe punishment was interrupted by a petition led by Colonel Scrope, former Governor of Bristol Castle, who was shocked at the inhumanity of the sentence and pleaded for clemency but to no avail.[123] Naylor had chosen to come to Bristol as it was the epicentre of religious dissent which had given birth to both the Baptists and the Quakers. A former Quartermaster in Cromwell's Army—where he used to preach before going into battle—Naylor was an early outspoken critic of slavery:

> Where can the innocent go out and not a trap laid to bring him into bondage and slavery to some of these spirits?[124]

After his imprisonment, Naylor's contemporary, rival and successor, George Fox, took up the mantle of anti-slavery protest in 1657 in Barbados with an epistle *To Friends Beyond the Sea That Have Black and Indian Slaves.*[125]

Quaker James Naylor being punished for blasphemy:
"whipping, the pillory, and boring his tongue with a hot iron".

Subsequently he tried to set up schools for Africans in Nevis, Barbados and on the American mainland, only for them all to be quashed.

After the short-lived republic and the restoration of the monarchy in 1660, Charles returned to Bristol as king in 1663 and was treated to a banquet in the Great House. Another feast was held here with the visit of his brother, King James II in 1687.[126]

Throughout Edward Colston's lifetime, religious dissenters, a significant minority of Bristol's population,[127] were hounded and bullied. In 1660 Government Commissioner Richard Ellsworth declared:

These... Monsters of Men with uss, are very, yea more Numerous, then in all the West of England... on this side [of] London; & here they all Confer, & have Their Meetings, att all seasons till 9 of the clock att night, & later, sometymes aboue 1000, or 1200 att a tyme, to the greate affrighting of the City [Bristol], as to what wilbe the Consequence thereof, If not restrained.[128]

As a result of this 'restraint' many dissenters paid for their beliefs with their lives.

Also in 1660, Bristol Quaker Jonas Langford landed in Antigua to make the first sugar fortune there; he was followed by Christopher Codrington II in

1668. Codrington's standing in Barbados had soured after accusations of theft and murder, and he took windmill technology to his *Betty's Hope* plantation in Antigua while he quietly grew his operations, leasing Barbuda in the process. Erstwhile Governor of Jamaica, Thomas Modyford, expanded the sugar industry from Barbados to Jamaica in 1666, before dying in 1671. This left the way open for the ruthless Beckford dynasty to prosper and become super rich in Jamaica.[129]

‖ **1660s**—Demand for African labour for the sugar plantations intensifies.

The high attrition rate in the plantations amongst workers combined with the rapid expansion of the sugar industry contributed greatly to this increased demand for labour. This demand was initially being met by enslaved Africans, indentured servants and penal labour. However it was the former that became the predominant source of labour as the century progressed. There were several reasons for this. First, by the 1660s the value of enslaved Africans had made them a more attractive financial proposition than indentured servants. Second, the number of enslaved Africans available far outweighed the supply of labourers from England. Third, the mortality rate amongst Europeans in the Caribbean was higher than that of enslaved Africans.

Up until the 1660s these three groups of forced labourers had literally been thrown together on the plantations, there was little segregation between them and their treatment and conditions of work were similar. No matter the origins of their bondage, chattel slave, prisoner or servant they were:

> ...chattels; their labour was organized and maintained by violence. Floggings and brandings left bodies scarred beyond the imagination... "the distinction, often made, between selling their labour as opposed to selling their persons makes no sense whatsoever in real human terms." The same Devil controlled all.[130]

The ensuing revolts, which involved all of these groups, terrified the plantocracy who feared above all the rebellious alliance between slaves and servants. One solution to their problem was to divide these groups, to create a hierarchy amongst them and encourage distrust. These divisions were formally introduced in the slave and servant code of 1661 in Barbados, which later became the model for similar codes in Jamaica, South Carolina, Antigua and St Kitts. The resulting legal and social separation laid the foundation for the servants to become "a labour elite, as artisans, overseers, and members of the militia, who, bearing arms, would be used to put down slave revolts".[131]

Meanwhile on 2nd November 1661, William Colston was 'restored' to Bristol and appointed alderman of the city once again; he was also made Deputy-

Lieutenant before retiring from active civic life in 1664. On completion of his apprenticeship in 1662, his son Edward's life is again shrouded in mystery; tradition states that he was working abroad in his father's trading concerns as a factor, probably based in Lisbon, Portugal.[132]

In 1663 Sir John Knight, cousin of sugar refiner John Knight Jr, became Mayor of Bristol. The climate in the aftermath of the restoration of the monarchy in 1660, which included fears of republican insurrection, allowed Knight to set about purging the Quaker community. This led to one of the most violent periods of religious persecution in Bristol's history. Hundreds of Baptists and Quakers were imprisoned, some tortured and others transported to the West Indies as penal labourers. Quakers claimed that Knight wanted "the rooting of us, and the generation of us, out of this city".[133]

> **1664**—Sir William Penn [Quaker William Penn's father] appointed Great Captain Commander, under the Duke of York, preparatory to the successful engagement with the Dutch fleet, commanded by Opdam, on the 3rd of June, off Harwich.

At the time of the Restoration Admiral Penn had switched sides and had left the Parliamentarians for the Royalists. His reward was a rapid rise in the ranks to become the overall commander-in-chief of the Navy and colleague of the celebrated diarist Samuel Pepys, who was a naval administrator at this time. Whilst his duplicitous father was reaching the zenith of his career in the English state, young William Penn appeared in Bristol as a preacher among the Quakers in 1668.[134]

> **1670**—Sir John Knight, M.P. having informed the King that the Mayor (John Knight [Jr.], sugar-refiner) and most of the Council were fanatics, Sir Robert Yeamans was sent for by His Majesty, and committed to the Tower. The Mayor was then sent for and examined; when the contrary soon appeared... the informer was obliged to beg pardon of the King on his knees.

Ultra-Tory former Mayor Sir John Knight, royalist and arch repressor of the dissenters in Bristol, denounced the Council and his own cousin because of their perceived puritan leanings. The accusations were eventually proved false after the intervention of Mayor John Knight (Jnr) and the innocent Robert Yeamans was duly released.

Also at this time in the Americas, another of the Yeamans family was making a name for himself. In 1671, Barbadian planters were expanding into Carolina; in their vanguard was Sir John Yeamans. As Carolina's first Colonial Governor he founded Charles Town (Charleston) on the Ashley River and had the dubious honour of being the first to import enslaved Africans into the fledgling State. This 'entitled' Yeamans to a 100-acre bounty for each of the 200 people he brought to the colony, which also enabled him to secure the largest plantation, much to the chagrin of his fellows. Charleston, as the port became known, was to become the centre for handling a large number of the enslaved indigenous population as well as for receiving vast numbers of enslaved Africans for the American continent. It would also be here in Charleston harbour, nearly 200 years later, that the first shots of the American Civil War would sound out during the Confederate attack on Union held Fort Sumter, heralding the end of slavery in the United States.[135]

Edward Colston

As we have seen, Edward Colston came from a powerful and well-connected family with contacts in Bristol and London. Complete with his Bluecoat education, apprenticeship with a premier mercantile trading company in London and overseas interests as a 'mere merchant' in the Mediterranean, he was well groomed to become one of the leading lights in the Royal African Company.

The Royal African Company

Edward Colston's time abroad, acting as a factor for the Colston family business, was key to his future success with the Royal African Company. These activities laid the foundation of his becoming a major supplier of goods to be traded on the Guinea coast, by garnering contacts and knowledge around the Iberian Peninsula and into the Mediterranean. According to the Port Books of the City of London Colston started shipping goods such as worsted hose and Spanish wine to and from London by 1672.[136] In 1673 he finally sought admission to the Mercers' Company after paying a small fine for his neglect—he should have taken up his membership in 1662.[137]

Immediately after the restoration of the monarchy in 1660, Charles II granted a select group of London merchants a monopoly over the African slave trade, with the formation by charter of the 'Company of Royal Adventurers Trading to Africa'. Because of the second war with the Dutch (1665–1667), which the English lost, the company ran into debt and was reformed as the Royal African Company (RAC) in 1672 with James, Duke of York, becoming its Governor.

The Charter of the Royal African Company states:

"We hereby for us, our heirs and successors grant unto the same Royal African Company of England... that it shall and may be lawful to... set to sea such as many ships, pinnaces and barks as shall be thought fitting... for the buying, selling, bartering and exchanging of, for or with any gold, silver, Negroes, Slaves, goods, wares and manufactures..."

Witness the King at Westminster the seven and twentieth day of September [1672]

BY THE KING [CHARLES II][138]

This charter determined the limits of RAC activities from North Africa to the Cape of Good Hope and also defined the right to buy and sell enslaved Africans. It gave locations on the West African coast for their purchase and included projections for where the trade might be expanded. It concludes by claiming an economic justification for this trade in humans:

The Slaves they purchas[e]d are sent, for a Supply of Servants, to all His Ma[jes]tie's American Plantations which cannot subsist without them.[139]

Recent estimates suggest that the Royal African Company purchased and then transported 170,000 enslaved Africans across the Atlantic between 1672 and 1713. Of these approximately 36,000 died of dehydration, dysentery and scurvy during the crossing.[140] The cargos included women and children as young as six, with each being branded with the letters 'DY' for Duke of York and later, after James's accession to the throne in 1685, 'RAC' for Royal African Company. By 1675, the island of Nevis had become the main RAC entrepôt for slave trading in the Caribbean.

'Elephant and Castle' badge of the Royal African Company.

Edward Colston and his family were deeply involved in this early phase of the Atlantic slave trade. In 1674, William Colston became a member of the Royal African Company, joining the organisation by acquiring £400 worth of stock transferred from the holding of George Day, a founding member of the enterprise.[141] The Colston family were soon trading textiles of huge value and quantity, such as sletias and calicoes which were specifically required for acquiring enslaved Africans.[142] In that year William's transactions with the RAC amounted to over £3,000 in textiles alone.[143] Edward's brother Thomas was also involved; in 1679 he traded yet another commodity, a massive £600 worth of beads, also exchanged for enslaved Africans.[144]

Tragedy struck the family on 16th December 1675 when William, Colston's second son, was stabbed to death in Lisbon. William junior, another trader in the family business, was killed probably as result of a religious brawl; an Englishman called Hutchinson was implicated and on his return to England he was apprehended and brought to trial—he was acquitted through lack of evidence as had already happened in Portugal.[145]

‖ **1677**—First mention of a Bristol coffee house in the tenure of John ‖ Kimber in High Street.

Newly imported commodities such as tea, coffee and cocoa became the drinks of the masses and, as they all need sugar to sweeten them, sugar was "a rarity in 1650, a luxury in 1750, and had been transformed into a virtual necessity by 1850".[146] Quantity wise, 1lb of tea required 15lbs of sugar, which demonstrates the relative size of the sugar trade. Another lucrative by-product of sugar was molasses, which could be distilled into rum or 'kill devil'—it would become the 'spirit of choice' in the Americas. Tobacco too was becoming more and more important as national consumption kept increasing. As well as being a major importer, Bristol responded by becoming a prominent maker and seller of 'Shagg' tobacco, snuff, 'Segars' (cigars) and even clay pipes themselves.

Edward Colston joined his father as a member and shareholder of the Royal African Company on 26th March 1680, after buying £500 of stock from Captain Francis Wilshaw. He then "took the Oathe and was admitted a member"[147] quickly rising in rank to become an 'Assistant' within a year of joining.[148] This was not a minor role:

The word *Assistant* is somewhat of a misnomer suggesting the role of operative or subordinate; in practice these men were company executives. The entire burden of decision-making in the huge organisation that was the RAC was carried out by the Assistants and their committees that met multiple times a week. This day-to-day commitment to running the company's business tied its managers to living in London or its environs.[149] The Assistants, twenty-four of the wealthiest investors, effectively ran the company, decided its policies and direction and, of course, resourced, organised and managed its substantial slave trading arm.

Wilkins gives an example of Colston's day to day management of the RAC:

Edward Colston was present at the Courts held on August 16th and 18th 1681 when it was resolved 'that the Committee of Goods be desired to report Cargoes for the Shippes'. Hired by the Committee of Shipping being approved of by the Court; the *Charles* to receive her Negroes from the Gold Coast and the *Swallow* for Two hundred and Tenn Negroes from New Callabar. *Supply* for Two hundred and Eighty Negroes from Old Callabar, and *Good Hope* for Three Hundred and Twenty Negroes at Angola.[150]

So Colston was, in modern parlance, "on the board of the company" and eventually became Deputy Governor from 1689–91.[151] Holding these positions of power within the RAC provided Colston with plenty of 'insider knowledge' and the authority to act on this information. He was thus ideally placed to extract maximum profit from every stage of the 'triangular trade'.

Investors in the RAC were a select group limited to around 200 very wealthy people. Within this group Colston was a member of a further financial elite, the top 5 per cent, personally investing £1,600, equivalent today to millions of pounds.[152] On top of the increasing value of his shares were the dividends he collected; seven in all, amounting to £860, a fortune worth several millions more. Colston also acted as a money-lender to the RAC, furnishing it with loans of thousands of pounds at generous rates of interest (for himself). Outside of these financial investments Colston made further profits by trading commodities to the company for the purchase of enslaved Africans. Finally, the Colston family had a significant fleet of ships which it is likely the RAC hired as 'slaving vessels' at lucrative freight charges.[153] On 21st November 1681 Edward Colston's father, William, died at the age of 73 years; he was buried in All Saints Church, Bristol. Edward's legacies from his father included land and buildings at Hambrook in the Parish of Winterbourne, one thousand pounds of lawful money of England and a warehouse in St Peter's Churchyard.[154] After his father's death Edward further ingratiated himself with the mercantile elite in his native city through money lending:

"1682, June 15th. [Bristol Corporation] Received of Mr Edward Colston, of London. M'chant, £1,800, for which he is to have a Citie Seale, next Sealing day, at 5 p. cent; this money was to pay off a Seale of Ann Lysons... £1,800."

"1683, December 10th, Edward Colston, merchant was admitted to the freedom of the City, being the son of William Colston, deceased."

"1683, December 17th Mr Edward Colston, being a free Burgess of Bristol and a meire [mere] merchant, son of William Colston, merchant, decd [deceased], a late member of this Society [Merchant Venturers, Bristol], was admitted into the liberties of the same Society." The following undertaking was given:–"I do promise to be obedient to the rules and constitutions of this Hall, and will pay Mr Treasurer, and the Clerk and the Beadle, the accustomed fees. (Signed) EDWARD COLSTON."[155]

By becoming a free Burgess Colston was entitled to carry out commercial activities in the city without financial penalties; it was also a requirement to join bodies such as the Society of Merchant Venturers.

Colston's younger brother Thomas died during 1684 and bequeathed his house in Small Street, Bristol to Edward. Their widowed mother resided there, having vacated her house in Wine Street on the death of her husband William in 1681, and continued to do so until her own death in 1701.[156] Edward inherited Thomas's business in Small Street, along with a partnership in a sugar refinery in St Peter's churchyard, that traded with St Kitts. St Kitts, and its close neighbour Nevis, was the springboard for English and French expansion into the West Indies in the first half of the seventeenth century. It was the very same sugar refinery that had been founded by Robert Aldworth. Aldworth had been succeeded by Giles Elbridge, his son John Elbridge, Henry Willoughby and then Edward Colston with partners Captain Nathaniel Wade and Sir Thomas Day.[157] Colston, Wade and Day invested more money into the St Peter's churchyard refinery in 1689 but it would only last another seven years. After a more than 80 years continual production this sugar business was ended and sold to the Corporation for £800 in 1697. By then the premises consisted of a sugar-house, warehouse, counting-house, cooperage and private dwelling house.[158]

Kidnapping Knaves

Colston might have been involved in managing and profiting from the trade in enslaved Africans through his involvement in the RAC but, outside of illegal activities, Bristol merchants were not heavily involved in the trade at this stage.[159] The use of coerced labour in the Atlantic colonies was not something new to the Bristol judiciary or merchants. In its semi-legal forms such as indentured servitude or penal labour, or in its illegal forms such as 'spiriting'[160] and kidnapping, the practice was commonplace. The latter though would be publicly exposed by an unlikely figure…

1685—Feb. 6, the King [Charles II] died at Whitehall, of a fit of apoplexy, in the 55th year of his age.

Within a day, baronet Sir George Jeffreys was made Lord Chief Justice of the King's Bench and, by 18th February, the future King James II had published two papers, taken out of the late King's strong box, to prove he died a papist. This was the first of many attempts by James to justify taking the country back to Catholicism; he was crowned King on 23rd April. In response to these efforts James the Pretender, the Duke of Monmouth, landed at Lyme in Dorset on 1st June and proclaimed himself King at Taunton on 20th June. After this proclamation the Pitchfork Rebellion began with the Pretender swelling his army with untrained yokels along the way to his first major target, Bristol. The Duke got his rag tag army to Keynsham and actually crossed the County Bridge but didn't press home his advantage as Chilcott recounted:

Monmouth's rebellion, in 1685, is said to have failed in its object only by the duke's refraining to invest Bristol: when pressed to do so, the duke's compassionate answer: "God forbid that I should bring the calamities of fire and sword together on so noble a city," (the Duke of Beaufort having declared that he would set the town on fire in that event) naturally raised a sympathy for his cause; we find accordingly that Bristol was not forgotten in Judge Jeffreys "Progress."[161]

This cost Monmouth dear, he took a circuitous route back to Sedgemoor and was soundly beaten on 6th July by James's professional army led by the Earl of Faversham and Lord Churchill (the latter, a former Recorder of Bristol, went on to become the Duke of Marlborough and victor at Blenheim). It was a massacre: the King lost about 30 men killed and just over 200 wounded but at least 1,400 of Monmouth's men died in the fighting and pursuit. The rebels were tracked down by Colonel Kirke; "Kirke's Lambs", noted for their savagery, hanged or slaughtered anyone they caught. This wasn't enough for King James who wanted a 'fuller vengeance'. He recalled Kirke and appointed Chief Justice Jeffreys who would broker no defence and abused those he sentenced. Jeffreys arrived in Bristol in September and started his assize with the following statement:

Rebellion was like the sin of witchcraft, and Bristol had too many rebels who had added to the ship's lading[162]

To his great annoyance only six 'rebels' could be found, of whom three were reprieved and three hanged on Redcliffe Hill. He then switched his assault to the city's magistrates. For thirty years they had commuted prisoners' death sentences to transportation for life to work on plantations in the Americas, and in so doing made profits from this forced labour which they pooled and shared out.[163]

1685—Judge Jefferies [Jeffreys] accuses Bristol aldermen and justices of kidnapping English people to serve on their plantations in the Caribbean and Virginia.

Derek Robinson once more:

His [Jeffreys'] mission was to punish the rebels who had supported Monmouth's rebellion, and he spared neither himself nor them. In Devon and Somerset he had 233 prisoners hanged, quartered and gibbeted. Twelve were executed in Pensford, eleven in Keynsham. Jeffreys also sentenced about 850 to transportation as slaves to the West Indies, and it's interesting to see how well he knew their market value. He advised the king (James II) that they were in great demand and that His Majesty should therefore take care over deciding who got them, because they were worth £10 a head, if not £15.[164] No doubt some Bristol merchants were licking their lips, but James gave the prisoners to his queen and some of his courtiers to sell.

Jeffreys then moved to Bristol and opened his Assize at the Guildhall. He was in a foul temper when he arrived—he suffered from kidney stones and drank steadily in an effort to kill the pain—and the small number of rebels in the dock made him angrier. Six death sentences and several lashings were the most he could achieve. Jeffreys had never trusted Bristol, and this poor showing confirmed his blackest suspicions. After a series of blistering remarks, he became impatient with his own moderation: 'Come, come, gentleman,' he snapped, 'to be plain with you I find the dirt of the ditch in your nostrils. Good God! Where am I? In *Bristol*?'

The mayor, Sir William Hayman, and the aldermen were present in court, all gorgeously robed, and Jeffreys decided to give them a lick with the rough side of his tongue.

'Sir!' he barked. 'Mr Mayor, you I mean, kidnapper! And that old justice on the bench'—pointing at Alderman Lawford—'an old knave—he goes to the tavern, and for a pint of sack he will bind people servants to the Indies. A kidnapping knave! I will have his ears off, before I go forth of town.'

Clearly, Jeffreys knew all about the Bristol justices' racket. He flung a paper at the Town Clerk and ordered him to read it. The court—half of them fascinated, the other half terrified—listened to a detailed account of several kidnappings, culminating in an attempt by the mayor to have an alleged pickpocket transported for life.

Jeffreys exploded with rage. 'Kidnapper!' he shouted. 'Do you see the keeper of Newgate? If it were not in respect of the sword which is over your head, I would send you to Newgate, you kidnapping knave. You are worse than the pickpocket who stands at the bar. I hope you are men of worth. I will make you pay sufficiently for it!' And he did: he fined Hayman £1,000 on the spot...

The mayor and his friends paid for their offence, but they paid in cash, and discreetly. For all his crusading zeal to punish disloyalty, Jeffreys preferred to hang only the poor rebels and sell pardons to the rich ones. He took a large fortune out of the West Country. One example alone indicates the scale of the demands: Prideaux, son of a former Recorder of Bristol, paid him £15,000.[165]

Hayman, Edward Colston's brother-in-law, was fined £1,000, not for 'kidnapping' but for the vague offence "for suffering a boy committed to Bridewell to go beyond the sea". His fellow aldermen, however, Sir William Clutterbuck, Sir Robert Cann, John Lawford, John Napier, William Swymmer and Robert Kirke were ordered into recognisances, "with sufficient sureties, the principal £10,000 and the sureties in £5,000 each, to appear to answer an indictment at the King's bench for kidnapping".[166]

In some cases, disaffected convict transportees helped fuel the slave-based economy in the Americas, while others escaped and went 'on their own account' by becoming pirates—leading to the advent of the Golden Age of Piracy. One of the convicted rebels from the Monmouth Rebellion, Azariah Pinney, had his sentence of death commuted and was transported to the island of Nevis in 1685. Within a short space of time he acquired the family's first plantation, an interest the family would keep and add to right up until the 1830s and emancipation.[167]

Towards the end of James's reign, the Dissenters seemed to finally get a break, in the words of Derek Robinson:

Relief came with astonishing suddenness. In the spring of 1687, James II suspended all penal laws against Dissent, liberated those in gaol and declared that all sects were free to worship in public according to their faith. The fact that he did all this for the benefit of Roman Catholicism scarcely dampened the joy of the Dissenters. For the first time, they were free under law. But as I have said before, it's easier to change laws than people. In Bristol discrimination went on. The records of the Merchants Society (the Merchant Venturers) for 1711 show that Charles Harford, a merchant, applied to join and was rejected because he was a Quaker. Just to make its position quite clear, the Society passed a resolution: 'in future no professed Quaker should be admitted.[168]

Slave trader

In the meantime, Edward Colston was carrying on with his duties at the RAC and increasing his money-lending and mortgage broking on a large scale. Wilkins illustrates more of his actions:

> November 16, 23, December 1 1686 To Edward Colston Borrowed on Company's [RACs] Bill of debt for 3 months at 5 per cent £1,250. By Edward Colston his Dividend 160 guineas.

During 1686, at a most inconvenient time, Colston demanded the complete repayment of his loan to Bristol Corporation, when their total debt was £16,000. This almost pushed the Corporation into financial disaster.[169]

Monmouth's Rebellion and other obligations had pressed heavily on Bristol and expenses had been stretched to the limit. Wilkins speculates that the reason for Colston's change of heart regarding his loan was his disagreement with the policy of the Corporation; he would have no dealings with those who didn't share his values, especially if they were of a religious nature. As Wilkins says, "He never hesitated in using the power of his purse".[170] In this instance the Corporation was forced to offer securities on prime property in order to placate Colston in the short term before paying the remainder, including legal charges, to Thomas Edwards senior.[171]

Wilkins uses Colston's behaviour to his debtors to demonstrate his thoughts and character. For example, in 1692, after refusing the invitation to take over a debtor's property, Colston demanded that his unfortunate victims continued to work for nothing so that he was paid in full. Between 1686 and 1713 Wilkins cites some 23 court cases where Colston is involved in financial litigation, each time trying to extract his 'pound of flesh'.[172]

| **1689**—Feb. 13, [William and Mary] proclaimed King and Queen.

After William and his Dutch army landed in England, James II's position became untenable and he fled the country. Both the House of Commons and the House of Lords then agreed that James had abdicated, and that the throne was thereby vacant. Within 11 days William and Mary [Stuart] had become joint sovereigns. Seizing this opportunity, on 8th January 1689, Edward Colston transferred £1,000 of his RAC stock to William, Prince of Orange thereby putting him "on to a good thing".[173] This was clearly a political manoeuvre to bring the new monarch into the RAC, but it also happened to coincide with the point at which the stock reached its highest value in the company's history. Colston continued to buy and sell shares in the RAC until he ended his stockholding in 1691. Two weeks after this major transaction with the new

King, Colston took the oath of Deputy Governor of the RAC. This meant he became second in command of the entire organisation, sitting on all of the RAC committees.

Edward Colston's meteoric rise to the head of one of the most powerful English trading companies of the period was further enhanced in June 1689 when he was given the task of leading negotiations between the RAC and the Spanish over the "Asiento for Negroes".[174] The Asiento was the contract endorsed by the Spanish government for supplying enslaved Africans to the Spanish 'New World' colonies. The RAC had previously dabbled in selling slaves to agents of the Asiento from 1680–87 and the formal monopoly in slave trading to the New World was greatly sought after.[175] Colston would have been an ideal candidate for negotiating this treaty with his recent knowledge of managing and directing the African trade, previous mercantile experience in the Iberian Peninsula, and, we might suppose, command of the Spanish language.

In addition to the profits from the slave trade that Edward Colston accumulated in his time in the RAC, it is reckoned that he owned and operated a fleet of 40 ships at the peak of his activities, at least some of which he inherited after the deaths of his father and brother in the 1680s.[176] It is claimed that he sold these in 1689 netting another not inconsiderate sum when the cost of an ocean going vessel in the period varied between £2,500 and £10,000.[177] Eighteenth century historian Barrett claimed that Colston famously "never insured a ship and never lost one".

The legend of the dolphin on Colston's crest comes from the following incident according to Wilkins:

> One of his ships, returning from the West Indies heavily laden sprung a leak which the crew was unable to stop. The water was rapidly rising in the vessel, when a dolphin was sucked into the aperture whereby the vessel and crew were saved.[178]

‖ **1690**—First major slave revolt in Jamaica—begins in Clarendon.

From the very beginning of the occupation of Jamaica by English forces in 1655 the geography of the island made it difficult for the invaders to truly control it. The mountainous interior provided opportunities for relatively large groups to hide out and survive, plus it was excellent terrain for guerrilla warfare. After the invasion by Penn and Venables, several groups headed for the hills, including Spanish colonists, freed African slaves and indigenous Taíno. These groups intermingled at various points and became known as 'Maroons' (from the Spanish word 'cimarron' meaning 'runaway' or 'unruly'). The English were unable to fully suppress these Maroons so in the years after 1660 they ignored them and concentrated on developing the sugar plantation system on the coastal plains. This involved increasing the number of forced labourers; by 1673 there were 9,500 enslaved Africans on the island.[179]

There were a series of risings in 1673, 1678 and 1685–86, each involving hundreds of enslaved Africans. Many of these were successful in that surviving rebels were able to escape into the interior, in some cases defeat their pursuers and either form new Maroon groups or join existing communities. Despite counter-insurgency missions, brutal punishments and exemplary executions of captured rebels, the English were still unable to crush the insurgents. Their failure to tame the island's interior left two main groups of Maroons, the Leeward in the west of the island and the Windward in the east.

In 1690, four hundred enslaved Africans rose up on a plantation in the parish of Clarendon:

> [They] disposed of the person in charge of stores and, after seizing all the arms they could carry, proceeded to the next estate where they killed the white overseer and set the house afire. The troops were called out and twelve of the rebels killed in the ensuing engagement. In the course of the following month, sixty women and children and ten men surrendered. With 318 of them still at large, however, the Governor…feared "that (it) will be very dangerous to the mountain plantations". This group of rebels eventually joined ranks with the Leeward gang already established in the mountains "and greatly strengthened their party, having good arms and plenty of ammunition".[180]

The increasing strength, confidence and resilience of the various Maroon communities in Jamaica led them to successfully raid settlements and plantations for provisions and arms, whilst evading parties of soldiers and settlers sent to hunt them down. As we shall see, they would remain a serious thorn in the side of the British occupiers into the eighteenth century.

> **1691**—March 4, an earthquake was felt in Bristol; Edward Colston, esq. purchased of the Corporation 2 acres 3 quarters and 37 perches of pasture-ground, on St Michael's Hill… on which he built the Alms-house and Chapel, and three other messuages. The alms-house contains twelve men and twelve women. Trustees, the Society of Merchant-Venturers [endowed 1696]. The charge of building and finishing this house amounted to about £2,500 [opened 1695]; Richard Lane, sugar-baker, mayor, occupied the great house, St. Augustin[e]'s Place.

After serving his statutory two-year stint as Deputy Governor of the RAC in January 1691 Colston gave up the post but continued to serve on several committees; this was unusual as normally the sitting Deputy Governor would go on to serve in the top job of Sub Governor. In the following year, 1692, Colston ceased to be involved in the Royal African Company. Colston's departure on the brink of becoming the head of one of the most important English trading companies is curious. It may have been the consequence of his insider knowledge of the challenges to the RAC's monopoly and the organisation's financial weaknesses.[181]

During Colston's 12-year tenure in the RAC he helped organise and manage the shipping of 84,500 enslaved Africans to the Americas. Of these, only 65,200 Africans survived the crossing with 19,300 dying on the voyage, including several thousand children—a 23 per cent mortality rate. Of the enslaved Africans embarked on RAC ships, 49 per cent were men, 37 per cent women and 14 per cent children under the age of 10 years.[182]

In 1693 Edward Colston sat for one of four portraits, the first with artist Sir Godfrey Kneller the country's leading portrait painter of the day. In 1920 Wilkins stated that Kneller's portrait of Colston resided in St Bartholomew's Hospital, London. Another portrait he had at Mortlake was transferred to his school on St Augustine's Back and then on to Colston's School at Stapleton where it remains to this day. A more famous portrait by Richardson was handed down from the Corporation of Bristol to Bristol City Council and the last example resides in the Merchant Venturers' Hall.[183]

‖ **1696**—Board of Trade and Plantations set up by the British.

Hugh Thomas noted in *The Slave Trade*:

Another difficulty was that the company [RAC], largely an enterprise of London merchants, was from the beginning of its life denounced and often outmanoeuvred by interloping merchants and captains from 'outports'— principally Bristol, a great port from the Middle Ages onwards which by 1700 had become Britain's premier sugar and West Indies harbour. The city's distilleries and sugar refineries... on the Rivers Avon and Frome, were kept busy by the import of much raw sugar and molasses. (Bristol was also Britain's chief port for shipping, and kidnapping, indentured servants, many of whom came from Ireland.)[184]

By investing in early exploration and colonisation the Society of Merchant Venturers' overseas interests had greatly expanded. This led to plantations in the Americas and, to protect their trade in tobacco in the seventeenth century, the society helped suppress the growing of tobacco in Gloucestershire.[185] To augment their use of forced labour, which included indentured servants, convicts and prisoners of war in their plantation colonies, the Society campaigned to become involved in the transatlantic slave trade. As Charles Clark states in his history of the Society:

> For nearly forty years the Bristol merchants engaged in a truceless warfare as champions of free trade with Africa against the would-be monopolists of London.[186]

The "would-be monopolists from London" is a direct reference to the Royal African Company who, as we have seen, through Royal Charter, claimed exclusive rights to trade on the West coast of Africa. Throughout the 1690s the public propaganda war between the RAC in London and the Society of Merchant Venturers and other provincial merchants intensified as both sides lobbied (and bribed) in the background in order to gain or retain political influence over the Atlantic slave trade.[187]

In 1698, during the reign of William and Mary, the wishes of the Merchant Venturers were granted by Parliament and the African trade was opened up to maritime merchants across the country. As a consequence, the numbers of enslaved Africans transported across the Atlantic on English ships rapidly increased, more than tripling within 15 years. Pettigrew calculates the effect on mainland America alone:

> In the fifteen years prior to the 1698 act, slavers transported close to fifty-five hundred slaves to the American mainland. In the fifteen years after, that figure increased by nearly 300 percent to more than fifteen thousand.[188]

Within ten years of the overthrow of the Royal African Company's monopoly, Bristol's African fleet had grown to almost sixty vessels. As the slave trade expanded the RAC went into a protracted and terminal decline; by 1729 its market share had reduced from a high of 100 per cent in the 1680s to 4 per cent. It ceased trading in slaves in 1732 and was finally dissolved in 1752.[189]

1699—May 20, Christopher Codrington, esq. [III] fellow of Allsouls, Oxford, made Captain-General and Governor of the Caribbee Islands [Caribbean], in the room of his father. Col. Codrington, [II] deceased.

The Sugar Barons continued to rule with a rod of iron and their need for labour in the Caribbean grew and grew. The massive supply of enslaved Africans made their numbers superior to all other ethnic groups and by 1700 they comprised 80 per cent of all residents in the English possessions. Of the estimated 300,000 workers shipped to America and the West Indies from

England, Scotland and Ireland during the seventeenth century, it's estimated that some 200,000 of them were either indentured servants, many of whom were forced by poverty to give up their 'freedom', those convicted of crimes and sentenced to penal servitude or those 'spirited' by 'kidnapping knaves'—abducted children or adults.[190] It's a fair assumption that amongst these there were political and religious opponents of the merchant elites who ended up 'going west', or being 'Barbadosed'. In Bristol, as we have seen, there is evidence that dissident religious non-conformists such as Quakers and Baptists were specifically targeted for transportation to the colonies. This appears to have been particularly prevalent after the restoration of the monarchy in 1660 and the subsequent criminalisation of these politico-religious sects.[191]

> **1702**—Feb. 21, the King [William III] thrown from his horse in riding from Kensington to Hampton-Court, which broke his right collar-bone. March 6, he died, in the 52d year of his age.

Anne, daughter of King James and youngest sister of the late Queen Mary, became Queen on St George's day, 23 April, aged 37 years. She was the last of the Stuarts to reign.

Nicholls writing in *Bristol: Past and Present* states that Jeffreys did not stamp out the practice of kidnapping and quotes a local annalist writing in the reign of Queen Anne:

> There is not a brick in the city but what is cemented with the blood of a slave. Sumptuous mansions, luxurious living, liveried menials, were the produce of the wealth made from the sufferings and groans of the slaves bought and sold by the Bristol merchants. From the first cargo of human flesh sent to Ireland until the abolishing of the abhorrent traffic, they traded largely in the living commodity. In their childlike simplicity they could not feel the iniquity of the merchandise, but they could feel it lucrative; advancing it as a reason for certain privileges.[192]

Philanthropist and Loyalist

As well as being mainly resident in Mortlake from 1689, Edward Colston's interests included being a Governor and benefactor of Christ's Hospital (formerly in London, known as Bluecoat school, now in Horsham, West Sussex) from 1684. In addition to this he added to his philanthropy—see 1691—by building Almshouses and a chapel on St Michael's Hill in Bristol. In 1696, after one of Colston's ships turned up after being missing for some years, he applied to the Merchant Venturers to make room for "six poor sailors in our almshouse". Colston, having initially written off the missing ship, then "sold both ship and cargo and applied the proceeds to the relief of sailors".[193]

His 1691 Almshouses cost him £8,500 and his total outlay in London for various institutions was £6,100 with the lion's share of £2,500 going to St Bartholomew's. He also chipped in for churches in Tiverton, Devon and Manchester and £540 for educating and clothing 12 boys and 12 girls in Mortlake.[194]

> **1702**—Edward Colston, esq. proposed to increase Queen Elizabeth's Hospital [QEH], by a further endowment from himself, for 100 boys instead of 44, provided the Corporation would erect a fabric equal to their reception; but this was not agreed to.[195]

Colston had initially endowed QEH in 1695 when he paid for an additional six spaces for more boys to be educated.[196] One year after his mother's death, Colston wished to make another larger endowment to QEH (sometimes referred to as the 'City School') but was rebuffed by the Corporation after his conditions were turned down. He had been deeply involved in the High Anglican and strictly Tory scheme for "Dissemination of religious and moral instruction" and the political and religious conditions were apparently too harsh for a Corporation with a large Whig presence. Seemingly by way of consolation, Bristol Corporation commissioned a portrait of Edward Colston by artist Jonathan Richardson, one of the three foremost painters of the day.[197] This popular portrait was engraved and sold as a print back in the day.

Some recent letter writers to the *Bristol Post* believe that it was at about this time of his life that Edward Colston decided to cease slave trading activities and switch fully to philanthropy.[198] Some have even suggested that he underwent some kind of "religious conversion" and renounced slavery.[199] Unfortunately, there is little or no evidence for this. In fact, as we shall see, Colston returned to the 'vile trade' both as an investor and a political advocate—if he ever went away from it.

Colston's 'fixer' in Bristol was Thomas Edwards senior, attorney-at-law of Redland and Broad Street; his turnover in fees in 1690 was so great that he was able to buy the Somerset manor of Clapton-in-Gordano for £4,350. The connection with Colston was mutually beneficial as Edwards' standing in the local community blossomed throughout his management of Colston's extensive affairs in the west. This was despite Edwards' political affiliation; he was described as a 'Whig Dissident'. As we have seen, Colston was particularly litigious and Edwards reaped the rewards, also being Colston's legal adviser to his many charitable associations. In his private life Edwards senior was

St Peter's Hospital (formerly Aldworth'
Colston's Sugar House, Bristol's
oldest sugar refinery).

Badge of the Society for the
Propagation of the Gospel in
Foreign Parts.

interested in the Bristol Society for the Reformation of Manners, or Morals as we would say today, and was involved in setting up the Corporation of the Poor in 1696, in Colston's old St Peter's sugar refinery. [200]

Colston's relationship with Edwards senior was further cemented in 1703 when Thomas Edwards junior (who would become Colston's replacement as MP for Bristol in 1713) married Colston's niece Mary. They settled in Filkins Hall, Oxford which was possibly a dowry gift from Colston.[201] Mary was the only daughter and heir of Sir William Hayman. Hayman was a West India merchant with a 500-acre plantation in Jamaica who had married Mary Colston—Edward Colston's sister—in 1670. Hayman had been made sheriff of Bristol in 1679 followed by mayor five years later when he was also knighted. As we have seen, he was the 'kidnapping knave' accused of trafficking children by bloody Judge Jeffreys in 1685; he ultimately died in 1702 aged 77.

Other recent commentators in the *Bristol Post* (2017) have suggested that the last thing on Colston's mind was the perpetuation of his name; this simply isn't so, as historian Wilkins explains in his entry for 1706:

> Edward Colston had survived all his immediate near relatives. His will shows that he has no near kinsman bearing his name. Onwards and increasingly so he disposes of his wealth for the perpetuation of his name and charitable purposes.[202]

On 2nd July 1708, the vicar of Temple Parish, Bristol, the Rev. Arthur Bedford,[203] proposed Colston as a corresponding member of the Society for Promoting Christian Knowledge (SPCK), and the Society asked Bedford to enquire of Colston if he would accept. The reply was favourable, "provided it don't oblige him to write frequent letters." Colston fell out with Bedford soon after as he had the temerity to differ from him in politics.[204] A prominent, passionately devoted High Anglican layman, Colston went on to become an early leader of the SPCK [205] but this again, as Wilkins' research shows, didn't stop him continuing with his extensive trading:

> ...wine, oil, bayes, raisins, currants, "perpetts"[206], timber, silk, indigo, serges, sarsaparilla, coppras, soap, sugar, iron, alum, powder, groceries, draperies, "sletias", wax, hides, figs, etc., ... It was not till 1708—when he had reached his 72nd year—that he was "inclined to retire from business," as he himself states in one of his letters. When he actually did so—if ever he did—is not known.[207]

As we have discussed, commodities such as perpetts and sletias were important currency on the Guinea Coast for purchasing enslaved Africans.

1709—Edward Colston, esq. purchased of the widow of Alderman Lane, sugar-boiler, the great house on St Augustin[e]'s Back, and established it as a hospital, with a master and two ushers, for 100 boys, to be fed, clothed, and instructed in writing and arithmetic, till they should attain 14 years, with £10 each as fee of apprenticeship. The expense of erection and endowment, all in his life-time, was £40,000. The estates and lands and ground-rent produced at this time £1,318 15s 6d. The charge of fitting up the school and dwelling-house was about £11,000.

The Great House was initially purchased by Edward Colston's committee of Merchant Venturers (after Colston's first approach to the Merchant Venturers in 1706 for a hospital school) in 1708 for £1,500 before eventually being sold somewhat dubiously to Colston himself for the smaller sum of £1,300 in 1709.[208]

At about this time Colston chose the Society of Merchant Venturers to act as trustees and administrators of his new Colston Hospital Trust which controlled his school, a role that they carry out to this day.[209] Brown and Harris again:

In spite of his many benefactions, Colston was an intolerant man. He was a Tory, and a supporter of the High Church party in religion, and it is to be noted that when he established a school of his own, the children of Dissenters were rigorously excluded, and books containing any political doctrines savouring of the Whigs were forbidden. It is very likely that he attempted to attach some conditions to his offer in 1703 [1702], and that it was refused in consequence.[210]

Edward Colston had also been a member of the Society for the Propagation of the Gospel in Foreign Parts (SPG) since 1704.[211] The SPG were a sister society to the SPCK. One of the founding roles of the SPCK was to act as a sort of unofficial governing body for charity schools throughout Britain, setting standards for existing ones and promoting new ones. Both Societies were founded by Dr Thomas Bray, the former to counter the influence of Roman Catholic and dissenter missionary activities in the colonies. Sugar Baron Christopher Codrington III, who died in 1710, gifted two of his Barbados plantations to the SPG. For the first decade of their ownership the SPG branded their enslaved Africans with the word 'SOCIETY' on their chests.[212] They not only kept 300 slaves working there but imported fresh captives every year to keep the numbers up.[213] Despite their belated support for abolition from 1783, the SPG kept its slaves and its plantations up until the 1834 emancipation of the enslaved in the British Empire, collecting £8,558 (equivalent in 2016 to £10.3 million by GDP per capita conversion) for 410 enslaved Africans in compensation. The two SPG plantations were called *College* and *Uphill* and were situated in the Parish of St John. Just prior to emancipation in the mid-

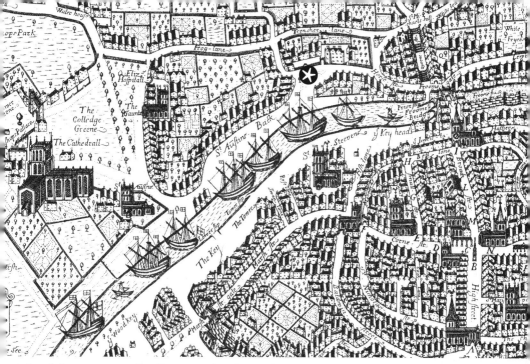

A detail from James Millerd's 1673 map of Bristol showing the Cathedral and Great House (at the top of St. Augustine's Back, marked with an asterix).

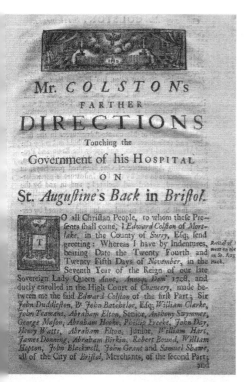

Colston's School (Hospital) settlement after purchase of Great House Sugar Refinery.

Codrington's *Betty's Hope* plantation, Antigua, after restoration in 1994.

1820s the plantations were yielding in the region of £2,500 per annum (about £2.5 million in 2016 by GDP per capita).[214]

1710—Nov. 25, Edward Colston and Joseph Earl, esqrs. returned to Parliament for Bristol.

On the occasion of his triumph in the elections, Colston returned briefly to Bristol and spent what's thought to be his last time in the city. Up until Colston's election, all of Bristol's MPs were declared 'non-partisan'; he was the first to be returned as a member of a party, in his case he was a High Tory.[215] The Bristol Loyal Society was founded by his supporters later in the same year with Edward Colston as president and Henry, second Duke of Beaufort, as one of its patrons.[216] Leading members included Colston's slave-ship owning nephew Francis, and William Hart, son of former Bristol MP Richard Hart. The Loyal Society acted as the main organisational base for the Tory party in the city. Within five years its members would be suspected of Jacobite sympathies, see 1715.[217]

In the early eighteenth century, Bristol's population was around 20,000 and of those, around 3,500 Freemen were eligible to vote, the highest number outside of London. The city returned two MPs to parliament.[218] As the century wore on the population grew by a factor of five, but the number of voters only grew roughly by a factor of two, while elections became more and more violent and corrupt. Even so, the franchise in Bristol was more democratic than down the road in Bath.[219] Bristol had been a town and county in its own right since 1373, meaning the Corporation had its own courts, two sheriffs, and an undersheriff. These were augmented by a Mayor and a Recorder with each of the city's 12 wards having their own Aldermen, on top of these there were 28 common-councilmen. The town clerk had to be a barrister of at least three years standing and acted as judge at the quarter sessions. Queen Anne updated the 1373 charter in 1710 and cemented the position of the self-appointed Council officers whose positions by now were fixed for life. Public voting was non-existent with no democratic process, leading to a cosy cartel that lacked ideas and innovation. As historian Mike Manson noted:

> Perhaps even more alarming was the shadowy role of the Society of Merchant Venturers... [who] represented the merchants of the city and exercised control over the river and the port. It has often been said that the secretive freemasonry was the real power behind the throne. To muddy waters even more membership of the Merchant Venturers and the Corporation was largely interchangeable.[220]

1711—Edward Colston endowed the Boys' School in Temple-street, of which parish he was native, for the instruction of forty boys, and new clothing them every year.

Increasingly partisan, Colston interfered in the school's curriculum to limit "contamination" of the pupils' minds by non-conformist religious thought. He insisted that a clause be added to the rules of the school where any books used by the children should be vetted by the Bishop and the SPCK and have in them "no tincture of Whiggism".[221]

1711—Two privateers, named the *Duke* and the *Duchess*, commanded by Wood[e]s Rogers and Stephen Courtney, which had been fitted out by some merchants of Bristol, to cruize against the Spaniards, in 1708. In August, this year, they arrived in the Downs, after encompassing the world in three years two months; having on board, as pilot, the famous Capt. Dampier, author of 'Voyages, &c.' In one of these ships also came home Alexander Selkirk, who had resided alone on the Island of Juan Fernandez nearly five years, by whose history De Foe was indebted for his 'Adventures of Robinson Crusoe.' In 1712, John Rumsey, esq. presented to the Bristol Cathedral a pair of large candlesticks, of the plunder of this expedition, which cost him £114.

Privateers were commissioned by the British state during the War of Succession to attack Spanish shipping and possessions. Many sailed from Bristol and, nationally, Rogers' cruise was the most successful; as well as the marooned sailor Selkirk, they brought home a Spanish treasure ship. Money from Bristol's recent official involvement in the slave trade was invested in this cruise; second Captain Thomas Dover, who represented the backers' interests, was originally a medical doctor who is remembered today in Bristol for being the first to offer his services free of charge for the poor in St Peter's Hospital in 1695. Between the years 1701-1706 Dover became a slave-ship surgeon and then a slave-ship captain before part funding Rogers' cruising voyage. Speculators like Dover and Rumsey doubled their money and privateering cruises such as this were one of the factors that brought the Spanish to the negotiating table.

1711—The Custom-House in Queen-Square [commenced building 1709] completed, which cost £2777 7s 5d.

The construction of the Custom House reflected the steep rise in economic activity in the city brought about by Bristol's direct involvement in the transatlantic slave trade after 1698. The building was an important symbol in the growing mercantile architectural landscape of the city in the eighteenth century. It was targeted and destroyed by arson during the 1831 'Reform riots'.

The South Sea Company

1711—Bristol Corporation and Society of Merchant Venturers begin two-year campaign to stop the Royal African Company regaining monopoly status, arguing the importance of the slave trade to Bristol's economy.

Despite associations with the monopolistic Royal African Company (RAC) twenty years previously, Edward Colston had a significant role to play in the campaign by Bristol's merchant elite to retain access to the West African slave trade. In 1711 he presented a petition to Parliament "requesting that the trade to Africa should be open to all her majesty's subjects".[222]

During the same year he also became involved in one of the most infamous episodes in British economic history with the creation of the South Sea Company (SSC). A huge national debt had been built up during the Spanish War of Succession and members of the new Tory government came up with a plan to pay this off. This involved creating a private/public partnership company to break the stranglehold of the Whig dominated Bank of England which hitherto had controlled the national debt. In April 1711, the plan for the proposed SSC was revealed to a caucus of forty or fifty Tory MPs. It was approved with the "greatest enthusiasm and with surprise at the merit of the project".[223] It's likely that Colston was amongst this group of Tories who were privileged with this insider knowledge of the SSC plan which relied on future access to Spanish America and the lucrative slave trading monopoly known as the Asiento. As we have seen, Colston was familiar with the Asiento through his dealings with the RAC. So when the opportunity arose in 1711 it was no surprise that he immediately became a Commissioner responsible for taking subscriptions to the SSC.[224]

Also that year, Lady Mary Hayman, Edward Colston's only surviving sister, died aged 70. As Colston had remained unmarried and had no children, the heir to his fortune, at least on paper, was his only surviving younger brother Richard. However, (Sir) Richard Colston left Bristol in 1660 to become the English Consul at Marseilles and never returned.[225] This left Lady Hayman as the remaining direct heir. With her death the inheritance passed on to her daughter Mary and her husband Thomas Edwards junior.[226]

Bishop Robinson's runic inscription inside Bristol Cathedral, just feet from Colston's SW Tower, translates into "Man is but a heap of mouldering dust".

1711—Sept. 3, Dr. Robinson, Bishop of Bristol, made Lord Privy Seal, in the room of the Duke of Newcastle, who was killed by a fall from his horse.

John Robinson, who had been ordained Bishop of Bristol in 1710, attended the Congress of Utrecht in 1712 as one of the two Plenipotentiaries, effectively the chief negotiators for Britain. The Congress, effectively a series of peace treaties, marked the end of the War of the Spanish Succession (1701–1714). It led to the re-apportioning of Spanish and French territories in Europe and the Americas to the British and their allies.[227] Robinson, as 1st Plenipotentiary, signed the treaty in April 1713. After it was brought about through his 'instrumentality', he was made Bishop of London on his return to England in 1714.[228]

Bishop Robinson was not just negotiating over territorial claims in Utrecht but also access to trade, particularly the slave trade. The Asiento was a major prize, giving Britain the right to be the sole supplier of slaves to Spain's colonies in South America for thirty years. Control over this trade had long been recognised as a source of huge financial gain as one Dutch slave trader stated:

Everyone knows that the slave trade is the source of the wealth which the Spaniards draw from their Indies, and that he who knows how to supply the slaves will share this wealth with them.[229]

Bishop Robinson was the last of a long line of Bristol's 'diplomatist prelates' and, in all probability (because of the pairs connections with Bristol Cathedral and the Asiento) Edward Colston and Bishop Robinson knew one another. As already stated, Colston used Robinson and the SPCK to vet the books used in Temple School.

1712—The Dock at Sea-Mills was begun—this was about the commencement of that enormous wen upon the face of funding-speculations, the 'South-Sea Bubble'. In 1718, the King [George I] was appointed the Governor of the company. In June 1720 the stock rose to 890. In September it fell to 150. In January 1721, the King gave orders to discharge such of the Directors as held offices under the Crown; and in February the Lords resolved that their declarations of dividends was a villainous artifice, to delude and defraud His Majesty's good subjects. The whole history of South-Sea is curious and instructive.

On 6th June 1712 Queen Anne addressed Parliament with the news that: "I have insisted and obtained that the Asiento or contract for furnishing the Spanish West Indies with negroes shall be made with us for 30 years." In order to bring this about, officials in Madrid were given handsome fees and King Phillip V of Spain was lent one million pesos to buy shares in the South Sea Company—this was in addition to 28 per cent of the initial stock. Queen Anne received 22.5 per cent of the initial stock.[230]

1713—Treaty of Utrecht ends the Spanish War of Succession: Britain takes over the *Asiento*, the contract to supply Spanish America with slaves.

Wilkins explains the basis of the *Asiento*:

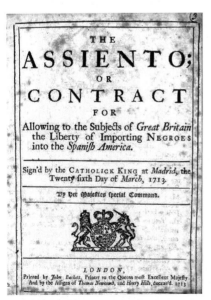

THE

ASSIENTO;

OR

CONTRACT

FOR

Allowing to the Subjects of *Great Britain* the Liberty of Importing NEGROES into the *Spanish America*.

Sign'd by the CATHOLICK KING at *Madrid*, the Twenty-sixth Day of *March*, 1713.

By Her Majesties special Command.

LONDON,
Printed by *John Baskett*, Printer to the Queens most Excellent Majesty: And by the Assigns of *Thomas Newcomb*, and *Henry Hills*, deceas'd. 1713

The Asiento trade agreement between Britain and Spain.

By the Treaty of Utrecht the *Asiento*—the Spaniards were prevented from forming establishments on the African Coast by the Bull of Demarcation ('*Inter caetera*') of Pope Alexander VI. (1493), which forbade their acquiring territory to the east of the meridian line 100 miles west of the Azores. They would therefore supply their American possessions with slaves only by contracts with other powers—or contract for supplying the Spanish colonies with 4,800 negroes annually, which had previously passed from the Dutch to the French, was transferred to Great Britain; an English Company was to enjoy the monopoly for a period of thirty years from May 1st, 1713.[231]

As was the case for previous Portuguese, Dutch and French holders of the Asiento, the profit from the slave trade was augmented by illegal contraband goods mostly smuggled in slave ships. This was in addition to the permitted annual 500-ton trade ship. These goods were sold to the Spanish colonies at inflated prices where demand was high; they also constituted unfair competition with taxed goods from Spain and became a major drain on Spanish Crown income. The British government duly sold the Asiento contract to the newly formed South Sea Company.

For Bristol's merchants the Asiento was "the most popular feature of the Treaty of Utrecht".[232] It triggered a shipbuilding boom for Bristol that lasted centuries; the first half of the eighteenth century saw James Hilhouse building his Snows and Brigantines for the Guinea trade, and in the latter half Sydenham Teast with his Guineamen. Ships' names included *Colston, Hayman* and *Freke* and *Serleon, Bonny, Angola* and *Calabar Merchant,* reflecting dealers and destinations respectively.[233]

In February 1713, according to '*Tovey's Local Jottings*', Bristol's mayor, aldermen and common council presented a 'humble' petition to Parliament:

> That the chief dependence of the inhabitants of this city for their subsidence is on trade, the greatest part of which is to her majesty's plantations and colonies in America and the coast of Africa, which employs great numbers of handycraftsmen in building and fitting out ships, and in the making and manufactures of wool, iron, tin, copper, brass, &c., a considerable part whereof is exported to the coast of Africa *for buying of negroes,* which trades are the great support of our people at home and foundation of our trade abroad. And we shall ever pray, &c.[234]

> **1713**—Sep. 7 [Monday], an election for Parliament commenced, in which Sir William Daines was the favourite of the low party, Mr Thomas Edwards, jun. of the high party, and Col. Joseph Earl divided both parties. The expenses were £2257 9s. 7d., including 'Bonney's note for printing, £27.'—The contest lasted till the Tuesday se'nnight, and broke up with broken heads, in every respect a drawn battle.

It's thought Thomas Edwards junior was recommended to the "Tory zealots in the Loyal Society" by Edward Colston on his retirement from Parliament in 1713. By now Bristol's Loyal Society were getting a reputation as "a set of rakehells, who kept up a drunken club to carry on treasonable designs". They fell into disrepute because they were suspected of having Jacobite sympathies at a time when the Stuart dynasty was about to be replaced by the Hanoverian line in Britain.[235]

1713—Nov. 2, Mr. Colston's birth-day, the annual dinner of the Loyal Society. Mr. Colston being aged, he was not present, but represented by Henry, duke of Beaufort. [In the Cathedral, affixed to the canopy of the stall now assigned to the Archdeacon of Dorset, are three small carved shields, bearing this gentleman's armorial ensign, and his initials E.C. The venerable philanthropist was a daily attendant upon divine service, and just previous to his decease had made a contract to re-pave the whole of the choir with marble, at his own private cost, to the amount of £600.]

Also in 1713, Colston subscribed £250 towards the cost of rebuilding the tower of All Saints' Church in Bristol and a further £100 to 'beautify' the chancel. As a token of gratitude, Colston's dolphin crest and a pineapple were placed as a vane atop the tower (they were taken down in 1728 and replaced by a globe and cross, the copper dolphin and pineapple were sold off a year later). "To such lengths did the 'cultus' of Colston grow!" stated Wilkins in 1920.[236]

1714—Oct. 20, the coronation-rejoicings [of George I] in the city were disgraced by attacks, in the evening, upon the windows of Dissenters. The house of Mr. Stephens, a baker, in Tucker-street, was entered, partitions were broken down, boxes and drawers forced open, and bread, plate, and other goods, plundered, upon pretence of the provocation given by Stephens and his son in defending their persons and property. Two people were killed and several wounded. A Quaker, who stood in the entry, endeavouring to persuade the mob to desist from their violence, was by one of them knocked down and trampled upon in such a manner that he died the next day. One of the mob was shot in the head, as supposed by young Stephens, and died a few days afterward. Stephens, jun. ran another through the body, but the wound did not prove mortal. Thirteen of the depredators were committed to Newgate; but the greatest criminals absconded.—Upon application of the Magistrates, His Majesty sent a special commission to try the rioters in custody: three of the judges and four counsellors arrived Nov. 25, and the proceedings lasted nearly a week. About ten persons, indicted as rioters, were each fined twenty nobles and imprisoned three months, to give security for nine months more; one, indicted for felony, was ordered to be whipped; the rest were acquitted.

The riot and subsequent court case precipitated an astonishing attack on Edward Colston's name and character via a pamphlet in the form of a letter (see Appendix 2). Wilkins called it "The Charge of Immorality against Edward Colston" where Colston was accused of being a 'Jacobite', political fanatic, hater of dissenters and, by implication, having improper sexual relationships with his sister Ann. This attack on Colston may seem over the top, but it has to be seen in the context of the insurrections around the country planned by Jacobite sympathisers in the following year—1715.[237]

The General Election of February 1715 was a controversial affair when the Whigs, who dominated Bristol Corporation throughout the century, 'fixed' the election. Despite the Tories, including Thomas Edwards junior, receiving more votes than the Whigs, Colston's prodigy Edwards lost his Bristol seat. The "partiality of the Whig sheriff" was given as the reason for this but Edwards' appeal was quashed.[238] As a result of this rebuff Colston retaliated and took his ire out on Temple School because its parishioners didn't vote Tory. In July 1715, the SPCK received a 'curious' letter from Temple parishioner William Carey of Bristol in which he complained:

Temple School is "sinking". Mr Colston has told the trustees not to clothe the boys whose parents voted against his kinsmen (his heir Mr Edwards and Captain Freetinge) at the last election. Subscriptions have been withdrawn. Will the Society interpose its good offices?

After failing to get re-elected for Bristol in 1715, Thomas Edwards jun. took the seat at Wells in 1719 previously held by 'family'—his wife's cousin, another Edward Colston, nephew of Edward Colston 'the philanthropist'. Edwards then held Wells as a Tory MP until losing it in 1735. The following year his wife died. She had inherited much of her uncle's substantial fortune in 1721, but it then passed to Edwards' three daughters in accordance with the terms of Colston's will, leaving him in dire financial straits. His younger daughter Sophia, said to be worth £20,000 at the time of her marriage in 1737, didn't help her father, who was so deeply in debt that he couldn't afford the rent on his chambers in Middle Temple. He was then ousted from Filkins Hall and died intestate in 1743, the administration granted to Sophia.[239]

1715—Oct. 2, discovery was made of a design to seize this city for the Pretender; whereupon the militia were mustered, the gates shut, and canon placed at several of them, and divers of the citizens (including William Hart, esq.) were apprehended and committed to the Marshalsea, on suspicion of being in the interest of the Pretender, or not well affected towards His Majesty's person and government.

The previous month Colston's nephew Francis had been accused of distributing a seditious Jacobite pamphlet, although the charges were later dropped. To show the seriousness of the potential revolt the Earl of Berkeley rushed to Bristol with a large body of troops to suppress any rebellion. Major-General Wade (not Colston's former partner from St Peter's sugar refinery) went on to Bath and seized 200 rebel horses, ten chests of fire-arms, a hogshead full of swords, three canon and a mortar amongst other items. The prompt action by Berkeley and Wade and the failings of the rebellion in the North led to the capitulation of the Jacobite rebellion in the West.

The Loyal Society conspirators were shipped to Marshalsea prison in London though they were eventually freed.[240] Colston was no stranger to the prisons of London and every year "went through Whitechapel prison and the Marshalsea to shower his money in freeing the most deserving debtors incarcerated for small sums, and in one case he sent £3,000 to liberate the poor in Ludgate prison."[241]

One of the executors of Edward Colston's will was banker Henry Hoare who was enmeshed with Colston in South Sea Company dealings and shared several political and religious affiliations. The family bank, C. Hoare & Co., was founded in 1672 on Cheapside in the City of London by Henry's father Sir Richard Hoare. Still operating today, it is Britain's oldest modern bank and originated from a goldsmith's business.[242] Edward Colston opened an account there in December 1703[243] and joined the "landed aristocrats and gentry, MPs and office-holders, clergymen, and some people with city interests" who made up the bank's well-connected clientele, alongside its primary mercantile and commercial business concerns. As economic historian Laurence noted:

> A very high proportion of [the bank's] customers were MPs, especially Tory MPs and minor office-holders, with a few occupants of great offices of state... Many of them were high churchmen and were associated with the societies for the reformation of manners and the charity school movement, both of which had strong support from Tories. The Society for Promoting Christian Knowledge (SPCK)...opened an account at Hoare's Bank in 1711; and the Society for the Propagation of the Gospel (SPG), founded in 1701...opened one in 1719. Henry and Benjamin Hoare were themselves involved with both societies, as well as with many other causes supporting charity schools and parochial libraries.[244]

As we have seen Colston was a very wealthy, strident Tory loyalist, eventually becoming an MP, and had close connections with both the SPCK and the SPG. It is likely that some of these connections were a product of his relationship with the Hoare family or were the reason they became acquainted in the first place. Richard Hoare was a Tory MP at the same time as Colston and also held the post of Sheriff of London and Lord Mayor. He was also one of the original

Right: Edward Colston and the South Sea Company. The lower section mentions Colston's South Sea Company stock and Henry Hoare.

EDWARD COLSTON, ESQ.

J. Richardson pinx.   J. Cochran sculpt.

THIS distinguished philanthropist, was born at Bristol, Nov. 2d, 1636, became a Spanish Merchant, and realised a large fortune. He founded a School at Bristol upon the plan of Christs Hospital, built several Alms-houses, and endowed various charitable institutions, not only in that city but in different parts of the kingdom.

Mortlake y⁹ 9ᵗʰ February 1718

Pay unto d Mr M. Humphreys two hundred eleven pounds the dividend due on seaven Thousand pounds being all my stock in y South Sea Companys books for halfe a years interest due at Christmas last, & this shalbe your sufficient Warrant.

Edward Colston

He gave 6000l. for the augmentation of small livings; 2000l. to St. Bartholomew's Hospital; a like sum to Christs Hospital, and very large sums for benevolent purposes. He died Oct. 11, 1721, and was buried at the church of All Saints, at Bristol, where a monument is erected to his memory & a sermon ann⁸ʸ preached on his birth-day.

Mortlake y 15ᵗʰ January 1716

Pay to mr Henry Hoare or order my dividend on seaven Thousand pounds being all my stock in y South Sea Companys books for two halfe years at three pᵉ¹ each due at Mid-summer and Christmas last, & these shalbe your sufficient Warrant.

Edward Colston

To mr John Grigsby Accomptant to the South Sea Company

directors of the South Sea Company (SSC) and a supporter of its founder and first Governor, Robert Harley. Links between the Hoare family and SSC 'insiders' were to prove crucial in the financial dealings of the bank and its well-connected customers (including Edward Colston) during the turbulent years of the 'South Sea Bubble'.

The Hoare family bank was not just holding accounts for its hundred plus customers but also facilitating their involvement in the burgeoning stock market, particularly in the SSC. In some cases the bank appears to be acting as an agent, managing the purchases and sales of SSC shares on behalf of their clientele.[245] Two manuscript authorisations signed by Edward Colston, show that he held at least £7,000 of shares in the South Sea Company in 1715 and 1716 and one of them indicates that he used Henry Hoare to distribute his dividends.[246] By mid-1719, Colston's stock holdings had increased to £7,840 and he was raking in £470 in dividends each year. This was a significant investment, the base sum worth more than £19 million and the dividends alone more than £1 million in 2016 (by GDP per capita conversion).[247]

Investigations into the dealings of Hoare's bank in the SSC suggest that with their 'insider' knowledge the Hoare family were able to successfully advise their tight political and religious network of customers about when to buy and sell stocks.[248] There is some evidence for this in Edward Colston's case. In the autumn of 1719, less than a year before the 'Bubble', he purchased an additional £500 of bonds in the SSC and then authorised the selling of a significant portion of his stock holdings in the company, depositing £3,890 in his account in Hoare's bank. At the time of the sale Colston purchased a 'diamond buckle' for £24 (about £60,000 in 2016, by GDP per capita conversion) as a gift for Henry Hoare.

The 'insider' knowledge and efficacy of Henry and Benjamin Hoare's dealings in the SSC is demonstrated by the £28,000 profit that they made out of the 'Bubble', whilst other less privileged investors were bankrupted.[249] From the proceeds Henry bought land and constructed a mansion at Stourhead in Wiltshire which became the family seat.[250] For Colston the personal and financial relationship with the SSC and the Hoare family liberated significant profits. For comparative purposes, the dividends he received from his investments in the SSC alone were in excess of that which he was to bequeath to Bristol upon his death.

Many people in Britain have heard of the 'South Sea Bubble' and can recount stories of the summer of 1720 when herds of investors scrambled to buy shares in a company which supposedly had no concrete business, just an enticing façade. This perception of financial behaviours has been challenged by economic historians but the 'Bubble' story hides a much darker and unpalatable truth. The whole SSC edifice was built on Britain gaining the Asiento through war and thus expanding its part in the transatlantic slave trade. At the base of all the financial blather and wheeler dealing was horrific human suffering, which has rarely, if ever, been part of the story; a perennial feature of sanitised British history.

Major investors like Edward Colston, who were aware of the huge profits that could be made from successful slave trading, knew exactly what they were getting involved in. In the period of Colston's investment in the SSC, from 1711 until his death in 1721, the Company's ships embarked 15,931 enslaved Africans, with 12,951 surviving the passage into chattel slavery in the Spanish Americas; a death toll of 2,980 and a mortality rate of almost 19 per cent.[251] This hard, cold fact sits in stark contrast to popular stories about the 'terrible' financial losses of public figures such as Isaac Newton, who also famously invested in the SSC.[252]

Even at over 80 years of age, Colston couldn't stop accumulating land and property with his vast wealth. In 1717 he purchased monopoly rights over an important trading river, the Warwickshire Avon, which gave access to Bristol, via the Severn estuary, from the Midlands and the future manufacturing centres of Birmingham and Coventry:

> **1717**—November Purchase of Profit of Navigation for boates of in and upon the river of Avon—This was a tripartite indenture for the Warwickshire Avon between Thomas lord Viscount Windsor in the Kingdom of Ireland and Baron Mountjoy of the Isle of Wight in the first part. Edward Colston of Moortlack [Mortlake] in the County of Surry [Surrey] Esquire of the second part and Thomas Edwards senior of the Citty [City] of Bristol Esquire, Thomas Edwards Junior of the Middle Temple London Esquire and Robert Carr of London aforesaid mercer of the third part.[253]

'Keep my memory green'

> **1721**—Oct. 11, died Edward Colston, aged 85 years. He gave £100 towards erection of the organ of St. James Church, and left more than £100,000 among his relatives, notwithstanding his immense public largesses.

Edward Colston has long been remembered in Bristol in the role of the 'Great Philanthropist', lavishing the city with countless gifts. Some commentators have suggested, albeit with little evidence, that Colston was 'humble', that he didn't want the scale of his philanthropy to be known and that the thought of prominent monuments would be an anathema to him. These Christian caricatures of unrestricted kindness and modesty are perhaps what some of his fans would have liked Colston to be. The evidence suggests something different.

There is still some confusion concerning how much of the enormous wealth Edward Colston accumulated that he actually gave to charitable causes, where it was given and what proportion came as bequests after his death.[254] It is true that a philanthropic record actually exists as part of the memorial to Colston in All Saints Church in central Bristol. Chiselled into a huge vertical tablet is a detailed chronology of his benefactions and the claim that in Bristol they "have exceeded all others", as if to literally 'set in stone' why he should be venerated. Through studying this memorial, a close reading of his comprehensive will and other contemporary sources it is possible to piece together a detailed record of his philanthropy (see Appendix 3).

Edward Colston's final will was proved on 18th December 1721 and the executors named as "Thomas Edwards, sen. Thomas Edwards, jun. And Francis Colston Esquires and Henry Hoare and Robert Carr". Alongside the executors were the Society of Merchant Venturers who were already acting as trustees for Colston's School on St Augustine's Back. As outlined in the Will, their role was to act as Colston's theological 'commissars', monitoring those individuals and institutions who benefited from his charity. The Society of Merchant Venturers were given power to withdraw payments from those who strayed from his strict religious doctrines or allowed non-Church of England believers to partake. Colston may have used the Merchant Venturers but it is clear he did not wholly trust them to carry out this task, particularly in relation to Colston's School. In the Will he empowers his executors and nominees to oversee the Merchant Venturers and to act if:

> ...by Connaivance or otherwise they have consented or encouraged the Educating said Boys in any Principles of Religion contrary to or dissenting from our present established Church or bound them out Apprentices to Masters dissenting therefrom they immediately give notice to them desiring it may be amended it being wholly contrary to my Inclinations and Itencons [intentions] that they should be brought up in any Principles repugnant to the Church of England now established by Law.[255]

In the case of such a transgression the executors were to contact the Governors of Christ's Hospital (Bluecoats School) in London who had certain legal rights over Colston's School or to seek legal advice.

In addition to the large sum he left his family members (estimated to be £100,000) Colston bestowed £13,145 (equivalent to £31.5 million in 2016 by GDP per capita conversion) in charitable donations. Of this sum he gave a modest £2,440 (£5.8 million) to causes in Bristol, with the majority going to London or small sums spread across parish churches and schools in England.[256] However, Colston did not intend these gifts to be merely handed out to the poor or distributed widely. They were typical of his previous benefactions; either targeted for institutions he had already created, with strings attached or in order to propagate his staunch religious outlook. For example, from rents and profits of his landholdings he set aside £100 per annum for twelve years to support those apprenticed from his Hospital School on St Augustine's Back and the Temple School (now St Mary Redcliffe and Temple), but with one important condition:

> ...it is my express Will that no pson [person] or psons [persons] shall have or receive any benefit or advantage of this One hundred pounds p Ann [per annum] that shall not in all things conforme to the present established Religion of the Church of England.[257]

Another £660, in small sums per annum, he handed over to Ministers for sermons to be preached in parish churches all over Bristol, the city gaol and to the boys from his school at the Cathedral on his birthday, 2nd November.[258] The sermons were to be based upon those he was already sponsoring during Lent and would cover:

> severall Subjects relating to the Primitive Discipline and Usage of the Church of England....the nature and Constitution of the Catholick Church... the Excellency of the present Church of England...the Censures of the Church vizt Excommunication Penance Restitution Baptism...frequenting the Comunion against the Pope's Supremacy and the Errors of the Romanish Church...Confirmacion frequenting the Publick Worship Our Saviours Meritorious Passion Confession...Publick and Private Absolution...Publick and Private Repentance...

These theological 'gifts' also had significant strings attached; the members of the Merchant Venturers were to observe the sermons and withdraw the money if:

> the said Minister shall be negligent in the faithfull performance of what is above appointed and recomended to them...Then such Gift to cease.[259]

A further £480 was set aside for four 'Charity Schools' in city parishes on the condition that the:

> Inhabitants shall resolve on and actually sett up such a School and continue and maintain it...in the Principles of the Church of England[260]

In fact, apart from his payments for improvements to Bristol's churches, it is hard to find any charitable donations in his will which did not carry orthodox religious caveats that excluded dissenters, Catholics and many others.

Outside of the bequests that are listed in detail in his will there are the sums Colston gave away during his lifetime. Accurately calculating these figures is difficult as the sources disagree. For example, the largest sum he donated was to set up and maintain what became Colston's school. On the memorial in All Saints this is listed as "about ... [£]40,000", whereas a source from 1784 claims: "the charge for first setting up this hospital [school], and making it convenient for the purpose, amounted, it is said, to about [£]11,000".[261] Another, contentious issue is Colston's supposed donation of £20,000 to the London poor during a famine in the winter of 1708–1709. No reference to this huge sum appears on the memorial in All Saints Church, neither is it referred to in a number of sources. If these large and approximate sums are included then the total monies Colston gave away in his lifetime exceeds £83,000; in the region of £200 million in 2016, by GDP per capita conversion. Adding the bequests from his will, he donated in all about £63,000 to causes in Bristol.

Colston was meticulous in detailing his bequests and this was mirrored in the plan for his funeral which opens his will of 1712:

> ...I committ my Spiritt to God who gave it and my body to the Earth from whence it was taken to be decently buried in All Saints Church in the City of Bristoll in the Grave of my Ancestors in the Evening without any manner of Pomp or Ostentation...

So far, so good, from the modesty perspective; though there is a big BUT coming....

> Save only that my Corps shall be mett at Lawford's Gate by the poor Men and Women of my Almshouse on St Michaels Hill and also by the poor boys of my Hospitall [School] on St Augustines Back together with the six old Seamen maintained by me in the Merchants Almeshouse in the Marsh as likewise by all the Boys of the Charity School in Temple Street cloathed and taught by me and from thence accompanied by them to the aforesaid Church directly...

The nature of this funeral supposedly "without any display" can also be gauged by the costs of the items on Colston's wish list. These ranged from coaches, horses, Postilians, Porters and Pages to silver candlesticks, plumes of fine Ostrich feathers and velvet palls. The following gives a selection of the major items (over £10):

An Elm Case, Covered with the best Velvet, a double
Silver'd Plate with inscription, Coat of Arms and Flower;
3 Pair of Silver Chaced handles, and set off with 2 rows
of best Silver'd Nails .... £14 0s. 0d.
A Hearse and 6 horsses, 7 days at 35s. per day .... £12 5s. 0d.
3 Mourning Coaches and 6 horsses, 8 days .... £36 15s. 0d.
8 Men in black to attend to Bristol, with Sadle horsses
7 days at 10s per day...£28 0s. 0d.
9 dozen of Buckrum Escutcheons for room, 30 s .... £13 10s. 0d.
48 Buckrum Escutcheons Verged with Silver, 24 Shields,
and 12 Chaps for the hearse and horsses, being 2 setts......... £10 10s. 0d.
12 Banners and 2 sets of Pencils for ditto .... £12 0s. 0d.[262]

In all, the forty items cost £237 (over £500,000 in 2016 by GDP per capita). Toward the end of his life Colston decreed that his sister Ann's remains should be exhumed from Mortlake church and interred with his own on his death "since it was her desire that her bones should lie in the same grave where I shall be buried". Ideally he wanted her bones to be carried in his own coffin to All Saints church in Bristol.[263]

Colston's funeral in Bristol was a grand affair despite the weather; here's an eyewitness account:

> The day of the arrival of the procession in Bristol was a gloomy one; the rain had all day descended in torrents yet the streets were lined with people, and every window along the route was crowded with spectators. The Merchants gathered in their hall, and met the corpse at the entrance to the city; the grey-haired, weather beaten mariners from King street, clad in their rueful black coats, and the aged men and women from St Michael's almshouses, new clothed, marched feebly before them, thirty in number, whilst 146 boys from Temple and Colston schools led the van, chanting the 90th Psalm, to the church of All Saints, all hung in black. Five hours, says Silas Told, did the procession take from Lawford's Gate to the church, which it only reached at midnight of Saturday, October 28th, amid the light from flaring torches and the sobbing sound of falling rain. 'Southwell, Codrington, Harrington, Trye, Haines and J. Downing, Esqs., were ye bearers.'[264]

The funeral is a useful metaphor for the contradictions in how Colston wanted to be remembered. Although he claimed the virtues of modesty and lack of pretention, and others have claimed them for him, in fact Colston wanted to be feted by those who had benefited from his charity and he clearly wanted to propagate his memory after his death.

One issue that Colston was clearly aware of was his lack of a direct male heir to carry on the family name. Consequently, he stated in his will that if his grandniece Sarah married, then her husband had to take the Colston name within six months or be disinherited.[265] In fact it took until 1755 for this to transpire, although it was through the marriage of his grandniece Sophia rather than Sarah. Sophia married Alexander Ready, who changed his name to Colston by Act of Parliament. The Colston family retained Filkins Hall well into the nineteenth century but by the twentieth it was in ruins; the present main house is a rebuild.

After Colston's death the process of memorialization began. It is claimed that some of Colston's executors were governors of St Bartholomew's Hospital, London[266] and through this connection they commissioned another St Bart's governor, Rococo architect James Gibbs, to design the architectural frame that became Colston's tomb in All Saints Church in Bristol. Gibbs in turn recommended his long-term collaborator John Michael Rysbrack to create Colston's effigy. The statue's head was based on Jonathan Richardson's 1702 portrait of Colston which was formerly hung in the Lord Mayor's parlour of the Mansion House,[267] and the terracotta macquette of the statue is in Bristol Museum and Art Gallery. Pevsner describes the statue thus "Rysbrack's outstanding reclining figure is urbane and dignified".[268]

Tombs and statues are one element of commemoration, but to really perpetuate the memory of a person's life after their death, physical ceremonies and rituals are even better. Today in Bristol four charities still exist which are descendants from the eighteenth century. They were formed in memory of the philanthropist by sections of the Bristol elite and represent their political divisions:

- The Colston—or Parent—Society, founded 1726 with ties to St Mary Redcliffe Church
- The Dolphin Society founded in 1749 by the Tories
- The non-aligned Grateful Society founded in 1759
- The Anchor Society founded in 1769 by the Whigs[269]

Their job was to execute Colston's wish to "Keep my memory green" through philanthropy, ceremony and memorialisation.[270] As we shall see, these organisations were to flourish in the Victorian period, more than a century after Edward Colston's death.

Slavery, Rebellion and Abolition

The Corporation

Within three decades of the opening up of the slave trade to Bristol merchants in 1698, the port had become the main slave-trading centre in Britain. It had outstripped its main rival, London, which went into a gradual decline, and Liverpool, although on the rise, was still a minnow compared to Bristol. From 1725 until the mid-century, 20, 30 or even 40 or more vessels left Bristol each year for the West African coast to purchase thousands of enslaved men, women and children and transport them into a life of forced labour.[271] Between 1728 and 1732 Bristol's slave-ship voyages were peaking at nearly 50 and carrying well over 10,000 enslaved Africans per annum, while Bristol's merchants were also pioneering the business of shipping the enslaved to Virginia and from one North American colony to another.

Analysis of the investors in the slave ships that set out from Bristol has shown that there were three occupational groups involved, tradesmen or manufacturers, ship masters and merchants. The last group was by far the largest and the trade in the pre-1750 period was dominated by about 20 merchants who, as leading investors, acted as agents and organised the majority of the voyages from Bristol (see Appendix 4).[272] Prominent were James Day with 57 voyages between 1711 and 1742; Isaac Hobhouse with 68 voyages between 1721 and 1746 and, the largest trader of them all, James Laroche with 104 voyages between 1727 and 1766. Over the whole period of slave-trading (1698–1807) Richardson estimates that 290 agents were active in Bristol, of which 52 were responsible for organising almost three-quarters of the 2,100 slave-ship voyages.

The eighteenth-century slave trade was thus organised and financed by a small but dominant group which, although representative of the landed gentry and merchant class, did allow a measure of social mobility. Some tradesmen and ships' masters were able to transition into the merchant elite through the opportunities provided by acting as slave-ship agents, though connections with established mercantile families still determined access to political power. Thirty-two of the 50 or so leading agents were members of the Society of Merchant Venturers and half of these became masters of the organisation. Many of this select group of agents were also common councillors (17), sheriffs (16), aldermen (10) and mayors (11), demonstrating the close links between economic and political power in the city. Richardson noted:

> all the [slave-trade] agents who held political office were closely connected with the established mercantile families of Bristol, whether by birth or apprenticeship[273]

The profits from all three sides of the triangle, trading commodities such as brass, textiles and guns to purchase the enslaved, selling these captives for profit in the Americas and then purchasing cash crops such as sugar, coffee and tobacco to be sold in Britain, could be huge. These in turn allowed the investors to purchase or hire more ships, more commodities and the cycle multiplied each time the vessels returned to Britain. Thus within a few years the Bristol mercantile elite became fabulously wealthy and carefully protected their economic interests by consolidating their political power. As mentioned before, at the heart of this was control of the port and of the city through the Corporation. These were effectively in the hands of the Merchant Venturers.

There were several ironies to all of this which were partially exposed by the writer Daniel Defoe. Defoe was not enamoured with Bristol's corporate governance at all; writing in the 1720s he stated:

> The greatest inconveniences of Bristol are, its situation, and the tenacious folly of its inhabitants; who by the general infatuation, the pretence of freedoms and priviledges, that corporation-tyranny, which prevents the flourishing and increase of many a good town in England, continue obstinately to forbid any, who are not subjects of their city soveraignity, (that is to say, freeman,) to trade within the chain of their own liberties; were it not for this, the city of Bristol, would before now, have swell'd and encreas'd in buildings and inhabitants, perhaps to double the magnitude it was formerly of.[274]

Defoe had originally been paid by the Royal African Company to write political tracts to defend the company's monopoly against calls for the 'freedom' (sic) to trade in enslaved Africans. Organisations of provincial merchants (such as the Society of Merchant Venturers), interloping traders and entrepreneurs cynically exploited popular ideas of 'liberties' of the 'freeborn Englishman' in order to force millions of Africans into plantation slavery and to make a fortune in the process.[275] It was highly ironic to Defoe that for all their bluster about 'freedom' and 'free trade' the Bristol merchant elite were protecting their slice of the pie from 'outside' traders just as the RAC had attempted all those years before.

> **1724**—Sept. 24, died Sir William Daines, alderman of Bristol, and several times its representative in Parliament. He was succeeded by James Dunning, esq.

Born in Norfolk County, Virginia, Daines had tobacco plantations in Virginia and Maryland and came to Bristol in the 1680s. He took the seemingly usual route through Bristol's ruling hierarchy, common councillor 1691–1702, sheriff 1694–1695, Master of the Society of Merchant Venturers 1698–1700, mayor 1700–1701 and alderman from 1702 until his death aged 68. He had two stints as MP for Bristol representing the Whigs, 1701–1710 and 1715–1722, before ill-health forced his retirement. He complained that it had cost him £10,000 to represent the city, though he was less forthcoming on the relationship between his civic and political offices and his fortune made through trading in the plantation economy.[276]

In 1707 and 1725 Sir Hans Sloane, the Anglo-Irish physician, naturalist and founder of the British Museum, published in two volumes his *A Voyage to the Islands Madera, Barbados, Nieves [Nevis], St Christophers [St Kitts] and Jamaica*.[277] Sloane's books inadvertently showed the harshness and brutality of the slave masters. Within 50 years these words would be picked up by campaigners Anthony Benezet and John Wesley, who quoted Sloane verbatim in their popular anti-slavery pamphlets. One high impact description they used is as follows:

> …the Punishment for crimes of Slaves are usually for Rebellions, burning them, by nailing them down on the ground with crooked Sticks on every Limb, and then… burning them gradually up to the Head… For Crimes of a lesser nature, Gelding or chopping off half of the Foot with an Ax. These punishments are suffered by them with great constancy.[278]

> **1727**—Sir Abraham Elton, bart. and Baron Scroop [Srope] chosen representatives in Parliament for Bristol. 'Mr Hart sold his election.' This gentleman was the leading capitalist in the clothing-trade.

Violence and intimidation were not uncommon during Bristol's elections for Parliament, but the blatant corruption of 1727 was a new phenomenon.

William Hart, previously a member of Colston's 'rakehell' Loyal Society—who had been imprisoned for his role in the Jacobite rebellion of 1715—was the sole Tory candidate for this election. He took a £1,000 'bung' from fellow candidate Abraham Elton II while others eligible sold their votes for between one and five guineas each.[279]

Sir Abraham Elton II was a second Baronet who followed his father into Parliament; Elton senior, with his partner Gabriel Wayne, had founded the Conham Copper and Brass works just outside of Bristol in 1698.[280] Both Eltons were leading Merchant Venturers as well as Sheriffs and Mayors of Bristol. Like his father, the younger Elton combined his duties at the brass works with those of being a slave trader with his brothers Jacob and Isaac. He left Britain for a few years after losing most of his money in the South Sea Bubble of 1720. Elton II was MP for Taunton before taking his Bristol seat in 1727; the Elton family owned the largest house in Queen Square as well as a mansion in north Somerset called Clevedon Court.

Hudleston gives an overview of Bristol's economy in the eighteenth century in the 1931 guide book *How to see Bristol*:

> To give some idea of the profits of a successful cruise, it may be stated on the authority of existing documents that about 1727–28 a cargo of 270 slaves could be obtained at a cost of £2 15s per head, paid in the shape of iron and copper rods, cotton fabrics, spirits, etc., and could be sold in Jamaica for nearly £31 per head, making a gross profit of £7,600, or vastly more than the value of the small vessel engaged in the transit. As the demand for negroes increased prices rose in Africa, but there was an equivalent rise in the West Indies, and the profit was still £28 per head when Clarkson began his crusade [in 1786].[281]

1728—July 23, Baron Scroop [Scrope] chosen Recordèr of Bristol, upon the resignation of Lord Chief Justice Eyre, who had filled the office for upward of twenty years.

Latimer states:

> John Scrope, M.P. for Ripon in the previous Parliament, and now a candidate (1727) for Bristol, may fairly be styled one of Fortune's favourites. The son of a merchant dwelling in Small Street, Scrope, when very young, took part with several other Bristolians in Monmouth's rebellion, and subsequently acted as agent between the Whigs and the Prince of Orange, making one voyage to Holland dressed in women's clothes. After the revolution he adopted the law as a profession, and in 1708 he was appointed one of the Barons of the Scotch Court of

Exchequer, practically a sinecure office, for which he received £500 a year, while Queen Anne subsequently granted him a pension of £1000 in consideration of his having given up his practice at the English Bar. Having resigned his judgeship in 1724 (though he continued to enjoy its title by courtesy), he was now Secretary and a trusted lieutenant of Walpole.[282]

In July, 1728, Scrope was appointed Recorder of Bristol, and as a member of the Government "rendered local merchants great service in Parliament by opposing the attempts of the African Company to monopolise the slave trade".[283] Scrope was grandson of Colonel Adrian Scrope who was executed after the Restoration as one of the regicides of Charles I. Scrope's pal, Robert 'Cock Robin' Walpole, was Britain's first Prime Minister and amazingly made a 1000 per cent profit on his shares in the slave-trading South Sea Company. He sold just before the bubble burst.[284] Scrope died at the age of 90 and his fortune went to the descendants of his sister Anne who predeceased him. Anne married Henry Fane whose family owned the Westbury Tithes for over 150 years. Fane was also clerk to the Society of Merchant Venturers from 1701 to 1726.

‖ **1730**—Beginning of first Maroon war in Jamaica (ends 1739).

The runaway slaves and indigenous Amerindians, who had founded the Maroon settlements in the late 1650s after the British capture of Jamaica, remained undefeated for more than 70 years. They had been bolstered with recruits after revolts of the enslaved in 1673 and 1690 and effectively controlled large areas of the interior of the island. By the 1720s they were several thousand strong and apparently able to move amongst the enslaved Africans in the plantations receiving intelligence whilst fermenting rebellion and mutiny. Fears amongst white colonists reached a peak in 1730 when repeated attempts to suppress them had failed and they appeared to be emboldened. Several military units were moved to Jamaica in order to eliminate the Maroons once and for all. As a result, throughout the 1730s, Jamaica was wracked with guerrilla war as the Maroons defended their territory, inflicting several stinging defeats on British Army and Navy units in the process.[285]

In 1734, before going to France to continue his studies, 25-year-old Scotsman David Hume took up a post as a clerk to Bristol merchant, African trader and future banker Michael Miller of 16, Queen Square. The employment didn't last long though as the future historian and philosopher had the temerity to correct his employer's English, "I tell you what, Mr Hume, I have made £20,000 by my English, and I won't have it mended" Miller retorted.[286] Hume would go on, with Adam *'Wealth of Nations'* Smith, to refine the idea of the Enlightenment, while Miller would eventually buy the Great House at Henbury. The very same house that former 'Pagan and a Slave' Scipio Africanus had served in until dying at the age of 18 in 1720; Scipio is now famously interred in nearby Henbury churchyard.

> **1735**—Aug, in this month the equestrian statue of King William [III] was erected in Queen-square, after a model presented by Rysbrach [Rysbrack]. It cost £1,800.

Arrowsmith's Dictionary of Bristol states that nearly all the expense for the statue was borne by the Corporation and the Society of Merchant Venturers. The choice of William in lieu of Queen Anne—in a square named in her honour—is a strange one, especially after William had snubbed Bristol on his return to England from the Battle of the Boyne in 1690. Was William chosen in gratitude for granting the charter of 1698 legalising the slave trade to Africa for the 'outports'? The idea for a brass statue was originally promoted by slave trading Whig MP Abraham Elton II and Thomas Coster in 1733. According to Dresser, critics attributed their actions more to their interest in the brass industry than art.[287] It should be remembered however that the Eltons were a prominent slave trading family in the Whig interest, far more likely to support a sculpture of King William than a Tory with Jacobite sympathies.

> **1736**—Slave revolt in Antigua: plans to massacre whites fail, and the plotters, including skilled millwrights, coppersmiths, sugar boilers, masons, butchers, carpenters etc. are executed—five broken on the wheel, six gibbeted, 77 burned alive.

The planned uprising in Antigua, which had been preceded by an earlier plot in 1729, was discovered in the nick of time and the lucky escape sent shockwaves through the Caribbean planter class. According to British authorities:

> "all the white inhabitants of this island were to be murdered and a new form of government to be established by the slaves among themselves" as they were determined to "possess the island…entirely"[288]

The leader of the revolt was Coromantee[289] slave Prince Klaas, who came up with the idea of blowing up the entire Antiguan plantocracy in one go, whilst they were celebrating a royal occasion. Prince Klaas is commemorated today on the outskirts of the Antiguan capital St John's with a sculpture depicting him summoning his supporters with a conch shell.[290] Despite the failure of the uprising, the threat of future revolts convinced many colonists to leave the Caribbean islands and relocate to the apparently safer conditions of the North American mainland.

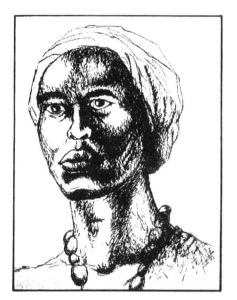 

Left: Nanny, one of the leaders of the Jamaican Maroons.
Right: Prince Klaas memorial in Antigua.

At this point Bristol's 'Golden Age' was in full swing, driven by the proceeds of slavery, followed by privateering and industry, and it was no mere coincidence that copper and brass production had taken off in the city. The raw materials were available, and so was the market. Copper was revered in Africa and had been known as 'red gold' since medieval times. After the opening up of the slave trade in 1698 it became the currency of choice for traders to the Guinea Coast; from rods and bars, to pots and pans. It had even been traded pound for pound for gold in trans-Saharan commerce. In Colston's time textiles had been coveted by West African slave-traders but by the eighteenth-century copper and its alloy brass were the goods most sought after. The mass production of copper-based items was a major factor in Bristol's leading role in the slave trade as the products were easily and cheaply made in the area.

1737 also saw the formation of the exclusive Tory *Steadfast Society*, based in the venerable White Lion Inn in Broad Street. As a result the society was also known as the 'White Lion Club'.[291] It was this organisation that was responsible for choosing Bristol's Tory candidate for Parliament for the next 89 years.

Awash with money, Bristol Corporation instigated plans for the building of the Exchange in 1738 and within six years the project was completed at the massive cost of £50,000. The Exchange became Bristol's most prestigious building of the eighteenth century. Architectural historian Andrew Foyle stated that the building was "in the highest canon of C18 civic design" and that it was "likely to appeal to Bristol's mercantile oligarchy".[292]

1739—British treaty with the Jamaican Maroons: under the leadership of Cudjoe, they gain their freedom and are given 1,500 acres in return for helping to capture other escaped slaves.

The First Maroon war in Jamaica ended with the British offering a compromise, after it became clear that a military victory was out of the question. As far as they were concerned the key objective was to cut off escape routes for the enslaved and lessen the threat of an island-wide rebellion that could unite Maroons and slaves. After the signing of the treaty and the suppression of recalcitrant Maroons and rebellious slaves, the British colonists certainly felt safer in their beds.[293] However, they may have chopped one head off the 'Hydra of revolts' in the Atlantic colonies but another soon grew.

1739 was also marked by the 'Stono Rebellion' in South Carolina on the North American mainland. This uprising was inspired by the freedom and land offered by the Spanish in Florida to those slaves who escaped from nearby British colonies. Carrying a banner reading 'Liberty' before them, the rebels burned several plantations, killing more than 20 colonists. The revolt and attempted escape of the enslaved Africans to Florida was violently suppressed by slave holders, with many executed. The colonists mounted the severed heads of the rebels on stakes along major roadways to serve as warning for other slaves who might consider revolt. Despite this brutality, further risings of enslaved Africans occurred over the following two years in Georgia and South Carolina. The 'Stono rebellion' proved that the slave-based colonies of mainland North America were not free of the virus of revolt.[294]

The Methodists

In the same year as the Stono Rebellion, John Wesley came to Bristol at the request of George Whitefield the 'leader of the Great Awakening'. Whitefield had been the first Anglican minister to bring religion to the neglected inhabitants living just outside the city in Kingswood. He needed someone to succeed him who was capable of preaching outdoors to mass audiences and John Wesley was his man, initiating the advent of Methodism. In the late 1730s, prior to coming to Bristol, the Wesleys spent a formative time visiting the colony of Georgia in America, witnessing first-hand the brutality of slavery. Both John and Charles Wesley wrote about the 'horrid cruelties' at the time and the irony of then coming to Bristol at the peak of its involvement in the trade wasn't lost on them.[295] Here's one of Charles Wesley's recollections from his journal of 2nd August 1736:

> I heard much, and heard more, of the cruelty of masters towards their negroes... The giving a child a slave of its own age to tyrannise over, to

beat and abuse out of sport, was, I myself saw, a common practice. Nor is it strange, being thus trained in cruelty, they should afterwards arrive at so great a perfection in it; that Mr Star... [for example, should] first nail up a negro by the ears, then order him to be whipped in the severest manner, and then have scalding water thrown over him, so that the poor creature could not stir for four months after.[296]

The intervention of Whitefield and Wesley in and around Bristol sparked a religious revival amongst the very people the Church of England had hitherto turned its back upon. Since the 1650s there had been Baptist ministers from Bristol preaching in Kingswood, but they had for a time been prohibited by a law banning non-conformists from holding services within five miles of the city's walls. Many of the new congregations consisted of colliers and their families who lived a tough and brutal life in an area which had also become home to 'wrongdoers', beyond the reach of the law. To paraphrase Bristol's Mayor of 1727, the people of Kingswood were considered "a barbarous and ungovernable people". The Mayor's assessment (at least the ungovernable bit) was proved right later that very year when the colliers struck at the hated toll houses. A cosy cartel of Bristol's MPs, Mayor and Aldermen made up the turnpike trustees, controlling the roads into and out of Bristol. After forcing through a rise in the tolls, the people rebelled. The colliers set fire to the toll houses and then promptly began running them for their own profit![297]

With his brother Charles, Wesley worked tirelessly to establish what was to become the Methodist (Wesleyan) Church and they found Bristol's poor underbelly fertile ground for their preaching. In their first year they created the New Room in Broadmead and then a school at Kingswood. Illustrating how slavery was never far from his mind, John Wesley wrote in 1744 about the 'blood and guilt' of Bristolians engaged in the trade:

To the captains employed in this trade... every merchant who is engaged in the slave-trade... every gentleman that has an estate in our plantations... Is there a God? ...Have you no sympathy, no sense of human woe, no pity for the miserable?[298]

And then he followed it up in 1755 with a pamphlet entitled *Explanatory Notes Upon the New Testament* where slavers are referred to as "man-stealers" who were "the worst of all thieves, in comparison of whom highwaymen and house-breakers are innocent!"[299]

Further compounding John Wesley's dislike of the slave trade was his acquaintance of former slave-ship sailor and Colston's old boy, Silas Told, who he had first met in 1740 and converted to Methodism in 1748. Told had witnessed the inhumane treatment of enslaved Africans and had several times

A detail from William Hogarth's *Industry and Idleness, Plate 11; The Idle 'Prentice Executed at Tyburn*. The preacher Silas Told—the former Colston schoolboy and slave ship sailor who became a prison chaplain—comforting the condemned and asking, "are you afraid to die?"

been treated cruelly himself by ships' masters. Told recorded these incidents in his memoirs which were published after his death and added to the weight of incriminating evidence against the trade.[300]

Another sailor who had been treated savagely was Robert Barker who had served aboard two Bristol slave ships in the 1750s. He wrote up his experiences in a pamphlet published in 1760 and entitled *The Unfortunate Shipwright or Cruel Captain*. It outlined in particular how he and others had suffered on board the *Thetis*, where the captain had apparently been poisoned by the chief mate Robert Whapshutt and ship's surgeon, John Roberts. At the behest of Whapshutt and Roberts, Barker was tormented by female slaves who the pair had already sexually subjugated. On a later voyage Barker lost his sight and was given a pension by the Merchant Seamen's Hospital in Bristol. This was rescinded by the Merchant Venturers after the publication of Barker's pamphlet, allegedly because it contained "several falsehoods".[301]

Meanwhile, now living in America, George Whitefield didn't campaign for abolition but wanted Americans to treat the enslaved with more kindness and compassion—'amelioration'. This compromising stance would delay anti-slavery campaigners on both sides of the Atlantic from seeking emancipation for over a century. Unheard of at the time, Whitefield preached directly to the enslaved and even tried to set up a school for African-Americans. He also made the following observation:

94

As I lately passed through your provinces, I was touched with a fellow feeling of the miseries of the poor negroes... God has a quarrel with you for your cruelty... It is sinful... to use them worse than brutes... Nay, some, as I have been informed by an eye-witness, have been, upon the most trifling provocation, cut with knives, and had forks thrown into their flesh... or been cruelly whipped... My blood has almost run cold within me when I have considered how many of your slaves have neither convenient food to eat, nor proper raiment to put on.[302]

Thanks in no small part to the system of transatlantic slavery, Bristol became one of the cradles of Britain's later Industrial Revolution. Many of Bristol's products and innovations were used in the African trade: ceramics and brass, 'guinea pots' and 'guinea kettles', 'guinea guns' and 'guinea gunpowder', pewter mugs, window and bottle glass, bangles and manilas (used for currency), shackles and thumb screws. Literally fuelling Bristol's 'dark satanic mills' was water power from the rivers Frome and Avon, and coal power from the mines of Kingswood. At the time of the Wesleys' arrival there were over 70 pits large and small being worked. The lure of profits made by supplying commodities to the African trade by some leading Quaker manufacturers, such as Abraham Darby, seemed to overcome their religious aversion to the slave trade.[303]

Not long after coming to Bristol, John Wesley had a couple of interviews with the then Bishop of Bristol, Joseph Butler, who wanted him to stop preaching. Wesley disobeyed him. Here's Bristol Cathedral's take on these meetings:

[But] at the name of Joseph Butler we must make respectful pause. This great divine and philosopher lies buried in the Eastern Lady Chapel, and Southey has written his stately eulogy on the monument in the north transept. In the now ruined Bishop's Palace he lived for twelve years, and here, I suppose, took place that historic interview with John Wesley, wherein Butler pressed his characteristic dislike of the methods of the great evangelist. It was in the Palace gardens, walking by night, that the Bishop asked his chaplain (Josiah Tucker) the ominous question about nations going mad.[304]

Wesley was wrongly accused of offering sacraments such as baptism within Methodist society meetings and was charged with "fanaticism—encouraging irrational behaviour among those who listened to him". Bishop Butler was concerned about decay in Britain's religious life and the two clashed.[305] The Reverend H. J. Wilkins, writing in the 1920s, thought highly of Bishop Butler and put him forward as one of Bristol's great sons and daughters who could perhaps share some of Edward Colston's limelight. He said of Butler "Of all post-Reformation Bishops he had the greatest intellect and did for Christianity a work the significance of which is still valid and vital." Interestingly, Wilkins didn't include either John or Charles Wesley on his list of 'Bristol greats'.[306]

The Methodists, just like the Baptists and Quakers before them, were a driven people having themselves been persecuted for their beliefs. From the start Whitefield and Wesley were miserably treated "sometimes the butt of slanderous tongues, at others mobbed, ducked and stoned".[307] During 1740, the New Room was attacked by a crowd whilst John Wesley was preaching. John Wesley's protégé John Cennick was perpetually harangued and abused at Upton Cheney in Gloucestershire while trying to preach and George Whitefield's colleague, William Seward, was killed after being struck by a stone while preaching in South Wales.[308] As we shall see, this repression may also explain why all three religious sects had empathy for the plight of enslaved Africans, encouraging them to speak out against slavery.

As the mid-seventeenth century approached, Bristol passed its apogee as the pre-eminent British slaving port. In 1743, both Bristol and Liverpool were launching on average 25–30 slave trading voyages each year, with London trailing well behind at less than 10. However, after 1747, Liverpool accelerated away from its competitors reaching more than 40 voyages a year, whilst Bristol began a slow decline towards the end of the century.[309]

From merchants to bankers

It is often assumed that early philosophers and scientists of the Enlightenment held progressive views regarding the slave system. However, this was not always the case and in fact the opposite was true in many instances. Peter Fryer in his seminal history of black people in Britain, *Staying Power*, isolates three eminent enlightenment thinkers who propagated the idea that Africans were inferior to Europeans and thus provided a justification for slavery. Sir William Petty, a founder of the Royal Society, expressed the opinion that Africans and Europeans were dissimilar physically and "differ also in their Natural Manners, & in the internall Qualities of their Minds". As we have seen, the philosopher John Locke was an early investor in the RAC, apparently managing to "reconcile a belief in the inalienable rights of man with the view that black slavery was a justifiable institution". But this was not all; Locke argued that even a child recognised that "a Negro is not a Man". Fryer also slates David Hume by saying:

> However embarrassing all this may be for historians of western philosophy, there is worse. Locke's successor, the great empiricist David Hume, came out openly as a racist. White people, he claimed, were naturally superior to all other races.

These influential thinkers of the seventeenth and mid-eighteenth centuries laid the foundations for the later development of racist ideology as a justification for the enslavement of Africans.[310]

In contrast, an 'enlightened' member of the Enlightenment, French philosopher Montesquieu, published *The Spirit of the Laws* in 1748. In this sarcastic and biting critique of the supporters of slavery he declared "that the state of slavery is in its own nature bad. It is neither useful to the master nor the slave."[311] This is the same year that Hume expressed his views on the subject and demonstrates that there was a significant ideological split amongst European thinkers. *The Spirit of the Laws* was hugely influential and portions of if it were published in the press throughout the late eighteenth century.

1750—The Company of Merchants Trading to Africa takes over the Royal African Company's role in slave trading, with membership of 237 Bristol merchants, 157 London merchants and 89 Liverpool merchants.

The RAC was dissolved two years later, formally marking the end of an era of Royal control over the African trade. The company's terminal decline since Colston's departure in 1692 was paralleled by the expansion of free trade within Britain's dominions. This change was reflected in the actions of the successor to the RAC, the Company of Merchants Trading to Africa, which became an important pro-slavery lobbying body.[312]

The huge amount of wealth that was being extracted by Bristol merchants from both trade in the enslaved and their labour in producing commodities in the Caribbean plantations was reflected in the move to diversify into banking and money lending in the mid-century. In 1750, Onesiphorus Tyndall, a West India slave-merchant and dry-salter; Isaac Elton; Harford Lloyd; William Miller, a grocer; Thomas Knox, and Matthew Hale founded the first private banking partnership in Bristol. Originally called 'Bristol Bank', it soon became known as the 'Bristol Old Bank' as another concern, set up by others with West India interests, also opened on Corn Street two years later.[313] This pattern was to continue through the rest of the century and into the nineteenth: "England's second city had banks springing up like mushrooms. There were thirteen in Bristol by 1811".[314]

The financiers were closely linked with the organisers of the slave trade and in some cases were directly in business together. The idea that those who financed the business of slavery were distanced or unaware of the horrors they were profiting from is scotched by the following example. Bristol banker, Onesiphorous Tyndall and his partner in the slave trade, Isaac Hobhouse, callously discuss issues of supply and demand in the midst of human misery:

Jamaica agents inform Isaac Hobhouse and his partner, Onesiphorus Tyndall, that two-fifths of the slaves on board one of their ships had died on the passage, many more had died after landing, and several were almost valueless. But the writers conclude with the encouraging intelligence that there was an immediate demand for 1,000 good negroes, and fine cargoes will make agreeable sales.

Hobhouse's ruthlessness in the slave trade was matched by that in his other business dealings, as demonstrated by this example of lying to secure a commercial advantage:

In the struggle between Bristol (and Liverpool) and Glasgow over the import trade of tobacco with the American colonies Isaac Hobhouse took a leading role. The complaint was that Glasgow, by evading customs duties, undersold the southerners. By the mercantile influence 'the persecution reduced the northern tobacco trade to insignificance for many years, to the great joy and profit of southern competitors'. A letter written by Mr Isaac Hobhouse, an eminent Bristol merchant, admitting that the charges against the Glasgow firms were untruthful, is among the Newcastle MSS in the British museum.[315]

On a national level, in his book *William Pitt the Younger*, William Hague states:

For two and a half centuries ship-owners had plied their trade with human cargoes across the Atlantic... there had been no interference from governmental authority.[316]

Hague gives the impression that the British slave trade was solely a laissez-faire operation with little or no relationship with government. However, another recent former Tory minister, Jonathan Aitken, points out in his book, *John Newton—from Disgrace to Amazing Grace* that this wasn't so:

After eight months on the coast [1753] Newton was complaining about 'stagnation of trade'. He was having difficulty in filling the holds and lower decks of the *African* until he visited the largest slave factory in Sierra Leone on Bence Island. The reinforced walls and gun emplacements that protected it against attacks from native Africans were paid for with an annual grant of £10,000 voted for maintenance of the Royal African Company's forts in West Africa by the House of Commons in London. It was a reminder that the British Parliament was complicit in supporting the trade from which Newton earned his living.[317]

James Fort (modern day Accra, West Africa) engraved from a painting by Nicholas Pocock, Royal Academician and former Bristol sea captain. Pocock was Bristol's foremost maritime artist.

Resistance on slave ships

Newton, a sailor turned slave-ship captain, later to become an abolitionist, observed a particular form of resistance of enslaved Africans several times during the transatlantic crossing: the ship-board insurrection. He stated:

> One unguarded hour, or minute, is sufficient to give the slaves the opportunity they are always waiting for. An attempt to rise upon the ship's company, brings on instantaneous and horrid war: for, when they are once in motion, they are desperate; and where they do not conquer, they are seldom quelled without much mischief and bloodshed on both sides.[318]

Such an insurrection occurred on a Bristol slave ship the *King David* in 1750. The vessel left Calabar in the Bight of Biafra bound for St Kitts in the Caribbean with a crew of 30 and carrying 350 enslaved Africans.[319] During the voyage, one of the Africans who could speak English gained the trust of the Captain, Edmund Holland, and as a result, some other captives were unshackled and were able to move about freely. Several weeks into the middle-passage, a number of the crew became ill, and several died, significantly reducing the numbers and capability of those who remained. After days of plotting, on 8th May 1750, as the vessel entered Caribbean waters, the enslaved Africans seized their opportunity:

> At 5:00 am, the slaves aboard the *King David*, none of whom was in shackles at the time, rose in sudden revolt. The leader of the uprising quickly directed his fellow rebels to the captain's quarters to confiscate the weapons he had seen there on numerous visits. The revolt was swift and efficient. Within a few minutes, the Africans had secured the arms, killed the captain and five others and taken control of the vessel.

After throwing nine of the captured crew overboard to reduce their fighting strength and chaining the rest to the deck, the victorious Africans debated where to take the ship. They rejected the dangers of sailing back across the Atlantic, deciding instead to secretly make land in the Guadeloupe island group. Unfortunately, two crew members who accompanied a party of Africans ashore were able to warn the French authorities. After a five-day chase the *King David* and its insurrectionary crew were run down by a French ship carrying a hundred armed men and they were recaptured.[320]

This example of a shipboard revolt demonstrates the problems captive Africans faced on attempting to escape from slave ships. Obviously once the vessel had left the African coast there was literally nowhere to escape to, leaving little option but to rise in violent rebellion with the aim of taking control of the vessel. As demonstrated by the *King David* incident, this took careful planning, subterfuge, organisation and choosing the opportune moment to have any chance of success. These moments included crew negligence, reduction in crew strength by sickness, disunity between the sailors and officers, sometimes in situations of mutiny, storms, and attacks by pirates.[321] The closed environment of the ship and the brutal nature of the slave trade made such revolts violent affairs which necessarily pitted the crew against their desperate captives, as Taylor explains:

> Sailors may not have cared about the fate of the Africans on board once they reached the Americas, and other than their own salary, they may not have cared about the profitability of the voyage or about how many Africans survived the passage. Some were filled with hatred and self-righteousness, while others surely felt compassion and perhaps even remorse for the obvious brutality of the slave trade. But regardless of how crew members felt about the voyage in particular or the slave trade in general, they all valued their own lives, and this provided the first line of defence against slave revolts.[322]

A shipboard revolt by enslaved Africans.

Despite the well-founded fears of slave-ship crews and the violence of shipboard insurrections, when the enslaved did take control of vessels it did not mean indiscriminate massacres. Often the victorious Africans realised they needed at least some of the crew to navigate and sail the vessel; they often spared those who posed no threat to them such as 'boy' sailors or those who had treated them well and, as their primary aim was to escape the ship to safety on land, massacre was not necessarily a sensible step. Taylor notes:

> Although large numbers of sailors were...killed in the many revolts that occurred, on the whole unnecessary violence, cruelty, and vengeance do not seem to be typical of the slaves' actions. Indeed, reports of large-scale crew massacres at the hands of revolting slaves are not a common occurrence in the historical record.[323]

The relatively benign reaction of the enslaved during and after successful revolts, considering their desperate circumstances, was not necessarily matched by the captains, officers and crew of slave-ships. Punishments for failed revolts involved public execution, flogging and torture on board ship, though their use was moderated to a certain extent by the monetary 'value' of the enslaved and the financial demands of their 'owners' who sponsored the voyage. These kinds of punishments should also be contextualised. In the pre-democratic, largely monarchical societies of this period, terror of this sort was regularly wielded against the landless, the heretic and the insubordinate.

Two years after the ultimately failed revolt on the *King David* another Bristol slave ship, the *Marlborough,* was seized by more than four hundred Africans. The enslaved Africans, originally from Bonny and the Gold Coast, launched the insurrection a couple of days sail out from West Africa. Some of the crew were killed in the revolt whilst others were executed or thrown overboard until the rebels were satisfied the survivors posed no threat. They ordered the remaining eight sailors to turn the ship round and within a couple of days they were back off the coast of Bonny. After a disastrous attempt to make land in the overloaded ship's longboats which led to their loss and the death by drowning of about 100 Africans, fighting broke out between the Bonny and Gold Coast ex-slaves. Despite this setback, using the skill of the sailors to get close to the shore and in sight of other vessels, 270 Africans from Bonny managed to escape to land as free men and women. The Gold Coast contingent on board the *Marlborough* then used the ship's muskets and guns to outwit and defeat another Bristol ship, the *Hawk*, which attempted to board them by force. The rebels apparently escaped out to sea, heading for the Gold Coast; their fate remains unknown.[324]

So how prevalent was this kind of resistance by enslaved Africans during the middle passage? Research has suggested that, on average, one in ten transatlantic slave-ship voyages experienced insurrections of some form or other. However, the statistics suggest that the chances of successfully seizing a ship were low (perhaps one in five) and those of then returning to Africa were even lower (perhaps one in nine). As Behrendt et al note:

> If, as estimated earlier, 10 per cent of all slave vessels experienced revolts, a guess at the proportion of slaves regaining land with free status would be less than one-tenth of 1 per cent.[325]

Of the 2,081 slave ships leaving Bristol between 1698 and 1807 that are logged in the *Trans-Atlantic Slave Trade Database*, 35 (1.7 per cent) are tagged as having some form of explicit 'African resistance'(see Appendix 5). Of these, eight are marked as 'vessel attacked from shore' referring to attempts to release the enslaved by force on the West African coast. Half of these attacks appear to have been successful, leading to the vessel being 'cut off' and presumably lost, with the enslaved making their way to shore and perhaps even to freedom. The remaining 27 incidents are listed as 'slave insurrection', of which four appear to have been successful (including the *Marlborough*). However, this small number of insurrections may not be a true reflection of explicit on-board resistance. Slave-ship captains were often reluctant to report such incidents as it questioned their reputation and reliability in delivering their human cargo, so the figures may be significantly larger. In any case, the effect of resistance of this sort upon the slave traders was much greater than it first appears. One group of researchers estimated the financial and human effects:

> Between 1680 and 1800, nearly 6.6 million slaves left Africa for the New World. The model predicts that without shipboard or coastal resistance the number of people moving across the Atlantic from Africa would have been nearly 9 per cent greater. Put another way, in the long eighteenth century alone, resistance resulted in nearly 600,000 fewer slaves crossing the Atlantic and forced European consumers to pay higher prices for

plantation produce. In effect, Africans who died resisting the slave traders as well as those who resisted unsuccessfully, but survived to work on the plantations of the Americas, saved others from forced migration to the Americas.[326]

The prevalence of shipboard insurrection can be gauged by a brief study of the most prolific Bristol slave ship, the *Black Prince*. Owned by James Laroche, who as we have seen was Bristol's predominant slave trader in the eighteenth century, the vessel made nine slaving voyages to West Africa between 1750 and 1768, the largest number of any Bristol ship. On the seventh voyage, in 1762, the ship arrived at Cape Coast Castle on the Gold Coast and spent eight months in the area whilst a cargo of 438 enslaved Africans was assembled. Toward the end of this long period, in February 1763, a first plot by the captives to seize the ship was discovered and put down by flogging the ringleaders. The *Black Prince* duly sailed for Antigua; within three days a second insurrection was thwarted and ten of the plotters were chained together and whipped. Eventually the ship reached St John's in Antigua where the 394 surviving Africans were sold.

On her ninth and final slaving voyage the *Black Prince* experienced an insurrection of a different sort. The ship left Bristol bound for West Africa in December 1768 with 45 sailors on board. Three weeks into the voyage, off the Cape Verde islands, the crew mutinied and seized the ship. Setting the captain, officers and unwilling crew adrift in a longboat, the mutineers then sailed across the Atlantic to Brazil. They landed at Pernambuco, at this time a Portuguese colony, where they left 11 of the crew. The remaining mutineers then turned pirate and were last heard of seizing a French slave ship and running the *Black Prince* aground off Cape Francois in the Caribbean. A furious Laroche wrote to Viscount Weymouth—Secretary of State for the Southern Department responsible for dealings with Portugal—demanding the repatriation of the mutineers to Lisbon or London in order for them to stand trial and, almost certainly, face execution.[327] It is clear from this, along with many other examples, that the violent rejection of maritime hierarchy, coerced labour and brutality was not solely confined to chattel slaves.

The beginnings of a movement...

1754—April 5, a general election. Candidates for Bristol, Richard Beckford, esq. [Tory], who polled 2283 votes—Robert Nugent, esq. [Whig], 2622 (both returned)—Sir John Philipps, bart. [Tory], 2217.

Richard Beckford and Sir John Philipps were both Tory Steadfast Society candidates who tried to end the controlling Whig influence of Bristol in Parliament. Beckford was in Jamaica during the entire election and, of his three questions in the House, he only asked one on behalf of his Bristol electorate. He died in 1756 occasioning another election for his seat which was won by Jarrett Smith esq. with a large majority. Beckford left an estate worth roughly £120,000, mostly in Jamaica. It included nearly 1,000 slaves, two cattle pens and three prime contiguous sugar estates in Westmoreland parish.[328]

Beckford's older brother Alderman William Beckford—also known as 'negro whipping Beckford' when Lord Mayor of London—was even wealthier; when he died in 1770, he was the first commoner in England to be worth over £1 million. His son and heir, William Thomas Beckford of Fonthill, inherited not only the £1 million but also an annual income in excess of £100,000.[329] Spectacularly, this younger Beckford, the 'Fool of Fonthill', managed to blow nearly all of his inheritance within a generation, one lasting legacy being Beckford's Tower on top of Lansdown. Built in 1827, the three-stage tower is 157 feet high and topped with a gilded lantern, the gold domed roof glistening down over the Avon Valley from Bath to Bristol to this day.

The aforementioned chaplain of Bishop Butler, Welshman Josiah Tucker, was a supporter of Robert Nugent and, thanks to Nugent's preferment, went up the clerical hierarchy, ultimately becoming Dean of Gloucester in 1756. Tucker had a great interest in trade and politics and as early as 1749 predicted that the American colonies would leave Britain. He came to the attention of the Bishop of Norfolk who asked him to write a pamphlet entitled *Elements of Commerce and the Theory of Taxes* for the instruction of the future King George III. Published privately, it has been argued that this document influenced some of Adam Smith's ideas for his *Wealth of Nations* (ideas such as sweeping away monopolies and duties which impeded trade and commerce in Britain). Tucker would go on to become one of Bristol's leading abolitionists.[330]

In 1759, Philadelphian Anthony Benezet, the acknowledged founder of the transatlantic abolition movement, published his first anti-slavery tract. Of French Huguenot descent, Quaker Benezet started America's first African Free School in 1750 and, inspired by the anti-slavery stance taken by early Quakers such as James Nayler[331] and George Fox, he reached out to others opposed to slavery. Benezet tirelessly corresponded with French, British and American enlightenment abolitionists including Benjamin Franklin, Abbé Raynal and Benjamin Rush; regardless of their religious affiliations, whatever their nationality, he wanted to get slavery banned. The Society for the Propagation of the Gospel unfortunately resisted Benezet's overtures.

|| **1760**—Portrait of Robert Nugent MP painted by Thomas Gainsborough
|| to mark his re-election, unopposed, in 1759.

Madge Dresser and Sue Giles state in *Bristol and Transatlantic Slavery*:

Clare Street was built in 1775 and named after Viscount Clare, formerly Robert Nugent, who was MP for Bristol for 20 years from 1754. He was involved in the 1750 Act which replaced the London based Royal African Company with the Company of Merchants Trading to Africa. The RAC had lost its monopoly of the slave trade to Africa in 1698, but it was still responsible for the management of trade in Africa, and for the maintenance of the English trading forts. The new company gave merchants from Bristol and other provincial cities a say in the running of the African trade. The portrait in the Lord Mayor's Office shows Nugent holding a copy of the Act for the Regulation of the Slave Trade.[332]

From 1760, Colston Parade was laid out just south of St Mary Redcliffe Church.

|| **1760**—Tacky's slave rebellion in Jamaica—400 rebels are executed. || Quakers in Britain ban slave-trading amongst their followers.

The revolt of the enslaved in Jamaica in 1760–61, known commonly as Tacky's Rebellion, was a massive uprising involving around 1,500 men and women. Over more than a year, in a series of raids and skirmishes, the rebels killed 60 white colonists and damaged the economy of the island to the tune of a quarter of a million pounds (equivalent to around £500 million in 2016 by GDP per capita). The brutal suppression of the revolt led to the deaths of over 500 black men and women, either killed in battle, executed, or through suicide. Another 500 rebels were transported from the island for life. One contemporary writer commented on the impact of the uprising:

> "Whether we consider the extent and secrecy of its plan, the multitude of the conspirators, and the difficulty of opposing its eruptions in such a variety of places at once," wrote planter-historian Edward Long in his 1774 *History of Jamaica*, this revolt was "more formidable than any hitherto known in the West Indies"[333]

The latter half of the eighteenth century eventually saw a reawakening of people's consciences and the anti-slavery movement was formed. As we have seen, Saint Wulfstan had started the work in the eleventh century in Bristol but the lessons had not been learned. Anti-slavery ideas of the Enlightenment had had little effect in preventing the African slave trade from taking off and, ultimately, enslaving and displacing millions.

In 1765, a musician to the court of George III, Granville Sharp, became involved with the slave trade when he met a patient of his brother who was so badly injured that he had been left for dead. Black teenager Jonathan Strong's 'owner', David Lisle, had beaten him "upon his Head with a Pistol till the barrel and Lock were separated from the stock" and then abandoned him to the streets of London. William Sharp, Granville's brother, was also the King's doctor and he treated Strong as best he could and then had him admitted to St Bartholomew's Hospital. It took Strong over four months to recover and on his release the brothers gave him money for food and clothes and got him a job as a footman for a pharmacist near William's practice.

Two years later Lisle spotted his onetime slave and, astonished to see him still alive, followed him home and had him kidnapped in order to get his 'property' back. Lisle sold him on to a Jamaican planter but while awaiting shipping, Strong managed to get a letter to Granville Sharp. The case went before the Lord Mayor of London and the well-connected Sharp managed to win Strong his freedom against all the odds; this started a lifelong campaign against slavery by the former. Sharp, now 32 years old, became the leading 'go to' defender of black people in the capital and an early leader of the British abolition movement, becoming the 'father of the cause'.[334] In 1769 Sharp published *A Representation of the Injustice and Dangerous Tendencies of Tolerating Slavery in England*, arguably the first modern anti-slavery tract.[335]

1767—Jonathan Strong legal case begins: a slave in England was agreed to be free from transportation if they were not guilty of any crime.

Also in 1767, in an early example of 'gun boat diplomacy', six British slave ships, the *Indian Queen, Duke of York, Nancy*, and *Concord*, of Bristol, the *Edgar* of Liverpool, and the *Canterbury* of London,[336] were involved in a massacre at Old Calabar, modern day Nigeria. Bristol Captain James Bevan deemed that local potentate Grandy King George was charging too much for his slaves and when a power struggle developed between Grandy and his nearby rival, Duke Ephraim of New Calabar, Bevan sided with the latter. Grandy and his followers were tricked into a meeting on Bevan's ship and ambushed. Grandy escaped but one of his brothers was decapitated and some 300 were killed trying to flee in their canoes after the slave ships opened fire. Two 'princes', another of Grandy's brothers, Little Ephraim, and nephew, Ancona Robin, were promptly enslaved by the British. They miraculously made it to Bristol where eventually they were freed by Charles Wesley and his associates. John Wesley reported the case to Benezet in 1774.[337]

1770—French writer Abbé Raynal publishes work calling for a 'Black Spartacus' to arise and avenge slavery, which the author calls a crime against nature.

"Power of the Purse"—Merchant and enslaved African woman—early engraving. Portrayals of the enslaved in literature crucially helped change public opinion against the slave trade.

Bristol's 'boy poet' Thomas Chatterton attacked the slave trade in his poem *African Eclogues*. Other writers also started to critique slavery both in print and in the theatre in Bristol, reflecting "the local diffusion of Enlightenment ideas and their impact on attitudes towards the slave trade".[338]

‖ **1774**—John Wesley publishes anti-slavery tract *Thoughts upon Slavery*.

From 1772, John Wesley was in contact with Granville Sharp and, through him, with Anthony Benezet. Together they formed a 'triumvirate against slavery', subsequently joined by Olaudah Equiano, Thomas Clarkson and William Wilberforce. It was Sharp who gave Wesley a copy of Benezet's *Guinea Trade*[339] and, deeply impressed, Wesley reworked it by shortening and improving the prose. The pamphlet, retitled *Thoughts Upon Slavery*, was even harder hitting, immediately becoming a best seller throughout Britain and appearing in 13 editions in the United States.[340] Benezet was happy for his work to be used in this way and gave his blessing—the goal of abolition being central to his life's work. Modern Wesleyan historian, Gary Best, believes that the impact of *Thoughts Upon Slavery* has "not received the historical recognition it deserves",[341] while Benezet historian Maurice Jackson believes it was *the* major influence on the Methodists, who obtained nearly a quarter of a million signatures in a petition against the slave trade just after John Wesley's death in 1791.[342]

To this day some people try to justify European involvement in the transatlantic slave trade by saying "Africans traded Africans". Here is Wesley's (and Benezet's) take on this type of pro-slavery propaganda in *Thoughts upon Slavery*:

> That slave-holding is utterly inconsistent with mercy, is almost too plain to need a proof. Indeed, it is said, "that these Negroes being prisoners of war, our captains and factors buy them, merely to save them from being put to death. And is this not mercy?" I answer, (1.) Did Sir John Hawkins, and many others, seize upon men, women, and children, who were at peace in their own fields or houses, merely to save them from death? (2.) Was it to save them from death that they knocked out the brains of those they could not bring away? (3.) Who occasioned and fomented those wars, wherein these poor creatures were taken prisoners? Who excited them by money, by drink, by every possible means, to fall upon one another? Was it not themselves? They know in their own conscience it was, if they have any conscience left. But, (4.) To bring the matter to a short issue, can they say before God, that they ever took a single voyage, or bought a single Negro, from this motive? They cannot; they well know, to get money, not to save lives, was the whole and sole spring of their motions.[343]

Wesley and Benezet clearly recognised that the involvement of British merchants, purely for monetary gain, had not only encouraged expansion of slavery in Africa but had also led to internal wars and instability.

> **1774**—At the general election, the votes in Bristol were, for Henry Cruger [Whig], 3565—Edmund Burke [Whig], 2707—Matthew Brickdale [Tory], 2453—Lord Clare [Robert Nugent, Whig], 286. Burgesses who voted, 5384.

Did this surprising election result, which put the Whigs into total power in Bristol for the first time in many years, represent a waning of interest in the slave trade or worries over the revolution brewing in North America? Henry Cruger won on a 'radical' Whig ticket but was most concerned about British and American matters. His family had interests in the slave trade and he defended slavery as "the practice of every civilised nation" and "considered a sudden and total abolition ruinous in the extreme".[344] Cruger's supposed radicalism came from his admiration for journalist and populist politician John Wilkes, who in the 1760s had introduced the petition to parliamentary debate and revived the use of political pamphlets.[345] However, as Poole and Rogers note, the political inconsistencies were glaring:

> [Cruger] saw no contradiction between a libertarian radicalism, the defence of property and legal rights before an intrusive state…and chattel slavery; presumably because Africans in bondage were denied subject-hood.[346]

Cruger later became an advisor to the Society of Merchant Venturers over tactics for defending their interests in slavery and also introduced a number of pro-slavery petitions to Parliament. He eventually retired to America and in 1792 was elected to the senate of New York State.[347]

John Wesley, on the other hand, had no time for 'radical' politicians and, being a Tory at heart, voted for the likes of Brickdale despite their clear pro-slavery stance.[348] Apologists for Edmund Burke, the other winning candidate in the 1774 election, often represent him as a pioneering abolitionist because of his views on slavery and the slave trade.[349] This is somewhat of a misrepresentation. It is true that Burke wrote a work, *Sketch of the Negro code*, in 1780 which has been interpreted as an early anti-slavery tract.[350] However, the *Sketch* is merely a series of guidelines for the regulation of slavery, full of revealing references to the "uncivilised" nature of the enslaved "savages", giving us an insight into Burke's world-view. As late as 1792 he stated:

...the cause of humanity would be far more benefitted by the continuance of the trade and servitude, regulated and reformed, than by the total destruction of both or either.[351]

Burke's position that slavery could be gradually reformed away was predicated on protecting the long-term interests of the plantation owners and the idea that civil law could regulate its excesses. Ironically this was precisely the position that apologists for colonial slavery took once they were under significant threat from the abolitionists in the nineteenth century.

Burke lost his Bristol seat in 1780; though he went on to support Pitt, Fox, Wilberforce, Sheridan and Canning with various Abolition Bills against King George III, who hated abolitionists. The king was aided by his son, the future William IV, who, as the Duke of Clarence, led the opposition to the abolitionists in the House of Lords. In one debate Lord Barrington, the grandson of Bristol MP Sir William Daines [see entry for 1724], claimed that slaves "appeared to him so happy that he often wished himself to be in their situation..."[352]

1776—American War of Independence seriously disrupts all transatlantic trade in Bristol.

The war had dire consequences for the working poor of the city who lost their jobs and found it hard to find food for their families. C. Roy Hudleston stated in his overview of Bristol's economy in the eighteenth century in the 1931 guide book *How to see Bristol*:

...the commerce of Bristol had suffered a terrible shock by the revolt of the American colonies, which wrought havoc amongst the mercantile firms, and reduced for a time the trade of the port by fifty per cent.

It was even worse in the West Indies where the enslaved starved; the problem of withering agriculture and restricted supplies was compounded by hurricanes; 15,000 died on Jamaica alone between 1780 and 1787.[353] The Admiralty responded by sending Lt. William Bligh to the Pacific to obtain bread fruit trees; although he famously failed, a second expedition successfully introduced the trees to the islands. Few of the enslaved would eat the fruit however.[354]

It's interesting to note that at this time the combined wealth created by the thirteen 'free' United States was minuscule when compared to the British sugar producing islands of the West Indies; of those, by far and away Jamaica was the most productive, exceeding the American colonies' wealth creation by a factor of five.[355] It wasn't the most productive Caribbean island, though; in the 1780s, the French islands of the West Indies exported £9 million of goods back to Europe compared with Britain's dominions at £5 million; the top earner was Saint-Domingue—formerly part of Hispaniola, now modern day Haiti. The island imported 18 per cent of all enslaved Africans into the Americas, twice as many as the United States, and its soil was five times as productive as Jamaica's.[356] So for the British economy, at least in the short term, losing the American colonies wasn't a complete disaster. However, the huge importance of the Caribbean slave economy for both the French and the British would make it a geo-political battleground in the 1790s.

1776 also saw the launch of Scottish philosopher Adam Smith's seminal work *Wealth of Nations,* published in London by Bristolian Thomas Cadell. The book was hugely important and firmly against the institution of slavery on the basis that it was economically inefficient, rather than morally wrong. It heavily influenced William Pitt the Younger who went on to say in the House of Commons in April 1792 "There is no nation in Europe that has… plunged so deeply into this guilt as Britain."[357] But, as we shall see, Pitt had other motivations for attacking the slave trade.

|| **1778**—House of Commons appoints a committee to investigate the
|| British slave trade.

On 28th January 1782, presumably so as to counter the emergence of anti-slavery sentiment, the inaugural meeting of the West India New Society was held at the Bush Tavern in Corn Street, with Richard Bright as secretary.[358] The society was revived from an older organisation and became the Bristol merchants' main instrument in their dealings with Government. Bitter opponents of abolition, Thomas Daniel along with his 20 year old son Thomas junior joined the organisation. The latter stayed a loyal member for over seventy years and held every office from treasurer to secretary to chairman. The title of the organisation morphed into the West India Association which at its height had related bodies in London, Liverpool, Glasgow and Dublin.[359]

Another important member of the West India New Society was the prolific slave trader James Laroche. Sheriff of Bristol in 1764–5, Laroche, was of Huguenot descent and followed his father's footsteps in becoming the MP for Bodmin in 1768. In Parliament, though, he primarily represented Bristol's slaving interests, defending the city's "stand for free trade in slaves". As a result, Laroche and the Bristol MPs were 'paid' in handsome gifts of wine from the Corporation. Like other Bristol merchants he had a major house in Queen Square and on the proceeds of the slave trade bought the mansion Over Court near Almondsbury. He married into the Yeamans family, prominent Bristol merchants who owned plantations in Antigua. Laroche was forced to mortgage these estates for £7,000 in 1774, before going bankrupt in 1778. This was probably due to accumulated losses from his contested parliamentary elections and the American Revolution. However, it is argued, it was his support for George III during the latter that earned him a baronetcy.[360]

1780—Matthew Brickdale, esq. [Tory] and Sir Henry Lippincott, bart. [Tory] chosen representatives in Parliament.

After the superstar MP Edmund 'Paddy' Burke lost his seat, the Bristol electorate resorted to the tried and tested method of appointing their own plutocracy of mayors, sheriffs and prominent members of the Society of Merchant Venturers to Parliament. Lippincott, a tobacco merchant, died a year later and was replaced by another Tory, George Daubeny, who had interests in sugar refining, banking and glass-making. All of the MPs were pro-slavery. George 'the vain' Daubeny had beaten New Yorker Henry Cruger into second place by 'attracting' voters with free dinners at the *Full Moon* in Stokes Croft with cries of "[try] the difference between American bull and the roast beef of Old England". Daubeny's conduct was so blatant that Parliament was petitioned by 1,000 disgruntled Bristolians on a charge of "[his] many acts of bribery and corruption and other partial and illegal practices and proceedings." In an affray during the election, two of Cruger's supporters were shot and killed by a Tory ship's captain and the ensuing enquiry was less than satisfactory. A satirical engraving deriding Daubeny's election victory of 1781 shows an African semi-obscured behind a statue of Liberty holding a 'cap of liberty' on a staff. The other statue was that of Law.[361]

Meanwhile the Corporation incensed the local populace by acquiring the Mansion House in Queen Square and refurbishing it at great public cost with new chandeliers and carpets. The building was used by the oligarchy to receive prestigious visitors and host banquets, thereby maintaining the Bristol elite's legendary reputation for hospitality. This symbol of excess was to be targeted and destroyed during the Reform Riots of 1831.[362]

1783—Public outrage in England when the case of the Zong *becomes* known: the captain threw sick Africans overboard because of a shortage of water—the owners could claim insurance if the deaths were necessary to save the ship, but not if they died of 'natural causes'.

In 1781 the master of the slave ship *Zong*, Luke Collingwood, in an attempt to guarantee insurance payments for an ailing cargo of slaves, had decided to jettison 123 live Africans, still shackled in their irons, into shark infested waters off Jamaica. Although Collingwood's reasoning was based on financial considerations, he tried to mask the murders by claiming that his decision had been made due to a shortage of water. This explanation didn't ring true because a third group of Africans were thrown overboard even after rainfall had replenished the ship's reserves. While the 'live cargo' was insured, the underwriters would not pay up for property that could be deemed 'losses at sea'. The *Zong's* master believed that killing the Africans would constitute reimbursable losses. However, the underwriters in London refused to pay; the owners sued; and a case proceeded based on infamous deliberations about whether or not the 'cargo' could legitimately be claimed for under the terms of the insurance.[363]

Freed slave and abolitionist Olaudah Equiano alerted Granville Sharp to the *Zong* case and the latter took part in a second trial which attempted to get convictions for murder. After failing to 'prosecute the murders', Sharp subsequently went to the Court of Admiralty but the charge was thrown out. In both cases the judge sided in favour of the owners, prominent Liverpool merchants and mayors. Even though the case was only reported in one newspaper it became a cause célèbre and did more to publicise the horrors of the slave system than anything else at the time. Furthermore, it established Sharp as a force to be reckoned with and, within a few years, led to the formation of the 'Committee for Effecting the Abolition of the Slave Trade'.

On 7th July 1783, Harry Gandy, a Bristol Quaker and former slave-ship captain, wrote to William Dillwyn, a 'go-between' for the anti-slavery triumvirate, Benezet, Wesley and Sharp, about his voyages to Africa. On his first voyage in 1740, Gandy had witnessed a revolt on a slave ship just off Barbados and on his second voyage he vindicated Benezet's observations from *Some Historical Account of Guinea*:

"I have carefully pursued Anthony Benezet's Tracts on that subject [and had] never had such reflections arise, as I never experienced before doubtless owing to my formerly being less convinced of the iniquity of such traffic than I am now." He went on "a six and twenty years residence in the West Indies gave me a full opportunity of knowing the cruelties exercised there on the slaves, having in the ways of the trade frequented almost all the English Islands, and some of the Dutch, French and Spanish." He added, "I can therefore confidently affirm that Anthony Benezet, and others quoted by him, are by no means exaggerated."[364]

Gandy's vindicating statement was included in the 1788 edition of Benezet's *Some Historical Account of Guinea*.

1784—Commenced an election for representatives in Parliament that lasted thirty-seven days. The votes were, for Matthew Brickdale [Tory], 3458—Henry Cruger [Whig],—3052—George Daubeny [Tory], 2958—Samuel Peach [Whig], 373.

In 1788 Brickdale presented a petition to maintain the slave trade on behalf of the Bristol Corporation and many of the city's commercial interests. Brickdale, an Honorary member of the Merchant Venturers, was formally described as 'clothier and undertaker' but this hid a family interest in the slave trade. His father John had been a co-owner of the slave ship *Loyal George* with Isaac Hobhouse and he became a real thorn in the side of abolitionist William Wilberforce in Parliament.[365] Representing Bristol's Tory Steadfast Society, Brickdale inherited a huge fortune of some £100,000 from his father but spent prolifically on his election contests, ending his days in straightened circumstances.[366]

Thomas Clarkson

Come June 1785, cometh the hour, cometh the man. Sharp, Wesley, Equiano and the Quakers were in desperate need of someone to galvanise their anti-slavery campaign in Britain; that person was 25-year-old novice Anglican clergyman, Thomas Clarkson from Wisbech, Cambridgeshire. As a student and having absorbed Benezet's works in particular, Clarkson won a prize essay competition critiquing the slave trade at Cambridge University. The horrors revealed to him during his research coursed through his mind and made Clarkson stop on the road to Wades Hill in Hertfordshire. The thought then occurred to him: "…if the contents of the Essay were true, it was time some person should see these calamities to their end".[367]

Unknown to Clarkson at the time, he had committed himself to one of the greatest of all human rights movements. The first step on this historic road was the concentration of the abolitionists' efforts, and these were helped by the contribution of the Quakers whose commitment and organisational skills had been built up over many years in business. Improved means of communication between London and the provinces also helped; the fledgling postal service and the new express coaches were now running on superior toll roads so that the travel time between Bristol and London had come down from about three and a half days to just 16 hours.[368]

> **1786**—Thomas Clarkson's Ess*ay on Slavery and Commerce of the Human Species* published.[369]

The original subject of Clarkson's prize-winning essay was *Anne Liceat Invitos In Servitutem Dare?* (Is it lawful to make slaves of others against their will?). After he translated it into English it became a bestseller, gaining significant plaudits and influence amongst abolitionists and the wider public.

As Clarkson's influential anti-slavery essay was distributed in pamphlet form, one of his most bitter future opponents, Thomas Daniel junior, became sheriff of Bristol. Before moving to Bristol in 1764, the Daniel family were a leading mercantile dynasty from Barbados, where they had been since the mid seventeenth Century. Daniel's father—another Thomas Daniel—was known as a 'respectable merchant' and his firm of T. Daniel & Sons based in Bristol became the principal sugar importer from Barbados. Thomas junior was born on the island in 1762 and went on to have a meteoric rise through the ranks of Bristol's corporate and mercantile elite. He was a freeman by the age of 21, elected member of the corporation at 23 and High Sheriff of Bristol at 24. Wealth was clearly a factor in this rise through the hierarchy; for example, Daniel complained that after his sheriff's dinner at Michaelmas (29th September) 1787, he was a whopping £600 out of pocket.[370]

This year also saw the launching of yet another financial institution in Bristol by some members of the West India interest. The 'New Bank' was set up by Levi Ames, John Cave, Joseph Harford, George Daubeny and Richard Bright.[371] Ames, Cave, Daubeny and Bright all had direct financial interests in the slave-system, whether through 'owning' slaves and plantations or through trading in the enslaved. Others, like Harford, were supplying commodities to the merchants to trade in West Africa.[372]

> **1787**—*Committee for Effecting the Abolition of the Slave Trade* founded in London: Thomas Clarkson visits Bristol on fact-finding mission about the slave trade.

The Committee was formed on the 22nd May 1787 and led by Granville Sharp who, after 25 years fighting slavery, became the figurehead, while Clarkson became the main driver of the movement on the ground. Their first act, against Sharp's wishes, was making the pragmatic choice to first strive for abolition of the slave trade, with emancipation to follow. It's unlikely they thought it would take another 51 years to fully achieve their goals!

When a pleased John Wesley heard the news that Clarkson was striving for an Act of Parliament, he wrote to his friend, the Quaker banker and abolitionist, Samuel Hoare:

> I have long wished for the rolling away of this… reproach not only from religion, but to humanity itself… Mr Clarkson's design strikes at the root of it. And if it can be put into execution will be a lasting honour to the British nation… With men this is impossible; but we know all things are possible to God! What little I can do to promote this excellent work I shall do with pleasure.[373]

The Abolition Committee was in dire need of a representative in Parliament and had identified the talented Hull MP and Evangelical Christian, William Wilberforce, only a year older than Clarkson. To facilitate this, London abolitionist Bennet Langton contrived a dinner party at his home to which Wilberforce and others like Samuel Johnson's biographer James Boswell and portrait painter Sir Joshua Reynolds were invited. Unusually tongue-tied, Clarkson failed to pop the question and it was left to the host, Langton, to do the necessary. Wilberforce replied that, "provided no person more proper could be found", he would pledge himself to take up the subject in Parliament.[374]

Within weeks Clarkson started his fact-finding mission by going to the 'fountain heads' of the slave trade, Bristol first and then Liverpool, early the following year. On approaching the city, young Clarkson was suddenly filled with dread on realising the magnitude and danger of what lay ahead:

> On turning a corner... at about eight in the evening, I came within sight of it [Bristol]. The weather was rather hazy, which occasioned it to look of unusual dimensions. The bells of some of the churches were then ringing; the sound...filled me, almost directly, with a melancholy for which I could not account. I began now to tremble, for the first time, at the arduous task I had undertaken, of attempting to subvert one of the branches of the commerce of the great place which was then before me... I questioned whether I should ever get out of it alive.[375]

On his arrival, Clarkson had a letter of introduction to Harry Gandy who in turn introduced him to sympathetic Quaker families including those of James Harford, Matthew Wright, and Thomas Bonville. He met Quakers George Fisher and Walter Chandler soon after. For a while these were his only friends and acquaintances in the metropolis of the West. On asking around, Clarkson found that the people of Bristol talked openly about the slave trade and were acquainted with various aspects. Although they all seemed to loathe it—his word was 'execrate'—no one seemed to think of its abolition. Clarkson didn't know it at the time but he was pushing at a slightly open door—as well as Bristol's Quakers, the city's Methodists and Baptists had been denouncing the iniquities of the slave trade for several years.

Clarkson made other good contacts within the city hierarchy, including the aged Dean Josiah Tucker, the Reverend Dr John Camplin and attorney and deputy town-clerk of Bristol Corporation, Mr Burges. Clarkson was aware of Tucker's work and in the Dean's 1785 *Reflections on the Disputes between Great Britain and Ireland* noticed Tucker had passed a severe censure on British planters for the inhuman treatment of their slaves. The Dean took a great interest in Clarkson's quest and wanted all of the latest news, especially regarding the abolition of the slave trade. He became a 'warm supporter' of both Clarkson and the cause. Camplin of All Saints, ironically the Colston family church, would also defend Clarkson's position, while Burges became his informant and advisor within local government.[376]

Clarkson's initial goals were to get information on the natural produce of Africa, the procurement and treatment of enslaved Africans, the loss of British seamen involved in the slave trade, and the quantity and value of imports and exports. The Abolition Committee required hard evidence regarding these goals, ideally eye-witness testimony, in order to both undermine the propaganda of the apologists and to bring the hitherto largely hidden realities of slavery to the public and Parliament's attention. The problem was where to start; obviously anyone who had financial interests in the trade was unlikely to spill the beans.

Clarkson immediately got wind of ill treatment of sailors and on 3rd July pursued a slave ship named the *Brothers* which was waiting in port at Kingroad to depart, where a free black sailor named John Dean had been cruelly treated by Captain Jeffrey Howlett. In Clarkson's words:

> The report was, that for a trifling circumstance, for which he was in nowise to blame, the captain had fastened him with his belly to the deck, and that, in this situation, he had poured hot pitch upon his back, and made incisions in it with hot tongs.

Other members of the crew had also been abused and of the complement of 40, 32 had died on that voyage.[377] As a consequence the ship's captain had great trouble recruiting for his next voyage—a party of would-be recruits became terrified on learning of the previous crew's fate and jumped ship immediately. Unfortunately for Clarkson, Dean had left Bristol for London but his testimony was corroborated by a new acquaintance of Clarkson's, Sydenham Teast, a slave-ship builder and trader to Africa. The importance of the account of John Dean's ill treatment is that it directed Clarkson's attention towards the plight of the slave-ship sailors.

In order to meet his goal of uncovering information on the ill usage of sailors, Clarkson began to gather evidence from ships' muster rolls that he found at Bristol's Custom House in Queen Square. Clarkson's decision to transcribe the evidence in the nearby Merchants' Hall was a puzzling one bearing in mind that the Hall was home to all of Bristol's West India and African merchants; it must have been like entering the lion's den. It may have been the influence of Dean Tucker that brought this situation about. Tucker had introduced Clarkson to the Custom House and the two regularly met in the Merchants' Hall. It was Dr Camplin, though, who became Clarkson's "warm defender" against these merchants when they, on learning of his intentions, began to "calumniate" (charge falsely or with malicious intent) against the abolitionist.[378]

It was in the muster rolls that Clarkson discovered that the city's slave-ship sailors died or failed to return home in shockingly large numbers. Of the 940 sailors that left Bristol on 24 slave ships bound for West Africa, 216 died (23 per cent) and 239 more (25 per cent) failed to return due to desertion or being left in

The Merchants' Hall

Merchants' Hall, the 'Lion's Den'. Thomas Clarkson transcribed slave-ship muster rolls here in 1787; off left is Marsh Street, off right is King Street.

Thomas Clarkson, with his box of African artefacts, in 1828.

the Caribbean so that ship owners could avoid paying their wages.[379] Clarkson went on to use the same technique in London and Liverpool, finally recording the details of some 20,000 sailors to back up his claims.[380] The figures proved that being engaged as a sailor in the slave trade was an extremely dangerous occupation compared to other maritime ventures. The high mortality and ill-usage begged the question as to why sailors took jobs on slave ships. One of the answers would become clear on Clarkson's return visit to Bristol from Bridgwater.

Other evidence soon came Clarkson's way, this time relating to the massacre at Old Calabar (see 1767), which he had heard about but not acted upon due to lack of proof. Henry Sulgar, a Moravian minister in the Maudlin Street chapel, put him in possession of copies of the real depositions which had been taken in the case of the King against Lippincott and others relative to the event, namely those of captain Floyd of the city of Bristol, who had been a witness to the scene, and of Ephraim Robin John and of Ancona Robin John, two African chiefs, who had suffered by it. Clarkson later said:

The knowledge of this tragical event now fully confirmed me in the sentiment, that the hearts of those, who were concerned in this traffic, became unusually hardened, and that I might readily believe any atrocities, however great, which might be related of them. It made also my blood boil as it were within me. It gave a new spring to my exertions. And I rejoiced, sorrowful as I otherwise was, that I had visited Bristol, if it had been only to gain an accurate statement of this one fact.[381]

Clarkson then looked into the ill usage of seamen in the newly returned slave ship *Alfred* and found several cases worth pursuing; one crew member had actually been killed after repeatedly being beaten over the breast by a knotted rope. Against his own judgement Clarkson was talked out of taking further action by deputy town-clerk Burges, who cautioned him against it on the grounds that the merchants would use every means at their disposal to defeat him, including bribery and prevarication. Clarkson was unhappy at having to drop this particular line of enquiry but determined himself to fight on, grasping each day in Bristol in order to "bring this evil nearer to its end".[382]

Clarkson had initially thought that Africa's natural produce could possibly substitute the trade in humans and to this end interviewed Sydenham Teast who had, as we have seen, verified the mistreatment of sailor John Dean on the slave ship *Brothers*. Teast was able to furnish details of some of Africa's natural products such as ivory, exotic woods, beeswax and palm oil. Another trader to Africa named Biggs not only gave samples of spices but also textiles made and dyed by Africans. Clarkson managed to augment these with more African material such as cloth and tulip wood supplied by Thomas Bonville and others.

The collection would go on to form the basis of the legendary 'Clarkson box' of African artefacts and produce that he would use to illustrate African culture and demonstrate African genius and talent; African people weren't 'sub-human' or merely 'beasts of burden', and could offer much more to the world than populating the slave trade.

After a brief sojourn in Bridgwater, Clarkson's Quaker friends then introduced him to Landlord Thompson of the *Seven Stars* in St Thomas Lane. According to Clarkson, Thompson was a very intelligent man who would have no connection with the slave trade. Accustomed to receiving discharged sailors, Thompson had declared that the credit of his house would be ruined if it were known that those under his care were sent into the slave trade. He then became the abolitionist's 'man on the ground', showing him around Bristol's bustling docks and bawdy ale houses. As we shall see, the *Seven Stars*, itself a remarkable survivor, is arguably 'the pub that changed the world'.[383]

It was Thompson who introduced Clarkson to the reality of the life of a slave-ship sailor, showing him the recruiting grounds in the pubs of Marsh Street. Clarkson realised that working on slave ships was a deeply unpopular occupation for mariners and through his endeavours to protect, rescue and get justice for sailors in Bristol he gained their trust. He found that sailors were extremely unwilling to do the merchants' dirty work, despite the promise of enhanced wages, and tried to avoid the slave trade as much as possible.[384]

To overcome this reluctance, ship owners resorted to organised impressment of various forms to force sailors to man their ships. These methods included 'crimping' and 'spiriting' which were used to trick, blackmail or force destitute sailors into service upon slave ships. Breward describes 'crimping' as the practice

...in which gullible and inebriated sailors were coerced into joining ships by the offer of advanced wages to pay off drinking and lodging debts, incurred through a compact between ships' mates and unscrupulous landlords.[385]

'Spiriting' on the other hand was a less subtle method of obtaining crew members, where unfortunate individuals were pressed into service by threat and abduction in the manner of the dreaded press gangs.

Clarkson returned again to the Merchants' Hall to transcribe the muster rolls from the Custom House, this time to gauge the relative losses of seamen from the slave trade compared with those of other trades from the same port. His conclusion was:

more persons would be found dead in three slave-vessels from Bristol, in a given time, than in all the other vessels put together, numerous as they were, belonging to the same port.

He also procured an account into Bristol's import and export of goods for the year 1786 in order to judge the comparative value of the slave trade versus other trades.

His most appalling discovery, though, was established when studying the actual ships that were being used to transport enslaved Africans. What he found shocked him. Two small vessels in particular drew his attention, both sloops, one of 25 tons and the other 11. The former was fitted out to carry 70 captives, the other 30, though Clarkson noted the latter had originally been "a pleasure boat for the accommodation of only six persons upon the Severn". Clarkson found it "incredible" that vessels such as these were going to be used for long deep-sea voyages, let alone carrying crew and their human cargo. From his calculations he concluded for the first vessel:

Hence, a grown person must sit down all the voyage, and contract his limbs within the narrow limits of three square feet….

And for the second;

The whole height from the keel to the beam was but five feet eight inches, three feet of which were occupied by ballast, cargo, and provisions, so that two feet eight inches remained only as the height between the decks. Hence, each slave would have only four square feet to sit in, and, when in this posture, his head, if he were a full-grown person, would touch the ceiling, or upper deck.[386]

A problem for Clarkson was that his early contacts in Bristol, although firmly against slavery, had little eye-witness knowledge of the trade or the plantations. One exception was Harry Gandy, his first acquaintance in Bristol and a former slave-ship captain who had actually been on two voyages. Although aged, he was willing to travel to London to state publicly all he knew and give evidence if required. Procuring others to do the same was proving a hard feat but after a few weeks Clarkson got a break when his friend Chandler managed to introduce him to a slave-ship surgeon named Gardiner. One of the owners of Gardiner's ship, the *Pilgrim*, possibly James McTaggart, had pointed Clarkson out to him as a person "whom he would wish him to avoid".

Gardiner furnished Clarkson with details on the different methods of securing enslaved Africans and on their treatment during the Middle Passage including details of various distressing scenes. He also mentioned the barbarous usage of seamen and concluded by saying "that there never was a subject, which demanded so loudly the interference of the legislature as that of the Slave-trade". Due to his humble circumstances, Gardiner was compelled to make yet another slaving voyage but he promised Clarkson he would keep a journal and present evidence to Parliament on his return if the opportunity arose. The opportunity didn't arise; Gardiner left Bristol for the last time on 28th July 1787 on the slave ship *Pilgrim* and died on the coast of Africa. When his journal was discovered amongst his belongings by Captain Charles Sloper and his officers it was buried with him "in great triumph"—much to Clarkson's disgust.[387]

Following his meeting with Gardiner, Clarkson had a chance encounter with another slave-ship surgeon who he had heard talking about the trade outside the Exchange. His name was James Arnold and he proved to be as willing as Gardiner in coming forward with information. Although, like Gardiner, he had been cautioned about falling in with Clarkson, Arnold's view was that it was a bad trade that ought to be exposed. With similar stories of maltreatment of slaves and sailors, Arnold was willing to testify against the trade and to this end agreed to give a sworn affidavit before his imminent next voyage. Depositions were accordingly made from Arnold's own words and Clarkson went with him to the residence of George Daubeny Esq., who was then chief magistrate of the city, where they were sworn in and witnessed "as the law required".

After his experiences in trying to get eyewitness accounts, Clarkson made this lament against the wall of silence he was fighting in Bristol:

> The owners of vessels employed in the trade there, forbad all intercourse with me. The old captains, who had made their fortunes in it, would not see me. The young, who were making them, could not be supposed to espouse my cause, to the detriment of their own interest.[388]

By this stage Clarkson had clearly realised that those with a significant share in the slave-ship voyages were reluctant to speak about the details of the trade. Ships-masters and first mates—basically captains and officers—had a different financial relationship to the trade than the waged or often impressed ship's crew.[389]

All this work and worry was beginning to put a strain on Clarkson's health and when his colleagues in Bristol urged him to take a rest, he agreed and went to Monmouth for a short break. Monmouth, like Bridgwater, had petitioned Parliament against the slave trade in 1785 and Clarkson was keen to know why. After a brief time away he anxiously returned to Bristol to continue his work.

Clarkson's friends had been busy while he was away in Monmouth and managed to procure a meeting with Alexander Falconbridge,[390] yet another ship's surgeon who had taken part in four slaving voyages. So far his witnesses, such as Gardiner and Arnold, were still engaged in the slave trade and therefore unlikely to give evidence in person or even return home alive. Clarkson was delighted to hear that Falconbridge had "done with the trade" and that he was more than willing to give information about it. Clarkson was quite overcome with Falconbridge's principled stand and his eagerness to give evidence either privately or publicly. Here is a brief synopsis of Falconbridge's information given over subsequent interviews:

> ...as far as relates to the slaves, that he confirmed the various violent and treacherous methods of procuring them in their own country; their wretched condition, in consequence of being crowded together, in the passage; their attempts to rise in defence of their own freedom, and when this was impracticable, to destroy themselves by the refusal of sustenance, by jumping overboard into the sea, and in other ways; the effect also of their situation upon their minds, by producing insanity and various diseases; and the cruel manner of disposing of them in the West Indies, and of separating relatives and friends.[391]

Falconbridge and Landlord Thompson both commended Captain Frazier as the only man sailing out of the port of Bristol for slaves who had not been guilty of cruelty to his seamen. Burges went further and said "That he knew but one captain in the trade [Frazier], who did not deserve long ago to be hanged." Falconbridge also spoke of the deplorable state of seamen on reaching the West Indies who were in "such a weak, ulcerated, and otherwise diseased state, that they perished there". Those diseased sailors that actually made it back to Bristol either died on their return or ended up in the Infirmary for months on end.

Of equal importance to Clarkson was the slave trade intelligence garnered by Thompson of the *Seven Stars,* everything regarding slave-ship sailors that passed in the port came to his notice. Thompson got wind of a group of sailors that had been tricked to serve aboard a slaver without being allowed to read their articles of agreement [contract of employment]. These included a particular acquaintance of Thompson's, a ship's mate called Sheriff, who, fearing he would never return alive from the African coast, needed rescuing.

As Thompson had rendered so many good services to Clarkson he felt compelled to act. Within an hour he had hatched a plan with one of his closest allies, Quaker Truman Harford, and the pair were off, rowing down river to the mouth of the Avon at Kingroad to board Sheriff's ship, the *Africa.* The captain being ashore complicated matters but after much anxiety as to what to do next, the pair decided to immediately take Sheriff off the ship and back to Bristol and safety. Clarkson left the captain his calling card, giving details of what he'd done and where he could be contacted, but nothing more was heard.

By now news had spread around the port that Clarkson was 'on the side of' the slave-ship sailors and three ailing crewmen of the *Thomas* begged him to look into the murder of fellow sailor William Lines before leaving Bristol. Lines' mother then approached Clarkson and pleaded for him to intervene; she also provided another four witnesses who claimed to have seen the mistreatment of her son first-hand. Clarkson interviewed the sailors and verified their accounts before proceeding to court. In order to make sure it went to trial, Clarkson avoided speaking to his ally Burges, the deputy town clerk, who had previously persuaded him to drop a similar case with the *Alfred*.

Before the trial at the Common Hall, Clarkson approached the Chief Magistrate and newly appointed Mayor, George Daubeny, to notify them of his intentions. At the start of proceedings the following day the bench was miraculously filled with slave traders and West India merchants; Clarkson immediately recognised this and later said:

> I shall never forget the savage looks which these people gave me; which indeed were so remarkable, as to occasion the eyes of the whole court to be turned upon me

What ensued was courtroom drama at its best; the bench got up and surrounded the mayor and began to whisper to him, then one of them turned and stared at Clarkson and said loudly "Scandalous reports had lately been spread, but sailors were not used worse in Guineamen [slave ships] than in other vessels..." The court then looked to Clarkson for a reply but he thought better of it. Another member of the bench then gave Clarkson the 'evil eye' before saying to the mayor:

> ...that he had known captain Vicars a long time; that he was an honourable man, and would not allow such usage in his ship. There were always vagabonds to hatch up things

He then made a 'dead point' at Clarkson and stared him right in the face, attracting the attention of the whole court in such an intimidating manner that Clarkson felt obliged to respond:

> You, sir, may know many things which I do not. But this I know, that if you do not do your duty, you are amenable to a higher court.[392]

Evaluating the situation the mayor looked directly on Clarkson and then his friend Burges, who was sitting as clerk to the magistrates and who had gone over to the mayor and whispered in his ear; all private conversation then ceased and the hearing was ordered to proceed. The four witnesses were then examined for evidence and the case well established before Captain Vicars was summoned to give his account. On being questioned, Vicars did not deny that there had been bad usage, but said that Lines had died "with the flux". His assertion went for nothing when balanced against the facts and an order was made to apprehend the chief mate. The next day the defendant, James Lavender, was called for and subjected to a 'rehearsing of the case' when he was duly sentenced to jail on 11th September. Lavender then had to lie at Newgate until the Lords of the Admiralty could order a sessions to be held for the trial of offences on the high seas.[393]

Subsequently Clarkson began to receive numerous first-hand accounts of the horrific treatment that the sailors and enslaved received on the transatlantic crossings:

Seamen, too, came from various quarters to apply to me for redress. One came to me, who had been treated ill in the *Alexander*, when Mr Falconbridge had been the surgeon of her. Three came to me, who had been ill-used in the voyage which followed, though she had sailed under a new captain. Two applied to me from the *Africa*, who had been of her crew in the last voyage. Two from the *Fly*. Two from the *Wasp*. One from the *Little Pearl*, and three from the *Pilgrim* or *Princess*, when she was last upon the coast.

Clarkson evoked his feelings after hearing the testimony from this group of sailors:

The different scenes of barbarity, which these represented to me, greatly added to the affliction of my mind. My feelings became now almost insupportable. I was agonized to think that this trade should last another day.[394]

Come November Clarkson finally finished his work in Bristol. Before leaving he carried out two last acts. The first was to go to Bath and secure the services of Richard Cruttwell, editor of the *Bath Chronicle*, the most respectable paper in favour of abolition in that city. The second was to:

lay the foundation of a committee in Bristol, and of a petition to Parliament from it for the abolition of the Slave trade. I had now made many friends… Mr. Joseph Harford, a man of fortune, of great respectability of character, and of considerable influence, had attached himself to the cause. Dr. Fox had assisted me in it. Mr. Hughes, a clergyman of the Baptist church, was anxious and ready to serve it. Dr. Camplin, of the Establishment, with several of his friends, continued steady. Matthew Wright, James Harford, Truman Harford, and all the Quakers to a man, were strenuous, and this on the best of principles, in its support. To all these I spoke, and I had the pleasure of seeing that my wishes were likely in a short time to be gratified in both these cases.[395]

Clarkson's claim that he initiated the Bristol Abolition Committee during his pioneering visit is supported by the fact that he knew personally at least seven of the 20 founding members and they had already assisted him in his endeavours.[396] His stay in Bristol would have a long-term impact on the abolition movement in both its organisation and methods. Clarkson developed his ideas and resolve to initiate other abolition committees around the country; he perfected the means of gathering evidence regarding ill treatment and impressment of seamen, along with first-hand accounts of the inhuman conditions the enslaved were kept in; and finally, he introduced African cultural items to the material he was collecting in an attempt to show the continent's potential. Whether or not the London Committee expected Clarkson to chase sailors to the mouth of the Avon and free them, or take ships' officers to court on charges of murder is another matter; the fact was he had delivered.

The information Clarkson garnered from sailors and their records managed to explode the myth propounded by West India merchants that slave ships were "so many nurseries for the marine (Royal Navy)". Allied with this myth busting, the exposure of the cruelties meted out to both sailors and the enslaved on the Atlantic crossings filtered into the public consciousness via the abolition groups that were now springing up around the country. Crucially, because of this concrete information from trusted sources, public opinion in Britain began to shift against the slave trade.

Working parallel to Clarkson in Bristol was abolitionist Hannah More who was born in Fishponds. Unusually for a woman in the eighteenth century she was well educated and successful; a playwright, poet, a leading literary figure—a member of the 'Bluestockings'[397]—she'd even been a campaign manager for Bristol MP Edmund Burke—but in middle age she was looking for spiritual guidance. More had read the religious text *Cardiphonia* and had determined to meet its author, the former slave-ship captain turned Anglican priest and belated abolitionist, John Newton [see also 1750].

Through Newton's influence she joined the Clapham Sect whose members were chiefly prominent and wealthy evangelical Anglicans. They shared common political goals concerning the liberation of slaves, the abolition of the slave trade, along with penal and educational reform. The group would go on to include William Wilberforce, Zachary Macaulay, Henry and Marianne Martineaux. However, Hannah like her earlier mentor Dr Samuel Johnson was a Tory, and neither of them nor the Clapham Sect wanted to change the status quo, just end some of the miseries associated with it.[398] Confusingly yet another Newton was also a mentor to More, this time it was her old Latin tutor the Rev. James Newton of the Bristol Baptist College. A staunch abolitionist, Newton would go on to influence a generation of missionaries and local activists, such as the radical bookseller Joseph Cottle.[399]

As we have mentioned, Prime Minister Pitt had already approached Wilberforce in order for him to be the spokesperson for abolition in Parliament, warning "that if he did not bring the motion in, somebody else would". Ideologically, Pitt was opposed to slavery on the basis that it was monopolistic, inefficient and backward; however, there were other economic and geo-political reasons for his stance. Historian C. L. R. James argued that it was the particular nature of the system of slavery in the Caribbean in the late eighteenth century which determined his agenda. Pitt realised that although Britain dominated the supply of slaves and therefore labour from West Africa it was the rival powers, principally France, that were benefiting. Pitt discovered that around 50 per cent of the enslaved Africans sold in the British West Indies were being repurchased by French colonies, particularly Saint-Domingue (Haiti).

After the independence of America, in 1783 this French possession alone doubled its production of sugar becoming "incomparably the finest colony in the world and its possibilities seemed limitless". Britain was 'cutting its own throat' economically; it arguably had enough slaves of its own to sustain its plantations. Allied with this was the fact that other colonies such as India could easily and efficiently produce cash crops like sugar and cotton without having to resort to slavery; "Indian free labour cost a penny a day". Pitt and others realised that the abolition of the slave trade would do far greater damage to Britain's rival powers than it would to its own economy, making it an attractive proposition, unless of course you were a member of the West India lobby.[400]

In November 1787, after conversations earlier in the year with Pitt and abolitionists like the Reverends James Ramsay and Thomas Clarkson, John Newton finally convinced Wilberforce to make abolition his life's work. In his biography of Newton, Jonathan Aitken states that Wilberforce's concerns had centred firstly on his own ability to compromise his principles in order to accommodate his opponent's prejudices when trying to win their support for the cause; secondly, how he would cope with unfair insults, name calling and other stigmas; and thirdly, how he would square the circle between his secular life as a campaigning politician and his spiritual life as a committed Christian.[401]

Wilberforce was right to be worried about the ramifications of his decision, as within a few short years his likeness was being burnt in effigy by West India planters and runaway slaves in Jamaica were referring to him as 'Saint Wilberforce'. In stark contrast this man was on almost every other topic profoundly conservative. When later in life he reflected upon the 'greatest of all causes' that he had taken part in, it wasn't the abolition movement he chose but the introduction of Christian missionaries to the Indian subcontinent...[402]

Action and reaction

‖ **1788**—First public meeting of Bristol Abolitionists held in the Guildhall.

The first meeting in January 1788 was well attended and included a group of women who became subscribers. A petition for the abolition of the slave trade was launched at the event and a committee was formed just eight months after the London one had been established. The Bristol Abolition Committee was the first outside of the capital and was followed by Manchester and then Plymouth; it consisted of twenty leading ministers and merchants across most religious denominations except, curiously, Methodists. At least two of the merchants had West India interests.

Leading Anglicans were Dean Josiah Tucker of Gloucester Cathedral, also Rector of St Stephen's Church, and Reverend Dr John Camplin, Vicar of All Saints, both of whom were vehement critics of Methodism and were in Hannah More's circle of friends. The remaining Anglican was Dr John Hallam, Dean of Bristol Cathedral. Non-conformist ministers included Presbyterian/Unitarian John Prior Estlin and dissenting minister Reverend Thomas Wright. They were joined by Baptist ministers Reverend Caleb Evans, an old adversary of Wesley's, especially over the question of the American colonies, and the Dean of Broadmead Baptist Chapel, Alderman John Harris.[403] The professionals were Dr John Wright of Bristol Royal Infirmary, solicitor and former slave-ship captain Harry Gandy (Quaker) and Dr Edward Long Fox, later famous for his treatment of mental illness and his role in the Bristol Bridge massacre.

The largest group were the merchants and manufacturers: Mathew Wright (Quaker); William Peter Lunell (Society of Merchant Venturers (SMV) Warden 1793 and Master 1812, Castle Green Congregationalist Meeting House) who was nominated Secretary and Treasurer; John Collard Esq (Unitarian and plantation owner in Jamaica); Alderman George Daubeny (SMV Master 1784 and Steadfast Tory MP for Bristol 1781–1784); Joseph Coates (Corn St. wine merchant); Joseph Harford Esq (SMV Master 1796, banker, brass manufacturer) who was nominated Chairman; Thomas Rutter (brush and bellows manufacturer, Quaker); Joseph Beck Esq (Gentleman, Quaker); and Edward Griffiths (member of Bristol Corporation).[404]

Eight hundred Bristol people signed the petition (out of a population of about 60,000) and, according to Robert Hall, co-pastor at Broadmead Baptist Chapel, it was a great feat "considering that no application has been made to any". He went on to say, however, "much opposition is made by the merchants and the dependants who are many, perhaps most of them engaged in it".[405]

These formal organisations entered the history books but at the same time a number of informal social networks were also operating in the abolition movement. These contained people who were working for the same goal but

John Wesley Preaching before the Mayor and Corporation of Bristol, 1788, by William Holt Yates Titcomb.

who had differing political and religious perspectives. On the face of it the Abolition Committee was dominated by men but these social networks also provided an environment in which women could play a major role. For example, committee member Quaker Thomas Rutter was married to Methodist Charles Wesley's daughter, Susannah. Hannah More's circle of friends included Selina Mills, the Anglican daughter of Quaker bookseller and publisher Robert Mills. Selina was a teacher at the school of the sisters More in Park Street and then took over the running of it before marrying anti-slavery activist and Governor of Sierra Leone, Zachary Macaulay, in 1799.[406] By the middle of the 1790s these abolitionist circles would be joined by radical writers such as the Romantic Poets and scientists such as Beddoes.

In the arena of popular culture, writers and performers were also at work on the question of slavery. In the theatre there had been plays in Bristol about the cruelties of the slave trade performed in the early eighteenth century when Thomas Southerne dramatized Aphra Behn's novel *Oroonoko*. It was reprised by impresario John Hippisley in the 1760s and criticism of the trade also appeared in the Bristol press from the 1770s. In a similar vein, journalist William 'Count' Combe, serialised articles about the 'respectable merchant' and the 'fair retail dealer'. These were augmented in the 1780s by abolitionist writers such as 'Benevolous' and 'Brittanicus'—the latter being the pen name of none other than Baptist preacher Robert Hall.[407]

At a national level, and following on from Wilberforce's announcement in December 1787 that he would introduce a motion to abolish the slave trade in the new session in Parliament, John Newton published his pamphlet *Thoughts upon the African Slave Trade*.[408] The following month Hannah More backed this up by presenting her own anti-slavery poem *The Black Slave Trade*, and Ann Yearsley published an even harder hitting rival to Hannah's entitled *On the Inhumanity of the Slave Trade*. Yearsley's story is an interesting one. She was 'discovered' by More when delivering milk to her house; Hannah realised her literary talent and had her poems published. Ann at this time was impoverished because her family had been made destitute by enclosures in Clifton perpetuated by the Merchant Venturers. Unfortunately, Yearsley and More fell out over money that had been placed in a trust. More felt that Yearsley was incapable of running her own financial affairs, but Ann needed the money to try and enhance her children's education. More publicly denounced Yearsley for her ingratitude and Ann promptly lost the majority of her patrons.[409]

In March 1788, John Wesley made one of his regular visits to the city and preached on the burning question of the slave trade. The sermon he gave was interrupted by what he described as a "supernatural occurrence":

A vehement noise arose, and shot like lightening through the whole congregation. The terror and confusion was inexpressible. The benches were broken in pieces, and nine-tenths of the congregation appeared to be struck with the same panic. In about six minutes the storm ceased. None can account for it without supposing some preternatural influence. Satan fought lest his kingdom should be delivered up.[410]

‖ **1788**—Committee of the British Privy Council examines the slave trade.

John Newton, former slave-ship captain and Alexander Falconbridge, former slave-ship surgeon, both gave evidence to the Privy Council, along with Bristolians Harry Gandy, Sydenham Teast, the Society of Merchant Venturers, and the controller of the Port of Bristol. In charge of the proceedings was the president of the Committee on Trade and Plantations, Charles Jenkinson,[411] who owned land in the West Indies and even had a slave ship named after him. The pro-slavery lobby thought they were onto a winner with 'their' president but he proved to be surprisingly fair minded; he wanted statistics and reports from everyone concerned with the trade—the slave traders, the slave owners, the merchants, the missionaries, the colonial legislature and even other slave trading nations. He wanted space comparisons between troopships and slave ships and asked the British envoy to Warsaw what happened when serfs in the Austrian controlled part of Poland had recently been freed.[412]

‖ **1788**—Dolben Act passed, to regulate the number of slaves carried in
‖ British ships.

The Bill was to "mitigate sufferings of the negroes during their passage to
the colonies by the prevention of overcrowding". The Act decreed that slave
ships must not carry more than 1.67 slaves per ton up to a maximum of 207
tons burthen, after which only one slave per ton could be carried. Even then,
transported convicts still had twice the space of enslaved Africans. Prior to
the Act Clarkson had witnessed as many as three slaves per ton being carried
on some wholly inappropriate vessels. Latimer stated that "the measure
was vehemently opposed by the African merchants in London, Bristol and
Liverpool". The slave traders argued in Parliament and the House of Lords that
their businesses would be ruined if the bill became law. Matthew Brickdale, MP
for Bristol, seconded the motion for rejecting the Bill, but the opposition was
ineffectual and the measure became law.[413]

Indignant at this course of events and a reduction in their profits, Bristol's
West India planters and merchants convened a meeting through the Society
of Merchant Venturers at Merchants' Hall in April 1789 with William Miles
presiding. An influential committee was appointed to defend "a traffic on
which the welfare of the West Indies and the commerce and revenue of the
Kingdom so essentially depend". The majority of the committee came from the
Corporation and included the aforementioned Aldermen Miles (SMV Warden
1789), Harris, Daubeny (SMV Master 1784), Anderson, Brice, Sir James Laroche
(SMV Master 1782), Thomas Daniel junior (SMV Warden 1789, Master 1805
and 1834), Evan Baillie, Richard Bright (SMV Master 1792), John Fisher Weare
(SMV Warden 1778), Robert Claxton, John Pinney, James Tobin and Philip
Protheroe.[414] They met under the auspices of the *New West India Society* and
a petition was signed by 11 people representing Bristol's African Merchants,
23 from the West India Merchants and Planters and 34 from manufacturers
connected to the trade, including ship holders.[415] Sitting MP Henry Cruger
submitted the petition to Parliament.

The inclusion of Aldermen George Daubeny and John Harris in the
last list is very interesting. Only the year before they had joined the Bristol
Abolitionist Committee founded in the Guildhall. Apparently in the interim
they had changed their minds and wanted regulation of the slave trade rather
than abolition. Daubeny and Harris later teamed up commercially in 1795 by
forming a combined sugar refining business. Harris, a Baptist himself, became
Mayor in 1790 and in July 1791 had to deal with anonymous threats to destroy
the Baptist, Presbyterian and other dissenting churches in Bristol. He put army
units on alert just one day's march from Bristol, but they weren't required. At
the time there was unrest all around the country with people influenced by
the republican and democratic ideas of the French Revolution. The threats

in Bristol came from reactionaries under the 'Church and King' banner with support from "eversomore".[416]

Young radical and staunch abolitionist Robert Hall, who was a star speaker on the circuit in the city, fell out with his fellow Baptists, the Rev. Caleb Evans and Alderman Harris, at the end of 1790. Whether this was because of his radicalism or his anti-slavery stance is not known. It is fair to say that both Evans and Harris were compromised to a certain extent by their commercial links with the West India merchants. Hall would return to Bristol late in his career. The conflict between financial interest in the business of slavery and religious ethics amongst merchants and manufacturers would be a continuing dilemma.

Another who could have been compromised in this way but wasn't, was Unitarian Minister Dr John Prior Estlin, whose congregation contained many pro-slavery merchants. One of these, Richard Bright, actually paid for a replacement Unitarian Meeting House in Lewins Mead that was finished in 1791![417] In addition to being a minister, Dr Estlin ran an Academy on St Michael's Hill which churned out a number of students with radical free thinking ideas. One of Estlin's sons, John Bishop Estlin would become an ophthalmic surgeon of note and would follow in his father's anti-slavery tradition, as indeed in turn would his grand-daughter, Mary Anne Estlin; both descendants would fight for worldwide abolition through the nineteenth century. The minister's friends included Robert Hall, Joseph Priestly, Anna Barbauld, Coleridge and Southey.

The West India lobbyists were wrong footed once again in 1789 by the anti-slavery campaigning of Clarkson and his cohorts. The new Abolitionist Committee in Plymouth had found a plan of the Liverpool slave ship *Brookes* by which Clarkson managed to show graphically the inhumane means by which 482 slaves were packed in, and this was post the regulations laid out in the Dolben Act! Four years previously the *Brookes* had actually carried 740 enslaved Africans, more than 50 per cent greater than shown in the famous plan.[418] It became known simply as *The Print* and copious copies were made and models distributed throughout the land. Their visual impact is as strong today as it was in the eighteenth century.[419]

Other visual devices included Josiah Wedgewood's "Am I not a brother" seal which was initially used for letters but was soon made into snuff boxes and cuff-links. American statesman Benjamin Franklin said the design was "equal to that of the best written Pamphlet".[420] To pile on the pressure, Olaudah Equiano launched his seminal autobiography from the perspective of the enslaved, *The Interesting Narrative*,[421] which became a bestseller—Hannah More, Rev. Frank Wills and Thomas Clarkson were amongst the subscribers. William Cowper penned one of his best poems *The Negro's Complaint* which spread like wildfire in both verse and song:

Forc'd from home and all its pleasures,
Afric's coast I left forlorn;
To increase a stranger's treasures,
O'er the raging billows borne,
Men from England bought and sold me,
Paid my price in paltry gold;
But though slave they have enroll'd me,
Minds are never to be sold.[422]

The *Brookes* ship plan in particular stirred up the 'West India interest' nationwide; consequently the merchants decided to increase the levy on a barrel of sugar or rum and bale of cotton from *1d* to *6d* in order to fight the growing public sentiment with their own propaganda campaign.[423]

One of the last-minute witnesses for the Committee on Trade and Plantations that was investigating the slave trade was James Arnold, one of two abolitionists recruited by Clarkson when he visited Bristol in 1787; the other, Gardiner, as we have seen, had died on the African coast during a voyage on the slave ship *Pilgrim*. A surgeon's mate and then surgeon in his own right, Arnold was able to furnish the committee with up-to-the-minute information on how slaves were sometimes traded using hostages and force.[424] This was the practice of ensuring that a deal for the purchase of slaves was honoured by holding captive members of African slave trading families. The evidence didn't win the day, but the seeds of abolition were well and truly sown.

Partially due to Liverpool's rise in prominence, Bristol lost its second city status and consequently its influence on national matters was on the wane, but it was still a plum post for politicians seeking a prestigious and challenging constituency. Here's historian David R. Fisher's take on Bristol's situation:

Despite its large electorate, of which a significant proportion was non-resident, control was securely in the hands of the long-established political clubs, led by a comparatively small number of men from the propertied and mercantile classes. Local government was carried on by a closed, self-electing corporation, notorious for its extravagance and mismanagement and deeply unpopular with the majority of Bristolians.[425]

The Reverend James Ramsay, a prolific pamphleteer and anti-slavery campaigner, was the first high profile casualty in the fight for abolition, which had become quite vicious; he didn't have the resilience of an Equiano. It would get even more fractious over time. Ramsay wrote two hard hitting pamphlets against slavery in 1785 and these elicited contrary pamphlets from the pro-slavery lobby in Bristol, most notably from West India merchant James Tobin.[426] However, the figure who apparently applied the verbal coup de grâce was Crisp

Molyneux, MP for King's Lynn and a plantation owner on the island of St Kitts. Ramsay collapsed and died after Wilberforce's abolition motion was postponed. Molyneux arrogantly boasted to his son on St Kitts, "Ramsay is dead—I have killed him".[427]

In the election of 1790 the winning candidates in Bristol were John Holroyd, Lord Sheffield [Whig—Constitutional Club, yellow] and Henry Charles Somerset [Tory—Steadfast Club, blue], the Marques of Worcester—who later became 6th Duke of Beaufort. Unusually these candidates weren't from Bristol's merchant elite but were chosen by Bristol's political clubs and, like all of Bristol's MPs during this period, supported their pro-slavery stance in Parliament. It became increasingly apparent to the leading abolitionists that the only way to break the powerful West India lobby's hold in government would be radical democratic reform or even republican revolution on the model of the previous year in France.

> **1791**—House of Commons rejects motion of William Wilberforce to introduce [another] Abolition Bill. Celebrations on Brandon Hill [and it is claimed that the church bells were also rung in celebration throughout Bristol.][428]

Prominent amongst the petitions against abolition was one from the Bristol's *New West India Society*, who were clearly using Abolition Committee methods against the abolitionists. In their 1789 petition they insisted:

> That the petitioners learn with serious alarm that, on the proposed investigation in the Committee of the House Of Commons of the petitions against the slave trade, a motion will be made for its entire abolition, on which trade the petitioners conceive, the welfare and prosperity, if not the actual existence, of the West India Islands depend: that it has been found by recent enquiries, conducted with the greatest exactness, that the African and West India trade constitute at least three-fifths of the commerce of the port of Bristol, and that if, upon such a motion a Bill should pass into a Law, the decline of the trade of the city of Bristol must inevitably follow, as the African trade and the great West India commerce, connected therewith and dependent thereon, form so considerable a part of it, and this to the very great loss of the petitioners, and to the ruin of thousands of individuals who are maintained thereby, but who are not sensible of the impending danger...[429]

At this time the largest concentration of absentee West India landowners in Britain could be found in the suburb of Clifton, city of Bath and the surrounding countryside around Bristol; in fact, Bath was the Las Vegas of its day, attracting all types of moneyed people both high and low to its gaming tables and brothels during 'the season'.[430]

In his *History of the Society of Merchant Venturers*, John Latimer gives a damning snapshot of the slave trade at this time:

The trade was not abolished until nearly twenty years afterwards, but the number of Bristol ships rapidly declined at an early period, and the conduct of the ship captains who continued to frequent the slaving ports had a powerful influence in rendering the commerce unpopular. In 1791, whilst Lord Sheffield, MP for Bristol, was denying the right of Parliament to suppress the traffic, six English ships of which three, the *Thomas*, the *Wasp* and the *Recovery*, belonged to Bristol, bombarded the town of Calabar [again] for several hours, to compel the native slave dealers to sell at the price fixed by the captains, a great many innocent blacks being killed and wounded during the cannonade. In denouncing this outrage in the House of Commons, Mr. Wilberforce stated that the facts were perfectly known in Bristol and Liverpool, where the act of the captains was deemed so meritorious that they had been furnished with new appointments.[431]

John Wesley died in March 1791, aged 87. An anti-slavery campaigner to the end, his last ever letter was written to William Wilberforce to bolster him after the defeat in Parliament:

If God be for you, who can be against you? Are all of them stronger than God? O be not weary in well doing! Go on, in the name of God and in the power of his might, till even American slavery (the vilest that ever saw the sun) shall vanish away before it.

The letter revitalised Wilberforce and immediately after Wesley's death he launched another anti-slave trade petition, asking the Methodist Conference for help. They responded with a massive 229,426 signatures and were aided by a further 122,978 from non-conformist groups. 350,000 people out of Britain's population of around eight million was no mean feat.[432]

The rejection of the Bill was a huge set-back for the abolition movement and it took some while for the leaders of the movement to regain their enthusiasm, especially when the Bill failed again in 1795 by just seventeen votes. By this time Hannah More had started writing and selling 'Cheap Repository Tracts' to promote the thoughts and ideals of the Clapham Sect. These inexpensive pamphlets aimed at the 'literate poor' were a direct propaganda response to the radical publications that were circulating in Britain as a result of the French Revolution, particularly the works of Tom Paine.[433] Paine's *Rights of Man* (1791), which was widely read in Britain, presented a significant threat to the rigid class hierarchies by promoting republican ideals of suffrage and liberty.[434]

Leading Baptist Caleb Evans died in August 1791 and the void he left was filled temporarily by the Rev. Joseph Hughes who had promised Clarkson in Bristol in 1787 that he would 'willingly serve the abolitionist cause'. True to his word, as well as remaining a keen abolitionist, in 1791 he became an enthusiastic 'Anti-sacherite' in the first wave of sugar boycotts; according to Clarkson, by 1794 an estimated 300,000 British families were boycotting West Indian sugar.[435] Evans's post wasn't permanently filled until the arrival of Dr John Ryland in December 1793. Ryland's anti-slavery credentials had been confirmed in 1788 in correspondence with abolitionist Rev. John Newton who sent him this letter:

> As you are a friend to Liberty and Mankind, you will not be sorry to hear that I have a pamphlet in the press upon the African Slave Trade. On this subject I can write as an eyewitness and something more, for I was too long actively engaged in it. As the business is now coming before Parliament I thought myself bound to declare what I know.[436]

Dr John Ryland was the son of Rev. John Collett Ryland who "did more than any man of his time to promote polite learning amongst Dissenters".[437] John junior was appointed pastor of Broadmead Baptist Chapel and combined this with being principal of the Bristol Baptist College; he held these roles for the next 32 years. In 1792 Ryland was one of the founders of the Baptist Missionary Society before becoming secretary from 1815; from its commencement over 100 Bristol students became missionaries and these included the abolitionist and modern-day Jamaican national hero William Knibb.

To compound the worries of conservative abolitionists such as Wilberforce and More, the French revolutionary government, partly in response to the massive armed uprisings of the enslaved in Saint-Domingue (Haiti), abolished slavery in the French colonies in February 1794, effectively instituting the doctrine of the 'natural rights of man' across ethnic divides.[438] This dramatic step emphasised the stark political differences between gradualist and conservative abolitionists and their radical counterparts who sensed a new, faster and more effective route to full-scale emancipation: republican revolution in Britain. For example, one of Thomas Clarkson's prized possessions was a souvenir stone from the Bastille which, on his visit to Paris just after its storming, was still being demolished. He chose a stone from a prison cell wall with a carved message from an unfortunate inmate, and he kept it on his desk at all times to remind himself of one potential route to abolition and emancipation.[439]

In Bristol these radical elements soon began to surface. Bristol printer and bookseller John Rose produced an inflammatory pamphlet on Bristol's corporate governance in 1792 in the mode of Thomas Paine's *Rights of Man*. Here, in addition to criticising the Corporation's lack of financial transparency, Rose pointed out that, unlike in London, the Common Councillors were a self-elected body:

> The offices of Mayor, Alderman and Common Council of the City of Bristol, are what ought not to exist in this country...They are a local tyranny; a partial oppression; an arbitrary government within a limited one; a self creative, self existing-evil...[440]

Friends of Ann Yearsley had helped her set up a radical circulating library in Hotwells in 1793, and two years previously the Calvinist publisher and abolitionist, Joseph Cottle, had established his book shop in the High Street, not far from the Exchange. These were in addition to Bristol's Free Library in King Street where one of the most popular borrowed books of the time was Abbé Raynal's anti-slavery epic *A Philosophical and Political History of the Settlements and Trade of the Europeans in the East and West Indies*.[441]

Radical writing was one thing, but on the streets of Bristol disputes that once would have been fairly minor were ending in bloodshed. A disagreement about tolls on Bristol Bridge led to public protest that had a terrible outcome. In the vanguard of the Bridge Trustees was pro-slavery ex-MP George Daubeny, one of three magistrates who inflamed the situation. The mismanagement by Daubeny and his colleagues directly led to the Bristol Bridge massacre of 30th September 1793 when troops opened fire on demonstrators and onlookers, killing 14 people and wounding more than 40.[442]

Treating the many dying and wounded that night in the Infirmary was abolitionist Dr Edward Long Fox who was so incensed by the events surrounding the massacre that he set-up an unofficial investigation. The Corporation, suspicious of the motives of 'Jacobin' Fox, promptly denied the Doctor and his colleagues the premises for a public inquiry. Venue after venue was withheld in which to conduct it. In the end they had to hold their inquiry in secret and even though their case was strong, the tenuous state of the country meant that legal proceedings could not be brought about. No doubt thanks to the enlightened principles of doctors such as Fox, Bristol Infirmary's mantra at this time was "that all persons, without regard to country, colour or dialect, who are accidentally injured, are on application immediately admitted, without any recommendation whatsoever".[443]

Dr Fox would go on to lead local protests against Pitt's suspension of Habeas Corpus in 1794, whereby His Majesty's government could arrest anyone on suspicion of having committed a crime and detain them indefinitely without bringing specific charges. These draconian measures were a direct response to the spread of republican ideas in the wake of the French Revolution. The repression by the state was only one aspect of the divisions in the country that were arising at this time. In a letter to his brother, Fox wrote that he was of the opinion that his involvement with the proposed public inquiry had both prejudiced his career and made him enemies for life.[444]

In yet another example of Bristol Corporation's abuse of power, none of the chief protagonists such as George 'Twig Pigeon' Daubeny and his co-magistrates, including the then Mayor, were brought to account. For over 100 years after the massacre "give 'em Bristol Bridge" was the cry of Bristol's malcontents.[445] Several handbills, pamphlets and poems were published regarding these events with perhaps Quaker poet Robert Lovell's *Bristol: A Satire* being the most well-known.

By now publisher Joseph Cottle had been introduced to the radical writers Robert Southey and Samuel Taylor Coleridge by Robert Lovell. Southey and Coleridge embarked upon a series of public lectures in the spring of 1795 which became increasingly radical and included attacks on slavery and colonisation. It was through sharing these ideas and the platform, literally, with Coleridge that he met scientist, physician and radical democrat Thomas Beddoes. Beddoes at this time was running a TB clinic in Hotwells, Bristol, that would eventually become the world changing Pneumatic Institute. That same year Coleridge made the acquaintance of William Wordsworth who, like Beddoes, had been a supporter of the early phases of the French Revolution.

The following year Coleridge's lectures, including an extract from *On the Slave Trade* were published in the short lived but influential periodical *The Watchman*. Other topics included the *Essay on Fasts* (attacking the fusion of church and state power) and reports on radical orators and writers who had been imprisoned for treason and sedition. Beddoes, Lovell, Southey, Thomas Poole (a radical neighbour of Coleridge's in Nether Stowey, Somerset) and Dr Edwards of Birmingham supported the magazine which was founded in Bristol's most venerable pub, the *Rummer Tavern*. Printing partners Biggs & Cottle published *The Watchman* journal every fortnight from March to May 1796. Prior to setting up the magazine Coleridge had innocently asked his friend Clarkson to advise him on how to get subscribers but instead of getting the wise counsel he expected, he got a full-blown business plan, most of which he ignored. Coleridge was indignant and wrote to a friend:

> I have called him [Clarkson] the moral Steam-Engine, or the Giant with one idea—Heaven knows! How well I love and how very highly I revere him. He shall be my Friend, Exemplar, Saint—anything, only not my Counsellor in matters of Business.[446]

The journal's impact was far reaching and it's amazing to think that Cottle had innocently introduced Southey and its biggest protagonist, Coleridge, to

Radical Romantics triptych
(Samuel Taylor Coleridge, Ann Yearsley and Robert Southey).

staunch government advocate Hannah More at Barley Wood just two years before. They had anti-slavery in common however. Southey once famously called tea "the blood sweetened beverage".

Despite the existence of these radical currents, Hannah More's conservative tracts sold in their millions; circulated by middle class 'respectable societies' amongst the poor in their cottages, schools, hospitals, prisons and among the army and navy. The majority of the Cheap Repository Tracts were aimed at 'reforming the morals' of the working classes through simple tales and retellings of bible stories. However, a few were written by abolitionists in the Clapham Sect. Due to their popularity, many thousands of tracts were sold overseas and when Harriet Martineaux visited America in 1834 she found that Hannah More was heard of everywhere: "She was certainly much better known than Shakespeare".[447]

After publishing his autobiography, *The Interesting Narrative*, in 1789, Equiano went on a five-year book tour of Britain and Ireland to great acclaim. He came to Bristol in about 1794 and had the foresight to get Josiah Wedgewood to vouch for him should he be apprehended by the dreaded press gangs—not unreasonable when you consider he'd been abducted and enslaved several times before. War with France meant press gangs were on the loose again and port cities such as Bristol were a dangerous place for working class white men, let alone black men.[448] John Wesley read *The Interesting Narrative* on his death bed and was outraged to read:

a man who has a black skin, being wronged or outraged by a white man, can have no redress; it being a *law* in all our Colonies that the *oath* of black against a white goes for nothing. What villainy is this![449]

In 1795 Samuel Taylor Coleridge gave a lecture to a Dissenting audience in St Mary Redcliffe Church.[450] Coleridge described the opposition his talks generated in a letter to fellow radical and poet George Dyer:

[Coleridge had] endeavoured to disseminate the truth… [but found that] the opposition of the Aristocrats is so furious and determined, that I began to fear, that the good I do is not proportional to the Evil I occasion— Mobs and Mayors, Blockheads and Brickbats, Placards and Press Gangs have leagued in horrible conspiracy against me. The Democrats are as sturdy in support of me, but their number is comparatively small.[451]

The contribution to the movement for abolition of these various literary protesters, including the Bristol coterie, is assessed by Irish historian Nini Rodgers:

By the beginning of the nineteenth century, anti-slavery had triumphed in imaginative literature in Britain and Ireland. It was still possible for the next half century to publish pamphlets, articles, memoirs and historical works defending slavery but for poets, novelists and the authors of children's fiction, the guardians of sensitivity and feeling, it [the slave trade] was no longer respectable.

This was an important victory, most significant perhaps in nurturing hereditary anti-slavery commitment and the spreading of a general public consciousness that the trade and the system itself should be combated. But it occurred at the very time when the cotton gin was invented, the United States spread west into rich hot lands of Louisiana, the mills of Lancashire (and, for a time, Belfast [not to mention Bristol, especially after 1838]) imported more and more bales; while Britain drove the slave and sugar frontier forward in the Caribbean, her capital pouring into her new colonies of Trinidad and Demerara and priming the take-off into similar expansion in Cuba and Brazil.

Economic development and consumer demand produced more poetry, more novels, more sweetmeats, more cotton goods and more slavery…[452]

‖ **1795**—Start of Second Maroon War in Jamaica (ends 1796).

It took £500,000 (equivalent in 2016 to £656 million by GDP per capita) and 5,000 British soldiers and militia eight months to put down this rebellion by 500 Maroons. It was originally sparked by the British seizing and incarcerating six Maroon leaders, thus violating the treaty signed in 1739 after the First Maroon War. After months of brutal and bloody guerrilla warfare the British commander Major-General George Walpole, who had come to admire the fighting skills of the Maroons, offered another peace treaty to which they agreed. However, the treaty was not adhered to by the Governor or the Assembly of Jamaica. Maroon land was seized, their leaders were rounded up, flogged and jailed and eventually the whole remaining group of 568 were transported, some in irons, to Nova Scotia. It was a cynical double-cross that enraged Walpole and led to him leaving the army to engage in a public campaign to force the British government to stand by its promises.[453]

Early in 1796 Clarkson married his sweetheart of four years, Catherine Buck; she too was a radical, keen abolitionist and supporter of the French Revolution. Clarkson considered women to be the intellectual equal of men and derided the way "homage is paid to their beauty, very little is paid to their opinions".[454] Bright and bubbly, she was an instant hit with the Coleridge, Southey and Wordsworth families, living for a time amongst them all in the Lake District until ill health forced her home to Suffolk in 1806. On the way she had to be treated in Bristol by Beddoes, first in 1804 and then 1805, until Beddoes finally managed to make her well again.

Also in 1796 Thomas Daniel the Younger became an alderman and the following year, Mayor of Bristol. From 1800–1821 he was partner in the banking firm of Ames, Cave & Co. while already being a leading member of the Society of Merchant Venturers. His prominent role in the city's most influential governing bodies made Alderman Daniel well placed to shape Bristol's mercantile destiny throughout the early part of the nineteenth century. Francis Greenacre described him as "Merchant, ship-owner and West India planter, he was also one of the most powerful defenders of slavery".[455]

As already stated, other defenders of the slave trade were Bristol's representatives in Parliament. Lord Sheffield proved himself a strong adversary to Wilberforce and Clarkson, right from his election in 1790 to his standing down in 1802. Sheffield collaborated with other pro-slavery MPs such as Liverpool's Colonel Banastre Tarleton in order to scupper the abolitionists. Just prior to being elected for Bristol, Sheffield had published a pamphlet against abolition and, in 1792, repudiated the use of petitions in Parliament, questioning their validity. There was great irony in this as it was the 'right of petition' that had enabled outports such as Bristol and Liverpool to become 'officially' engaged in the transatlantic slave trade in 1698. In the general election of 1796, Sheffield stood again for Bristol and was elected with Charles Bragge—later Bathurst— another pro-slavery MP.

Opposition was still growing to the trade however. In 1797, the Rev. George Heath, historian of the city, wrote:

The ardour for the Trade to Africa for men and women, our fellow creatures and equals, is much abated among the humane and benevolent Merchants of Bristol. In 1787, there were but 30 ships employed in this melancholy traffic; while the People of Liverpool, in their indiscriminate rage for Commerce and for getting money at all events, have nearly engrossed this Trade, incredibly exceeded London and Bristol in it, employ many thousand tons of shipping, for the purposes of buying and selling God's rational creatures, and are the venders (*horresco referens*) of the souls and bodies of men and women! To almost all the West Indian islands!!![456]

The Rev. Heath, and a little earlier, the romantic poet Robert Lovell in his aforementioned poem of 1794, *Bristol: A Satire*, roundly condemned the slave trade and Bristol's involvement in it. Strangely though, they did not for one moment—in their praise of Edward Colston—wonder as to where the 'liberal Benefactor' got his money from. Here Heath twice eulogizes about Colston, first under *Of the different Classes, Manners, Customs, Peculiarities*:

The Birthday of *Mr. Colston*, Nov. 13th, that liberal Benefactor to this City, is observed here with great ceremony. As soon as the 12th of November is over, at 12 Midnight, the great Bells at *Redcliff* are rung muffled; and so are all the Bells of the City, in turn, till dawn of day; and from thence until the close of this Holiday. Also various charitable Societies meet, dine, and deposit their Contributions in honour of his memory.[457]

And then under *Account of some eminent persons*:

Edward Colston Esq. was born here in 1636, lived in *Small-street*, where he was a very successful Merchant, never insured a Ship and never lost one, and acquired a very large fortune, the principle part of which he expended in doing good... What adds greatly to his character, is, that he performed his principal works of Charity in his life and health; he delighted in beneficence, was an excellent and eminent example to the opulent of posterity, and deserves, in Bristol, something more than the ringing of Bells to perpetuate Memory; a Statue of Brass, on a Pedestal of Marble, erected on St. Augustine's-place, opposite to the School he founded.[458]

Defeat and victory in the Caribbean

1798—Toussaint L'Ouverture, leader of African slaves, wins full control of Haiti.

In his declaration at Saint-Domingue in 1793, Toussaint made the following plea: "Unite, brothers, and fight with me for the same cause. Uproot with me the tree of slavery."[459] Toussaint's revolutionary call to the enslaved and their allies in Saint-Domingue (Haiti) not only helped inspire the first successful modern rebellion against slavery but sent a shockwave reverberating across the Caribbean, the Americas and eventually the World. Saint-Domingue was the jewel in the crown of pre-revolutionary France and economically the most important European colony in the world. As Hochschild relates:

> It [Saint-Domingue] produced more than 30 percent of the world's sugar and more than half its coffee, not to speak of cotton and other crops... The colony's eight thousand plantations accounted for more than one third of France's foreign trade, and its own foreign trade equalled that of the newly born United States. St Domingue's annual production of sugar and other crops was roughly double that of all the British West Indian islands put together. No colony anywhere made so large a profit for its mother country.[460]

More than 500,000 enslaved Africans, one of the largest concentrations of labour in the world, worked their brutal lives away to make planters and merchants in Saint-Domingue and France fabulously wealthy. That was until the revolution of 1789 and the news of the fall of the Bastille, as Hochschild recounts:

> The colony's superintendent wrote, "the blacks are all in agreement...that the white slaves have killed their masters...and have come into possession of all the goods of the earth"[461]

The nature and importance of Saint-Domingue as a colony made it both vulnerable to a revolt of the enslaved and a prize which all European powers coveted. In August 1791 the rebellion exploded, with the enslaved unleashing decades of seething hatred for their oppressors whilst carrying the vision of the 'natural rights of man', an idea that was being lauded by the revolutionaries in Paris.

The response of the British was a little known but massive military campaign in the Caribbean from 1793–1801. Involving more than 100,000 soldiers and sailors aboard hundreds of ships, it featured the largest maritime expedition to

Toussaint L'Ouverture, leader of the Haitian Revolution

ever leave Britain. The primary aim of the campaign, according to the Secretary for War Dundas, was "security", or as the overall Commander of the operation stated more clearly:

> ...to prevent a circulation in the British Colonies of the wild and pernicious Doctrines of Liberty and Equality.[462]

In practice this meant both the military suppression of French revolutionary forces (mainly freed slaves) and the re-establishment of chattel slavery where it had been overthrown. A secondary objective was to take advantage of the divisions created by the French Revolution to seize control of French possessions. The targets of the invasion included St Lucia and Martinique in the Windward Islands, Guadaloupe in the Leeward Islands and the jewel in the crown, Saint-Domingue. British agents exploited the split between the royalist French slave-holders and the revolutionary government in Paris which was in the process of abolishing slavery outright. The agents organised shipments of arms to support the French planters and British forces were rewarded with their whole-hearted cooperation when they began landing on the French possessions in late 1793.[463]

Supported by the French royalists, British forces were initially successful in capturing ports and towns on the coasts of the various islands. However, the politicians and commanders had made two fatal errors. First, they underestimated the determination, organisation and fighting qualities of the ex-slaves, many of whom were veterans of wars in Africa and well versed in guerrilla tactics. Second, surprisingly, as the British had been resident in the Caribbean for nearly two hundred years, they did not account for the toll that the climate and disease would take on their own forces. As heatstroke and dehydration punished the unprepared soldiers, yellow fever and malaria tore through their ranks, killing tens of thousands.[464]

The five-year struggle in Saint-Domingue eventually ended in a disastrous defeat for the British forces. Ground down by constant guerrilla warfare, surprise attacks and the effects of disease they were forced to withdraw after Toussaint's army of 14,000 experienced troops bore down on Port-au-Prince in October 1798. The situation in the other French possessions was little better. In Guadeloupe, the initial invasion in April 1794 by British troops supported by royalist slave-owners was swift and successful. Within a month, however, a small force of French Republican soldiers landed, armed with both muskets and the declaration of emancipation from the revolutionary government. They were soon joined by hundreds and then thousands of ex-slaves who forced a British regiment to surrender. The French commander of the operation, Victor Hugues, went on to successfully invade St Lucia in 1795, defeating a British force of over a thousand troops. Once again British forces were forced to flee the island, along with the French slave-holders.[465]

The spirit of revolt spread into islands that were already controlled by the British. In 1795, as British troops struggled to crush Toussaint's forces in Saint-Domingue, French Republican troops landed in St Lucia and the Second Marooon War broke out in Jamaica, the 'hydra of revolt' exploded in Grenada. Led by Julien Fédon, the son of a French jeweller and a freed African slave, the rebellion aimed to abolish slavery, grant citizenship to former slaves and overthrow British colonial rule. Fédon wanted to create a new black republic, modelled on the success in Guadeloupe. After executing British settlers, looting and burning their houses, destroying plantations and capturing the governor, Fédon retreated to the mountains. More than half of the 28,000 slaves on the island rallied to the cause, and it took over a year and the deaths of 7,000 rebels before British forces were able to crush the revolt. Fédon was never captured and remains a hero on Grenada to this day.[466]

The human cost of the five-year Caribbean campaign to the British was immense. Recent studies suggest that more than 50,000 soldiers and sailors died between 1793 and 1798. To put this figure in context, it is estimated that 3,500 British servicemen lost their lives at the battle of Waterloo. Another 10,000 Caribbean army and navy veterans were discharged from service, most of them crippled for life by wounds and disease, whilst several thousand more deserted during the campaign. The financial bill to the British state was astounding; with reliable estimates suggesting it was in the region of £16 to £20 million pounds. This equates to tens (if not hundreds) of billions today.[467]

The defeat of British forces by revolutionary armies principally made up of African ex-slaves had other political effects. It convinced many, both within the officer class and in Parliament, that slavery had to be abolished because otherwise similar rebellions would eventually occur in the British slave colonies with the potential outcome of losing control of the entire Caribbean.[468] One senior commander, Brigadier-General Thomas Maitland, who negotiated the withdrawal from Saint-Domingue, wrote that it would be useless to try to suppress the rebels as they were fighting for a "Negroe free Government arising out of the ruins of European Despotism…We have no business on that Island". An MP, recognising the impact of the anti-slavery elements of the French Revolution, argued in the House of Commons that:

> To be a match for France in the West Indies, we must meet her with her own weapons; we must adopt, towards our negroes, the same line of conduct she has observed towards hers: we must follow her example.[469]

There was an irony about this comment which urged Britain to follow revolutionary France's lead. In July 1794, nearly seven months after the historic decree for the abolition of slavery in all French territories, an internal counter-revolution was launched against the revolutionary government. Supporters of the 'natural rights of man and the citizen', that is, those who believed in the universality of human rights regardless of land and property, were ousted, imprisoned and in some cases executed. This bourgeois seizure of power destroyed many of the most progressive elements of the revolution and eventually led to the dictatorship of Napoleon Bonaparte in 1799.

Three years later Bonaparte completed the defeat of the Universalist rights of man by re-establishing slavery in the French colonies and launching an invasion of Saint-Domingue to carry this policy out. Despite bitter resistance, slavery was re-established in Guadeloupe and Guyana, but the numerous and battle-hardened rebel forces in Saint-Domingue proved a much tougher prospect. Although their leader, Toussaint L'Ouverture, was captured by the French a few months after the invasion, the rebel armies were triumphant, leading to the independence of the Republic of Haiti on 1st January 1804.[470] Over more than a decade of war the rebellious slaves of Haiti had defeated the greatest imperial powers in Europe, proving to the world the possibility of liberation from the bondage of slavery.

The importance of the dramatic events in Haiti was not lost on the radical abolitionists in Britain. In a letter to Coleridge dated 19 Feb 1804, Southey wrote of Clarkson's excitement about the victory of the enslaved in the Caribbean and its ramifications:

> He [Clarkson] is in high spirits about the Slave Trade, for the West India merchants will not consent to its suspension for five years, to prevent the importation of hands into the newly conquered islands [Tobago and St Lucia]; and what from that jealousy, and from the blessed success of the St. Domingo negroes, I believe we may hope to see the traffic abolished.[471]

After being shipped to France and contending with a cold winter imprisoned in a fort in the Jura Mountains, Toussaint died on 7th April 1803, ten months after his capture. Coleridge wrote that he had more "true dignity of character" than his captor Napoleon,[472] while Wordsworth's penned a sonnet that concluded:

> Though fallen thyself, never to rise again,
> Live, and take comfort. Thou hast left behind
> Powers that will work for thee; air, earth, and skies;
> There's not a breathing of the common wind
> That will forget thee; thou hast great allies;
> Thy friends are exultations, agonies,
> And love, and man's unconquerable mind.[473]

It was a fitting tribute to the legacy of hope that Toussaint—perhaps Abbé Raynal's Black Spartacus—had helped create for millions of enslaved Africans.

Abolition of the slave trade

An unexpected consequence of the Act of Union between Britain and Ireland in 1801 was the weakening of the cause of the pro-slavery parliamentarians; the new wave of Irish MPs didn't, in the main, have a direct interest in the slave trade. By contrast the Bristol electorate carried on returning pro-slavery MPs. Former Sheriff of Bristol and West India merchant, Evan Baillie, succeeded Lord Sheffield for the Whigs and Charles Bragge (Bathurst) for the Tories, both representing the city until 1812. Bathurst opposed the Bill to abolish the slave trade right to the bitter end while Baillie apparently abstained. In 1804 Baillie had written to his son Peter in Bristol complaining about the "unaccountable way" abolition had seized all parties in government and that he was seriously considering reducing his West India interests.[474]

1803—Last slaving voyage out of Bristol: the *Alert* carries 240 enslaved Africans to Jamaica.

The effects of war on overseas trade, the economic recession of the 1790s and the advantageous position of Liverpool, have all been debated by historians as reasons for the decline of Bristol as a slave-trading port in the latter part of the eighteenth century. Another important factor was the lack of investment in the port facilities in the city which made it less competitive than its rival in the north west of England.[475] In 1803, in a belated attempt to correct this disparity, the Merchant Venturers and Bristol Corporation formed the Bristol Docks Company in order to build and manage the Floating Harbour.[476] The £250,000 raised came primarily from five Bristol families whose wealth was generated either directly or indirectly from slaving and West India estates. Leading shareholders were Richard Hart Davis with 80 shares and Thomas Daniel and John Weare with 70 shares each. Davis and Daniel were appointed onto the board of directors.[477] Alderman Daniel was subsequently made Master of the Society of Merchant Venturers in 1805.

Not all of Bristol's leaders thought the scheme to modernise the docks was the answer, the Common Council only giving its consent by a single vote. Tory MP Charles Bathurst (previously Bragge) promoted the project before a committee of the House of Commons, while his Whig counterpart, Evan Baillie, opposed it with support from other mercantile dynasties, such as those of the Bright, Gibbs, Protheroe, King, and Pinney families. They strongly condemned the proposal primarily because it placed the entire harbour in the hands of a private company and also they reckoned that their vessels did not require dock accommodation.

The net result however was swingeing port dues that favoured the shareholders, and, by default, the West India merchants, but dissuaded others;

Latimer cited two examples of this imbalance that led directly to cries of malpractice and abuse:

in 1818 that a large local business might have been transacted in indigo, which was extensively used by the West of England clothiers; but that the dues imposed on it, being seven times greater than those levied at Liverpool, had put a stop to importations. A few years later, when steamboats had begun to ply to Ireland, a little packet of 270 tons burden, sailing weekly to and from Cork, was charged £468 per annum for dock dues and £104 for Mayor's dues; while a ship of 400 tons [such as Thomas Daniel's Bristol built 1807 West Indiaman *Steadfast*], making a yearly voyage to the West Indies, paid £15 6s. *5d.* in respect of both imposts.[478]

There was clearly a conflict of interest; Bristol's merchants desperately needed to modernise in order to retain their competitiveness but still wanted to maintain their own cosy cartel at the expense of others.

By now the abolition movement had been stalled for over ten years, Prime Minister Pitt having switched his focus towards Britain's war with revolutionary France. Pitt introduced draconian sedition laws in the 1790s and suppressed campaigning of any kind, including that for the abolition of slavery. There followed though, almost miraculously, several factors that came together to make the abolition of the slave trade possible. Pitt died in 1806 and his successor, Lord Grenville, was more sympathetic, or at least less distracted, in taking up the cause. Grenville was able to take the fight directly to the House of Lords and counter the main enemy of abolition, the Duke of Clarence, head on. As mentioned previously, Clarence, the leading proponent of the West India interest, would go on to become King William IV.

In the House of Commons, Clarence's chief pro-slavery ally was Liverpool Whig MP Banastre Tarleton, who had seen active service in the American War of Independence, where he been accused of a war crime. The Tarletons were directly involved in slavery: the family shipping company was one of the top four slave trading firms in Liverpool. For 15 years Tarleton had been having an affair with Bristol actress, talented writer and celebrity figure, Mary 'Perdita' Robinson. Famously Robinson had also been the first public mistress of the future King George IV, the Duke of Clarence's older brother. It was Robinson who had written many of Tarleton's speeches which were renowned for attacking and mocking abolitionists. Ironically, after their relationship ended, Mary turned to writing hard hitting anti-slavery poems.[479]

At just the right moment the anti-slavery lobby switched tactics. Maritime lawyer and fervent abolitionist, James Stephen, cleverly came up with a scheme to limit the slave trade to France and its allies while still appearing 'patriotic'. Stephen's argument was that although the Royal Navy had cleared the seas of French, Dutch and Spanish ships during the war with Napoleonic France, neutral vessels, mostly American flagged and British owned, were helping French colonies in the West Indies to thrive, replenishing their slaves and transporting their goods. In 1806 Wilberforce was about to trundle out yet another Abolition Bill when he was approached by Stephen to try a different tack in the name of the war effort, hence the 'Foreign Slave Trade Act'. Tarleton eventually smelt a rat and proclaimed that the abolitionists "were now coming by a side wind on the planters" but to no avail. The actual Bill to abolish the slave trade throughout the British Empire soon followed and was finally passed after 20 hard years of campaigning.[480]

1807—British slave trade abolished by Act of Parliament 25th March 1807.

Calling it the "most glorious measure, that had ever been adopted by any legislative body in the world" in order for the king to save face, Prime Minister Grenville was then forced to resign in order for George III to finally give his ascent to the Act. The Commons had voted by 283 to just 16 to abolish the slave trade. Clarkson called it "a Magna Carta for Africa" and it moved his friend Wordsworth to pen a sonnet *To Thomas Clarkson*.[481] John Newton lived just long enough to see this happen, dying nine months later at the age of 82. His hymn *Amazing Grace*, written with poet William Cowper in 1773, went on to become the anthem of abolition, especially in the United States.

Despite the so-called cessation of 'Trade to Africa', it was reported in Bristol that from 1795 to 1811 there was still an ongoing traffic in enslaved Africans, even after abolition. The finger of guilt was pointed firmly at several of Bristol's West India merchants, including Thomas Daniel, who were trading directly with the West Indies and 'Demarary' [Demerara[482]]. Their ships returned to Bristol via Africa and moored at Hungroad near the mouth of the Avon. Here the enslaved were quietly slipped ashore at Ham Green House—at the time owned by prominent West India merchant Richard Bright—and then transferred on to West India bound ships for the labour starved plantations. Initially the penalty for trading in slaves was pecuniary but in 1811 it became transportation for life, followed by the death penalty, later reprieved.[483]

1808 saw the publication of Thomas Clarkson's two volume autobiographical history of the abolition movement. Coleridge, Clarkson's pal and the only person who called him 'Tom', was so impressed he bought 25 copies to give to his friends. Coleridge raved:

Nothing can surpass the moral beauty of the manner in which he [Clarkson]… relates his own [part] in that Immortal War—compared with which how mean all the conquests of Napoleon and Alexander![484]

Contemporary historian Adam Hochschild rates it very highly as well:

> The book, particularly its first 150 pages on his first horseback trip to Bristol and Liverpool, remains perhaps the greatest memoir of a political organizer ever written.

Clarkson's two volumes would be published again in 1837, along with his seminal *An Essay on the Commerce and Slavery of the Human Species*.

Dresser sums up the mood of the people both locally and nationally after the first decade of the nineteenth century:

> Bristol's mercantile elite had failed in their opposition to abolition and were now faced with the challenge of political reform at home and emancipation abroad. For the moment, this challenge could be deflected by an appeal to patriotic unity. But once peace descended, both the enslavement of Africans and the plight of the English working classes would become bitterly contested topics, in both Bristol and the nation at large, in the decades to come.[485]

With the tide turning, both of Bristol's MPs stood down in 1812. True to his word after abolition, Evan Baillie began reducing his West Indies interests and acquired yet more land and estates in his native Scotland. After representing the city's West India merchants in five successive Parliaments, Charles Bathurst was presented with a 'piece of plate' from some of his grateful constituents. The solid silver 'tripod candelabrum' included the Bristol coat of arms, weighed 532 ounces and cost 700 guineas. Another accolade given to Bathurst was the naming of the basin created at the confluence of the rivers Malago and Avon in his honour, the Bathurst Basin.[486]

In a dramatic political coup in 1812, Alderman Daniel was instrumental in wresting control of Bristol Corporation from the Whigs which showed his prowess as an assured political operator. His "complete omnipotence in corporation affairs" reportedly earned him the sobriquet "King of Bristol".[487] The coup ended the Whig supremacy over the Bristol Corporation that had prevailed since the Glorious Revolution of 1688.[488]

> **1812**—Oct. 19, at the general election, after eight days polling, Richard Hart-Davis and Edward Protheroe [senior], esquires, were returned. The votes were, for Mr. Davis [Tory], 2910; for Mr. Protheroe [Whig], 2435; for Sir Samuel Romilly [Whig], 1685; for Mr. Hunt [Independent], 455. The number of persons polled was 4500.

Cigarette card (c1900) showing smut-stained view of The Exchange in Corn Street—
'Orator' Hunt spoke on top of his favourite nail outside the Exchange in the 1800s.

White Lion Inn (centre) in Broad Street, home of the Steadfast Club.

During the 1812 election, radical reformer Henry 'Orator' Hunt's opponents included not only the West India merchants of Richard Hart Davis for the Tories and Edward Protheroe senior for the 'Old Whigs', but also Sir Samuel Romilly, a Progressive (and 'official') Whig reformer and committed anti-slavery campaigner. As it turned out, Romilly was beaten by a combination of the Tory and Whig wings of the West India interest which, Latimer stated, "heartily concurred in detesting the anti-slavery principle of Romilly". The election was a fiery affair, the violence and corruption being exceptional and much money spent on winning the election with 'bludgeon boys' aplenty; Hunt was accused of inciting the mob to attack the Council House and even Hart Davis's home—and that was during just the first day of polling! To top it all, Protheroe's supporters placed two cannons outside the Exchange and aimed them directly at Romilly's HQ in the Bush Tavern opposite. In their defence the 'pranksters' said that the guns weren't loaded…[489]

Throughout the contest Hunt and Romilly failed to set up a coalition of their own and succumbed to the "scurrilous press, the party funds, the hired bludgeon men, and the pettifogging lawyers"[490]. The victory of the pro-slavery candidates came at a significant financial cost. The *Bristol Times* of 2nd August 1862 published a detailed account of the Tory party's outlay during the elections of 1812, which amounted to £29,429 14s. 7d. (equivalent in 2016 to £26 million by GDP per capita) paid through the Steadfast Club.[491] The large sums of money invested in the election by the West India interest to defeat the anti-slavery candidates reflected the significant financial interests that were being threatened by the end of slavery.

> **1813**—From Feb. 26 until March 11, a select committee of the House Of Commons (Michael Angelo Taylor, esq. in the chair) was engaged in trying the merits of the late Bristol election. The petitioners were, Mr. Hunt and four of the electors.

The threats and violence of the 1812 election prompted Hunt to request an investigation at the highest level. These complaints were subsequently rejected by the committee.

Corruption, Reform and Emancipation

Suppressing the slave trade

With disruption in Europe still ongoing after the Battle of Waterloo in 1815 and the final defeat of Napoleon, the cause of emancipation from slavery was side-lined in Britain. The strategy that the original abolitionist committee had agreed in the 1780s, that of banning the trade, had been chosen for two reasons. First, it had been a pragmatic step to try to overcome a smaller hurdle than going for full emancipation as the French revolutionaries had done. Second, it had been believed by many abolitionists that cutting off the supply of imported Africans would eventually lead to the demise of the slave system in the Caribbean altogether. William Wilberforce naively assumed that the "common kindness" of many of the plantation owners would suffice and even Thomas Clarkson stated:

> Who knows but that emancipation, like a beautiful plant, may, in its due season, rise out of the ashes of the abolition of the Slave trade.[492]

They were quite wrong and failed to see that collective interest amongst the economic elite in combination with state power overrode "common kindness" or gradualist ideas of liberation.

But, what of the now banned slave trade? Initially the British government did not try to exert pressure to promote its abolition internationally. On paper the ending of the Napoleonic wars offered a great opportunity to enforce

154

international agreements between the European powers. However, when the first diplomatic conference arose at the Treaty of Paris in 1814, Huzzey notes:

> British statesmen expressed little interest in spreading British abolitionism abroad and the government was not predisposed to dictate anti-slavery conditions as part of the peace negotiations. It was Wilberforce and his abolitionist allies who objected, raising fearsome new petitions against a resurrection of this branch of the Atlantic slave trade.[493]

Fears amongst the public that abolition would be left out of the treaty and outrage that Saint-Domingue was going to be recognised as the possession of the newly restored French monarch produced a huge reaction, larger in many ways than when the original 1807 Slave Trade Abolition Act was passed.[494] While the Emperor of Russia and the King of Prussia were in London they were presented with Clarkson's evidence against the trade and "1,370 petitions with hundreds of thousands of signatures" were delivered to Parliament; it has been estimated that "one-fifth to one-third of adult men" in the country signed these documents.

In Bristol the shift in public opinion was demonstrated by a series of "great public meetings" in 1813 and 1814 which were called to condemn the slave trade and assert its abolition in the post-war peace conferences. Rather than being fringe events, these large gatherings were now being presided over by the Mayor. For example, in July 1814 at such a meeting several resolutions were passed which summed up the popular feeling in the city. These included: "Perish commerce rather than live the slave trade," and "a negro is a man!" Witnesses claimed, "the audience wept at the tales of horror which were recounted" and one newspaper report stated:

> Weep on my generous countrymen…you may exult, you may even luxuriate in the thought that all the chords of your heart are vibrating in perfect unison with the sympathies of a whole nation…Sir this traffic in human flesh is an infernal traffic and could have no other origin than the malignancy of fiends and furies of hell.[495]

This massive popular pressure for an international ban on the slave trade guided British government policy at the subsequent Congress of Vienna (1814-1815). Even hardened reactionaries such as the foreign secretary Lord Castlereagh and the lead negotiator the Duke of Wellington bowed to public sentiment over abolition.[496]

Although the outcomes for abolitionists of these and other international conferences were limited,[497] the stage had been set by popular pressure for military action against slave traders. By 1819 the Royal Navy had a permanent squadron of vessels stationed off the coast of West Africa. Their job was to intercept and seize slave ships leaving the continent, whilst politicians tried to achieve bilateral anti-slave-trade treaties with other European powers to allow them to 'legally' search vessels.[498] This kind of activity was not new to the Royal Navy; in fact, it had been born of conflict. After 1794 the navy had crushed French trade to and from the Caribbean as part of an economic war. Capturing slave ships and their valuable human cargo had been a central part of the strategy, but not for humanitarian reasons; they allowed free passage and sometimes provided escorts for British slave ships and those of their allies Spain and Portugal.[499]

At this early stage there was little opposition to naval operations against slavers as it suited the aims of a number of political factions. Obviously most abolitionists and the general public that supported them were in favour of the operations as a way to suppress the trade.[500] Although the Royal Navy had protected and engaged in British slave trading activity for the best part of two centuries, their new Atlantic policing task suited their expanding importance in protecting the empire.[501] For fervent British imperialists the vision of 'ruling the waves' could now be given a moral justification. Even some self-interested economic groups, such as Caribbean slave-holding planters and manufacturers that traded slave-produced commodities were in favour, as maritime anti-slaving operations damaged their European competitors. As a result, the West Africa Squadron (WAS) grew in size, reaching its peak in the mid to late 1840s with more than 36 vessels and 4,000 sailors. Although this was a significant commitment of warships and personnel (about 15 percent of naval vessels and 10 percent of the workforce) this was not reflected in the quality of kit. Most of the ships sent to the WAS were old second line vessels that were too slow to catch the faster slave-carrying clippers and with too few ships to carry out effective anti-slavery operations the WAS was handicapped from the very start.

In reality, many plantation owners responded to the dearth of enslaved Africans caused by the 1807 act by illegal trading and then latterly by creating "breeding" programmes, some of which involved feeding their slaves better, providing safer working conditions and in some cases even basic maternity and health care. Some slave-holders even bragged about these 'improvements' and the success of their endeavours to increase the number of enslaved Africans that they 'owned'.[502] Late historian of the Caribbean, Richard Hart, commenting on the slow progress of the abolition movement, noted:

> The fact that the anti-slavery sentiments of many prominent British abolitionists were an expression of their bourgeois economic interests and/or a reflection of the currently ascendant bourgeois philosophy, and were not identical with those of slaves, helps to explain the gradual

nature of the proposals they offered for bringing the brutal and degrading system of slavery to an end. It was indeed only by intervening on their own behalf that the slaves were able to bring to the problem the urgency it deserved.[503]

It would be a combination of revolts of the enslaved in the plantations, unrest amongst the disenfranchised in Britain and a revived and radicalised abolition movement that would finally succeed in toppling the hated slave system.

News concerning the fortunes of the abolition movement, the struggles for enfranchisement and decisions concerning the slave colonies made in Westminster was not just reaching the plantocracy in the Caribbean; it was also filtering through to the enslaved. This incendiary information often exaggerated or embellished through word of mouth, sometimes inspired refusals or revolts. This was often due to the belief amongst the enslaved that they had been freed by decree in London and the planters were hiding it from them or because of the perception of uprisings or emancipation of 'British slaves' (the working class) in the 'motherland'. News of the latter not only provided encouragement but, from a tactical point of view, suggested that it was the right time to act.

In 1816 just such a situation arose after news that Parliament was working on schemes to ameliorate the conditions of slaves in the Caribbean reached the island of Barbados. A rumour spread amongst the enslaved that they were to be freed and one of the leaders of the ensuing rebellion, Nanny Grigg, a literate domestic servant, was heard to say:

> ...that they were all damned fools to work, for that she would not, as freedom they were sure to get....And that the only way to get it was to fight for it, otherwise they would not get it; and the way they were to do, was to set fire, as that was the way they did it in St Domingo.[504]

The 'Bussa Rebellion' as it is known, was named after its principal leader African born Bussa and broke out suddenly on Easter Sunday. The festivities were a useful cover for the enslaved to make their final clandestine preparations. Over 70 estates were affected by the uprising, with cane fields and buildings fired as beacons for the revolt. The resident whites fled, and martial law was declared, though there was no massacre of the 'masters' by the rebels. The response of the authorities in crushing the rebellion was, however, brutal:

> Only 2 whites were killed in the fighting but probably about 100 slaves, with a further 144 executed, 170 deported, and innumerable floggings. Roaming slaves were shot on sight and Negro houses burned...Captives were commonly tortured to extract confessions or to incriminate others.

Convicted rebels were publicly executed in different parts of the island and their bodies—sometimes just their heads—in many cases exposed on their home estates…[505]

Despite the defeat of the rising and the terror inflicted upon the enslaved by these atrocities, the unrest and fears of revolt were ever-present. One Barbadian planter wrote ominously:

The disposition of the Slaves in general is very bad. They are sullen and sulky and seem to cherish feelings of deep revenge. We hold the West Indies by a very precarious Tenure, that of military strength only and if they do not change at home their system of reduction I would not give a year's purchase for any Island we have.

A speaker in the Barbadian assembly re-emphasised these fears and referred to both the influences of the successful revolution in Saint-Domingue and the rumours of emancipation in stating:

The Insurrection has been quelled but the spirit is not subdued, nor will it ever be subdued whilst these dangerous doctrines which have been spread abroad continue to be propagated among the Slaves. It behoves us to be upon guard—to keep watch that we may not again be caught so shamefully unprepared. The comfort and happiness of our families require it—the safety and tranquillity of the Island call for it. We must all determine to sacrifice our private interests for the public good. It is a duty which we owe to our Constituents—it is a duty which we owe to our Country.[506]

Abolitionist William Knibb, who was to play a major role as witness to a future rebellion of the enslaved, arrived in Bristol in 1816, aged 13, along with his older brother Thomas. Knibb's employer, John Gardner Fuller, had transferred his printing business to St Augustine's Place in the city and brought the two young apprentices with him. Fuller had abolitionist sympathies and clearly had an influence on his two charges.[507] The Knibbs attended the Broadmead Baptist Chapel under the leadership of Dr Ryland and both went on to attend Missionary School.[508] On graduating Thomas went to Jamaica and on his death in 1824, William volunteered to replace him as missionary-schoolmaster, just days after getting married. This would turn out to be a life-changing decision.

1821—Nov. 13, the centenary since the death of Edward Colston, whose munificent benevolence has been celebrated in our own time by three [several] societies, the Dolphin [named after his crest, which tradition says was assumed from the circumstance of a fish of that species having stopped a leak in one of his ships at sea], the Anchor, and the Grateful, dining together, and contributing, on removal of the cloth, to a charitable fund for distribution during the succeeding year. The Dolphin Society consists chiefly of Tories and Churchmen; the Anchor, Whigs and Dissenters; the Grateful composed chiefly of such as pride themselves in having been "Colston's Boys," yet among whom, (though Chatterton was one, we have not heard that his memory has been toasted) profess to be exclusively neither. This year the collection for charity alone at the Dolphin, where 171 dined, amounted to £406 17s.—at the Anchor, £450 14s. 6d., out of which the charge for dinner and wine for 150 guests was defrayed; and at the Grateful, £190, exclusively for apprenticing poor boys and relieving women in child bed.

Thomas Daniel, who was the most powerful representative of the West India interest, continued his meteoric rise through the civic and political structures in Bristol. By 1807 he was president of the Colston Society, in 1816 the Dolphin Society, and he continued to be leader of the Tory Steadfast Society, governor of Bristol's Incorporation of the Poor, sponsor of the Prudent Man's Bank, and treasurer of both Red Maids' School, and Queen Elizabeth Hospital School. Other interests included iron importing from Sweden, brass manufacture and coal mines in Bedminster. He went on to become one of the three founding trustees of the Clifton Bridge Trust in 1830 and founding shareholder in the Bristol and Clifton Zoological Society.[509]

The increasing political and economic power that Merchant Venturers such as Daniel were exploiting led to a split in the bourgeoisie in Bristol. By 1823 merchants and business people had tired of the combined exclusivity of the Society of Merchant Venturers and Bristol Corporation, along with exorbitant dock dues among many other grievances. Consequently, they set up their own organisation, the Bristol Chamber of Commerce, one of the last major cities to so do. From the outset they had a fight on their hands. The major cause for concern was that the Merchant Venturers in particular had not been fully representative of the rising business class since the late eighteenth century. On top of this there were accusations of favouritism, nepotism and corruption. 'A. Burgess'—reckoned to be the nom de plume of Whig accountant John Barnett Kington [see 1836]—complained that the Corporation tried to subvert the Chamber and that the Port and Corporation offered various personal inducements—in other words, bribes—to get their way.[510]

Once more unto the breach...

‖ **1823**—Founding of the Anti-Slavery Committee in London.

The group's full title was the 'Society for Mitigating and Gradually Abolishing the State of Slavery throughout the British Dominions' and was set-up in London by veteran campaigners including Zachary Macaulay and new man Thomas Fowell Buxton who would succeed Wilberforce in Parliament in 1825 on his retirement. The continuing failures to emancipate the enslaved had led to this revival in the abolition movement, although campaigners were still clinging to the idea of a gradualist path through amelioration of the conditions of the enslaved, that is, that slave-holders should treat the enslaved in a more compassionate manner.

The founding of the new Society in London stimulated the formation of similar groups around the country. Locally a branch—the 'Bristol Auxiliary'— of the Anti-Slavery Society was launched with Thomas Clarkson addressing the first meeting. One of the leading members of the Bristol branch was once again the long serving campaigner William Peter Lunell, Treasurer and Life Member. He was joined by Committee members such as Quaker Joseph Storrs Fry [I] of the chocolate dynasty; Unitarian Dr Lant Carpenter, father of social reformer Mary—he had come to Bristol in 1817 to succeed minister Dr John Prior Estlin; and sugar refiner Samuel Blackwell, father of Elizabeth, Britain and America's first woman doctor. The group was sometimes labelled the 'Bristol Humanitarians'.

As a result of the re-emergence of Britain's anti-slavery committees, Wilberforce submitted a Quaker petition to Parliament in March 1823 and Buxton followed it up with a motion in May "to obtain a commitment to bring slavery to an end":

That the House should agree on a date (not specified) after which the children born [to the enslaved] should be born free;

That those already alive on that date should continue to be slaves for the remainder of their lives, unless they were earlier manumitted;

That those who remained slaves should however have the right (as those in the Spanish possessions), whether or not their owners agreed, to purchase their freedom at a price to be fixed by a competent authority.[511]

In response to this weak proposal which deferred full emancipation for at least two generations and offered no hope of freedom for the majority of the enslaved,

Parliament came up with the following resolution at the end of the motion's debate:

> That it is expedient to adopt effectual and decisive measures for ameliorating the condition of the slave population of his Majesty's colonies.

> That through a determined and persevering, but at the same time judicious and temperate enforcement of such measures, this House looks forward to a progressive improvement in the character of the slave population, such as may prepare them for a participation in those civil rights and privileges which are enjoyed by other classes of his Majesty's subjects.

> That this House is anxious for the accomplishment of this purpose at the earliest period that shall be compatible with the well-being of the slaves themselves, with the safety of the colonies, and a fair and equitable consideration of the interests of private property.[512]

The problem with these supposed "effectual and decisive measures" was that the reforms would only be imposed on 'Crown Colonies' which had no elected assemblies. The politicians apparently hoped that other colonies could be 'persuaded' to enact laws to ameliorate the condition of the enslaved; a naïve and weak assumption to say the least. The failure to use the power of Parliament and the strong resistance of the plantocracy across the British Caribbean limited the effect of the reforms and essentially left their implementation in the hands of the slave-owners.[513]

Historian Richard Hart argues that "the British Government [had] set its face firmly against emancipation at an early date and failed even to consider the setting of a timetable".[514] Hart also cites the ministerial arguments that slaves were not yet 'morally fit for freedom' and speculates that the Government's nebulous ideas regarding slavery would have stalled the process for another 50 years. It appears, for many in government the main purpose of 'amelioration' was to stave off the possibility of immediate emancipation and the threat that posed to "the interests of private property".

Regardless of the various gradualist plans, there were greater forces at play, in particular the agency of the enslaved, something that the government could not easily control. One minister fearful of the potential for yet more unrest in the Caribbean stated bluntly:

> The question to be decided is, how civil rights, moral improvements and general happiness are to be communicated to this overpowering multitude of slaves, with safety to the lives and security to the interests of the white population, our fellow-subjects and fellow citizens.[515]

It was to be the action of enslaved Africans in British possessions in the Americas, in conjunction with the new anti-slavery committees throughout Britain, that would galvanise the campaign. In response, from 1823 to 1832, the West India planters in the Caribbean reacted by aggressively attacking the government's efforts to meliorate slavery. According to Claude Levy "They not only devised schemes to nullify effective reform but threatened to secede from the empire and seek protection from the United States".[516]

‖ **1823**—Slave rebellions in Jamaica and Demerara (now part of Guyana).

Following the abolition of the slave trade in 1807, West India merchants searched for other supplies of slave labour and expanded the plantation system into new possessions such as Trinidad and Demerara. In 1815 the Dutch finally ceded the latter to Britain in a 'colony swap'. Hitherto Demerara, on the north-east Caribbean coast of South America, had been cultivating coffee inland but, with the arrival of the British, production was switched to sugar on the fertile lands of the coast. Sugar prices dropped in the 1820s so British owners ordered their overseers on the island to increase productivity. In practice this meant every slave was put to work (even heavily pregnant women), for longer hours and with the whip at their backs.[517]

In 1823 news of the formation of the Anti-Slavery Committee in London and of "Parliament's vague declaration about the need for reforms" reached Georgetown, the capital of Demerara.[518] A rumour then spread widely that an emancipation bill had been passed by Parliament and that the colony's rulers were withholding the news from the enslaved. Hart continues:

> The rebellion [in Demerara] that commenced on August 18, which took the form of a refusal to work, had the support of 13,000 slaves. Its potential vitality had however been sapped by a belief on the part of the rebels, inculcated by the devout and sincere Christian missionary...Rev. John Smith, that it was morally wrong to take the life of another human being. Needless to say, this view was not shared by the plantation owners and the Government.

> They [the enslaved] seized the guns on the plantations but, as their leaders had no plan for offensive action, they made no use of these weapons. They did no more harm to the supervisory personnel than to put them in the stocks so as to prevent them from taking action. Even when the troops and militia moved against them, unleashing a ruthless and indiscriminate massacre, they made no violent response.[519]

The coordinated rebellion, which spread over 37 estates, was brutally crushed by British Army regiments over several days, with more than 250 of the enslaved killed in the fighting or in the aftermath. Those considered ringleaders were shot, their heads were cut off and nailed to posts, whilst others were sentenced to solitary confinement, flogging and death.[520] Hart continues:

> Quamina, one of the principal leaders, was assassinated and his bullet-riddled body was publically exhibited. The ailing missionary John Smith was falsely accused of encouraging the rebellion, tried by court martial and found guilty, but died in prison.[521]

Ironically, it was the death of the missionary Smith at the hands of the Demerara plantocracy that outraged the public and the media in Britain, rather than the mass executions, mutilation and torture of hundreds of the rebels. Over 200 petitions were received by Parliament and MPs denounced the actions of the colonial authorities in Georgetown on the floor of the house.[522]

Serious unrest amongst the enslaved in British Caribbean possessions was not confined to Demerara. In Jamaica in 1823 and 1824 a series of conspiracies were uncovered by the authorities. In December 1823 eight enslaved Africans from the parish of St Mary were executed for planning a revolt and over the following months further plots were discovered in the neighbouring parishes of St. George, St. James, and Hanover along the northern coast of Jamaica. In mid-July 1824 an insurrection broke out in the *Argyle* and *Golden Grove* estates in the parish of Hanover.[523] These groups remained in communication with each other and organised to resist collectively, along with rebels from a neighbouring estate, *Alexandria*. A large military force was sent to suppress the revolt, so the rebel slaves left the plantations and hid out in the bushes, fighting the militia until their capture a few days later. Eleven rebels were executed by the authorities, another four were hanged elsewhere on the island, whilst others were transported or flogged. Enslaved Africans had to be restrained from interfering with the executions and one of the rebel leaders claimed that the revolt had not been subdued but that "the war had only just begun".[524] This would soon prove to be true.

Concerned about the length of time emancipation of the enslaved was taking, Leicester born Quaker social reformer and radical Elizabeth Heyrick published a ground-breaking and widely circulated pamphlet *Immediate not Gradual Abolition* in 1824. In it she stated that gradualism in anti-slavery politics was "the very masterpiece of Satanic policy", the fear of total loss by asking for too much had frightened abolitionists into asking for too little. Heyrick reckoned that "Truth and justice make their best way in the world when they appear in bold and simple majesty" and insisted that campaigners act "with more the spirit of Christian combatants, and less of worldly politicians".[525] With help from the female wings of the Anti-Slavery Society, and despite negativity from William Wilberforce, Heyrick's influence finally helped formalise immediate emancipation as Society policy by the end of 1830.

In the Bristol election of 1826, the Whig West India merchants re-selected Henry Bright, the son of Richard, one of their number, who had originally stood for Bristol in 1820, in place of Edward Protheroe senior. For the Tory interest, the Steadfast Club refused to help Richard Hart Davis and invited banker Philip John Miles to stand instead. Hart Davis issued an address but then declined to stand for Alderman Daniel's Steadfast Club; this caused the club's dissolution.[526] The Steadfast Club had for many years been allowed to nominate the Tory candidate.[527] Despite all of these shenanigans, pro-slavery candidates Bright and Hart Davis were finally elected.

One reason cited for their lack of faith in Davis's candidature was his inability to pay campaign expenses after an ill-judged parliamentary investment the year before. The refusal of help for Davis's campaign may also have been down to some of the petitions he presented to Parliament which suggested a weakening of his resolve over slavery. In May 1824, Davis presented a Bristol petition for an inquiry into the dubious trial of the Methodist missionary John Smith in Demerara but two weeks later voted not to condemn the trial. Also, in June he presented another Bristol petition for the gradual abolition of slavery.[528]

1827 saw the formation of the Bristol and Clifton Female Anti-Slavery Society which featured some high-status women. The organisation was based in Isaac Hobhouse's former residence in Cornwallis Crescent, then belonging to Lady Isabella King, who headed the new group. Their stated aims included the production of anti-slavery propaganda and the spreading of the resurgent West Indian sugar boycott, the latter gaining the ire of the West India Association who condescendingly accused them of "ill-informed puff". Prominent amongst the campaigners was Marianne Schimmelpennick (nee Galton) who hailed from a Birmingham Quaker family associated with Priestley's 'Lunar Abolitionists'. The previous year she had anonymously written an anti-slavery pamphlet debunking in great and learned detail the notion that the Bible condoned modern slave regimes. The organisation included Hannah More. Although not a wealthy body the Society managed to donate money to the London Anti-Slavery Society and to Baptist schools in Jamaica, even though the latter were being accused of stirring up 'insolence' and political sedition amongst the slaves.[529]

While the anti-slavery societies were reforming, the grip on Bristol's corporate governance exerted by the Society of Merchant Venturers—including the West India interest—was as tight as ever. The most powerful combination of Corporation leaders during the 1820s was that of Thomas Daniel and William Fripp the younger, who not only shared the same political doctrine but also family connections through marriage. Alderman Daniel's influence

Commercial Rooms,

BRISTOL, 15th October 1818.

AT a Meeting of the West India Association, held this day,
THOMAS DANIEL, Esq. in the Chair,

over political and economic bodies was exercised through his leadership of the Corporation, the local Tories and the West India Association, in addition to heading a large merchant and plantation enterprise. Along with these political and business interests he still found time to participate in the affairs of diverse civic bodies. Radical reformer and newspaper proprietor James Acland wasn't too impressed with Daniel or his sidekick Fripp, declaring in *The Bristolian* in 1828 that the former "misapplied the talents entrusted to his care" and that the latter was "a narrow minded zealot exhibiting tyrannical tendencies".[530] However, contemporary historian Graham Bush argues that there was nothing wrong with Corporation members as individuals; they had the perfect right to donate their vote, wealth or talents to whatsoever party they chose. Citing Thomas Daniel, Bush even suggested he was the best example of this fusion of political and economic power of Bristol's business elite, stating that Alderman Daniel and his protégés "watched paternally over affairs without the extremes of absolute rule".[531] This viewpoint wasn't held by many of the Bristol public as the explosive events of October 1831 would demonstrate.

Defoe's 'corporation-tyranny' was as true in the 1820s as it was in the 1720s. Over one hundred years of election violence, intimidation, bribery, lack of representation, blackmail, excessive corporate governance, gerrymandering, corruption and mismanagement led directly to the turbulent 1830s where reform of Parliament, reform of Municipal Corporations and finally emancipation held sway. It's clear that Bristol's leaders, whether Whig or Tory, used the Corporation, Society of Merchant Venturers, Bristol Dock Company and the West India Association to further their own economic and political interests and, on top of that, used the Colston Societies to enhance their popularity and influence through charity and patronage. Historian Jo Manton sums up the situation that led Bristol's working people to clamour for these reforms:

> ...the City Corporation was a fossilized relic of ancient glories, self-appointed, meeting in secret, jealous of power and largely devoted to picturesque ceremonial. They let the port, on which the city's greatness depended, decay; they left the work of sewering, paving, cleaning and lighting undone... 'out Parishes', including Bedminster, with a working class population of over 13,000 not incorporated in the city until 1835, had no effective local government.[532]

Like the vote of 1812, Bristol's 'Slavery Election' of 5ᵗʰ August 1830 was a violent and ill-tempered affair. Pro-slavery candidate Richard Hart Davis was the sitting member for the Tories and offered himself for re-election while Henry Bright, the West India interest Whig, stood down. Another pro-slavery candidate James Evan Baillie, son of previous Bristol MP Evan Baillie, stood in his stead only to be challenged by Edward Protheroe (junior) on an anti-slavery, pro-reform ticket. There is great irony in this as Protheroe's father, Edward senior, was formerly MP for Bristol in 1812 and strongly pro-slavery in the election of that year. The final candidate James Acland, editor of *The Bristolian* broadsheet, notorious for taking on the abuses of the powers that be, had recently been released from prison for libelling the Corporation. He was an uncompromising opponent of slavery [see October 1830] and stood for Parliament as a Radical.

This fractious situation was worsened by the bellicose character of the Whig candidates' agents; one was the outspoken member of an old Bristol slaving family and former Royal Navy officer Captain Christopher Claxton, who represented Baillie. He was the son of Robert Claxton who had been a West India merchant in business with the Protheroes from 1783 to the early 1800s. Although Christopher didn't take an official role in the Merchant Venturers, his younger brother William was the first salaried Treasurer of the organisation and the last secretary of Bristol's West India Association. The other Whig agent was the highly successful floor-cloth (a form of linoleum) manufacturer, reformer and Bristol Anti-Slavery Society member John Hare, who represented Protheroe junior.

Claxton in particular was renowned for his use of intimidation and violence; he organised gangs of pro-slavery thugs, leading to arson, assaults and attacks on properties. The *Bush Tavern* was Protheroe's headquarters, Davis used the *White Lion* and the *Rummer* was Baillie's heart of operations. All three pubs were within a 100m radius of one another and were the focal points of violence, suffering much damage. During an eve of poll meeting at the *Bush*, a wooden missile narrowly missed Hare and struck Protheroe on the head knocking him unconscious. Hare was no saint in this either; he refused a pistol duel with Claxton over a scandal sheet that he had produced and led his men on persistent forays against Claxton's forces.[533] This was the zenith of the days when elections could be bought and sold. The expenditure by the main protagonists on this occasion was huge; in the six elections during his 18-year tenure as a Bristol MP, Davis reckoned his total expenditure had "fallen just short of £70,000".[534] It was reputed that Baillie, on this one election alone, had laid out £18,000 and because of this Acland promptly petitioned against his return—the allegations being for bribery and intimidation—but he didn't pursue the case. A report in the *Bristol Mirror* of 31ˢᵗ July 1830 declared:

We believe that since the days of Brickdale, Burke, Daubeny, and Cruger, there has been nothing like it... Bands of music everywhere parade the streets with banners, and immense trains of sailors and mechanics armed, shout "Baillie for ever", and "Protheroe for ever", as they pass the several stations they throw into the teeth of each other a brave defiance... never within our knowledge have there been any thing like the immense quantities of placards—they cover every thing... The appearance of Queen-Square is curious—poor King William is, horse and all, covered with large posting bills...[535]

Racism also reared its ugly head during the proceedings, as Dresser states:

However undesirable Captain Claxton deemed Jews, Quakers and politically active women, he reserved his most profound contempt for Africans... "Hasty emancipation will ensure that the negro race, a barbarian in grain... will as surely retrograde... as his master will be ruined".

Dresser also notes that Claxton's language, which refers to inherent differences between 'races' and 'racial hierarchy', was a "newer strain of a specifically racialist terminology" entering the British political arena. Claxton's ire was not just reserved for enslaved Africans. The Claxton/Baillie camp made one outrageous slur after another culminating in the claim that Protheroe was Jewish while still insisting on calling him "Nigger Ned".[536]

In the end, Protheroe junior and Acland lost the 1830 election to the pro-West India interest candidates. Protheroe fell a few hundred votes short, whilst Acland, who was hated by the Bristol elite, only polled 25 votes. Even so, from the perspective of the abolition of slavery and enfranchisement, the election had not been a complete loss. As Marshall explains, instead it reflected changing attitudes among those who, in general, could not yet vote:

The 1830 election had not merely allowed Bristolians to declare themselves on the question of slavery in the West Indies. More significantly, it had provided an issue capable of moral application in the plantations of the Caribbean and transferrable to the streets of Bristol as the basis from which radical demands could arise. Eighteen years before Charles Sumner would denounce the alliance in the United States between "the lords of the lash" and "the lords of the loom". Bristol politicians had perceived the existence of links of a comparable nature between economic interests in the city.[537]

Just prior to the 'Slavery Election' George IV had died 'unlamented' and was succeeded by William IV whose coronation day in September was greatly celebrated in Bristol. During the same month future mayor, Charles Pinney,

167

one of the sons of wealthy plantation owner and West India Association founder member, John Pinney, presided at a meeting in the Guildhall. Pinney congratulated the French nation on the revolution during three days of July and complimented them on their "fortitude, moderation, love of order and respect for social rights".[538] Pinney, a complex man, had just a few years earlier been a contender for the hand in marriage of Wilberforce's daughter Elizabeth—until Wilberforce looked more deeply into his credentials. He then seconded the nomination of pro-slavery candidate James Evan Baillie as Member of Parliament and stated at the time:

> ...five-eighths of the trade of Bristol depended on the West Indies. He [also] advocated the education of slaves, so that they might ultimately be fitted for a similar position to that of the English peasantry.[539]

This statement demonstrates that despite their financial interests in slavery, Whig sentiment over enfranchisement and emancipation was causing reservations amongst some of the West India merchants. This was characterised by the softening of the pro-slavery stance towards gradual abolition; the question was how gradual?

'Compensation for the enslaved, our fellow subjects'

On 28th September 1830 a "numerously attended" meeting of the Wesleyan Societies and Congregations, in the Ebenezer Chapel in King Street, Bristol, resolved to petition Parliament for the "entire and universal extinction of Slavery throughout the British Dominions".[540] A public meeting followed on the 22nd October in the Assembly Room, Prince's Street which was reported under the heading 'British Colonial Slavery' and attracted hundreds of people. The meeting had been organised by the anti-slavery lobby, and it turned out to be a stormy event. True to form, Captain Claxton and his West India Association cronies attempted to seize control of the meeting by taking the stage and after a scuffle they were thrown out. Claxton only agreed to leave the building if he was accompanied by the chairman, his motive being to end the meeting; the incident also led to "the ladies present being forced to retire". After the 'Claxtonians' departed the chairman was replaced by a dissenting minister who just happened to be in Bristol, a Reverend Roaf. The meeting was called to order and the new chairman promptly declared that he was a 'friend of Abolition' and that his opinion was:

> ...I would say, let them [the slave-proprietors] have their property, or the worth of it, but let them not have absolute property on their fellows. One thing is certain: the feeling of the country is up on this subject.

Whoever looks dispassionately upon passing events must see that the abolition of the slave is fast hastening forward to completion. He must be convinced that slavery cannot much longer continue... As it is, let them come forward, assent to our principles, and state their claims; and, as we have participated in the sin, we will share in the punishment; as we have enjoyed the advantages of slavery, we will endure a portion of the disadvantages. We will remember the 2,000 planters resident in this country, but we cannot forget the 800,000 slaves enthralled in our colonies. Who thinks of compensating them for the sufferings they have endured? Let the planter bestow freedom upon the slave, and then we will consider the justice of his claim for compensation...

Acland proposed the first resolution, which challenged the idea that Britain had achieved enough by abolishing the Slave Trade, and that the actions of the West India proprietors in continuing to hold enslaved people was going against the wishes of the country:

1.—That this Meeting is of opinion, that Slavery is the immediate cause of the continuance of the Slave Trade—for that so long as the West India Planter is permitted to hold an absolute property in the lives of his fellow-creatures, so long must the inhuman traffic in such property continue. Resolved unanimously.

The motion was seconded by a Mr Tripp who then gave a brief account of the current state of affairs in the West Indies, particularly Jamaica, where he had resided for the last eight years. Acland then continued by stating that the moment for emancipation had come:

It is many years since the question of emancipation was first broached; but the wishes of the people have been disregarded. This, Sir, is the period when the country should speak with a firm voice, and demand the rights of humanity for the oppressed negroes.

He then railed against 'gradualism':

He who, by milk and water measures, would now endeavour to obtain the amelioration of the condition of the slaves, is not an honest friend to the cause of humanity; he who would say to Government, "When you and the West Indian proprietors have agreed among yourselves at what time it would be convenient for the slave to be emancipated, then let him go free," he who would say this, is not worthy to be associated in this righteous cause.

And that 'amelioration' had been a sham:

> The people, for 23 years, have been cajoled by the statement that this is not
> the time when emancipation can be safely effected; yet, during the whole
> of this period, very little has been done, by ameliorating the condition of
> the slaves, to prepare them for a state of freedom. Session after session
> have we waited, in hopes that the ministry, and those who call themselves
> our representatives, would attend to the voice of the people; and still
> there are 800,000 of our fellow-creatures wearing the fetters of slavery.

He argued that emancipation was a pre-requisite for genuine amelioration:

> The time is arrived when we should state our conviction of the necessity
> of giving them freedom—when arrangements should be entered into for
> the abolition of slavery, and the immediate amelioration of the condition
> of the slave.

Acland then attacked the racist stance of the planters which claimed that
subservience was an inherent quality of the enslaved. Instead he turned the
'nature' argument on its head by referring to 'nurture':

> They tell us that the slave is unfit to enjoy the blessings of freedom; and
> perhaps, in many cases, from the subversion of the intellectual powers,
> there may be some truth in the statement. Born in bondage, reared
> to the heritage of slavery, driven to his task by the whip of his driver,
> and deprived altogether of the rights of man, can it be at all a matter of
> surprise that his ideas should be slavish?

Even the 'reasonable' measure of freeing the children had failed to be
implemented:

> You are told, that it would be dangerous to emancipate the slaves all at
> once; but if a proclamation were issued to the effect that the children born
> of slaves should be free, would there be any danger in such a measure?
> (No)—Would any of the real interests, or the rights of the West Indians
> be invaded? (No) Then why not emancipate the unborn, those who are
> yet in the womb—who have not yet sucked the milk of slavery, and who
> are not yet reduced to the level of the brute? The very nature of the milk
> of the slave-mother would be changed by such a measure of justice, and
> by a consciousness that she was suckling *her* child and a *free* child. Is
> there any excuse for delay in this respect? (No) However much it might
> be urged that immediate emancipation would endanger the lives and the

properties of the planters, on account of the slave population being more numerous than the whites, there can be no excuse for turning a deaf ear to the demand for this act of justice.

Acland then put a second resolution to the meeting calling for a petition to Parliament which confusingly still contained the words 'gradual abolition'. This time the resolution was seconded by Mr J. W. Hall who briefly harangued Claxton for his actions earlier that day and during the previous election, where he condemned the captain's use of a mob of sailors for "the putting down of truth by clamour". After other observations he then ceded the floor to a Mr H. C. Howells who thought the resolution as it then stood capable of some amendment; he suggested that for "gradual abolition" they should substitute "total abolition at the earliest possible period". He went on:

Sir, we have been contending for gradual abolition for many years—for so many, indeed, that we are at last compelled to believe that gradual abolition means nothing less than perpetual slavery.

The well-informed Howells then countered pro-slavery arguments based on the fear of what would occur if the enslaved were emancipated immediately by recalling what happened in Haiti almost 40 years previously:

Let us not for a moment suppose that the voice of freedom will be the signal for massacre and plunder. The principles of human nature are opposed to the supposition, and the facts of history are opposed to it. There is no danger in emancipating the slaves. Give to me the dispatches declaring them free, and I will fearlessly go among them, dreading no violence from the liberated slave. Sir, the example of St Domingo is brought forth in proof of danger; and we are told that the slave, if made a free agent, will starve in preference to working. Sir, I believe human nature to be nearly the same everywhere as with us: there may be many who prefer a life of idleness to one of toil; but I have my doubts whether men of any colour, however ignorant, will endure starvation, when they may procure food by labour. I fancy black and white will be found equally ready to work rather than starve.

But, Sir, what are the facts to St. Domingo? 500,000 slaves were liberated in one day; and, instead of avenging themselves upon their original oppressors, they worked upon the same plantations, for the same masters, for five years and a half. This was after the proclamation of Polverel, sanctioned by the decree of the National Assembly, had given freedom to the whole of the black population of the French colonies. The previous struggles and consequent bloodshed were occasioned by the planters, who resisted by force the extension of the privileges to the free people of colour, which had been granted to them by the mother country. The massacres and conflagrations were occasioned, not by the slaves, but by quarrels between the white and coloured planters, and between the royalists and the revolutionists, who called in the aid of the slaves for the purpose of wreaking vengeance upon each other; and as to the insurgent negroes of the north, who filled that part with terror and dismay, they were originally put in motion, according to Malenfaut, by the royalists themselves, to strengthen their own cause and to put down the partisans of the French revolution. Under Toussaint, which is but another name for Washington, the whites lived happily upon their estates, and the negroes continued to work for them.

But the French, accustomed to arbitrary power, could not brook the loss of their whips; they were mortified and chagrined at the change that had taken place, and they ardently desired again to reduce the negroes to a state of slavery. They induced Buonaparte to fit out an expedition, under Le Clerc, for the reduction of the islands. They endeavoured to seduce Toussaint and the other native chiefs, from their duty, but in vain; and having in open violation of all faith obtained possession of that patriot's person, he was shipped for France where he died in a prison. And what was the next step for the French? They landed an army, not of men, but of dogs, and the wretched blacks were hunted like wild beasts, and torn in pieces by bloodhounds trained to the work of slaughter. Hundreds were enclosed in the holds of the invader's vessels and suffocated with brimstone; others were bound and cast into the sea; and it was the Sunday pastime of the wretches who sanctioned these disgraceful proceedings, to witness the miseries of others of the unfortunate sufferers who were delivered up to the fangs of the savage animals I have just alluded to. What could be expected but cruelty in return for such cruelties? But the evil which the blacks returned upon their oppressors was not equal to a tenth part of that which was first practised upon them. Such is the true history of the cruelties practised in St Domingo—cruelties originating in the whites, and fostered by political prejudices and a blind and bigoted faith. We live in a better time. We have sent out missionaries for a long period of years...

Howells concluded his historical analysis by pressing for his amendment which Acland agreed to and which was also carried unanimously by the meeting:

2.—That the period for demanding the total extinction of Slavery at the earliest possible moment in our West India Colonies having now arrived, a Petition be prepared, embodying the sentiments of this Meeting, in order to its presentation to our Sovereign—praying his Majesty's most gracious direction to his Ministers immediately to bring into the two Houses of Parliament a bill on this great question, which shall accord with the interest of humanity, the claims of justice, and the often expressed desires of the People of this Country

Richard Fry then stated:

As lovers of justice, I can scarcely think there is one present who will not admit that the slaves are not only entitled to freedom, but to compensation...

And proposed a third resolution:

3.—That this Meeting is of the opinion that the Slaves are entitled not only to freedom, but also to compensation for all their loss and suffering during the time they have been enslaved, and that the compensation to be given to the Slave-holders should be only to the amount of the loss which they can prove

George Lovell seconded the third resolution—which again was carried unanimously—by saying "The resolution appears so reasonable, so equitable, that a long speech in support of it is scarcely required". Other resolutions were passed with James Acland pointing out that the meeting had "been deprived of the company of several gentlemen, in consequence of the disturbances that have taken place" and that, with a touch of sarcasm, he felt "quite sure, however they may differ from us on unimportant minutiae". After thanks were handed out, especially to the stand-in chairman Rev. John Roaf, the meeting was wound up with nine cheers for "Liberty all over the world".

A petition to parliament was drafted, signed by Fry and Lovell, and published in the *Bristol Mercury*. It stated:

The PETITION of the undersigned INHABITANTS of BRISTOL and its Vicinity, agreed upon at a Public Meeting held in the City, on the 22nd day of October, 1830, Humbly sheweth, That it is with sentiments of great and unfeigned respect and loyalty, that your Majesty on behalf of 800,000 of our fellow-subjects, unjustly held in Slavery in your Majesty's dominions. That your Petitioners are of opinion that all persons held in Slavery are entitled, not only to freedom, but also to compensation, from those that have held them, for all the loss and suffering that they endured, during the time they have been enslaved.[541]

The very next morning James Acland defiantly responded to the previous evening's event by writing in *The Bristolian*:

Let Mr Claxton and all his forces try once more to put down public opinion... The people are aroused to a sense of justice by the home-proceedings of the enemies of humanity. Nor will they be put down by a few noisy dealers in slaves and sugar.[542]

Claxton would not be silenced and just days after the meeting he issued a placard of his own that contained six resolutions which he would have put forward "if the Chairman had acted with impartiality". He couldn't resist his most vitriolic invective for the leaders of abolition (though strangely Clarkson wasn't attacked):

I omit an infinite number of instances of Christian charity, and simply conclude by asserting that it is my opinion William Wilberforce has been actuated by vanity; Master Stephen, by a sort of madness; Z. Macaulay and Co., by profit; and Henry Brougham, by the use the Society is to him as a mean parasitical crew, through whose influence he hopes to obtain a high situation for life. That what all these leaders utter on the walk of mind, the march of intellect, the trot of reason, and the canter of new light, will in the end be found nothing but the gallop of humbug; real philanthropy belongs to none of them—all is cant and trickery.[543]

After the disrupted anti-slavery meeting a petition with 89 signatures was sent to Mayor John Savage calling for him to chair a second public assembly at the Guildhall to debate the issue of emancipation. The Mayor declined so the petitioners resolved to reconvene once again at the Assembly Rooms on 9th November. Once again fighting broke out as the Claxtonians attempted to seize the stage and drown out the speakers. There was some confusion as to who had requested the presence of constables, but nonetheless they waded into the crowd with staves attacking all and sundry. It appears the crowd gave as good as they got and finally the meeting was called to some sort of order. Claxton's arch-opponent James Acland wasn't at the meeting and on taking the stage the Captain took the opportunity to regale the crowd. He claimed that if the law of England "did not allow of any restraint upon the personal liberty of the subject... [then why was there] coercive labour in England as well as the West Indies". He also slammed the sugar boycotters as hypocrites, inadvertently exposing the pernicious extent of slavery produced goods throughout British society in the process:

Some persons are so conscientious on the slave question, that they will not eat sugar made in the West Indies. Dear sensitive souls! Do they ever use a cotton hand-kerchief? Do they ever use cotton clothing?—cotton furniture round their downy beds? Do they ever smoke a cigar, take snuff, or use tobacco in any shape. To be consistent, they should refuse also the one and the other—all these articles being raised by the slave-labour of the western world.[544]

Claxton then claimed: "…that the condition of the Slaves was comfortable—that they were generally well treated…" and that there had been amelioration of their condition, contrary to the previous speakers, and finished his rhetoric with a call for compensation for the slave-holders.[545] The raucous meeting wound up with a resolution to put the question of compensation to Parliament.[546] Although the petition never materialised this debate in Bristol over gradualism and compensation for the slave owners would be reflected across the nation and in Parliament over the next three years. Interestingly the debate over gradualism had already taken place within the anti-slavery camp.

In May 1830, at the annual general meeting in London of the Anti-Slavery Society, modest Thomas Clarkson had moved that Wilberforce chair the meeting "as the great leader of our cause" and in his last public appearance Wilberforce replied that there was "no person more dear to me than my valued friend and fellow-labourer". Despite this the 'gradualist' old guard were now confronted by new younger members who wanted immediate action. Taking their cue from Elizabeth Heyrick, the Female Society from Birmingham submitted a motion for the immediate end to slavery in the British Colonies. This was matched by Henry Pownall who proposed that the Society demand "that from and after the 1st January 1830 every slave born within the King's dominions shall be free". Buxton vainly expressed his disapproval and Wilberforce tried to silence the crowd's cheers of appreciation. Having forced his hand, Wilberforce agreed to put the resolution to a vote. An overwhelming majority carried the declaration to abandon the 'gradualist' approach to emancipation and press immediately for the 'entire Abolition of Colonial Slavery'.[547]

Writer Zerbanoo Gifford claims that the campaign against slavery "united Britain more than any other issue" and clearly there was a massive groundswell of support for emancipation in 1830. The problem was translating this popular pressure into government policy as most of the supporters of manumission couldn't vote.[548] By the end of the year the Bristol Auxiliary had followed its female sister society by officially writing to the London Committee to formally request a switch to immediate emancipation.[549] Incidentally, Wilberforce, unlike Clarkson, was opposed to the participation of women in collecting signatures:

...for ladies to meet, to go from house to house stirring up petitions—these appear to me proceedings unsuited to the female character as delineated in the scriptures.[550]

On 28th January 1831 'A Loyal and Constitutional Meeting' in opposition to reform was held at the *White Lion Tavern*, with Thomas Daniel in the chair.[551] Despite some wavering amongst the Whigs, it was clearly not in the interest of the West India lobby to support reform. The previous year had seen a sharp rise in agitation for an extension of the franchise, with mass campaigning bodies known as Political Unions being formed in most of the major cities in Britain. In light of this the Bristol Political Union had first been projected by James Acland in *The Bristolian* of October 1830.[552] This movement, which combined republican inspired radicals and gradualist reformers alike, gained momentum in November 1830 after the fall of Wellington's staunchly anti-reform government. For most anti-slavery activists, an extension of the franchise offered the possibility of breaking the hold on Parliament of the West India lobby. Hochschild describes the latter as:

a steadily growing, well organised bloc of more than 50 MPs [that] had West Indian landholdings or commercial ties...Their spokesmen were smooth and articulate types who professed themselves completely concerned about the slaves' welfare.[553]

It was a combination of the reform crisis, a massive rural uprising known as the Swing Riots and the threat of mass protest in the capital that led to the collapse of Wellington's Tory government in November 1830. Whig leader Lord Grey then stepped in to lead the country, but his reform bill was then scuppered by the Tory committees in early April and in response the Whigs asked for the dissolution of Parliament. Another election was called for the 28th April to 1st June 1831, leading to a landslide win for the Whigs. This was reflected in Bristol where there was no contest and the city returned two Whig MPs, James Evan Baillie and abolitionist Edward Protheroe junior.[554] Old Tory incumbent Richard Hart Davis issued an address as an Anti-Reformer but chose not to stand in the end in order to avoid the "mischiefs" of a hotly contested election. During the proceedings maltster and chemist William Herapath called on Bristolians to reform themselves; stating that:

[with] the king and his government on your side ...this is the last opportunity of getting quietly and constitutionally, at a trifling sacrifice, that reform which France, Poland and Italy have been obliged to bleed for.[555]

As a consequence the Bristol General Union was formed in June 1831 for the "mutual protection of those mechanics who might suffer from voting conscientiously" and to "keep a watchful eye" on the Members while gathering information regarding their use of "charitable funds". Leading the Union was William Herapath himself and a handful of other 'professional' men; the majority of the members though weren't "above the grade of mechanics, the more influential of the liberal party having kept aloof".

On the 19th September the Reform Bill was finally passed in the House of Commons by a substantial majority, only to be thrown out by the House of Lords on 7th October—this immediately led to radicals seeking abolition of the Lords. On the 12th October 1831, when 60,000 were walking in protest on St James's Palace to present an address to the king, new Bristol Mayor Charles Pinney gave permission for the 'party of progress' to meet at the Guildhall; numbers were so great that they had to reconvene in Queen Square. Among those addressing the crowds were Edward Protheroe junior (by now MP), John Hare, William Herapath and Dr Lant Carpenter, where resolutions were passed unanimously, along with the mandatory loyal address to the king, to great acclaim. Meanwhile the Tories, elated after their victory in the House of Lords, "were unsparing in their taunts and defiance".[556]

'The British slaves are rising'

The failure of the Reform Bill to pass through the House of Lords in early October 1831 was the straw that finally broke the back of the pent-up desire for reform amongst the masses. Huge political union meetings of up to 150,000 people were held throughout the country and when Parliament 'prorogued' [unsatisfactorily ending a parliamentary session] on the 20th October, Britain was "within a measurable distance of civil war".[557]

Protests and riots rocked England, spreading from the East Midlands to the South West. Hot on the heels of serious unrest in first Derby and then Nottingham, the Bristol Reform Riots of 29th–31st October changed the city forever. Targets for the rioters included the Corporation (Mansion House, Custom House and Excise Office), the clergy (Cathedral and the Bishop's Palace), the prison system (New Gaol, Bridewell, Lawford's Gate and Debtors Gaol) and the Dock Company (Toll Houses in Prince's Street and Cumberland Road). The houses of the wealthy on elegant Queen Square were also destroyed by fire as were their nearby warehouses alongside the docks.

One concerned and horrified witness to the destruction was William Wilberforce who was taking the waters at Bath, which also experienced a reform inspired 'riot', just 14 miles down the road. He wrote to one of his sons:

Not a single gaol is left undestroyed. The Bishop's Palace (and Deanery too I'm told), burnt to the ground. The Custom House ditto, Mansion House ditto... The redness of the sky from the conflagration was quite a dreadful sight.

Wilberforce was concerned with the popular discontent around Reform and continued his letter by saying that if there were any further "grumblings of the volcano" he would flee Bath for his son's country parsonage "before the lava burst forth".[558]

What angered the protestors the most was the stance of the generally hated anti-reformist Recorder of Bristol, Sir Charles Wetherell[559], and the position of the Anglican Church; some twenty-two Bishops had voted against the Reform Bill in the House of Lords, including the Bishop of Bristol. Wetherell's arrival in Bristol sparked the unrest and Charles Davies, one of the rioters hanged for his part in the affray, was alleged to have said that the cry around Bristol was "Down with the churches and mend the roads with them". In addition to the attacks on the Cathedral and the burning of the Bishop's Palace, anti-slavery campaigner Samuel Blackwell had to step in to stop the rioters descending on St Mary Redcliffe Church. Meanwhile the Bishop of Bath and Wells, as a precaution, had the drawbridge raised on his palace at Wells—the last time this act was to be performed.[560]

The riot in Bristol was put down by the military in brutal fashion. To this day the numbers of dead and maimed haven't been fully ascertained; they certainly ran into hundreds and the 'Butchers Bill' was without doubt greater than that for the infamous Peterloo massacre of 1819. The size of the protest movement led by the political unions and the shock of the violent unrest, allied with fears of republican revolution, allowed reformers to apply increasing pressure on Britain's rulers over the question of expanding the franchise. Mayor of Bristol Charles Pinney was later tried for his part in the riots under the charge of 'neglect of duty', but after the sixth day of the trial the jury returned a verdict of 'Not Guilty', and prosecutions against the aldermen were also subsequently withdrawn. Colonel Brereton, commander of the 14th Dragoons during the riots was less fortunate. He was also accused of negligence, committed suicide during his trial and became the scapegoat for the whole affair. Another officer, Captain Warrington, also of the Dragoons, was deprived of his commission. Of the 81 prisoners charged with being involved in the riots, four were hanged, one reprieved (apparently insane), 26 transported for life, seven 'banished' for up to 14 years and 43 sentenced to imprisonment and hard labour.[561] Pinney would go on to serve the Society of Merchant Venturers as Warden three times (in 1840, 1849 and 1852) and as Master in 1844.

After the events of October in Bristol, Thomas Daniel presided over yet another meeting of the anti-reformers on 1st December 1831 where *The Times* reported him as saying "anarchists, atheists, robbers and incendiaries were the only allies of Lord Grey's ministry".[562] Several of the West India merchants suffered damage to their property in the riots, including Daniel, Christopher Claxton and Charles Pinney, who all put in claims for compensation. Other West India claimants included James Cunningham, Benjamin Bickley and the Bernard family; Philip John Miles lost his house at 61 Queen Square and his warehouse behind it.[563]

On 22nd December 1831 Mayor Charles Pinney wrote the following revealing letter to Christopher Claxton, the firebrand organiser of pro-slavery activists in Bristol:

> ...more than ordinary exertions had been recently made there [plantations in the Caribbean], by societies formed for the express purpose of emancipating the slaves in the West Indian Colonies, and perhaps more indiscretion shewn in the choice of language applied to those more deeply interested in the West India properties; and the careless use of the terms, **liberty** and **slavery**, and the promulgation of ill-digested notions of the very elements of society, arising out of these discussions, and rendered acrimonious by the peculiar character of the times, engendered a spirit in Bristol, (a city to which the West India interest has always been and must ever be of so much importance,) the future influence of which has not yet been either fully weighted or felt. And it is worthy of note, that this spirit arose in direct hostility to the **leading interests** in Bristol, and a notion was inculcated with great industry among the lowest orders, that the great merchants, to whom they had been wont to look up with respect, were drawing their resources from human blood, and were collecting their revenues through the whip and slave driver. This feeling engendered the names of slave and master became easily transferrable, whenever the demagogue should find it an object worthy of his art...[564]

This letter reveals a fracture in the supposed relationship of patronage in Bristol, in that the "lowest orders" were showing "direct hostility" (rather than "respect") to the "great merchants" on the basis that the latter were deriving their power and wealth from slavery ("human blood"). Even more worrying for members of the Bristol elite such as Pinney was the fact that the social relation of 'slave and master' could be easily transposed from the Caribbean plantations to represent the power relations between the "lowest orders" and the "great merchants". Coincidentally, Pinney's letter was written a few days before the 'slave and master' relationship in Jamaica met its severest test.

The Emancipation Rebellion

‖ **1831**—Slave rebellions in Antigua, Jamaica and Virginia.[565]

Discontent began in Antigua in March 1831 after the planters tried to suppress gatherings of both the enslaved and black and white 'freemen' at the local Sunday markets. These crowds confronted military units sent to disperse them and over the following days the unrest spread to the plantations of which 22 were destroyed by fire. The colony's Governor concluded that their real cause:

> …was not the abolition of the markets. The "root of the Evil" which lay "much deeper" and which was therefore more difficult to remedy was the "state of feverish excitement" among the slaves who expected their "early and unconditional emancipation"… on "this fatal subject" the minds of the slaves were "evidently becoming daily more and more unsettled".[566]

These serious events in Antigua were greatly overshadowed by what was to follow in Jamaica only a few months later.

Caribbean Historian Richard Hart described the great Emancipation Rebellion in Jamaica of December 1831 as being "a sure indication that if slavery was not soon abolished from above it would be destroyed from below".[567] Hart summarised the uprising thus:

> The Emancipation Rebellion in Western Jamaica, commencing on the night of December 27, 1831, was the most extensive and effective of all the many rebellions in the Anglophone Caribbean area. Brilliantly planned and secretly organised under the leadership of Sam Sharpe [an enslaved Baptist Deacon], whose motivation was devoutly Christian, its central strategy was a general strike against slavery. This was supported by a military plan and an arson campaign, to be implemented if, as anticipated, the strikers' demands were not conceded.

> The rebellion was suppressed by the combined operations of the British military and naval forces and the militia, the final embers being extinguished in the first week of April 1832. 201 rebels were reported killed in action. Approximately 750 slaves and 14 free persons were convicted of acts of rebellion by courts martial and in the courts. Most of those placed on trial were sentenced to death. Others were given savage sentences of from 200 to 500 lashes of the whip, with or without imprisonment. Only 21 appear to have been sentenced to transportation.

The conduct of Sharpe and many of the other convicted rebels was exemplary. To the Minister of Religion who interviewed him in prison while he was awaiting execution, Sharpe made this firm declaration: 'I would rather die upon yonder gallows than live in slavery!'[568]

Also known as the 'Baptist War' or 'Christmas Rebellion'—initially the idea was for the enslaved not to work on Christmas Day—up to 60,000 slaves (out of a population of 300,000) were mobilised by Sam Sharpe and his supporters. Once again rumours of impending emancipation decrees from the King arriving in Jamaica helped stoke the fires of revolt. Sharpe was chief deacon in a Baptist missionary chapel in Montego Bay, was literate and had access to British newspapers. It is highly likely Sharpe knew that no emancipation bill had been passed (despite preaching the opposite to his congregation) and that England had been wracked with its own 'uprisings' due to the reform unrest in late 1831.[569]

The damage done to the island's economy was immense with more than 200 plantations damaged to the tune of £1.1 million (equivalent in 2016 to about £1.3 billion by GDP per capita). Of the 750 slaves who were convicted of rebellion at its bloody conclusion more than 340 were executed by hanging or shooting. It is interesting to note that of the 14 'free persons' who were convicted of aiding the rebels (and in some cases executed), two were white: a sailor and a plantation official. This small number of mixed heritage and white people may mask a

wider network supporting the uprising amongst 'free' Jamaican colonists. One group of Whites who were blamed and punished by the planters for the uprising, regardless of their complicity, were the Methodist and Baptist missionaries.[570]

The uprising was witnessed by William Knibb who afterwards was urged by his congregation to return to Britain in 1832 and join the campaign for slave liberation. Knibb returned to England from Jamaica just as the Reform Bill was being made law and on hearing the news declared "Now I'll have slavery down".[571] He toured the country and eloquently argued against slavery while describing his experiences in Jamaica. Before both Houses of Parliament, he explained how nonconformist churches

Sam Sharpe, leader of the Jamaican Emancipation Rebellion in 1831.

Co-joined uprisings in Bristol and Jamaica in 1831 as imagined by artist Rachel Hewitt.

were doing good work and how colonial oppression had resulted in appalling cruelty that was still being meted out to the enslaved. He then related that during the uprising he had to go into hiding himself as the planters wanted to murder him and other missionaries they blamed for the rebellion.[572] Some twenty Methodist and Baptist chapels were burnt down by White mobs and militia during the rebellion. Henry Bleby, the minister who had interviewed Sharpe, narrowly escaped with his life after being beaten and tarred; he was just about to be torched when some of his black supporters rescued him.[573]

Knibb was a good speaker and, more than any other witness, his powerful evidence convinced many that slavery had to be speedily abolished. In one powerful speech he laid bare the facts surrounding religion for the enslaved in Jamaica:

> I appear as the feeble and unworthy advocate of 20,000 Baptists in Jamaica, who have no places of worship, no Sabbath, no houses of prayer... the greater part of these 20,000 will be flogged every time they are caught praying... I call upon children, by the cries of the infant slave whom I saw flogged on Macclesfield estate... I call upon parents, by the blood-streaming back of Catherine Williams, who, with a heroism England has seldom known, preferred a dungeon to the surrender of her honour. I call upon Christians, by the lacerated William Black, of King's Valley, whose back, a month after flogging, was not healed.

Knibb continued "If Samuel Sharpe had been a nobleman fighting to free the Poles from Russian rule; Britons would have built a monument to him".[574]

In the aftermath of the rebellion, early Trade Unionist, printer and publisher (and later Chartist) Henry Hetherington described the enslaved Africans of Jamaica as "brothers" and was deeply sarcastic about "Christian civilisation" and the label "savages" which had been ascribed to the rebels. Writing in his *Poor Man's Guardian* in February 1832 he explained the difference between chattel slavery and 'wage slavery' and made some interesting comparisons between those butchered in Jamaica with the hundreds of people killed and injured in Bristol and Nottingham (also by the British military but this time in the reform riots of October 1831). Hetherington finished his article by stating that he stood unequivocally for immediate emancipation at the hands of the enslaved:

the poor blacks think for themselves, and have come, it seems, to a determination of no longer sacrificing their natural freedom, and all their privileges and interests as human beings, (for human beings they are, or at any rate have full right to call themselves) for the exclusive advantage of a foreign nation, that in return, treats them with the greatest possible cruelty and contempt—that looks at them as mere beasts of the field, without even allowing their claim to that humanity which is not only denied, but is ensured 'by law', to brute animals!

Ironically the whole article went under the auspices of Edward Colston's mantra "*Go thou and do likewise*" although in this case Hetherington was referring to the spread of revolts of the enslaved throughout Britain's Dominions.[575]

Throughout 1832, thanks in no small part to the first-hand accounts of the plantation system and the rebellion in Jamaica by eye-witnesses such as William Knibb, the reinvigorated anti-slavery movement was strengthened by public demands for emancipation. Petitions to Parliament were showing definitively that the highest proportions of support for emancipation were from the lower middle and working classes. The impact of the Antiguan and Jamaican revolts on Britain's ruling class was immense. From the military, politicians and even managers of plantations in Jamaica came stark warnings about further uprisings. The Naval Commander for the West Indies, Vice Admiral Charles Fleming, a witness before the parliamentary committee stated:

The only reason why [the slaves] are tranquil now is, that they... hope to be emancipated. If they were not freed, he declared, insurrection will soon take place...

With the ghost of the disastrous British campaign of the 1790s in Saint-Domingue (Haiti) haunting them, many in government realised that a widespread war in the Caribbean colonies was probably beyond the capacity of the military. That left one option: emancipation.

'Slavery was becoming a dirty word'

In June 1832, under Earl Grey's administration, the Reform Act was finally passed, doing away with 'rotten boroughs', increasing the number of seats in the Commons and enlarging the English electorate to about 20 per cent of all adult males.[576] In Bristol, unlike the newer cities of the midlands and north of England which in some cases didn't have any representation at all, the number of voters changed to a lesser, but still significant, degree.[577]

The first post-reform election was set for December 1832 and it was won in Bristol by the two pro-slavery candidates, ultra-Tory 'Conservative' Sir Richard Vyvyan in tacit coalition with the moderate Whig, James Evan Baillie. The Protheroe camp complained afterwards "the cause of Reform has been betrayed, and by the Old Whigs of Bristol".[578] Unfortunately it seems the 'old ways' were not going to be swept away in Bristol as easily as the reformers might have hoped, expected, or deserved:

> Evidence presented in support of an unsuccessful petition suggested that bribery remained endemic, and the activities of the newly formed Conservative Operatives' Association, a supposedly charitable body, were a particular cause of complaint. In 1833 the municipal commissioners produced a damning report on the corporation, concluding that it was 'a very unfavourable specimen' of the closed system and that 'the desire of power' appeared to be its 'ruling principle', even when this was detrimental to the city's interests.[579]

As soon as the new Parliament met in 1833, campaigning for the Slavery Abolition Act inside and outside the institution intensified; significantly the MPs that made up the pro-slavery lobby had been halved in size by the election of the previous year. The hitherto powerful figures that made up the West India interest recognised that their decades-long grasp on Westminster, that had protected the slave system and their financial interests, was beginning to slip. Consequently, they changed tack and began demanding compensation in earnest for the 'human property' that was going to be taken away from them. In the end these slave-holders pulled off one of the greatest swindles on the British tax-payer in history.

> **1833**—Emancipation [Slavery Abolition] Act was passed (becomes law in 1834) stipulating that slaves in the British empire will formally become free only after a four-year[580] period of 'apprenticeship'.

With the Emancipation Rebellion in Jamaica still resonating, the Government's first scheme for the nominal abolition of slavery was set at 1st

Jamaican schoolroom at the time of the Emancipation.

August 1834, the enslaved then being referred to as 'apprentices' with field hands working free of charge for 12 years and domestic servants doing the same for seven years. To sweeten the deal for the slave-owners, during the period of transition, they were to receive a loan from the Treasury of £15 million. To qualify for the loan each British Caribbean Island Assembly had to agree to enact statutes on similar terms. Unbelievably, Thomas Buxton, the parliamentary spokesman for the Anti-Slavery Society, initially supported the scheme but other members were so powerfully opposed to it that Buxton had to withdraw the Society's support. They then pressed for a reduction in the length of time of apprenticeship and requested that no compensation be given to the slave-owners.[581] After the initial scheme was rejected in Parliament a compromise was reached.

Finally, the Slavery Abolition Act in the British West India Colonies was given Royal Assent in August 1833 and was planned to come into force the following August.[582] In order to get the Act passed it was agreed, despite the opposition of many abolitionists, that the slave holders were to receive £20 million in compensation—now a gift and not a loan—from British tax-payers. This huge sum was equivalent to five per cent of the Gross Domestic Product and 40 per cent of the national budget in 1834. Translated to a proportion of the national budget in 2018 it has been conservatively estimated to be equivalent to about £240 billion.[583] Subsequent research has shown that the compensation claims numbered 46,000 and that slave ownership was not just the province of the super-rich but crossed over into the middle-classes.[584] The huge payment made to the slave owners forced the government to borrow £15 million from the Rothschild banking dynasty who benefited from the interest on the loan. It is astonishing that overall debt wasn't fully paid off until 2015—a lengthy 181 years of expenditure by British tax-payers.[585]

For many anti-slavery activists, the Emancipation Act was sullied by the huge amount of public money paid in compensation to the wealthy slave-holders whilst the enslaved received nothing. At a Public Meeting held on Brandon Hill on the evening of Monday 5th August 1833, it was announced that the printer of the *Poor Man's Guardian*, Henry Hetherington would take the chair:

> We are assembled this evening for the purpose of entering our protest against the grant of £20,000,000 to the slave owners, for emancipating their slaves; and this subject is of the very first importance to you, and to all who live by their labour, for the sum must, at last come out of the labour of the honest and industrious people of England (applause). Let me ask you in what does slavery consist? The advocates of emancipation, in Parliament, will tell you that it consists in ill-paid and unrequited labour: I say, then, that upon this principle, they should rather vote £20,000,000 to disenthrall and compensate the slaves of England (cheers).

Then the real nub of the matter:

> But what makes them now so anxious to liberate the slaves, and to compensate the planters? Why this: the slaves had resolved to be slaves no longer, but to liberate themselves; and the moment they resolve this, we kindly step in, generously resolve to give them that freedom which they had resolved to take, and to compensate their masters for the loss of that which they must have lost but for our interposition (applause)...

He continued:

> The *Times* says "they will no longer be subjected to the cart-whip of the driver; and that instead of that they will be placed under the protection of the law and the magistracy." I say, it is better for them to be slaves, as before. I happen to know something of what an English magistrate is made of; and I do not know whether I would not prefer to be subject to the whip of a Scotch slave driver, than to the will of an English magistrate (hear). I know that an English magistrate's protection is death and destruction to the poor man (applause)...

The speaker then asks who had more right to compensation:

What right, I ask, has the West-Indian planter to compensation? ("none.") Compensation is rather due to the slave for his many years of forced labour. If a man engage, in this country, in anything illegal and is wronged, they tell him it is useless to seek a remedy in law. If a man pick my pocket of a watch and pawn it, I can recover it of the pawnbroker, without paying him compensation. But the men now constituting what is called the Reformed Parliament, but which I call the Deformed Parliament (a laugh), care not how many millions they vote away, so long as it comes not out of their pockets…

Hetherington finished his speech by lambasting the aristocracy and the Duke of Wellington; the *Bristol Mercury* believed the meeting was under the auspices of the National Union of the Working Classes and contested the number of people said to have been in attendance. Estimates of the size of the crowd ranged from 300 (in the *Mercury*) to 2,000 in the *Bath Chronicle* and 5,000 according to Hetherington.[586]

‖ **1834** Revolt against apprenticeship on St Kitts.

Some sources claim that slavery was abolished in the British Empire on 1ˢᵗ August 1834 but in reality only the enslaved below the age of six were actually freed on this date. All others effectively remained in bondage as *unpaid* apprentices for given periods of time. The original terms of this so-called 'apprenticeship' had been moderated in the Bill to six years for field hands—the majority—and four years for the remainder.[587] Anti-slavery activists in Britain campaigned vigorously for this clause to be dropped from the Bill but it took the actions of the enslaved across the British Caribbean to force the issue. Rather than being a day for the celebration of emancipation, the 1ˢᵗ August 1834 became a flashpoint for protests, strikes and riots against the apprenticeship scheme.

When the Emancipation Bill and the 'apprenticeships' were announced by the Governor to a crowd of elderly enslaved Africans in Port of Spain, Trinidad on August 1ˢᵗ, they began chanting "Pas de six ans. Point de six ans" ("Not six years. No six years") drowning him out. Peaceful protests followed until a resolution was passed to abolish the apprenticeship system, making Trinidad the first British colony to completely abolish slavery.[588] In Antigua the Colonial Assembly debated the scheme and:

…decided that the conflicts that apprenticeship was likely to produce were too great; on this small island the planters had an effective monopoly of all cultivatable land and the field labourers thus found they had to work on the plantations if they were to eat. The island Assembly thus ended apprenticeship of its own accord, granting full freedom to all.[589]

Jamaican treadmill used as punishment during the 'Apprenticeship' period.

A similar approach was followed in Bermuda.

The question of whether freed 'apprentices' would be forced to work for their original masters or could survive without labouring on the plantations for a wage was crucial to the land-owners. This issue turned on how much access to land the newly freed had and their capability for sustaining subsistence agriculture. These were precisely the issues which had underpinned enclosure, the creation of landless proletarians from the peasantry and the rise of capitalism in Britain for more than two hundred years. In the British Caribbean the planters were aiming to replace the forced labour of chattel slavery with the coercion of wage labour for the landless.

The colonial assemblies of Trinidad, Antigua and Bermuda clearly made a tactical decision to free the enslaved based on the potential resistance of the 'apprentices', their access to land and thus subsistence. In other areas of the Caribbean, in different circumstances, the planters enforced the apprenticeship scheme and resistance to it was met by severe repression.

In St Kitts, a Wesleyan missionary complained:

And it was difficult to make them [the former slaves] understand how they could be "discharged of and from all manner of slavery, and absolutely and forever manumitted", and yet be compelled to work the greater part of their time for the same masters without adequate wages. Freedom and compulsory labour, without payment, and for no crime, appeared to them incongruous . . . and all my attempts to show apprenticeship was a part payment for absolute unconditional freedom were in some cases unsatisfactory. I am fully persuaded, therefore, that had the term "slavery" been retained with the modification of the present system, it would have been productive of far less confusion.

It seems the enslaved in St Kitts weren't as confused (or naïve) as the missionaries about the new Bill and its literally "binding" apprenticeship clause:

They were frequently heard to express that "they would give their souls to hell and their bodies to the sharks" rather than be bound to work as apprentices. Their watch-word, not limited to St. Kitts, was, "Me free; no bind; no work". [590]

This verbal resistance was matched by action. On 1st August, after being compelled to work, a strike by the newly 'apprenticed' workers commenced. It spread rapidly from estate to estate, leading the Solicitor General of the island, Robert Claxton, to state:

There is little doubt that emissaries have been sent from the leading gangs to the others, for the purpose of confirming them in their determination to strike work after the 1st of August. And it is to be lamented that the occasions and manner in which their missions have been conducted have hitherto remained undetected. The head people upon many estates, who have hitherto been confidential and trustworthy, have betrayed a reluctance to converse with their masters on this subject; and others have admitted the fact of the general combination to strike. [591]

By 6th August martial law was in force on the island and estate mangers began to punish the 'ring leaders' with public floggings and imprisonment. As a result, many hundreds of former slaves fled to the mountains in the interior, joining up with other 'runaways' who had gone 'marooning' and had not been seen for years. [592] A major military operation was launched to flush them out, whilst soldiers and militia burned the fugitive's homes and what little property they owned. Eventually sixteen of the leaders, including two women, were tried for rebellion; five were deported to Bermuda, the others each receiving 24 to 100 lashes. [593] News of the St Kitts revolt travelled across the British Caribbean colonies encouraging other 'apprentices' to resist.

In Demerara (Guyana) on 1st August, the 'freed' celebrated their emancipation:

It was a public holiday and many Africans who were now Christians attended religious services. Others danced in their homes, in their yards and in the streets and the merry-making continued late into the night. But a rude shock awaited all the ex-slaves early the following morning when they were ordered back to the fields and other workplaces. This caused great confusion since they failed to understand how they could have gained their freedom and still be forced to work in their detested old posts.

As a result, refusals to work and disturbances broke out in both the east and west of Demerara whilst the Governor desperately travelled the colony trying to restore order and restrain the planters who wanted to introduce martial law. They had already responded with floggings and sentences on the treadmill for men and women who resisted.[594]

Further north on the Essequibo coast there were work stoppages to which the planters responded by killing the livestock of the workers and cutting down fruit trees. This action was specifically aimed at removing subsistence from the ex-slaves so that they would have to continue to work for the planters. Over 700 'apprentices' refused to work in response and 40 soldiers from the British West India Regiment were sent to suppress the strike. The unarmed strikers gathered in a church courtyard and raised a flag to demonstrate their freedom and independence from the planters. When one of the leading plantation owners, Charles Bean, ordered the troops to open fire on the peaceful protest, the commander of the unit, Captain Groves, refused. The Governor arrived shortly after and managed to defuse the situation but subsequently several ring-leaders, including their 'captain' Damon were arrested and tried for rebellion. Despite the fact that the protests and strikes had largely been non-violent, four of the 'apprentices' were sentenced to terms of imprisonment and severe floggings, while two were sentenced to transportation to Australia. Damon was given the death sentence and was publicly hanged in Georgetown on 13th October 1834.[595]

On St Vincent the apprenticeship scheme was resisted on numerous estates on the island by protests and refusals to work throughout the period of 1834–1838. Women were at the forefront of these struggles and they often bore the brunt of the punishments meted out by the planters. Although measures to ameliorate the condition of the enslaved had supposedly outlawed the cruellest abuses, including the flogging of women, this statement proves it wasn't so: "in July 1833, when the abolition of slavery was a certainty, the local legislature in St Vincent insisted on retaining the flogging of women in its new slave codes".[596] The brutality also continued in different forms. On the estates female apprentices who transgressed were 'sentenced' to solitary confinement in complete darkness in rat infested cells, whilst a trip to the island's 'houses of correction' was a horrific experience:

The cage and gaols were scenes of terror and degradation for women. During the day, apprentices sentenced to hard labour in Kingstown had to work the treadmill, regardless of their age, sex or level of fitness. Their arms were strapped to bars above their heads and they were forced to tread on the revolving steps of the mill or have their legs hit by the steps. Observers claimed that in some houses of correction in the British Caribbean, the floors under the treadmills were splattered with blood... rape was reputedly common within the penal systems throughout the Caribbean, committed by the guards, drivers and male prisoners. Men and women were only segregated at night. Prisoners also frequently had to wear chains and neck collars, both during the day and at night.[597]

Flogging of male apprentices was commonplace and sometimes applied to women in the 'houses of correction'. Some magistrates placed apprentices in stocks. These punishments were meant to instil terror in the 'apprentices', to force them to work and obey their (ex) 'masters'. Despite this, resistance was widespread and not just realised in strikes or protests, but in the everyday experience. Female apprentices engaged in theft, absence from work, gave abuse and were insolent to their overseers and 'masters', carried out acts of vandalism and refused to pay the land-owners. Male apprentices were accused of idleness, neglect of work, absence, 'running away', drunkenness, 'disobedience' and carried out assaults on their overseers. The most common offence for both genders however, was 'withdrawal of labour' with women often leading the way. In 1835 alone, the magistrates on St Vincent recorded "2764 offences, of which 1287 were committed by women" out of a pre-emancipation population of 22,250.[598] One of the most rebellious estates on the island was *Arnos Vale*, a name synonymous with Bristol, where hundreds of apprentices were brutally punished "for insubordination, indolence and neglect of duty".[599]

As we have seen, in some British colonies, such as Trinidad, the protests of the 'apprentices' which began on 'emancipation' day in 1834 were successful. However, these acts should not be confused with benevolence on the part of the plantocracy. In Antigua and Bermuda, the decision to emancipate was made because the plantation owners realised that they could guarantee that the freed slaves would have to work for them in order to survive. In some cases it was also cheaper to pay a daily wage than to feed and house their 'apprentices'. In the colonies where the apprenticeship schemes were retained, opposition to the overseers, land-owners and magistrates over several years was both heroic and unrelenting. Historian Richard Hart noted:

The courageous resistance of these apprentices contributed materially to the decision of the British Government to recommend to the colonial legislatures the shortening of the apprenticeship period to four years. This resulted in slavery being completely abolished on August 1, 1838.[600]

Despite the end of 'apprenticeship' and the supposed 'full' emancipation in the West Indies, serious hardship continued for the newly freed enslaved. The plantations were still in the hands of the plantocracy who owned not only the land but controlled local government, the courts and also decided taxes and rates of pay. The 'free board and lodging' entailed working long hours and enduring restrictive practices such as the hated 'company shops' which were being introduced into the colonies just as they were being outlawed in Britain.[601] Slavery might have been abolished but the struggles of the new proletarians in the Caribbean colonies were just beginning.

From plantations to factories

It is estimated that approximately half of the £20 million claimed by slave owners in compensation for their 'loss' was paid to those resident in Britain. Detailed research for this book, carried out by the authors using the UCL *Legacies of British Slave-ownership* database, has demonstrated that those claimants who gave addresses in Bristol obtained about £430,208 for the ownership of an estimated 18,212 enslaved people (see Appendix 6); a conservative figure which agrees relatively well with previous estimates.[602] This huge sum was equivalent in 2016 to £520 million (by GDP per capita) or £1.84 billion (as a share of GDP), or around £6 billion in 2018 (as an equivalent share of the national budget in 1834). Whichever monetary comparison is made, it was a huge financial windfall. This might give the impression that slave-ownership was widespread in the city, but in fact the successful claims for compensation directly linked to Bristol were limited to only 97 individuals. This means that less than 0.1 percent (or 1 in 1000) of Bristolians owned enslaved people in 1834. Of this group, 49 claimants came from 21 family groups and many of these were linked by marriage and/or business to the remaining beneficiaries. These individuals and families were also concentrated in the west of Bristol. Almost two thirds of those who gave full addresses were resident in Clifton and three-quarters lived in Clifton, Redland, Westbury-on-Trym, Cotham or Hotwells.

In 2015 a BBC TV programme, looking at the distribution of the compensation money for slavery, implied that it wasn't just the province of the super-wealthy male elite, but that in fact the middle-classes and women were also beneficiaries.[603] Of the 97 successful claimants in Bristol, just over a quarter were female but they received only four percent of the total sum, typically as heirs through the death of male relatives. The idea that significant amounts of money were disseminated outside of the 'Clifton elite' is scotched by an analysis of the distribution and size of the claims. About half of the compensation money (£243,949) went to only *eight* individuals, most of whom were related or were already in business together. Ninety per cent of the compensation was taken by only 34 individuals, of whom only one was a woman.[604] The suggestion that a significant amount of the compensation money passed into the hands of women or penetrated directly into the middle classes in Bristol is not supported by the evidence.

So, who were the big winners amongst the wealthy male elite? Thomas Daniel, Bristol's 'Grand Old Man' of the West India interest, received the largest sum of any local merchant in compensation for slaves freed (£71,500). Along with his brother and business partner, John Daniel, they 'owned' nearly 4,700 enslaved people in plantations in British Guiana (Demerara), Barbados, Antigua, Nevis, Montserrat, Jamaica and Tobago. Their total bill to the British taxpayer was £137,000 (or £165 million in 2016 based on GDP per capita). Coming in second on the list was James Evan Baillie who along with his father Evan and brother Hugh pocketed £57,000 (£69 million) and their business partner George Ames, merchant and son of Levi Ames (who had set up the 'Bristol New Bank'), received £18,000 (£22 million). The Baillie-Ames business held more than 2,100 captives in shared plantations in British Guiana, Grenada, St Kitts, St Vincent and Trinidad. Third was future Bristol MP Philip Miles, West India merchant, banker and landowner who took about £30,100 (£36 million today) for more than 1,300 enslaved people in Jamaica and Trinidad. Many of these plantation holdings were shared with his nephew and business partner Thomas Kington who trousered £15,300 (£18 million) in compensation. Other notable figures who pocketed significant sums include ex-Mayor Charles Pinney who along with his brother John claimed £23,200 (£28 million) for more than 1,200 slaves mostly in Nevis. Richard Bright another leading member of the West India interest obtained nearly £12,000 (£14 million) for two Jamaican plantations and his son Robert and his business partner George Gibbs shared more than £4,000 for their holdings in Barbados and Jamaica.

It is clear that by far the 'big winners' in the compensation game were the Daniel, Miles, Baillie, Ames, Cunningham and Pinney families who were linked by both marriage and business relationships.[605] These six families 'owned' and had profited off the backs of more than 11,000 enslaved people and took the majority of the compensation money as a result. The super-rich certainly got richer after the emancipation bonanza. Despite the massive pay-outs, for many of Bristol's West India merchants and plantocracy, emancipation was a far greater issue for their interests in the Caribbean than the abolition of the slave trade had ever been. This was reflected in their commitment to retain slavery. Throughout the abolition struggle in the 1830s the West India Association fought a fierce rear-guard action along with their colleagues in London, Liverpool and Glasgow; in 1833–4 alone they disbursed £445 (equivalent in

2016 to about £500,000 by GDP per capita) to meet travel expenses.[606] Now that their cause had finally been lost, the plantocracy resident in the Caribbean and in Britain had to make some serious economic decisions about where to refocus their investments.

In 1835 the Municipal Corporations Act was finally passed which aimed at rooting out the organised corruption and nepotism that riddled many corporations (city councils) throughout England and Wales. Unsurprisingly, Bristol was targeted by the Act, although in 1836 Thomas Daniel was made chairman of the transition to the new Town Council. This was surprising, as Daniel had only recently asked local Conservative MP Vyvyan to try and exempt Bristol from the very same Act! Daniel was then asked to become Mayor again but on reflection declined due to conflict of interest; the Society of Merchant Venturers still owned prime, large and advantageous dockside wharfage.[607] Vyvyan retained his seat at the 1835 general election which he won with fellow Conservative Philip John Miles, who had previously been MP for Westbury and then Corfe (until it was disenfranchised in 1832). This was Bristol's first all-Tory line up since 1780. Vyvyan wasn't too enamoured with his constituents' wants or needs, and years later he would recall that "the Representation of Bristol was a most irksome duty, involving many small details of local business which interfered with great politics". His opposition to emancipation waned as soon as the £20 million in compensation had been garnered for the slave-holders.[608]

It's hard to judge from figures alone the impact of the monies involved in compensation upon the already immensely rich slave-owning families; however, we can gain some insight by examining the Miles family. Their plantation holdings in Jamaica and Trinidad rivalled those of Thomas Daniel and this was reflected in the amount of emancipation compensation money they received. Already a seriously wealthy man, Philip Miles had built his mansion at Leigh Court on the outskirts of Bristol between 1814 and 1818 in order to house his massive art collection which featured works by Poussin, Raphael, Claude, Rubens, Titian and even two works by Leonardo da Vinci and one by Michelangelo, a collection that would make many a sovereign head of state jealous. He had acquired the bulk of his collection from fellow art lover and former Bristol Tory MP Richard Hart Davis, and the public could view it by contacting Miles' counting house in Queen Square.[609] When Miles died in 1845 he was declared Bristol's first ever millionaire—leaving a fortune in excess of that sum.[610]

In the early 1830s, campaigner 'A. Burgess'—reckoned to be the nom de plume of John Barnett Kington—was described as the "most penetrating critic of the unreformed system". He was a Whig accountant "[though] no rabid party man".[611] His numerous letters, essays and tracts published in the *Bristol Mercury* attacked and criticised the corporate governance in the Corporation, the Bristol Dock Company, the Society of Merchant Venturers, the West India 'Monopolists' and even the fledgling Bristol Chamber of Commerce. These public interventions revealed the gross un-competitiveness of Bristol's dock charges—a major symptom of the city's commercial decline, with a strong whiff of the ever-present corruption—and played a part in the reform of these bodies during this turbulent period. At a celebratory 'Important Public Meeting' in the Guildhall on 1st February 1836 Kington recounted in his book the following assessment of the recent reforms:

> ...I advert to the several measures of parliamentary reform, of the abolition of slavery, the opening of the East India trade, the new poor law and municipal reform act; and I contend that the character of each is, in the highest degree, excellent—the effects so far as they have been tried and ascertained, purely beneficial (continued cheering)...[612]

This shows that the Whigs at least connected reform and abolition together as related struggles. The speaker's triumphant tone which suggested "The spirit of discontent and of violence has been deprived of its energy; the impending gloom is dispelled; peace and tranquillity have succeeded them" was wide of the mark. The New Poor Law introduced in 1834 sparked major unrest and would be seen as 'Whig treachery' while the transitional enslaved in the British West Indies were still suffering under the yoke of 'apprenticeship'.

Later that year the new City Council gave an order to Frederick Pickersgill of the Royal Academy to paint a portrait of Alderman Daniel to commemorate his long connection to civic affairs. The chronicler of Bristol, Latimer, complained that as the Corporation was £10,000 in debt at the time it would have been better if the commission had come out of the councillor's own pockets. The portrait cost 150 guineas and Daniel's expenses alone for going to London to sit for it were £24 8s 3d.[613] It appears the ways of 'Old Corruption' were buried pretty deep in the merchant culture of Bristol. Daniel finally surrendered his leadership of Bristol's Tories in 1836.[614]

In the seventeenth and eighteenth centuries chattel slavery and various other forms of forced and bonded labour had provided the engine for the mercantile and plantation systems of early capitalism to develop. The abolition of slavery in the 1830s marked the formal transition from this earlier economic form to industrial capitalism. The compensation money for 'emancipation' acted as useful 'start-up' funding for the West India merchants and plantocracy in Britain to become part of an industrial bourgeoisie, switching from slave labour to wage labour.

It had been a long journey for the Bristol mercantile elite; from small city traders via the commercial monopolies of 'mere merchants' and the Merchant Venturers in the seventeenth century to the slave owning and trading Caribbean plantocracy of the eighteenth that dominated the city in both a political and economic sense. Now this 'elite' were mutating once again, this time into a modern business class that would exploit and dominate the city into the twentieth century. Of course, most of their wealth and power had been built off the backs of forced or coerced labour, whether indigenous, Irish, African or from elsewhere in their 'Empire'. With the demise of slavery they turned their attention to the 'industrial' exploitation of the men, women and children of the Bristolian working class through the burgeoning 'factory system' and the construction of the transport infrastructure to supply it.

Bristol suffered a severe local economic depression as a result of the Reform Riots of 1831, when a large part of the city was in ruins. One of the most visible ramifications of this was that work was suspended on building the Clifton Bridge. Although many rightly thought the bridge 'an ornament', the stoppage demonstrated that Bristol was facing significant problems with financial investment partly because of the damage the riots had done to the city's reputation. Soon after though, other investment was readily forthcoming on ventures that would reshape Bristol's economic landscape. Very little of the £20 million handed out in compensation to the planters in the 1830s was reinvested in the British Caribbean. Instead wealthy ex-slaveholders in Bristol used these massive pay-outs from the tax-payer to finance new projects in their home city. The first mooted concern was the Great Western Railway (GWR) of 1833 which passed into being by an Act of Parliament in 1835; the second was the Great Western Steamship Company (GWSC) whose prospectus was issued in January 1836 and the third was the Great Western Cotton Factory (GWCF) which was inaugurated in 1837. The West India merchants' arrogant choice of slave produced 'King Cotton' to replace Bristol's waning sugar refineries and brass works was a slap in the face for Bristol's abolitionists; and in the background the city's tobacco and cocoa industries continued to grow.

Bristol's mercantile elite had taken the decision to link the city's fortunes with that of London rather than the plantations. As Marshall succinctly put it, "the list of the company's [GWR] original subscribers suggests a broad willingness to replace slaves with sleepers".[615] When they did look west across the sea, the shift in ship design was more to provide communication links with North America than it was to carry commodities to and from the Caribbean colonies.

While the future celebrated engineer Isambard Kingdom Brunel was working on modifications to the Floating Harbour at the time of Bristol's Slavery Election of 1830 and the Reform Riots of 1831, it brought him into "[a] valuable friendship and respect" of Christopher Claxton.[616] After his role as a "zealous partisan and advocate of what was known as the West India interest"[617], Claxton rose quickly in rank through various municipal positions: 'Corn Measurer' from 1832–1833 and then Quay-warden (modern day Harbour Master) for Bristol's Docks from 1833–1848, all the while being a half-pay naval officer. Symptomatic of the corruption at large, Claxton "brazenly flouted his duties" by accepting a £400 stipend for the office he held and then passing £50 of it on to an underling to actually perform these very same duties. This left Claxton free to accept the post of first managing-director of the Great Western Steamship Company in 1835. Knowledge of this cosy arrangement was apparently widespread and led to a torrent of complaints to the Council from angry merchants and ship-owners, but the Corporation remained "amazingly tolerant".[618]

Claxton contributed to the building of both the SS *Great Western* and SS *Great Britain* until the GWSC's bankruptcy in 1846; he also collaborated on Brunel's Clifton Bridge (amongst others). When the SS *Great Western* launched on the 19th July 1837, 50,000 people turned up to see Claxton crack a bottle of Madeira over the demi-figurehead of Neptune. After the launch 300 people enjoyed a banquet in the hull of the ship hosted by Chairman Peter Maze, supported by the Miles family and a multitude of Bristol's prominent merchants and ship-owners. On the return from her maiden voyage from Bristol to New York in 1838 the *Great Western's* cargo was primarily cotton for the newly opened Great Western Cotton Mills [GWCF] in Barton Hill.[619] Claxton outlived Brunel and died in Chelsea in 1868 at the age of 75, seemingly in partial obscurity. Today he's feted as one of the top ten members in the 'Our Heroes' section of the Clifton Suspension Bridge website, with no mention at all of the leading role that he took on behalf of the pro-slavery lobby.[620]

The GWCF was a huge plant in Barton Hill, east Bristol that was opened in 1838. Of the fifteen partners that invested in the business, at least seven of the belated 'cotton kings', Thomas Kington, George Gibbs, Robert Bright, Charles Pinney, Robert Case, George Ames and Henry Bush, had received compensation money as a result of the 'emancipation'. Others, such as Philip William Skynner Miles were part of families which had been remunerated. The GWCF employed around 1,000 workers, mainly low-paid young women and children. From the 1830s to the early twentieth century, workers endured long hours, high rates of industrial accidents and ill-health from the cotton dust and humidity. Moreover, they were subjected to wage cuts and fines by a series of unrelenting managers.[621]

This pattern of investment by Bristol West India merchants and Caribbean 'plantocracy' would be repeated across many new industrial concerns in Bristol and the South West (see Appendix 7). For example, Thomas Daniel invested in the GWR along with his banking interests. Although the Bright family were early opponents of the Bristol Dock & Canal Company (BDC), Robert Bright along with George Gibbs put their money into the scheme, Clifton Bridge, GWR (in which both were promoters and directors) and the GWSC. Edward Protheroe senior already had an extensive industrial empire of iron and coal mines in the Forest of Dean which benefited from the slavery windfall. The Cave family were involved in the manufacture of glass and vitriol, whilst the

Baillies invested in railways, banking and added to their huge tracts of land in their native Scotland. Other West India merchants switched their attention to markets in far-flung parts of the British Empire. Philip John Miles, who already had financial interests in rope, gunpowder, brass and glass manufacturing as well as banking in Bristol, refocused his Caribbean trading activities. Along with partner and nephew Thomas Kington and latterly his second son Edward their firm established commercial activities in Australia and New Zealand, shipping large amounts of colonial produce back to Britain. Edward Miles went on to run the business, becoming a director of the New Zealand Shipping Company, The Union Bank of Australia, The London and Westminster Bank, The Panama, New Zealand and Australian Royal Mail Company and, of course, a member of the Society of Merchant Venturers in Bristol.[622]

By 1839 Alderman Daniel was complaining about labour problems in the West Indies immediately after full emancipation. As chairman of the West India Association, firmly ensconced within the Society of Merchant Venturers, Daniel wrote to the Secretary of State for the Colonies. He advised the secretary of the difficulties "arising from an indisposition of the negroes to work for wages and in many cases to work at all" and with help from allied societies in London, Liverpool, Glasgow and Dublin, supported schemes to aid immigration of impoverished labourers into the West Indies from elsewhere in the British Empire. According to one source the Merchant Venturers were "strangely silent about the West India trade" both before emancipation and after. This was despite the numerous West India Association members within the Society. Clearly "slavery was becoming a dirty word".[623]

That same year, Thomas Daniel bought Stockland, a manor and village on the Devon-Somerset border, from Bristol Corporation. Bearing in mind the city's money troubles, this purchase does look somewhat dubious, particularly considering its history. The property, alternatively known as Stockland Bristol, had been in the hands of the city since 1541 when the then king granted it to the mayor and commonalty. In 1840 Daniel sold his plantations in Demerara to ex-slaves for a consideration of £2,000, with the proviso that his former plantations of *Sparta*, *Fear Not*, *Lima* and *Coffee Grove* be named 'Danielstown'. Today Danielstown is located 41 miles northwest of the capital Georgetown, the latter being at the epicentre of the Demerara rebellion of 1823. Daniel stood down as Alderman the following year, having had continuous membership of both the 'un-reformed' and 'reformed' councils for 56 years (from 1785 to 1841).[624]

The emancipation of the enslaved greatly increased the cost of sugar production. Consequently, Britain's West Indian possessions went into sharp decline, while continuing slave-based economies in Cuba, Brazil and the southern States of the US saw an improvement in trade. Duties on foreign sugar in Britain were removed while the domestic economy for sugar collapsed, plantations in Jamaica were abandoned and the sugar refineries in Bristol began to close. In 1830, 63 percent of Bristol's trade was with the West Indies; by 1840 it was 40 percent, by 1871 it had more than halved to 29 percent and by 1890 it had gone completely.[625]

In the twilight years of the West India Association, letters have survived in the Bristol Archives between Chairman Thomas Daniel and Secretary William Claxton. William, the younger brother of Christopher Claxton, had lost his fortune in the West Indies in 1831, but when the post of treasurer of the Society of Merchant Venturers became salaried it saved his bacon.[626] The letters are concerned with various issues affecting Britain's Caribbean colonies and subjects, in particular the shortage of labour. In one letter dated 6th July 1847 Daniel offers intelligence concerning vessels engaged for the purpose of "coolie emigration" from Calcutta and Madras for the 1847–8 season—"12 ships to British Guiana [Demerara] and 2 ships to Trinidad". In another dated 3rd August 1847 Daniel states that Africans were being shipped privately to the West Indies with the knowledge of Lord Grey. Yet another letter on 20th January 1853 from Cllr William Terrell concerned the welfare of West Indian possessions—in terms of commercial viability—noting that the 'calamity on Madeira', a source of poor labourers for Demerara in particular, had been adversely affected by a famine that had wracked the island in 1852.[627]

The correspondence between Thomas Daniel and William Claxton in the West India Association in the 1840s reveals a new phase in the exploitation of labour in the British West Indies. Caribbean historian Richard Hart explains the official policy in the Dominions, post-emancipation:

> …in the first place it was meant to ensure the dependence of the ex-slaves on the plantations for employment. Secondly, prevention of a scarcity of labour was one of the means by which the plantation owners were assisted to keep wages down to a minimum subsistence level…But of all the policies adopted by the establishment to ensure a continuous supply of cheap labour for the plantations and insulate the society against the necessity of raising the wages of agricultural workers, by far the most important and far reaching was the introduction of indentured labourers, at first from Africa and Madeira, then from China and finally from the subcontinent of India. Recruited in poverty stricken regions with no knowledge of why they were being taken to the Caribbean area, these indentured labourers were shamelessly exploited in conditions not easily distinguishable from slavery.[628]

Transatlantic slavery had come full circle, sandwiched between 'indentured servants' from Bristol in the seventeenth century and 'indentured labourers' from India in the nineteenth century. Albeit 5,000 miles and two centuries apart.

SS Demerara in distress in the Avon Gorge with the unfinished
Clifton Bridge tower, upper right

Investment from emancipation money had made Bristol an innovative centre for the design and building of steamships, though by the 1850s money was running out. With the demise of the Royal West India Mail Packet paddle steamer *Demerara,* which was badly damaged after launching and fouling in the river Avon in 1851, and the loss of the Government contract for mail packets to the West Indies, the writing was on the wall for shipping and allied industries such as ship-building. These had originally been stimulated by the African/West Indian trade in the early eighteenth century, but, now in decline, alternatives were being urgently sought.

Thomas Daniel died on 6th April 1854 at his home and office at No. 20, Berkeley Square, Clifton. He was described in *Bristol Worthies* as:

a man of large frame and capacious dimensions, with full face of rather florid complexion, wearing all round slight whiskers... Quite of the old fashioned type of man of business, much looked up to by the younger generation. His appearance at any of the gatherings, festive or otherwise, was hailed with hearty greetings.[629]

And in *Reminisces by 'L'* in the *Bristol Times and Mirror* of 9th April 1888 Daniel was described thus:

He was a Bristolian to the backbone, and liked the old city as much as he liked turtle, which is saying something, as he was a valiant trencherman [hearty eater], when the place boasted giants in gastronomy amongst its leading citizens.

Unlike Christopher Claxton's obituary, there are no apparent references to Daniel as a pre-eminent supporter and active defender of the slave-system. The so-called 'grey eminence' left an estate valued at £200,000 (worth in 2016 about £190 million by GDP per capita). The West India Association survived for just three more years and was wound up in 1857.[630] Daniel was buried inside St Mary's Church Henbury and, ironically, his memorial tablet is just 15 yards away from the grave of the enslaved African servant Scipio Africanus who is buried just outside. Sydenham Teast, the renowned eighteenth-century slave-ship builder is also buried inside the church with a splendid memorial.

Of Daniel's commercial legacy, his company, T. Daniel & Co., carried on in business until going bankrupt in 1894. Partly due to the rise in the popular consumption of sugar beet, the price of sugar had plummeted from £21 per ton in 1893 to £15 per ton in 1894, and the continuing decline in the sugar price

Thomas Daniel, erstwhile 'King of Bristol', in old age.

had prevented the liquidators from selling off the company's plantations to realise its assets. At the time T. Daniel & Co. owned seven plantation estates in Barbados (*Mellowes, Brewsters, Foursquare, Ruby, Joe's River, Balls* and *Wilcox*) along with one in Demerara (*Taymouth Manor*) and one in Jamaica (*Llanrumney*). Due to the bankruptcy a complete panic ensued in Barbados. Today the Thomas Daniel name lives on in Bridgetown, with a waterfront building bearing his name; other old Bristol names and businesses live on and are still represented throughout the island with adverts for Berger Paints and Embassy (Wills') Cigarettes, the latter under the slogan "Up de Ting".[631]

The Battle Cry of Freedom

The American Connection

On the run-up to the passing of the Bill seeking the Abolition of Slavery in 1833—and the controversies that surrounded compensation—some of the doyens of the anti-slavery movement either moved on or passed away. They were replaced by a new generation of activists, who were initially concerned with the flawed 'apprenticeship' system in the Caribbean and later switched their attention to the plight of enslaved Africans in North America—the numbers of whom exceeded those in the British Dominions by a factor of over three. The position of the American pro-slavery lobby was even more entrenched than the pro-slavery lobby had been in Britain, with deep divisions emerging between the Northern and Southern States and 'White Supremacy' raising its ugly head. This would all culminate in the calamity of the American Civil War some 30 years on.

There were a number of direct connections between abolitionist families in Bristol and their brethren in the United States; these were exemplified by the pioneering Blackwell family. After the shock of having his sugar refinery burn down in April 1832, Samuel Blackwell finally decided to leave Bristol and emigrate to America, taking his entire extended family of eight children and seven adults with him. They left a cholera ravaged Bristol in August that year aboard the *Cosmo* and settled in New York City. On arrival Blackwell immediately resumed his anti-slavery campaigning and met up with the editor of *The Liberator,* William Lloyd Garrison, founder of the New England Anti-Slavery Society in 1831. Garrison soon visited Blackwell's home and family where they immediately struck a chord, and he persuaded the talented Blackwell to bring out a slim book of poetic verses entitled *Anti-Slavery Rhymes.*[632]

Garrison also asked Blackwell for advice regarding which prominent abolitionists he should meet on his forthcoming trip to Britain: veteran parliamentary campaigner Wilberforce; leading Whig cabinet member and Lord Chancellor Brougham; or Wilberforce's successor in Parliament, Buxton? Blackwell pragmatically suggested Buxton as he was the spokesperson for the Anti-Slavery Society. Elizabeth Blackwell would later record: "at last Papa had found an anti-slavery passion to match his own, the two men were tinder to each other's emotions".[633] Being an abolitionist in New York proved to be no picnic however. The Blackwell's got into various scrapes, Samuel escaping thugs and arsonists, and even used their home to hide a whole family away from danger at one time. Their father, a minister, was targeted by a crowd who wanted to lynch him for his views. From his pulpit he had had the temerity to tell the congregation that "Even our Lord, Jesus Christ, was of a darker skin than we are".[634]

One victim of Bristol's severe cholera epidemic of 1832 was surgeon John Bishop Estlin whose increased workload had brought on an attack of 'disease of the lungs', leading to the possibility of terminal consumption. To recover he was advised to live in a warm climate and to this end travelled to St Vincent in the British West Indies, accompanied by his daughter Mary. They set sail in December 1832, for what turned out to be a stay of six months. Here he encountered slavery first hand and was duped into thinking "[that] the physical condition of the slave, as seen by him, was superior, in many respects, to that of large numbers of the poorer classes of his fellow countrymen". One non-slaveholding resident told him that there had been a recent great improvement "in the state of negroes" thanks almost entirely to Britain's Anti-Slavery Society. Despite this "he maintained that the moral evils of the system were greater than he had conceived". Within a decade, Estlin and his daughter Mary would fight as hard as anyone to slay the monster of American slavery.[635]

Both Hannah More and her great friend William Wilberforce lived long enough to know that the Act finally abolishing slavery in the British Empire had been passed. Both died in 1833, Wilberforce on 29th July, just three days after the final reading of the Bill and Hannah More on 7th September in Clifton at the age of 88. More was buried at the nearby village of Wrington in Somerset. When the funeral cortege left Bristol the church bells in the city tolled out.[636] Latimer doesn't seem very sympathetic to More's memory though "[she] outlived not only all the celebrated literary friends of her youth but, to a certain extent, her once considerable reputation as an author."[637] Pro-reformists Protheroe junior and Tom Macauley had met her in 1831 and ended up arguing with her about current politics, much to the dissatisfaction of the inherently conservative More. She subsequently disinherited Macauley—despite her great friendship with his parents. Macauley was sanguine about it, "I kept her friendship as long as she kept her wits". Hannah left £27,500 in her will, which was no mean sum for those days.[638] As we have seen, despite the success of the abolition movement in Britain, campaigners held significantly different political perspectives. They were still in disagreement right up until their deaths.

Just prior to his passing, a fading Wilberforce had met with American anti-slavery campaigner William Lloyd Garrison and British abolitionist George Thompson in Bath; they subsequently joined Wilberforce's funeral procession to Westminster Abbey. The eulogy in Garrison's *The Liberator* read: "[Wilberforce] had gone up to the bar of God with millions of broken fetters in his hand". *The Liberator* used exactly the same wording almost 32 years later after American president Abraham Lincoln was assassinated.[639] Before meeting Wilberforce, Garrison had taken Samuel Blackwell's advice and visited his successor in the Anti-Slavery Society, Thomas Fowell Buxton. Buxton looked at him blankly to begin with, confessing later that he was expecting to see a "black man". On hearing the explanation, American Garrison, the grandson of former indentured servants from England, remarked, "it was the only compliment [he] ever cared to remember".

One man who wouldn't back Garrison though was Thomas Clarkson, who had been 'got at' by the controversial American Colonization Society prior to his visit. The Colonization Society wanted enslaved African-Americans to be relocated to Liberia, sometimes forcibly. They had selectively used extracts from a letter Clarkson had sent to them which implied that the noted abolitionist supported their plan. Clarkson assured Garrison that he was neutral on the matter, subject to seeing more evidence that the Society was "indeed an obstacle to abolition"; unusually for Garrison he was "awed into silence".[640] Garrison then returned to the States with letters of endorsement from other leading British veteran campaigners such as Zachary Macaulay and Wilberforce himself; he was now the American heir apparent to Wilberforce[641] with the added dimension—in the agitator tradition—of a Thomas Paine.

In his early life Garrison was apprenticed as a printer, describing himself as a 'mechanic'. He had a great interest in literature, three of his early influences being the abolitionist poet William Cowper and Hannah More along with the more extravagant Lord Byron. Garrison's childhood was particularly tough as his father had deserted the young family and his mother had to foster out her children so that she could make a living. The print trade saved him where he shone as a newspaper man. Always a 'philanthropist', his other interests included temperance, pacifism and women's rights especially. Garrison became a driven man on hearing about—and seeing—the slave system first hand and was keen on racial equality from the start. He had also read the work of Elizabeth Heyrick in the late 1820s and was a convinced early American advocate of immediate emancipation.

The first editions of *The Liberator* were blamed for the Nat Turner revolt in 1831 and Garrison became a wanted man in the Southern States. When

Garrison first met Blackwell in New York in April 1833, the outside blinds had to be closed and the shades drawn, "secrecy was imperative, for Mr Garrison had many enemies". His enemies had tried unsuccessfully to kidnap him and send him to Georgia prior to his first trip to England, and two years later in 1835 he suffered physical violence from "sedate and proper Bostonians" who tied a rope around his neck and bundled him around Boston—a frightening pretend precursor to lynching.[642]

On 1st August 1834 the emancipation countdown clock began ticking in earnest throughout the British Empire. Among those celebrating in Bristol was Unitarian Dr Lant Carpenter and his family of three boys and three girls, all of whom shared his pride in the landmark event. The youngsters were concerned with the struggle to free the enslaved ever since they had childhood lessons from their father; Mary would later say that "knowledge of the wrongs of the slave was implanted in [their] hearts from childhood".[643] On her daily visits to the docks, Mary said she looked at every person of colour "as a man and a brother, regarded with particular interest and sympathy".[644] In later life most of the six Carpenter children contributed to the anti-slavery cause and Dr Carpenter, through his teachings, was also a great influence on his many students. These included Harriet Martineaux, the hugely influential Whig writer and social theorist.[645]

At around this time Martineaux undertook her famous 20-month tour of the States and while witnessing slavery first hand noted, "it is a totally different thing to be an abolitionist on a soil actually trodden by slaves". She concluded that slavery was as endemic in US society as the 'aristocratic spirit' was in Britain. Harriet reckoned that abolitionists in America faced a task as difficult as British reformers had when challenging the monarchy and the poor laws. Martineaux had heard "every species of abuse" about William Lloyd Garrison and determined to meet him in Boston in 1835—he didn't disappoint. Harriet regarded him as the "master-mind of the revolution". Historian Henry Mayer wrote "[Garrison] would transform the intensely materialistic, slave-ridden culture of Jacksonian America into a truer realization of republican freedom". Garrison moulded the thinking of the abolitionists through his ideas of immediacy and racial equality and goaded America into a new "martyr age" of reformation. To help the Garrisonian cause for abolition in America, Martineaux would enlist her Bristol friends over the coming years.[646]

Another abolitionist, Quaker activist Joseph Sturge, was born in 1793 in Elberton in South Gloucestershire just north of Bristol. He made his fortune as a grain importer and corn merchant in Birmingham and worked throughout his life for universal emancipation of the enslaved, pacifism and working-class rights. He believed in complete suffrage and was one of the new wave of British abolitionists pressing for immediate emancipation in 1831. According to one of Sturge's biographers, his devotion to the liberation of the enslaved was "[for him] not a question of political expediency but moral principle". Lord Brougham complained to Sturge about the evils of the indentured 'apprenticeship' system that had been introduced in the West Indies and how difficult it was to obtain clear evidence of its actual practice. "Then I must supply thee with proof" was Sturge's reply and twice set out to visit the Caribbean, first in 1834 and then, more famously, in his tour of 1836-1837.[647]

Conditions for the former enslaved had worsened after his first visit and when his second investigation revealed even greater abuses of the system it "made his blood boil". Sturge co-wrote and published a journal *The West Indies in 1837* which asked the pertinent question:

> ...if the Imperial Act is not to be administered in its spirit, which means according to the rules of an honest interpretation, for what object did the nation pay the ransom of £20,000,000 sterling? What have the negros, the objects of its benevolence and justice, gained but the exchange of a name, the privation of some of the necessaries of life, and new and more galling chains and punishments.[648]

Sturge pretty much concluded that it was all a con. Planter tyranny still reigned, 'apprentices' still had to ask their 'owners' for permission to marry and harsh sentences were meted out for minor offences. The punishments were barbaric and included the introduction of treadmills and the continued use of flogging.[649] The planters reduced the food they allowed the apprentices and, in some instances, made it difficult for them to even grow their own produce. Denying the newly 'freed apprentices' of the means to support themselves through access to food and fuel ensured they would have to continue working for their 'former masters'. His journal finished by stating:

> ...respecting the 'privilege' of selling provisions, is worthy of especial notice. It would have been a fit addition to have enumerated the consumption of air and water as 'privileges,' which the planters accorded their apprentices of their own free bounty.[650]

Sturge witnessed the unrest over the 'apprenticeship' scheme throughout the British West Indies and on his return to Britain helped galvanise the campaign to end the nefarious indentured scheme. His evidence to Parliament managed to help persuade the government to curtail all of the 'apprenticeships' on the same day. Total emancipation happened on 1st August 1838 throughout the British West Indies and Canada but excluding the possessions of the British East India Company and the Islands of Ceylon and St Helena.[651]

After his business failed in New York, Samuel Blackwell died in Cincinnati early in 1838 aged 48, where he had been experimenting with methods of refining sugar beet in order to try and defeat slavery produced sugar cane. By now the whole family had thrown themselves four-square behind the anti-slavery movement and it would shape the rest of their lives—at this time there were around 2.5 million enslaved African-Americans in the United States. In the short term though the family was destitute and had to set up a small private school to help make ends meet.[652] Against all the odds daughter Elizabeth managed to follow her dream of becoming the first woman doctor, in the process surmounting untold pressure and prejudice just in order to get educated. Like her father and siblings she would become a leading campaigner for all manner of social reforms.

William Knibb, back again in Jamaica by 1838, presided over one of the many thanksgiving services on the night of July 31st—the eve of full emancipation. He decked out his church with branches and flowers and hung portraits of Clarkson and Wilberforce. At midnight he pointed at the clock and proclaimed, "the monster is dying". The congregation took a coffin and filled it with a whip, chains and a punishment collar and carried it to an open grave where it was lowered and covered with soil. The coffin lid was inscribed "Colonial Slavery, died July 31st, aged 276 years". A coconut tree was planted alongside it as a symbol of liberty, an echo from American and French revolutions and now adopted by ex-slaves.[653] The following morning, 1st August 1838, victory had been won throughout the British Empire; nearly 800,000, men, women and children of African descent had officially been set free, an agonising fifty-one years after Thomas Clarkson first crossed the threshold of the *Seven Stars* public house in Bristol. In William Knibb's own words on that momentous night:

Never did I hear such a sound, the winds of freedom appeared to have been let loose. The very building shook at the strange yet sacred joy.

Knibb and others, on seeing slavery first-hand in the West Indies, had been profoundly changed. After emancipation, much to the consternation of the plantocracy and even some fellow Baptists, Knibb advocated that former slaves should have full citizen rights including the vote. Garrison and other American abolitionists, along with free Blacks in the Northern states, started celebrating the 1st August, Emancipation Day, in the West Indies, in preference to the 4th July. In the words of the future abolitionist Frederick Douglass, "[it was the most] illustrious among all the days of the year".[654]

At the moment of the abolitionists' greatest triumph, Wilberforce's two sons published the biographical *Life of William Wilberforce*. This book shamefully belittled a by now half blind Clarkson's achievements, along with that of many others, leading to the *Sunday Times* commenting "Everyone of common sense knows that the merit was Clarkson's and not Wilberforce's".[655] The re-writing of the history, placing Wilberforce at its centre, was to create a significant legacy.

For the next 150 years this narrative, which excluded not only leading activists, organisations and the mass movement that Clarkson helped inaugurate, held sway. It also explains why many people's perceptions of abolition begin and end with Wilberforce, clearly a major distortion of history.

As seen, throughout the 1830s and 1840s leaders of the American anti-slavery campaign carried on making pilgrimages to Clarkson's home; one of these would include African-American Frederick Douglass from Maryland who made his final dash for freedom on 3rd September 1838 after several failed attempts. Formerly called Frederick Bailey, to help hide his identity he changed his surname to Douglass (extremely well read he chose a character from Scott's *The Lady in the Lake*, adding the second 's' by mistake). It was risky for the enslaved to be able to read and write in a European language and young Frederick found that he had a natural aptitude for English; if found out, punishment was severe. As a fugitive he was in grave danger of being apprehended by New York's slave-catchers.[656] Douglass would go on to become one of the most formidable of America's anti-slavery campaigners, coming to Bristol twice in the 1840s to gain support for the cause.

In 1840 the British and Foreign Anti-Slavery Society founded by Joseph Sturge and Lord Brougham—the 1823 London Anti-Slavery Society had been wound up the previous year—hosted the World Anti-Slavery Convention in London's Exeter Hall with Thomas Clarkson as the keynote speaker. William Lloyd Garrison led the American contingent, which included Samuel May junior, but famously 'sat-out' the proceedings because the organisers wouldn't allow participation from women. Many attendees at the event were captured in a massive painting by Benjamin Robert Haydon and included many of the delegates listening to Clarkson; among them were Lady Byron, William Knibb of the Baptist Western Union in Jamaica and M. L'Instant of Hayti (Haiti)—but not Garrison. Lady Byron, after separating from her husband Lord Byron the poet, turned her talents to social causes such as prison reform, the abolition of slavery and ragged schools. With similar leanings, Byron went on to become a firm friend and supporter of both Mary Carpenter and Elizabeth Blackwell.

On the run up to the 1840 Anti-Slavery Convention, painter J. W. M. Turner, who had been a supporter of the anti-slavery movement for many years, decided to make a contribution to the cause by combining two horrific episodes from the slave trade into one painting. Historian Simon Schama put it thus:

> The first was the case of the slaver *Zong*, [see entry for 1783] and the second was the pursuit of slavers by Royal Navy cruisers [post 1807] of the African Squadron which had inadvertently tragic consequences that some in the abolitionist movement believed had made the inhumanity

Thomas Clarkson addressing the World Anti-Slavery Convention in London in 1840, with Joseph Sturge, William Knibb and Lady Byron in the audience—Garrison protested outside.

of the trade worse, not better. Hunted by the cruisers, slavers had been known to jettison their slave cargo.

The result was his painting *Slave Ship (Slavers Throwing Overboard the Dead and Dying, Typhoon Coming On)*; Turner, in his inimitable style, with just a few strokes of his paint brush, managed to convey the sheer horror of these actions in one brilliant masterpiece. It was lampooned and misunderstood as soon as it was displayed and ultimately left Britain forever in 1876, unloved and unwanted.[657]

Now residing in Boston's Museum of Fine Arts the painting has recently been reassessed. Schama commented: "It's quite simply the greatest union of moral power and poetic vision that British art ever accomplished". For historian Blackburn it is Turner's apocalyptical "multi-coloured Guernica".[658]

It's worth contrasting Turner's masterpiece with *The Death of Colston* painted in 1844 by Richard Jeffreys Lewis. It was prompted by the exhumation of Edward Colston's body during church renovations at All Saints in central Bristol. A provincial pot-boiler if ever there was one, the oil painting features a languishing Colston with female mourner behind, seated Anglican cleric to the fore and, dominating the left centre ground, a black maid about to kiss his proffered hand.

In *Slavery Obscured* Madge Dresser asks the questions:

> Does it imply a more complicated personal attachment between the bachelor philanthropist and his maid? Or does the artist mean it to represent, along with the clasped hand, a posthumous plea for reconciliation between the slaver and the enslaved? Whatever the answers to these questions, the picture's content and history aptly symbolise the way slave-trading activities have been both obscured and revealed in Bristol's collective civic consciousness.[659]

It might be added that it is another example of the civic symbolism of Edward Colston, in this case as a 'philanthropic pope', where even the enslaved reverently kneel to kiss his ring (literally).

William Lloyd Garrison's great friend and co-abolitionist, Samuel May junior visited Bristol in 1843 and secured the services of John Bishop Estlin to the Garrisonian cause. Influenced by the writings of Harriet Martineaux, the charisma of Garrison and the evangelism of Samuel May, Estlin would become the "ablest and best helper [in Britain] of recent years"—not only to the cause of abolition in the States but also women's rights. 'Won over' at the same time was Estlin's daughter Mary who followed in her father's footsteps and became a leading campaigner for both causes, nationally as well as in Bristol, along with her great friend Mary Carpenter.[660]

Boston born Samuel Joseph May was a Unitarian minister who championed several reform movements along with abolitionism; these included education, pacifism, temperance and women's rights. He was secretary of the American Anti-Slavery Society (AAS) and used his home in Syracuse, New York State, as a station on the Underground Railroad—an organisation that provided 'safe' houses for runaway enslaved African-Americans—he had even publicly taken part in the rescue of one such individual from the police. Known to his friends as 'the Lord's Choirboy'—because of his disarming innocence—he was violently attacked and burnt in effigy because of his views on the run-up to the American Civil War.[661]

Mary Estlin stepped up her abolitionist activities by becoming a leading member of the Bristol and Clifton Ladies' Anti-Slavery Society and turning it 'Garrisonian', despite it originally being an auxiliary of Joseph Sturge's British & Foreign Anti-Slavery Society. Working with Mary Carpenter she sent large quantities of articles to be sold at the Boston Anti-Slavery Bazaar and later wrote a letter to the organiser, Maria Weston Chapman, saying "[that she was] very glad to hear that the Bristol contributions sold well".[662] Chapman used the money raised to fund anti-slavery causes in the States. A women's rights activist as well, she also happened to be a big friend of Harriet Martineaux.

Prior to May's visit, Mary Carpenter had already been influenced by visiting American Unitarians. With help from John Bishop Estlin she had set up her first 'ragged school' in impoverished Lewin's Mead, Bristol, after a suggestion by the social reforming Boston minister Joseph Tuckerman, who had visited in 1833.[663] She really took to American anti-slavery campaigning after meeting New York minister Orville Dewey on his visit to Bristol in 1843. Garrison said of the Unitarians in England "religiously [they were] regarded as little better than infidels [but he found them] to be much better than their revilers and persecutors".[664]

Back in Jamaica, William Knibb died on 15th May 1845, having helped raise money to enable 19,000 of the former enslaved to buy their own land. On the 150th anniversary of emancipation in 1988 he was posthumously awarded the Jamaican Order of Merit, the highest civilian honour in the country and the first white male to receive it. Knibb has a passing mention in *Bristol: Past and Present*, where he was described on his death as "the eminent Baptist missionary".[665]

Mr Douglass comes to town…

In August 1845 the formerly enslaved Frederick Douglass was on the run again and embarked on a ship to Liverpool. Douglass had to leave the States in a hurry because he had written a blistering autobiography which exposed his own experiences of the brutality of slavery. He had also bravely 'named names' of his overseers, 'owners' and their families. The *Narrative of the Life of Frederick Douglass, an American Slave* caused such a stir that Douglass was advised to take the trip until the furore died down. His visit to Britain and Ireland also offered him the opportunity to start a lecture tour to talk about his experiences and help promote the American anti-slavery campaign. The following year he was joined by fellow abolitionists William Lloyd Garrison and George Thompson. Together they visited a seriously ailing Thomas Clarkson in August at his home near Ipswich. On seeing Douglass, Clarkson clasped his own two hands around one of Frederick's and exclaimed:

> God bless you Frederick Douglass! I have given sixty years of my life to the emancipation of your people, and if I had sixty years more they should all be given to the same cause.[666]

Capturing the mood of the country, Clarkson's wife Catherine advised the American abolitionists that although there was no pro-slavery lobby in Britain

John Bishop Estlin's Bristol Blind Asylum (c1850) which was replaced by the Wills Memorial Building in the 1920s.

Social reformer and stau[...] abolitionist Mary Carpent[...]

"too many seem to think that having paid 22,000,000 [sterling] to redeem our own slaves England has nothing more to do".[667] At the age of 86 on 26th September 1846, Thomas Clarkson passed away, five weeks after Douglass's visit. The real father figure of the abolitionist movement was dead. Considering himself 'half a Quaker' to the end, he was buried simply in the churchyard near his home at Playford Hall. The Quakers attending the funeral symbolically removed their hats, something they wouldn't even do for the Tsar of Russia. A plaque was finally unveiled to Clarkson in Westminster Abbey in 1996, 150 years after his death.[668]

At the same time John Bishop Estlin published his own important pamphlet *A Brief Notice of American Slavery and the Abolition Movement* with Samuel May acting as his research assistant.[669] He sent a copy to Clarkson but unfortunately it seems he was too unwell to read it. Four weeks after meeting Clarkson, Douglass and Garrison went by train to Bristol where they were greeted at Temple Meads station by Estlin himself and his daughter Mary. Garrison stayed in their home at 47, Park Street close to Brandon Hill, while Douglass stayed at nearby 2, Great George Street. The latter belonged to abolitionist soap-maker Herbert Thomas, future husband of Anna, one of Mary Carpenter's younger sisters. The house was also an occasional home for Mary. Estlin wrote to Samuel May that Thomas "would not allow my monopolising both". The following morning, they breakfasted and visited Estlin's Blind Asylum, the site now occupied by the Wills Memorial Building, where Douglass read parts of his *Narrative* to 60 men, women and children in the institution. Continuing his correspondence to May, Estlin wrote: "Their delight was extreme to feel him and question him. I think F.D. will never forget the scene".[670]

The campaigner's first public address was to a packed house at the fashionably new Victoria Rooms and was attended by Bristol Mayor John Haberfield with Garrison speaking first, followed by Douglass. Garrison felt his own performance was "dull and flat" and admitted that in front of such a select gathering of leading Quakers and merchants it took "all the warmth out of me". Douglass got rave reviews. Mary Carpenter said she could not remember a speech of such "powerful reasoning... touching appeals, keen sarcasm and graphic description". The *Bristol Mercury* reported that there were:

occasional tones in his voice—not unlike the growl of a lion—which hint at 'something dangerous' and which seem to indicate that he is a man not to be trampled on with impunity.

The *Mercury* reporter noted sarcastically that Haberfield had, at one time during the proceedings, filled a glass of water for Douglass: "What! A white man—a mayor—a man in authority—hand a glass of water to a Negro! Incredible!" Of more importance was that the mayor, who had chaired the

Frederick Douglass 'The Lion of the Occasion'—against an early Victoria Rooms postcard backdrop.

event, noted that Douglass's *Narrative* had been "extensively read in the city". Historian Laurence Fenton suggests though that some still doubted that it could have been written by an ex-slave, a sign of lingering prejudice. That night the exhausted abolitionists, along with 40 invited guests, had a soiree at the Estlin's home.[671]

The following day the star speakers addressed a 1000-strong audience of "a more popular cast" who had paid a tanner (*6d.*) each to attend. With people standing in the aisles to listen to the celebrated fugitive slave, Douglass was again, according to Garrison, "the lion of the occasion". Douglass's September speeches also touched the hearts of Bristol's 'lower orders'. Mary Carpenter had taken a boy along with her who had recently been in prison and whipped. The boy, who hadn't slept under a roof for several months, turned to Mary after the meeting and said "[he] understood what Mr Douglass meant because he had *felt it himself*".[672] Among those supplying items to the Boston Bazaar from Bristol that year was a woman who had obviously been moved by Douglass's recollections of lashings and family separations. She had donated a small ceramic figure of a market women and the accompanying inscription said:

214

I be a poor, hard-working body, tis true;
I works hard and lives hard, I knows that I do;
But I works hard for they as I loves to my heart,
And if I dont do't, they 'ont make my back smart.
We struggles together, my old man and I,
To settle the young'uns before we do die.
What we gets is our own, as I says, and we're free,
And happen what 'ool, tis a comfort to me,
That nobody never can tear me from he![673]

Another donation was from Sarah Ann White a pupil of Kingswood Infants School, sent with the following accompanying note:

This small piece of lace was wrought by the little girl whose name it bears, in the following way, she obtained from her mother a half penny, in lieu of one weeks sugar. With this, she purchased two farthing balls of cotton, and from these produced the lace, an instance of self denial worthy of imitation.

These were in addition to the regular consignment of Boston bound basket-ware produced by Bristol's Blind Asylum. There was an increase in donations which was attributed to the 'Douglass effect' leading one of the organisers to state:

There can be no doubt that much of the sweep of the Bazaar this year may be attributed to him [Douglass]—for from all I can learn the contributions from this [British] side of the Atlantic will be finer than ever

Bristol's contribution to the Bazaar was picked out for praise by the press who had been shown the artefacts prior to despatch.[674] Mary Carpenter and her coterie consistently supplied contributions throughout the late 1840s and these ranged from her own drawings and water-colours—along with those of her sister Anna and Lady Byron—to knitted socks and patchwork quilts from her scholars at the ragged schools:

Many a time did the girls freely work long hours beyond school-time to finish their patchwork quilts; and bare footed children who had been taught to knit, brought stockings made in secret to escape the eyes of their drunken parents and begged them to be allowed to send them to the poor slaves.

At the height of its popularity, around 300 volunteers worked in Bristol shipping articles to the Anti-Slavery Fair, which was held each Christmas at Boston's famous Faneuil Hall and generated gross proceeds of between $3,000 and $4,000 a year. Even Garrison was impressed with these contributions from the supporters in Bristol, "no family of people worked harder than the Unitarians in support of the Boston Bazaar".[675]

By the time Frederick Douglass returned to Bristol the following spring he was a free man. Some of his supporters in the north-east of England had bought his freedom for him, now making it 'safe' for him to return home to America. On 1st April 1847 he gave a farewell speech in Bristol, this time under the title 'Monarchies and Freedom, Republics and Slavery', again to great acclaim. The meeting was held under the auspices of the Bristol Auxiliary Anti-Slavery League in the Broadmead-Rooms and the following was reported in the *Bristol Mercury*:

> Mr Douglass concluded his address (which lasted nearly two hours), by expressing, in a strain of much impassioned eloquence, his grateful thanks for the reception he had met with from the citizens of Bristol. C. J. Thomas Esq. moved a vote of thanks to Frederick Douglass which was carried with much applause.[676]

Within three weeks Douglass was on his way home to the States, carrying with him a silver inkstand from his friends in Bristol; among those showering him with grateful praise and thanks on his departure from Liverpool was John B. Estlin who had followed him there.[677] At the end of his twenty month tour of Britain and Ireland, Douglass had amassed enough money and contacts to start up his own abolition newspaper *The North Star* on his return to America. This would go on to further cement his position as one of that country's greatest abolitionists.

In tandem with her friend Mary Estlin, Mary Carpenter kept up a steady stream of correspondence with American liberal circles. Samuel May arranged for Carpenter's book *Meditations* to be published in America, although to her annoyance under her own name. It sold so well that for a brief period she was better known in the States than she was in Britain. Carpenter was firm in her belief that anti-slavery shouldn't be used to muffle social injustice in Britain, as it had done in the past. She was also proud of her father's efforts to make the Unitarian church in Bristol a church for all, rather than solely for just a few aristocratic merchants. Mary's faith reached out to the whole of society and she was a great advocate for people's freedom attending, incognito, a Chartist meeting on Brandon Hill in 1847. The year after she avidly followed events in the press regarding France, Italy, Hungary and Russia, 'the year of revolutions', and wrote to a friend:

The world is beginning to awake to its true life; I firmly believe it… One true, strong spirit, with the armour of faith, will destroy a whole army of Goliaths.[678]

Carpenter wasn't wrong; massive changes were underway across Europe as the struggle for the end of monarchy and the creation of democratic republics intensified. As we have already seen, these struggles were closely linked to the abolition of slavery.

After the abdication of King Louis-Philippe in February 1848—due to the mutiny of his National Guard and clashes in Paris with republican crowds leaving fifty dead—a provisional government was formed in France. In a decree dated 27th April 1848, 250,000 slaves were to be freed within two months; most didn't wait for freedom and just claimed it when the new Republic was declared. All male slaves were to get the vote, the 'right to work' and social security for the elderly and infirm! The decree also sanctioned 26 million francs to provide schools, nurseries, clinics and labour courts for the ex-slaves in the colonies. Compensation of 6 million francs in cash and 120 million in government bonds was later paid to the slave-holding colonists. This was equivalent to about £5 million sterling in 1848, proportionally a similar amount to the British compensation of £22 million paid for 'freeing' 800,000 slaves in 1834. It was also at this time that France began to colonise West Africa.[679]

The Bloodhound Law

Frederick Douglass was not the only African-American fugitive turned abolitionist to make their mark in Britain and specifically in Bristol; in fact, there were several. One, William Wells Brown[680] visited the city several times in the early 1850s as part of a series of lecture tours of Britain on behalf of Garrison's American Anti-Slavery Society (AAS). Born into slavery in Kentucky around 1814, Brown successfully escaped at the age of 20 and, in the 1830s and 1840s, worked as a 'steamboat man', secretly running hundreds of other fugitive slaves to liberty across Lake Erie and on to Canada. Like Douglass, he was influenced by Garrison and *The Liberator* which led him to undertake speaking engagements on behalf of the AAS.

In 1849 Brown travelled to Britain as a US delegate of the International Peace Congress[681], with the aim of lecturing against 'American Slavery'. In April of the following year he was invited to speak at two events in the Broadmead-Rooms in Bristol. Both meetings were packed with hundreds of people eager to hear of his direct experiences of slavery in the American South, details of his escape and his views on abolition. Brown did not disappoint, using "eloquent" oratory and even anti-slavery songs to get his points across. In the first meeting he launched a blistering attack "showing how slavery had corrupted every

United States, your banner wears
Two emblems,—one of fame;
Alas, the other that it bears,
Reminds us of your shame.
The white man's liberty entypes,
Stands blazoned by your stars;
But what's the meaning of your stripes,
They mean your Negro-scars.—*Thomas Campbell.*

Anti-slavery flag from William Wells Brown's anti-slavery songbook—the
thirteen black stars on the banner represent America's slave states—note the
'Cap of Liberty' atop the flag pole.

institution of America, religious, political, social, and commercial".[682] A few days later at the second event, a "public tea-meeting" attended by 300–400 people, Brown rounded on support by many American churches for the slave-system. He claimed that:

the slavery doctrines preached by the clergy of America, had done more to spread infidelity there than anything else, for it was impossible that a man could at once be a Christian and a slaveholder[683]

Brown's oratory was matched by his writing, itself a quite remarkable story. After his escape from slavery he taught himself to read and write and went on to become the first African-American novelist with the publication of *Clotel* in 1853. Six years earlier he had penned his first book, the *Narrative of William W. Brown, a Fugitive Slave, Written by Himself*, which, like Douglass's first book, was published by Garrison's Anti-Slavery Office. Just before he left Bristol in 1850, Brown wrote a verse in Mary Carpenter's *Poetical Extract* notebook:

Fling out the Anti Slavery Flag,
And let it not be furled,
Till like a planet of the skies,
It sweeps around the world,
And when each poor degraded slave,
Be gathered near and far,
O, fix it on the azure arch,
As hopes eternal star[684]

He annotated it with the following sentiment:

O, may the day soon come, when my race shall no longer be regarded as fit for nothing but slaves, but shall take their place among the Freemen. Wm Wells Brown, Bristol April 15th 1850[685]

Brown's successful meetings in Bristol were followed a few months later by the visit of another remarkable African-American abolitionist, James W. C. Pennington.[686] Pennington, born into slavery in Maryland in 1807, ran away at the age of 19, leaving his large family behind, and ended up working in Brooklyn, New York as a coachman. The illiterate Pennington was taught to read and write by Quakers who had helped with his escape; an avid learner, he soon became a teacher and then entered Yale University as its first black student. After completing his studies, he became a minister in the Congregational Church and in 1841 wrote what is believed to be the first history of African-Americans, *The Origin and History of the Colored People*. He followed this with his autobiography *The Fugitive Blacksmith,* which was first published in 1849 in London.

Pennington made several trips to Britain, speaking and raising money for the abolition cause, and visited Bristol in October 1850. At a "densely crowded" meeting in the Broadmead-Rooms, Dr Pennington was introduced to the audience with the announcement that he had recently received an honorary doctorate from the University of Heidelberg. In a wide-ranging speech with several biblical references, Pennington tore into the origins and tenets of American slavery with a vengeance. He pointed out the contradictions between the practice of slavery and the reasons for the War of Independence and the Constitution, rhetorically addressing the 'founding fathers':

> Why did you not throw away British slavery when you threw away the British Sceptre? (loud cheers). Great Britain had been in the habit of sending over governors, and statutes, and decrees: and yet, after having submitted to them for years, you, on the 4th July 1776, declared yourselves independent, and threw away the British governors, statutes, and authorities—why did you not then throw away slavery? (cheers).[687]

He completed his speech by turning to the subject of escapees from slavery. Of more than three million enslaved African-Americans in the US, Pennington claimed, some 150,000 had escaped over the previous 20 years. Yet, he explained to his captivated audience, there was a new and growing threat to the liberty of these escapees, including himself. Pennington was referring to the Fugitive Slave Law which had been approved by the US Congress the previous month. The new law was the result of a compromise between the slave-holding states of the South and the anti-slavery Free-Soil party of the North.[688] It was quickly nicknamed the 'Bloodhound Law' by abolitionists, after the dogs that were used to track runaway slaves. The legislation allowed slave owners to reclaim their 'property' in northern 'free' states by coercing both officials and citizens to hand over escaped slaves under the threat of fines or imprisonment. The issue soon came to a head, particularly in Boston where bands of volunteers hid, and used force to protect fugitive slaves from the authorities and bounty-hunters. High profile escapees in the abolition movement, such as William Wells Brown and James Pennington, were certainly not safe. They were targeted by politically motived slave-catchers from the South, as were a fugitive couple who had recently become national celebrities.

Husband and wife, William and Ellen Craft, had engineered a remarkable escape from slavery in Georgia in 1848. Ellen, who was lighter skinned than her partner, pretended to be William's young 'master'. Using this ruse, they travelled hundreds of miles in first class compartments on trains and steamboats, fooling officials and passengers along the way, to gain their freedom in the North. This

Left: William Wells Brown.
Right: Ellen Craft in Mary Carpenter's *Poetical Extract* Book.

caused a sensation in the media and, after the passing of the Fugitive Slave Law, made the Crafts a prime target for slave-catchers. Despite being offered terms for a 'peaceable arrest' by one of the President's men, and guarantees that they would be 'repurchased' and then freed immediately, the Crafts rejected the offer on behalf of hundreds of other fugitives who they said "would have their freedom jeopardised by legitimising the law's operation".[689] To end the stalemate the AAS vigilance committee in Boston despatched the Crafts to Britain in order to team up with William Wells Brown who was now effectively trapped in Britain by the passing of the new law. They were met at Liverpool by prominent British abolitionists led by Harriet Martineaux who arranged for the couple to stay at Lady Byron's school in Ockham where they had a crash course in reading and writing.

In April 1851 William Wells Brown returned to Bristol along with William and Ellen Craft to speak at a crowded public meeting in the Broadmead-Rooms, followed by three evenings of lectures at the same venue to similar acclaim. To illustrate the lectures they were accompanied by an amazing 2,000 foot canvas with 24 vistas painted by Brown. These were "descriptive of the history and condition of the American slaves; his employments on the plantations etc together with interesting incidents in the life of Mr Brown".[690] Wells Brown spoke at the meeting summarising the contradictions in the US that would ultimately lead to the American Civil War. The *Bristol Mercury* reported:

The present was a most important crisis of the anti-slavery question. When he was in Bristol twelve months ago the fugitive slave bill had not passed the congress, but was under discussion; it had now become the law of America. They had been told of some of its bad effects, but were he to detain them for two or three hours he could not hope to unfold to them all the evils which resulted from that iniquitous act. Every steamer which crossed the Atlantic brought with it tidings of some of its evil consequences—not only of the recapture of slaves who had just made their escape, but of the dragging back to slavery those who had escaped years and years ago. They found, too, that the masters were making severe examples of those whom they captured, in the hope of deterring others from attempting flight.

The American union was founded on iniquity, because its condition was that it should keep one-sixth part of the people in chains (hear). The union committee in New York was foremost among the supporters of the fugitive slave bill. It was that committee which took the lead in seizing the poor slave Henry Long, who made his escape to New York some years ago from Virginia. He was taken and sent back and put up to auction by his master; and although a benevolent man followed him from New York for the sole purpose of purchasing him and restoring him to his wife, he was astounded to hear when the poor fellow was placed upon the auction-block that no man could buy him unless he bound himself in a bond of 3000 dollars to carry him to, and use him upon, a cotton plantation.

What was the American union to William Craft—what to the millions of slaves who were clinking their chains in the Southern states? If the union were shattered to-morrow, and the people of the free states were allowed to live up to their principles, it would be the better for the world, for then would there be another asylum besides England for the poor slave. The people of Massachusetts were generally favourable to the bondman, but they were bound down by the government, and the preachers who were carrying out the policy of the slaveholder. Depend upon it, the sooner that the union was abolished, the better would it be for four millions of people. He was glad to find that the people of England were getting a knowledge of the teachings of the preachers of America, so that if any of them came to this country the warmest reception they would meet with would be just none at all.

He could not conclude without alluding to the last act of the American congress before its separation. It was to pass a bill authorising the government to fit out a vessel and send to this country, where it might be in waiting to receive such of the Hungarian refugees as might be willing to start on a pilgrimage to the "land of the free" and the "home of the brave," as they called America (laughter). The slave-holders, slave-breeders, slave-dealers, and slave-oppressors had fitted out a vessel to offer a home to those who had been oppressed. How dared they fit out a ship to receive Hungarian refugees, when men, aye, and tender women, must come from their own shore to seek a refuge in Great Britain? (cheers.) Let the people of England teach them their duty. Let them say we value not your sympathy for the Hungarians or anyone else while you enslave and oppress one-sixth of your own countrymen (cheers). He was glad to find that all the meetings he had attended on this question had spoken out manfully, and, he would add, "womanfully" too (cheers). He was glad to see so many of the Bristol fair ones present to welcome one of their own sex who could not find a home in her own country. He rejoiced at the vastness and the spirit of that meeting. It would go forth to the United States' people, and would tell them that while they were professing hollow sympathy for the oppressed Hungarians, some of their own people were being welcomed on the British soil as refugees from the despotism of American liberty (loud cheers).

Leading Bristol activist John Bishop Estlin followed Brown. He defended the character of William Lloyd Garrison and challenged the position of the British and Foreign Anti-Slavery Society:

Mr Estlin proposed a resolution expressive of sympathy with that noble band of men and women in the United States who had showed zeal in the cause of the poor slave; and in so doing referred to the progress which had been made with the abolition movement in that country since the establishment of the American Anti-Slavery Society in 1830. The person who formed that society was William Lloyd Garrison, whose name he never mentioned without feeling for it some of that respect, if not veneration, which he felt for those good men of ancient times around whose characters and names holy writ had thrown a sacred halo. He believed the same power which had called forth an Elizabeth Fry to visit their prisons and gaols, to ameliorate the condition of their inmates, and which had raised up a Clarkson to put an end to the slave-trade, had likewise called forth Wm. Lloyd Garrison to give a death-blow to the monster crime of American slavery.

Mr. Estlin entreated his hearers to deliberately weigh Mr. Garrison's whole character before they came to the decision that he was a man not to be worked with. Because he had denounced the want of faithfulness in the preachers, he and those who, like him, had left the churches in which the pastors upheld slavery, had been proclaimed as infidels. He (Mr. Estlin) solemnly believed that Mr Lloyd Garrison had done more to uphold the sanctity of the Bible in America than those ministers of religion had done who had prostituted the sacred volume as an argument in favour of slavery. After some further remarks expressive of the gratitude which the friends of freedom owed to the ladies of the Bristol Anti-Slavery Society, who were, in fact, doing the work which the British and Foreign Anti-Slavery Society ought to do...

William Craft thanked the Bristol abolitionists for their financial support for the abolition movement in the US and, from a very personal perspective, railed against the continuation of slavery through ameliorative measures:

...[he] could not allow the meeting to close without returning his thanks to the Bristol ladies and to the pupils of the Blind Asylum for sending out contributions in aid of a movement which aimed at the emancipation of his enslaved relatives and countrymen. If God made men free, let his people exert themselves to break every bond. If he made them slaves, then, in God's name, return him and his wife to bondage. Let them not ask that the poor slave might have more food, more clothes, or that he might be flogged less—let their demand be that he shall be set free (cheers). He had himself a father, and a brother and sisters, and his wife had a mother and a grandmother, who were dragging out life in bondage, and he implored their efforts in their behalf (cheers).

The meeting then finished in the following manner:

At the request of the Chairman, Mrs Craft then stood forward from the retired situation which, upon coming upon the platform, she had taken up, so as to become visible to the audience, by whom she was cordially and repeatedly cheered. Her husband and Mr. Browne [sic] then sung a characteristic abolition song, and a vote of thanks to the Chairman terminated the proceedings.[691]

The following month the trio appeared for two nights at packed meetings in the Assembly Rooms in Bath where the headline read 'Mrs Craft "the White Slave" will be present'.[692]

Perversely, the passing of the Fugitive Slave Law concentrated the minds of people sympathetic to the plight of African-Americans and raised awareness of their situation worldwide. It also exposed divisions in the British abolition movement. In the flurry of public meetings in Bristol in 1850–1851, speakers such as MP George Thompson, John Estlin and others consistently and vehemently criticised the British and Foreign Anti-Slavery Society. They mocked the organisation for its impotence in censuring the pro-slavery American clergy and complained about its failures to popularise the African-American speakers and the massive effect that the Fugitive Slave Law had on them and hundreds of thousands of other escapees.[693] The more radical abolitionists in Bristol and elsewhere were on the right side of history in their understanding of the far-reaching effects of the new law in the US. The Fugitive Slave Law would turn out to be one of several slow burning fuses that eventually ignited conflict between the slave-owning states and the north in a brutal civil war.

William Wells Brown finally returned to the US in 1854 but only after his 'freedom had been bought' by the Richardsons, the very same family that had enabled Douglass to return home in 1847. In his five years in Britain, Brown travelled more than twenty-five thousand miles and addressed more than one thousand public meetings and lectured in twenty-three mechanics' and literary institutions. His extended visits to Bristol clearly made an impression:

Bristol has long sustained a high position, as a place from which the American abolitionists have received substantial encouragement in their arduous labors for the emancipation of the slaves of that land; and the writer of this received the best evidence that in this respect the character of the people had not been exaggerated, especially as regards the Clifton Ladies' Anti-Slavery Society.

And he paid high compliment to abolitionist John Estlin and his family who had supported both him and the Crafts:

Of the hundreds of British Abolitionists with whom I had the pleasure of shaking hands while abroad, I know of none whose hearts beat more fervently for the emancipation of the American slave than Mr. Estlin's.[694]

James Pennington stayed in Britain for two years until he too was 'purchased' by friends and sympathetic abolitionists he had met in England. On his return to New York, Pennington set up a committee to fight against racial segregation on the New York transport system, which finally achieved its aims in 1865. William and Ellen Craft carried on campaigning and remained in Britain until 1868. In 1860, to much popular acclaim, they published *Running a Thousand Miles for Freedom; Or, the Escape of William and Ellen Craft from Slavery*. Three years later William Craft returned to Bath to fight a different kind of battle. In a debate at the British Association over a paper entitled "[the] Comixture of

Races" which proposed 'racial hierarchies' and warned of the dangers of 'racial mixing', the following was reported:

> Mr Craft (a gentleman of colour) who was loudly cheered on rising, defended the African race... "Whenever the African race had had equal opportunities with the whites, they had shown that they possessed considerable intellectual ability, and many of them had risen to a very high position in society".[695]

The 1860s marked the rise of pseudo-scientific racism, later given credence by its link to the unholy marriage of eugenics and social Darwinism. These flawed and distorted theories originally founded by British and other European 'scientists' would blight the world for a century, justify colonialism and play a part in the deaths of millions. It is interesting to note that at their very inception, William Craft was there to take on the ideologues of these theories.

In 1851, a year after the passing of the American Fugitive Slave Law, Mary Carpenter lessened her anti-slavery activities. She was furious at the country where the supposedly free and educated people had once asked Europe "to admire and copy... the glorious freedom of their adored Union." In April, after stating they would never do such a thing, the authorities in Boston returned a fugitive slave to slavery; it was at this time that she strongly dissented from fellow abolitionist Dewey's views. Carpenter wrote to May accusing his nation of an "atrocious act... against humanity itself, against God." Even so, through her sister Anna, she still carried on supplying the Boston Bazaar with a parcel each year. Meanwhile she stepped up her campaigns for educational and prison reform in both Britain and the rest of the world, particularly in India.[696]

Events in West Africa in the early 1850s marked an ominous turning point in the Royal Navy campaign to suppress the Atlantic slave trade. There had always been an understanding in the West Africa Squadron (WAS) that, when in pursuit of slave traders, they could use greater levels of force against Africans than Europeans. Huzzey notes:

> Instructions to the squadron's officers suggested that violence 'may be exercised upon shore as well as at sea, and irrespective of the consent of the native government', when Africans were involved.[697]

Although the WAS had previously carried out raids on slave-trading settlements and burned villages, these were relatively minor incursions. In December 1851 the bombardment and invasion of Lagos in modern-day Nigeria on the pretext of an antislavery mission was a step-change in both tactics and eventual strategy in Africa. From this point on, the British state became increasingly aggressive in their military incursions, expanding 'anti-slavery' operations to East Africa in the 1860s and using threats to missionaries to justify further invasions. These 'bridgeheads', justified on abolitionist grounds, would provide the basis for the huge colonial expansion known as the 'scramble for Africa', which began to accelerate in the 1870s.[698]

The WAS was wound up in 1867–69, along with the British campaign against the slave trade. As to its effectiveness, Eltis states:

> even after doing violence to international law, the British could expect to detain at best one out of perhaps every three ships sent to Africa by foreigners. When it came to traders' profits, "they could induce a loss of only one venture in five in any long-run period"[699]

Despite the strategic failure to effectively suppress the Atlantic slave trade through maritime means, between 1808 and 1867, the Royal Navy intercepted 1,600 slave ships carrying approximately 160,000 slaves bound for the Americas.[700]

On 10th June 1855, ironically while convening an anti-slavery meeting at his home in Park Street, John Bishop Estlin died. A 'Garrisonian' to the end, his final letter had been one of resignation from the British and Foreign Anti-Slavery Society.[701] He had already expressed his views that the Society had become "culpably cool [in their anti-slavery feeling], under the sectarian and prejudiced administration" and in his last letter he complained that the organisation had: "[been guilty of] serious derelictions from fidelity (faithfulness) to the true interests of the cause".[702] It is likely that Estlin was referring to the Society's gaze being turned towards slavery in Africa rather than in the United States. Estlin was interred in the Lewins Mead Burial Ground alongside his wife and close to his father. Monumental tablets to him and his wife are in the nearby Unitarian meeting house and a bust, created by the famous Bristol sculptor Edward Baily, was displayed in Bristol Museum and Art Gallery.[703]

Estlin's daughter Mary carried on her anti-slavery campaigning by continuing to tour with fugitive abolitionists such as African-American Sarah Parker Remond. She helped set-up the London Emancipation Committee with Garrison's old pal George Thompson in 1859. The group was mixed by ethnicity and gender and included another self-emancipated fugitive, Ellen Craft, as well as Remond.

One of Mary's chief concerns was the material problems faced by the former enslaved and the impact of racism on their lives. She also increased her interest in women's rights to include women's suffrage where she was one of the founders of the Bristol branch in 1868, the fifth place in the country to set-up such a committee.[704]

She also actively, and successfully, fought the notorious Contagious Diseases Act with Elizabeth Blackwell and Mary Carpenter. They all got together for the last time in Bristol in 1869 for the annual meeting of the National Association for the Promotion of Social Science, where delegates discussed the vagaries of the Contagious Diseases Act and started the process to get it abolished. Mary Estlin died in 1902, a natural heir to her grandfather's friend and abolitionist, Anna Barbauld, a 'woman of letters' who had pioneered women's involvement in politics in the 1790s.

Lincoln's Emancipation Proclamation

After a surgical accident finished her career as a surgeon, Elizabeth Blackwell returned to the United States in 1857 and helped establish the New York Infirmary for Indigent Women and Children, staffed entirely by women with Blackwell as a director. It was the first of its kind and she was aided by her sister Emily who had also qualified as a surgeon. Funds were tight and to help raise money she returned to Britain to do a lecture tour emphasising the role that trained and educated women could make to society. One of her aims was to set up teaching courses for women doctors and nurses and space was provided. Overcoming social prejudice, the hospital got bigger and bigger, treating both black and white patients. On one occasion a black patient was objected to by white women because of the colour of her skin. Blackwell was called and immediately calmed the situation. She told the patients:

> If there is anyone here who does not wish to remain, we will make arrangements… But, if it is your desire to stay, please remember we have no room for intolerance here![705]

1861—Start of American Civil War; the war is fought largely over the issue of individual states' rights to determine whether they allow slavery.

When the American Civil War broke out in 1861, it stymied Blackwell's plans to educate women doctors but there was a huge demand for nurses. When the call came she organized the Ladies' Sanitary Aid Association to enlist and train volunteer women to serve as battlefield nurses for the Union. This didn't stop the hospital from being impartial; wives and widows of Confederate soldiers shared the same wards as wives and widows of the Union side. Equally, enlisted men shared the same facilities as ranking officers. Elizabeth told her staff at the time, "suffering does not take sides, and we, as the alleviators of suffering, must not, either".[706] New York was an unsettled place at the outset of the war with pro- and anti-slavery riots. Black people were targeted by having their homes ransacked and set on fire; later in the war, when the draft law for more Union soldiers was passed, these riots were repeated and intensified.

Unfortunately, all of these activities put a strain on Elizabeth's own health, but it didn't stop her applying for a charter to upgrade the Infirmary to a Medical College for Women as the war was closing.[707] She finally left America in 1869 and finished her days in Britain campaigning for preventative medicine, dying at her home in Hastings aged 89 in 1910.

The battle for the end of slave-holding tyranny in the States can be traced back primarily to the agitation generated by William Lloyd Garrison and *The Liberator* newspaper that he started in 1831. He played a huge role in turning America from being a country that tolerated slavery into one that nearly tore itself apart in order to abolish it. Through his newspaper he galvanised public opinion using "a prophet's power and a propagandist's skill" to tackle one travesty after another. *The Liberator* railed against the American Colonisation Society, the stance taken by America's churches, America's political parties (he finished off America's Whig Party and confounded the Southern orientated Democratic Party), the Fugitive Slave Law and even the US Constitution—he publicly burnt a copy of the latter two documents at a picnic on the 4th July 1854. In the preface to Frederick Douglass's autobiography of 1845, published by the Anti-Slavery Office that he had helped set-up, Garrison finished by exclaiming "NO COMPROMISE WITH SLAVERY, NO UNION WITH SLAVEHOLDERS". He was prepared for the North to cede from the South but in the end the Confederacy abandoned the North after abolitionist John Brown's raid on Harpers Ferry in 1859.[708]

This was all against the backdrop of the earlier fragmentation of the Spanish empire and American expansionism from 1830–1860; first Texas, then New Mexico, Oregon, California and finally Kansas. The Southern States wanted to turn each and every one of them into slave states so that the Confederate aristocracy could maintain their supremacy in the White House. Led by the South, the US was then casting its covetous eyes towards Cuba and Nicaragua as potential slave colonies. On each occasion the American Anti-Slavery Society, through *The Liberator*, tried to peg them back and make slavery "the question of the generation".

The Civil War not only brought the issue of emancipation of the enslaved in the Southern States to the forefront of political debate, it also created a brutal contradiction for some working-class Britons. These were workers involved in industries that relied on raw materials such as tobacco and cotton that were sourced from the Confederacy. Britain declared neutrality in the conflict, though it was initially unclear how this position would affect trade. In Bristol, tobacco manufacturers such as W.D. & H.O. Wills had kept a close eye on the political situation as their principal supplier was the United States. The company stockpiled tobacco leaf in advance of the war and sought out substitutes from China, Japan and elsewhere. Despite a 60 per cent rise in the cost of American 'leaf' during the first two years of the war due to the embargo and blockade, they rode out the crisis by increasing retail prices and taking a hit in profits.[709] The situation regarding cotton which was vital to the huge textile industries in Britain was to be far more serious.

Initially the Southern States adopted an informal embargo on exports of cotton to Britain and Europe in an attempt to obtain recognition for the Confederacy. By the time it was clear that this diplomatic tactic had failed, the North had instituted a blockade of the 12 major ports in the South. In response, British investors began to commission the construction and use of 'blockade runners', fast steamships that could outrun the Union navy. Using British ports off the coast of the American mainland as staging posts, notably Bermuda and the Bahamas, blockade runners would carry arms, munitions and other essential supplies into Confederate ports, bringing out cotton and other raw materials. This was evidenced in Bristol when the American Consul photographed the blockade runner PS *Old Dominion* tied up on St Augustine's Parade opposite Broad Quay; the ship had clearly been working on behalf of the Confederates, probably supplying cotton.

By spring 1862, as the blockade began to bite, stocks of cotton in Britain began to dwindle despite the efforts of the blockade runners. In October the owners of the Great Western Cotton Factory (GWCF) in Bristol dismissed 1,500 cotton workers in order to protect their investments. The factory remained shut for three years.[710] There was severe hardship amongst the unemployed workers and their dependants, particularly in the area local to the plant, Barton Hill. Eight months after the closure around 700 workers were still unemployed and one source suggests that as a result 70 children died in Barton Hill in 1863.[711] Certainly some workers and their families had no choice but to suffer the misery of Bristol workhouses as a result of the 'cotton famine' and the closure of the factory, whilst others were forced to emigrate to Australia.[712]

Initially Garrison was unsure of President Abraham Lincoln and his new-fangled Republican Party as throughout his life he had been suspicious of all politicians for their greed and corruption. The Republicans had arisen out of a combination of the 1850s "Americans Party" (or "Know-Nothings") and Kansas "Free-Soilers", they then had a meteoric rise out of a range of popular issues that included the abolition of slavery. In the early phases of the war Lincoln tried to keep the Border States between the North and the South out of the conflict by allowing them to keep their slaves, but it didn't work. Finally, his patience ran out and on 22nd September 1862 he decreed that to meet the exigencies of war the slaves in the areas still in rebellion within 100 days shall, on 1st January 1863, "be then, thenceforward and forever, free...". The announcement promptly affected three million enslaved African-Americans.[713]

On 28th January 1863, a public meeting was held in Bristol in response to President Lincoln's Emancipation Proclamation. Key-note speakers were

PS *Old Dominion* – **Confederate blockade runner in Bristol Docks.**

Kingswood colliery owner and future Bristol East Liberal MP Handel Cossham and veteran abolitionist and Garrisonian, George Thompson. Cossham led the argument to support Lincoln's Proclamation. Although most of the audience were supportive of the anti-slavery declaration the works manager of the GWCF, Archibald Vickers, argued that Lincoln's proclamation was a sham, a political manoeuvre "for the sake of maintaining the Union". Richardson notes:

> Judging by the applause and cheering, as well as the hissing and calls to sit down, Vickers had a core of supporters present that in all probability would have included some of the better paid men from the cotton works.

Although Vickers's amendment was out-voted by a significant majority, the 'cotton famine' demonstrated the differing constraints that class interest had on political ideals. During the meeting Vickers also objected to Thompson's presence stating that people in Bristol were well versed on the topic and that "[they] did not need a stranger such as Mr Thompson coming to instruct them on the subject." This occasioned loud cries of disapproval from Cossham's supporters and Vickers had to take back his words.[714] This was mild approbation for the veteran activist Thompson; while supporting Garrison on a US tour in 1835, it is claimed death threats against him could be heard on every street corner in Boston and he had to go into hiding at one stage.[715]

The owners of the GWCF were keen to protect their business and essentially their capital investments, hence their decision to shut the plant, despite the suffering that caused amongst the workers and their families. They and their own families, however, were not going to physically suffer as a result. Despite mealy-mouthed references to the evils of slavery, for owners and their overseers the main objective was to obtain supplies of cotton regardless of the position of the (enslaved) labour that produced it. For the cotton workers (whose voices are rarely heard in the sources) the situation was far more pressing, as they were directly constrained by their economic position as proletarians (i.e. those without property). They and their children were physically suffering. As for the mainly middle-class abolitionists at the meeting, Richardson states:

...the question arises as to what degree had pro-abolitionists been concerned about the exploitation of working-class women, men and children in Britain

Richardson also notes that in 1844, Bristol-born radical socialist and free-thinker Emma Martin, had criticised:

...philanthropic ladies who wept over the sufferings of people in distant countries while ignoring the exploitation of poor women in their own land.[716]

These issues of class interest versus political ideals and the associated power relations that constrained those without property were prevalent throughout the campaign for the abolition of slavery. From the very beginning these questions had confronted activists on the ground, close to the slave-system, such as Thomas Clarkson. When Clarkson had first come to Bristol he had been faced with having to understand the relationship of the slave-ship sailor to his 'masters' in order to achieve progress in the campaign. It was a lesson he learned quickly. However, for many other abolitionists these problems were far from their minds, a reflection of the distance they were themselves from the experiences of precarious workers who were within the system of slavery or dependent upon its commodities for their income.

Mary Carpenter had tried to engage working class women in anti-slavery activities but had been put off by John B. Estlin who thought the movement would be better served by the educated classes. Possibly one of the 'philanthropic ladies' Martin was referring to was Estlin's daughter Mary. She had remained a firm supporter of Garrison and during the American Civil War helped found the Ladies' London Emancipation Society in 1863. This group included her lifelong friend Harriet Martineaux.[717] The main aim of the Society was to support the Northern states by trying to advance British understanding of the Union cause. A big problem for the North was that the Confederacy, under Jefferson Davis, had been courting the European powers in order to press for nation status and had had some degree of success. Britain's Prime Minister Gladstone for example had indiscreetly commented on what a good job Davis had done on bringing the South together. Despite this the South was never formally recognised as a nation.

The stance taken by the rulers of Britain and other imperial European powers over the US Civil War wasn't based on morality despite some claims to the contrary. In fact, the calculations made by all these countries were based on the damage war would do to their own economies, the potential loss of their colonies in the Americas and what they could possibly grab for themselves. For example, France took the opportunity to try and control Mexico which made them open to allying with the Confederacy, whereas Spain recaptured the lost colony of the Dominican Republic. Recognising the danger of these diplomatic manoeuvres Lincoln ultimately threatened war with any power that sided with the South. This concentrated the minds of the British who recognised the danger that conflict with the Union would pose to transatlantic trade and to colonies such as Canada. Britain's position influenced the other European powers to not ally themselves with the Confederacy. The moral high ground assumed by the British over the abolition of slavery and the slave trade was greatly diminished by the government's attitude to the whole conflict. Clearly the morality of slavery played little or no part in these crucial decisions; as ever, economic and geopolitical factors ruled the day.

On 8th April 1864, during the war, the Senate passed the Thirteenth Amendment to the US Constitution, which finally abolished slavery throughout the United States. It was the ambiguity of the original Revolutionary Constitution, that allowed some States to be slave-holders and others to prohibit slave-holding, that so incensed Garrison, especially when the slave-holding Southern States ended up dominating Congress. The House of Representatives followed suit on 31st January 1865 and the Thirteenth Amendment was passed.

‖ **1865**—American Civil War ends; slavery abolished in the USA.

The war officially ended on 9th April 1865; the nearly 4 million African Americans being made free, they finally had their 'Jubilee'. Religious reformers as far back as Wycliffe had noted the biblical tradition of jubilee, which primarily restored land to its original owners, cancelled debt and freed slaves and bond servants every 50 years. This idea was championed by early Quakers such as James Nayler, Anabaptists like Francis from Welsh Back, Methodists in the vein of John Wesley and poet Samuel Taylor Coleridge in his 1794 *Religious Musings*. These ideas were further crystallised in the late eighteenth century and early nineteenth century writings of Jamaican Robert Wedderburn, the son of a Scottish slave master and an enslaved African with Maroon roots, who synthesised them into abolitionism using radical Christianity and Paineite republicanism. Jubilee, in preaching and song, inspired enslaved peoples throughout the Americas, including rebel slaves such as Bussa, Nat Turner and Sam Sharpe, to rise up and fight for freedom.[718]

Although compensation for their 'lost property' was fleetingly mooted for the American slave-holders, before the country came to arms, nobody received a penny afterwards. The whole country had been subject to the 'fortunes of war'. In the Reconstruction that followed, the Fourteenth and Fifteenth Amendments were passed, the former in July 1868 granting citizenship and equal civil and legal rights to African Americans. The latter, passed in February 1870, forbade both federal and state governments from denying or abridging the right to vote "on account of race, color, or previous condition of servitude". Land reform never got past the talking stage.

During her tour of America in 1873 Mary Carpenter was able to see her old abolitionist friends for one final time. She treasured her reunion with Garrison in Boston where the two by now veterans of the campaign "[had] pleasant chats about the great battle fought and won". She then managed to call in on Frederick Douglass in Washington. In between Mary visited homes which contained water-colours that she and her sister Anna had painted for the Anti-Slavery Christmas Fairs and, still campaigning, went to New York where she was horrified at the state of the prisons. From there her party sailed on to Virginia where Mary was "happy to land on that shore, the scene of such frightful struggles and know the slaves are free".[719]

Four years later Carpenter wrote her final letter to William Lloyd Garrison after having heard he was to visit England again:

> I shall be very proud to have you as my guest… The Anti-Slavery cause was my 'first love'; even from my earliest childhood my sympathies were enlisted in it. So please be sure to come here *straight* from Liverpool with your son, to my house, where you shall do in every way what you like… [Adding that if he felt strong enough he could meet] about 100 friends in the Red Lodge Drawing Room.

Garrison received the letter on 16th June and opening it with his London *Daily News* at breakfast, he annotated it thus: "It is probably the last letter she ever wrote. Blessed be her memory! W.L.G."[720] She had died in her sleep in the ground-breaking Red Lodge Girls Reformatory School that she had set up and bought outright with a legacy from Lady Byron in 1854. Her funeral cortege was half a mile long and at a public meeting in October 1877, £2,700 was raised for her reform schools and for a plaque to be placed to her memory in Bristol Cathedral. Strangely Carpenter's eulogies rarely mentioned her campaigning against slavery in the United States.

As part of the American post-war 'Reconstruction', Fisk University was set-up for freedmen and black students in Nashville, Tennessee. Desperately short of funds, one of the founders suggested a musical tour to help raise money; it proved so popular that the tour was extended to include Britain and Europe. In the 1870s the Fisk Jubilee Singers, as they were now called, made two performances in Bristol. Their forte was singing 'Negro Spirituals' and one of their most popular numbers was *Many Thousand Gone*: "The words include 'no more drivers lash for me', 'No more auction block for me', 'Many thousand gone".[721] They followed this up with four dates in November 1901 at the newly rebuilt Colston Hall during a Temperance Rally; it begs the question of what the singers would have thought if they had known that the Hall had been named after a pre-eminent slave trader.

Garrison, who first sounded his own note of Jubilee in a sermon in Boston in 1829, died on 24th May 1879; he had been a powerful firebrand leader of the American Anti-Slavery Society throughout its history. His hard-line radical ideas and actions, like publicly burning the US Constitution, occasionally split the Society right down the middle. As we have seen, Mary Carpenter greatly admired him although admitted she was "alarmed by the violence of his language and his torrents of invective against slave-holders".[722] Some commentators had depicted Garrisonians as "insane and irresponsible 'Anti-everything-arians'".[723] Garrison had been born in the age of Pitt, Jefferson and Napoleon and passed away when Gladstone, Grant and Bismarck were making their mark. One of the people reading a eulogy at Garrison's funeral was Lucy Stone who had married Elizabeth Blackwell's abolitionist brother Henry in 1855. Like many other prominent American women's rights activists, Stone had first cut her campaigning teeth on the issue of abolition and was indebted to Garrison.[724]

In 1868 Westbury College passed into the hands of Sir John Cam Hobhouse, Baron Broughton. The Hobhouses were descended from a long line of Bristol West India merchants; John's great uncle had been Bristol's second most prolific slave trader, Isaac Hobhouse. Like his father, Sir Benjamin Hobhouse, John took an interest in politics. Benjamin had, despite being from 'slaving stock', taken an opposing view on slavery and notably supported one of William Wilberforce's bills to abolish the trade in 1797. This was after he had unsuccessfully stood for Bristol in the election of 1796 in the Whig interest. Benjamin's first wife was Charlotte Cam and son John followed in her dissident footsteps. He was educated in the Unitarian faith by John Prior Estlin, helping him to become one

Miles bank note of 1844.

of the most conspicuous figures of the early nineteenth century. As a young man John was a friend of Lord Byron's and acted as his best man. Before becoming a politician, he was a strong advocate for the reform of the House of Commons. In 1819 he was briefly imprisoned at Newgate for a sarcastic indictment of the government at the time of the Peterloo massacre.[725]

The future Lord Broughton was MP successively for Westminster, Nottingham and Harwich, but after the Reform Act of 1832 he took a less radical stance and held several high-powered government posts, though in later years he championed child labour reform.[726] Nine years after his death The Factory and Workshop Act of 1878 finally saw the end of child labour in Britain. The law was applied to all trades, not just the cotton industry; no child under the age of 10 years was to be employed and education was compulsory for this age group. In addition, 10–14 year-olds could only be employed for half a day and women were to work no more than 56 hours per week. The campaign against the exploitation of working-class children's labour in Britain had been a long one, only making significant gains 30 years after the ending of slavery.

Throughout abolition and emancipation, opponents often claimed that Wilberforce and other abolitionists cared more about slaves than for the suffering of Britons. In fact, Wilberforce had remained consistent in his reactionary beliefs whether applied to the working class in Britain or the emancipated slaves in the Caribbean. For example, he stated that a rise in the wages of workers would "ruin...the whole of the commercial greatness of our country" and that the poor should accept that "their lowly path has been allotted to them by the hand of God; that is their part...contentedly to bear its inconveniences". He did not believe in universal suffrage and stated that once freed slaves in the colonies had been suitably educated by Christianity they would know their place in the social order as "a grateful peasantry".[727]

Concentration in Bristol's banking interests reached its zenith in 1877, when the 'Old Bank' originally founded in 1750 by Tyndall and his partners and which had swallowed up the 'New Bank' of Ames, Cave, Harford, Daubeny & Bright in 1826, merged with the 'Miles Bank' itself founded in 1752. The new institution was known as Miles, Cave, Baillie and Co. and represented the fusion of some of the most powerful families in Bristol with a legacy of wealth creation derived directly from the slave-system. In 1918, this financial institution was in turn amalgamated with the Union of London & Smiths Bank to form the 'National Provincial'. In the late twentieth century the National Provincial merged with the Westminster Bank to become 'National Westminster'; 'Nat West' to you and me.[728] This pattern of merchants creating banks with huge profits made from the system of slavery was repeated around Britain. In Liverpool, Arthur and Benjamin Heywood turned their fortunes from the slave trade into a bank which eventually became part of Barclay's. Thomas Leyland, Mayor of Liverpool and one of the richest men in the city from the profits of slave-trading, launched his financial institution in 1807. It eventually became the Midland Bank, which is now HSBC. Similar stories lie behind Lloyds; in fact, all the traditional 'high street banks' in Britain have a basis in the transatlantic slave trade along with, of course, the Bank of England.[729]

The Cult of Colston

Colston reinvented

Although the various charitable societies formed to further the legacy of Edward Colston were active in the eighteenth century, it is interesting that their heyday came during the Victorian era (1837–1901), more than a century after his death in 1721. The second half of the nineteenth century saw a glut of Colston nostalgia ranging from named buildings and streets to statues and stained-glass windows. So why was Colston so important, to the exclusion of so many other historic figures? And who was pushing all this tat and ritual on Bristolians?

In the twenty-first century we are used to hearing about Edward Colston as the 'great philanthropist' but this was not always the case. Writing in 1863, Tovey stated:

> But for a few years only has Colston been recognised as a Philanthropist; but for a few years has his light shone before men, and his character become manifest, in his support of six sailors in the Merchants' Almshouse, and more especially in the peaceful dwellings that rose at his command on St. Michael's Hill.

Tovey follows this up with a eulogy—or prayer—of truly epic proportions:

> Here, while the name of humanity endures, and the solemn testimonies of the dead are sacred, these walls will ever echo his name and proclaim his goodness; and the daily voice of the chapel-bell ever summon the

thoughts from the creature to the creator—for whose honour he laboured—to whom he gave the glory, and to whom he willed the praise.[730]

Tovey's opening sentence demonstrates that Colston's image as a philanthropist only became widely recognised in the Victorian period. Sally Morgan suggests that the origins of Colston's fame lie in:

the 'great philanthropic awakening' of the 1840s, a time of major social reform when, possibly for the first time, wealthy men were encouraged to see themselves as having duties to society at large.[731]

Studying the second quote from Tovey, which places Colston as some kind of saint in a holy hierarchy of 'goodness', in relation to the first, suggests something bizarre is going on. A super-rich merchant puts up six sailors in an Almshouse and apparently "while the name of humanity endures" he will be remembered. Morgan questions this dramatic hero-worship in relation to the reality of his philanthropy:

His [Colston's] reputation for philanthropy is puzzling to the modern mind, not only because of his unpalatable occupation, but because his little kindnesses seem very little indeed. He instituted a small school for poor boys who would afterwards become apprentices or sailors (probably working for Colston himself), from which Dissenters were expressly excluded. This exclusion might have been a blessing considering the school's spartan regime and joyless conditions. Children were constantly running away and were always in danger of being expelled if they became ill or developed a 'leprosy'. He also, as we know, founded an equally small and joyless almshouse, principally for ex-mariners who were possibly also Colston's ex-employees. In a period when it was notoriously hard to tempt men to work at sea, a time when potential sailors had to be press-ganged and were likely to jump ship at the first opportunity, the founding of these institutions might be seen less as an act of charity than as a pragmatic move to ensure a supply of trained labour from his school, and to encourage long service from his sailors through the promise of a place in his almshouse.[732]

Colston was selected to be an icon from a number of historical figures who had made philanthropic donations to the city. These included, amongst others, Robert Thorne, John Whitson, Robert Aldworth, William Chester and the Canynges family, who most Bristolians have never heard of.[733] Arguably the greatest Bristol philanthropist of all was Quaker industrialist Richard Reynolds, who died in 1816; he gave away in excess of £200,000 in his lifetime and is not remembered at all in his native city.[734] So what was special about Colston, why was he chosen and is the Colston 'we know' a real reflection of the historical figure? Spencer Jordan argues in his detailed study of Bristol elites in this period that Edward Colston should not be interpreted as:

> a static eighteenth-century inheritance but rather a cultural creation whose form and meaning had distinct temporal qualities reflecting the vagaries of dominant bourgeois ethics.[735]

Jordan's point is that the historical figure of Colston was being reinvented in the Victorian period to fulfil the perspectives of the Bristol business elite. 'Invented tradition' can be characterised as:

> ...a set of practices, normally governed by overtly or tacitly accepted rules and of a ritual or symbolic nature, which seek to inculcate certain values and norms of behaviour by repetition, which automatically implies continuity with the past.[736]

Ritual commemoration, celebration and memorialisation of Edward Colston in the Victorian public domain was crucial to propagating both the elite concept of Colston and the belief that this concept was validated by long-standing tradition. So, what were the ideas underlying this reinvention? Jordan argues that the reimaged 'Victorian' Colston legitimised:

> ...two broad aspects of the developing bourgeois value system: first, the ascendancy of individualism, both morally and economically, as a political system; and second, the right of limited but sustained private relief organised and distributed by those considered the city's moral and economic leaders. The ability to depict Colston as both 'merchant prince' and 'moral saint' was thus central to the perpetuation of the tradition throughout the nineteenth century.[737]

The organisations used for propagating this Victorian version of Colston were primarily the four charitable societies: the Dolphin, Anchor, Grateful and Colston (or Parent) Societies. Leading members of these associations were tied closely to other organisations of the Bristol elite such as the Society of Merchant Venturers and:

> ...by the mid-nineteenth century a Colston presidency was considered to be a particularly high-status position, attracting members from Bristol's leading families to the degree that some established transient dynasties, such as the Wills in the Anchor, Miles in the Dolphin and the Hare and Lucas families in the Parent.[738]

The key period of ritual for the four societies was the 1st–13th November each year, which was effectively a drawn-out public fund-raising activity culminating in Colston's birthday on the thirteenth. 'Colston Day' as it was touted, consisted of elaborate ceremonial processions, worship and banquets which grew increasingly more stylised and complex as the century wore on. Jordan provides a description at the mid-century:

> With the church bells ringing around the city events began early in the morning when both the committees of the Dolphin and Grateful met separately for breakfast…While the latter was an intimate affair, the former included 100 young apprentices who, after breakfasting together, formed a procession carrying banners and wands…The procession wended its way through 'great crowds' to All Saints' Church where the banners were placed around the tomb of Edward Colston, profusely decorated with flowers. After breakfasting, the Dolphin committee was met by apprentices and boys from Colston and Temple Colston Schools. A procession was formed with banners and bands which, after marching around College Green, continued to the cathedral for a service. The boys and apprentices then marched to the Exchange where each was presented with a new shilling and each apprentice three shillings and sixpence. 32 Members of the Parent met at the Colston Rooms in mid-afternoon and then, attended by boys and girls from Blue Coat School [Queen Elizabeth's Hospital], walked to St. Mary Redcliffe Church. The Anchor, with its nonconformist associations, failed to generate any tradition of divine service, only meeting for a dinner in the evening.[739]

The evening dinners organised by the various societies which marked the end of 'Colston Day' became important national events by the end of the century, attracting leading politicians including a Prime Minister. They were marked by speeches reflecting the political flavours of each society and involved numerous toasts, including to "the pious memory of Edward Colston".[740]

Perhaps one of the most interesting aspects of this whole Victorian charade was the fact that the much-vaunted charitable efforts of the Colston Societies were superficial, making up only 1.5 percent of the cost of relieving the poor in 1884. However, as Jordan notes:

> this should not lead one to understate the importance of philanthropy as ritual in the maintenance of urban power structures.[741]

Thus the ritual and ideological aspects of the 'cult of Colston' far outweighed the actual practical benefits to the 'poor'.

From the mid-century on, 'Colston Day' events were increasingly reported in the burgeoning local press, pushing the 'cult of Colston' to a wider audience. Jordan explains:

> The telling and retelling of the Colston myth each year in the dailies took on an obsessive attention to historic detail…the parades and dinners… received careful elucidation, including the dutiful recantation of speeches and the names of those attending. Poems, songs and cartoons…all became part of the annual commemoration.[742]

The 'cult' was even expressed in literary form in Mrs Emma Marshall's *In Colston's Days—A Story of Old Bristol,* a fanciful historical romance originally written in 1883. The book mixes fact with fiction, picking out actual characters from Bristol's past and giving them improbable roles. Stressing the perspective of Colston as 'moral saint' Marshall ends her Preface with the words "…the good name" of the great Bristol philanthropist is better than his "great riches".[743] Emma Marshall was described in 1907 as a writer of "pure and wholesome stories for the young".[744]

In this way over several generations the myths of the 'cult' that portrayed Colston as both 'merchant prince' and 'moral saint' penetrated the Bristol psyche and were fixed, to varying degree, in much of the populace. As part of this reinvention, strange quasi-religious stories about Colston were propagated. It was said that when his body was disinterred in 1843, more than a hundred years after his death, it was miraculously preserved.[745] Rumours abounded that samples of Colston's hair and nails had been secretly conserved and were worshipped by the Society of Merchant Venturers in the Merchants' Hall, like medieval religious relics.[746] Others claimed that Colston's philanthropy was due to a religious epiphany, a 'road to Damascus' moment that had turned his life towards giving rather than profiteering.[747] With these implicit references to St Paul and Jesus along with his explicit representation as the 'Good Samaritan' created in Bristol churches, the reinvented Edward Colston covered most of the Christian bases. However, unpalatable aspects of Colston's history, such as his leading role as an organiser and profiteer in the slave trade and his religious and political bigotry remained hidden or were ignored.

Bristol historian Taylor wrote in 1875:

> Three societies yearly assemble on "Saint" Colston's day (Nov. 2nd) and celebrate his memory with flowing cups and flowing speech; and at the same time more practically recognise his philanthropic character by the contribution of liberal alms to the poor that are always with us. Up to the end of 1874 the amounts severally collected by the Dolphin, Anchor and Grateful Societies have attained an aggregate of £115,243.[748]

Alongside these characteristics of the 'cult' was the creation of physical memorials to Colston which became prolific in the latter part of the nineteenth century. These took several forms, which are surveyed in the following section.

Colston over-memorialised

125 years after his death, the first modern memorial for Colston was created in 1846 on the replacement Guildhall in Broad Street. This was built from the design of R. S. Pope and, according to architectural historian Pevsner, is the earliest Perpendicular Gothic Revival town hall built in England. When looking at the building there are three statues by Bristol sculptor John Evan Thomas positioned in niches on both sides of the first-floor oriel window. On the left they represent Queen Victoria, Edward III and Bristol merchant John Whitson (founder of Red Maids' school). On the right are Bristol merchants John Foster and John Dunning along with Edward Colston nearest to St John's Arch. Each sculpture has hands above it holding their own coat of arms on suspended shields. Colston's statue represents the earliest public sculpture of him in Bristol, in the very street that historically represented the city's seat of power.[749]

In 1834 Liverpool, Bristol's great mercantile rival, began courting designs for St George's Hall to meet their need for a venue for festivals, meetings, dinners and concerts. Desiring the same for Bristol, the Colston Hall Company was founded in 1861. A potential central location had been provided three years previously when Colston's trustees, the Society of Merchant Venturers, purchased (in controversial fashion) the Bishop's Palace at Stapleton for their new Boys' School, freeing up the Great House.[750] The Colston Company then purchased the historic Great House and promptly demolished it. Designed by John Foster and Joseph Wood, construction work on the Colston Hall began in 1863. The building was planned to accommodate 2,500 persons and was eventually opened in 1867.

The hall has had a chequered life. On 1st September 1898 the original hall was destroyed by fire and its replacement—"erected on most approved plans, in which especial regard has been paid to the safety and comfort of the people"—could then hold over 4,000 people. It re-opened in 1901 and contained a fine, world class, organ installed at the cost of nearly £12,000 provided by the late Lord Winterstoke and previous directors of the Colston Hall Company.[751] The Colston Hall Company itself was then wound up in 1919 with the building being saved and purchased by Bristol Corporation, thereby becoming a source of great civic pride. The Hall was internally reconstructed in 1936 and after escaping the fate of so many Bristol buildings in the air raids of World War Two, the building was again destroyed by fire in 1945. It was not until the Festival of Britain was contemplated that permission could be obtained to rebuild it.

Colston's old school in the Great House before demolition.

On 7th July 1951, the present hall was opened by the Duke of Gloucester and a memorial tablet in the old entrance was affixed in what is now the 'Lantern Bar'.[752] The plaque is surrounded by three bas-relief plaques celebrating founding benefactors of the Colston Hall: Elisha Smith Robinson (of Robinson's the paper merchants and printers), Lewis Fry (Attorney) and Sir William Henry Wills (of Wills tobacco and snuff manufacturers). They are matched on the opposite wall by four similar plaques marking Joseph Storrs Fry [II] (of Fry J. S. & Sons; chocolate, cocoa and chicory makers), Alfred N. Price J.P. (Price Brothers, Stoneware Potters), Herbert Thomas and Christopher J. Thomas (both abolitionists, of Thomas, Christopher and Brothers; soap and candle manufacturers).[753] Most recently an adjacent building was demolished in order to facilitate a major refurbishment which added an extra wing to the Colston Hall. This was opened in 2009 and revised the hall's capacity to 2,075 with an additional 350 people being catered for in the newly created 'Lantern Bar', also built as part of the 2009 redevelopments. Redevelopment of the Hall's cellars is currently ongoing (due for completion 2019) and during the work artefacts from the site's Carmelite era were discovered.

In 1865, during the restoration of St Mary Redcliffe Church (1842–1880), Handel's window was re-sited leaving plain glass in the north transept. New Canon Henry Randall was keen to memorialise Edward Colston in this space. At the 1866 meeting of the Canynges Society[754], he argued that Colston was solely remembered in All Saints Church and that with the remodelling of St Mary's, now would be a good time to rectify the omission. He gave the

New Colston Hall in 1908, by Samuel Loxton.

committee a choice of a new spire or a new window and the members voted for a new window with £80 raised on the spot. However, other funding wasn't so forthcoming. It took the combined efforts of the Colston Parent Society and cadging from past and present presidents of the Dolphin, Grateful and Anchor Societies, to make it happen. Even then, according to Latimer, "The proposal was received with coldness".[755]

The window itself depicts the Good Samaritan and the Corporal Works of Mercy, which concern the material needs of others. It was finally erected in 1870 at a cost of £400. In the 1850s, Cruger Miles requested a memorial window for his late father, Philip John Miles, Bristol MP and West India Merchant [see 1831] who had died in 1845. The window, in the west wall at the end of the south nave aisle, shows Moses as a type of Christ.[756] Today in St Mary Redcliffe Church there's a contextual plaque explaining the role that Colston and other Bristol merchants played in the slave trade.

With the remodelling of the Cathedral in 1870, Bristol's mother church got in on the act of Colston memorialisation by naming the brand-new south-west tower after him. The 'Colston Tower' was completed in the late 1880s and in conjunction with this a site for a new stained-glass window was created in his honour, the massive 'Colston window', dominating the north transept. The latter is worth describing in detail. At its zenith in a canopy in the main octofoil of tracery, with a depiction of the Centurion before the Almighty, lie the words: AS MUCH AS YE HAVE DONE IT UNTO THE LEAST OF THESE MY BRETHEREN YE HAVE DONE IT UNTO ME

The letters 'EC' are picked out directly below, within its own tracery (a sort of inverted red triangle). There are then a surfeit of Colston's dolphin badges cascading down, two groups of three, picked out in silver against a blue background. Below this Cornelius and the Centurion have been inserted, interspersed by four shields; from left to right:–the See of Bristol, Society of Merchant Venturers, City of Bristol and See of Canterbury. Below these again are six episodes of the Good Samaritan above a bold inscription:

GO AND DO LIKEWISE (Lu.X.37)

To this day the parable of the Good Samaritan is used in various Colston ceremonies—the injunction "go and do likewise" has led the 'Good Samaritan' name being applied to many hospitals. Along the bottom border reads:

TO THE GLORY OF GOD AND IN MEMORY OF EDWARD COLSTON, 1636–1721

This is combined with a view of Colston's Great House reproduced from Millerd's Map of 1673. In addition, there are two further dolphin badges at

Details from the Colston Window in Bristol Cathedral. Top, Jesus and the Centurion. Middle, the shields of (left-to-right) the See of Canterbury, the Merchant Venturers, Bristol City, and the See of Bristol. (A 'See' is the area of a bishop's jurisdiction; a synonym for diocese). Bottom, two of the six scenes depicting the Good Samaritan.

the base of each corner.[757] Beneath it all is a brass plaque that states that the Dolphin Society raised the money from 1888–1890.

In the most recent official history of Bristol Cathedral in 2000, Canon John Rogan, states in the introduction: "The monuments bear witness to the economic expansion of England but with silence about the slave trade". He reasserts this point later in the book by saying:

> …with its thriving sugar trade, amongst other commodities, Bristol had close connections with the West Indies and there are reminders of that in the memorials. Edward Colston was one of the great benefactors to the city and also donated to the Cathedral. However, there is no echo anywhere of connections with the infamous slave trade. The houses of the merchants of the time survive. They said nothing of their commercial methods.[758]

Rogan's observation really does beg the question as to why the Cathedral continued to fail to highlight its own connections with slavery after the publication of the book in 2000. In early 2017, the Dean of Bristol Cathedral, David Hoyle, grabbed the attention of both local and national media by announcing that the Cathedral was considering removing the Colston window. Hoyle subsequently backtracked on this claim but failed to state which person or organisation had exerted pressure for the removal in the first place.[759]

After the construction of the Colston Hall came a plethora of roads and buildings named in his honour; Colston Street (c.1870) and, in 1887, Colston Villas were built in Armoury Square in Easton, east Bristol.[760] Then when it was decided to culvert the River Frome it allowed for the creation of a tree lined boulevard in what was to become Bristol's most prestigious thoroughfare, this was named Colston Avenue in 1892. Ultimately, 13 streets and roads in Bristol were marked in remembrance to Colston.[761] In 1895, a second public statue of Colston was erected in the newly created Colston Avenue. The bronze figure of Colston was the last of four major public statues of the Victorian era which were installed over an eight-year span. These included the Bristol MP and millionaire philanthropist Samuel Morley (1887), Queen Victoria (1888) and Edmund Burke MP (1894).[762]

Bristol's last two stained glass windows to Colston's memory were revealed in 1908 and 1921. The first was in All Saints' Church and situated above his Rysbrack monument and was sponsored by 'some citizens' at a cost of £400.[763] The second was commissioned by the daughter and son-in-law of Samuel James King, ship-owner of the Port of Bristol, when they gifted 'four lights' to the Cathedral in his memory. The four full length standing figures are of Edward Colston, John Cabot, William Worcester and Samuel Wesley, each surrounded by clear glass with shields of the city and See.[764]

THE CITIZEN OF THE CITY OF CHARITIES---AND RATES

"I'm so glad to see you again, Mr. Colston-Day, but, er, I'm rather busy just now!"

A cartoon from *The Bristol Magpie* in 1906 showing the increasing irrelevance of charitable donations from the Colston Societies in the face of pressure from foreign competition, growing unemployment relief and infrastructure projects: "I'm so glad to see you again, Mr. Colston-Day, but, er, I'm rather busy just now!"

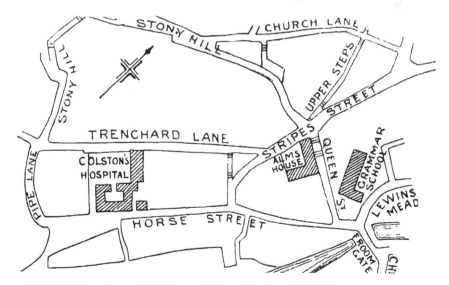

Rocque's Bristol street map (1750) pre-Colstonification (Hall, Tower, Statue, Street and Avenue)—mockingly known as 'Colston Corner' after remodelling in 2018.

Although the proliferation of buildings and roads dedicated to Colston was primarily a feature of the Victorian era, there was one major exception to the rule in the twentieth century. Between 1961 and 1973, the fourteen storey Colston Tower was erected in a prominent location on the centre adjacent to the existing Colston Hall. Designed by the late architect and broadcaster Michael Jenner, it had a major upgrade a few years ago with a clock face added high over a new exterior service lift. In addition to the clock, massive illuminated letters were added either side bearing the legend COLSTON TOWER. Wherever you are in central Bristol it is difficult to escape Colston's legacy, especially at night with his name in lights glowering down on all and sundry.

Schools and universities

As we have seen, much of the money bequeathed by Edward Colston and administered by the Merchant Venturers was allocated to education, in particular to Colston's Hospital which is known today as Colston's School. Despite the noble intentions of educating '100 poor boys', albeit under the draconian theological rules of Colston, the project was plagued with financial issues, mainly related to tight-fisted benefactors and administrators. After the death of Colston in 1721, it took almost 50 years and eventual legal action to force Colston's executors to produce all the money that he had bequeathed to the project. In 1842, the Society of Merchant Venturers was in court again when it was caught skimming Colston's endowments to the school. After six years and a legal battle, the Society was forced to pay the money they had taken back to the trust that ran the school.[765]

The Society of Merchant Venturers was faced with more serious problems in 1870 when the Liberal government attempted to reform education. One of a series of Education Acts was aimed at examining endowed schools to see if the money could be put to better use in expanding educational provision, particularly for girls. It also encouraged commissioners to alter or abolish "out of date and inappropriate rules laid down by long dead benefactors". The first reaction of the Merchant Venturers was to ask the Endowed Schools Commission for special exemption from the Act, an arrogant as well as naïve request, which was immediately refused.[766] They were soon faced by the Assistant Commissioner, Joshua Fitch, a fierce advocate of education for women and girls. Fitch after careful study of the curricula, methods, staffing, social class of the pupils and finances of endowed schools in Bristol produced a report in which he recommended:

...the practical abolition of Colston's and of Queen Elizabeth's Hospitals and of Whitson's Red Maids' School, all old schools with their own traditions and associations with the past. These foundations were to be

The foyer of Colston Hall and Colston Tower, 2018.

"scrapped" and their endowments to be applied in the establishment of a series of first, second and third grade schools.[767]

In his investigations Fitch had uncovered the lie that Colston's school was for 'poor boys' as the Society of Merchant Venturers had claimed. Instead it was based on a system of patronage where they and the so-called 'Colston Nominees' chose the pupils leading to a "school filled with middle-class boys".[768] Furthermore, and most worrying for the Merchant Venturers, Fitch's central recommendation was the immediate establishment in Bristol of schools to provide more accessible and better education for girls.

Fitch's report stunned the Merchant Venturers; they had been caught red-handed and faced dissolution of their privileged educational empire. They immediately stymied attempts to debate the report in the public domain. Over nearly four years the Merchant Venturers argued, stalled and refused to implement Fitch's measures until eventually a watered-down plan was agreed in October 1873. The Merchant Venturers decided to deal with the financial issues created by the agreement by making the boys' school mostly fee-paying, an ironic deviation from Colston's supposed institution for '100 poor boys'. Another part of the compromise they had to accept was the construction of a girls' school, something the Merchant Venturers were clearly reluctant to do. Over the next 15 years they variously ignored, delayed and then hoped the legal requirement for the girls' school would be forgotten. Finally, in 1891, Colston's Girls' School was established on Cheltenham Road.[769] The school may bear the name of the Merchant Venturers' icon, Edward Colston but, in keeping with his archaic views, it was an unwanted child of progress forced upon the reluctant Merchant Venturers.

Colston's Girls' School (CGS) buildings on Cheltenham Road were damaged by aerial bombing in 1941 causing its juniors to move to some houses on nearby Cotham Grove. The 1944 Education Act which introduced, amongst other measures, the Eleven Plus selection test for secondary admission meant that "girls in the Junior School had to compete on equal terms with the rest of Bristol" and were not guaranteed places at the upper school. Fearing the 'level playing field', many parents withdrew their children from the junior school over the succeeding years and it eventually collapsed in 1946. The following year the Local Authority took control of the buildings, employed the existing staff and a new primary school was created, unconnected to CGS. The school took the name Colston though it appears there was opposition to this as recounted by Head Mistress Sarah Dunn:

> Soon after its status was changed there was controversy, which spread to the columns of local papers, as to the propriety of its retaining the name of Colston. Happily, no official notice was taken of this smallmindedness.[770]

It is unclear whether this "smallmindedness" was an attempt by some to protect the (private) educational brand of 'Colston' from being sullied by association with a state school or if there was opposition to the school taking the name on the basis of Colston's nefarious history.

In 2015, the issue of Edward Colston's involvement in the slave trade was raised by a governor and a teacher at Colston Primary School. In 2017, the 70th anniversary of the founding of the school, an extensive consultation process involving staff, pupils and parents was launched. In December of that year, after a vote, the Governors decided to change the name of the school in line with the wishes of parents and pupils. Fittingly, the announcement of the change came the day before the international celebration of the Abolition of Slavery.[771] The new agreed name, 'Cotham Gardens Primary School', was launched in September 2018 and, despite the dire warnings of some Colston apologists, the sky didn't fall in.

Faced with similar calls from campaigners for change, in 2017 the principal of CGS decided to carry out an internal 'consultation' with the pupils. This carefully managed discussion was carried out in classrooms with students asked to write their views on pieces of paper. According to sources within the school a large majority of students wanted the school renamed with few, if any, dissenting voices. However, the students were never informed of the outcome of the consultation and it was quietly forgotten. Faced with the 'wrong answer' to the survey, the governors of CGS made an executive decision to ignore the views of their students and not to alter the name of the school.[772] In their statement to the media explaining their decision they claimed:

> Colston's Girls' School is directly descended from Colston's Hospital, a school which opened in 1710 for '100 poor boys', funded entirely by a large financial gift from Edward Colston (1636-1721).[773]

This contrived (and perhaps desperate) attempt to "directly" connect their school with the Colston legacy, and by implication with Edward Colston, was to enhance the feeling of an inalienable tradition in order to resist change. Of course, the statement not only failed to address the near two century difference between the founding of the 'school for poor boys' and CGS but also the fact that the Society of Merchant Venturers had been forced by central government to build a girls' school they never apparently wanted. It was a convenient distortion of history that has been all too present amongst the propagators of the 'cult of Colston'. An irony of this story is the fact that the Merchant Venturers had no difficulties in changing the name of other schools they had taken over in the city, without consultation and regardless of their 'traditions' or the feelings of those who had attended them.[774] The suspicion is that, as far as the Society of Merchant Venturers was concerned, their 'history', represented by the Colston brand, required protection whilst that of working class Bristolians was disposable.

Until fairly recently there has been a popular perception in Bristol that educational connections with Edward Colston were confined to two 'private' schools, the boys' (Colston's) and the girls' school (CGS).[775] However, the involvement of the Merchant Venturers in Bristol's major university led to representations of Colston appearing in higher education as well.

In 1885, the Society of Merchant Venturers took over the Bristol Trade School, renaming it the Merchant Venturers' Technical College (MVTC) and moving it to new buildings on Unity Street in central Bristol.[776] Rival to the MVTC was Bristol University College (BUC), associated with the Liberals and based on nearby Park Street. In 1899 the 'University College Colston Society' was formed with the aim of creating a university for Bristol.[777] The Tory dominated Society of Merchant Venturers was opposed to collaborating with BUC as it was perceived to be a 'Liberal' institution. However, in 1906 the MVTC was destroyed by fire, forcing the Merchant Venturers into working with the BUC in their plan for a dedicated university for the city. BUC struggled financially until 1908, when Henry Overton Wills, of the super-rich tobacco empire, made a donation of £100,000 allowing it to receive its Royal Charter and become the University of Bristol the following year. Unsurprisingly, Wills became the first Chancellor of the institution and he was memorialised in the massive Wills

Building, the late-gothic centre-piece of the university, which was constructed in 1925.[778]

The influence of the various benefactors and vested interests can be seen in the original arms for Bristol University. This had a ship and castle in the centre (the badge of Bristol) with a 'sun in splendour' representing the Wills family uppermost, an 'embowed dolphin' on the left signifying Edward Colston, a 'horse courant', the emblem of the Fry family, on the right and an open 'book proper' below symbolising learning. Bristol University re-designed the logo in 2004 but retained the dolphin representing Edward Colston.

In 2017, there were calls and a petition from students to rename the Wills Memorial Building because of the links between the Wills business empire and the use of slave produced tobacco. The students claimed that the:

> university was financed with "slave profited" cash and the name is a threat to the "diversity and inclusivity" of the university. [779]

A few months later the University announced it wasn't going to change the name as Wills had been a major benefactor and cited, without explanation, "duties of non-erasure of history".[780]

Bristol University's coat of arms and modern logo;
both feature Colston's 'Dolphin' device.

Dissent and Protest

Slavery obscured

The elite representation of Colston as a 'moral saint' created in the Victorian period did not go uncontested. It was first challenged by disclosure of his religious bigotry, then by criticisms of the manner in which he acquired his fortune and finally by exposure of his role in the slave trade as both a leading organiser and profiteer.

The *Handbook to Bristol and Clifton*[781] published in 1872, in the aftermath of the naming of Colston Hall, contained a frank quotation from Garrard's *Life of Colston* (itself published in 1852):

> His [Colston's] antipathy to dissent, it must be acknowledged, approaches the confines of bigotry.[782]

This open criticism suggests Colston was not as revered in the Victorian period as one might imagine and this may have been reflected in the lack of public support for one of his most famous memorials.

Despite the claim on a plaque on Colston's statue in Bristol city centre that it was "Erected by citizens of Bristol as a memorial of one of the most virtuous and wise sons of their city" the idea did not come from popular demands by the "citizens of Bristol". It was the brainchild of one person, James Arrowsmith, a wealthy businessman who owned the largest printing and publishing company in the city and was president of the Liberal dominated Anchor Society. He announced his idea to erect a statue to this "son and benefactor of the city" in October 1893 and in March the following year a fund-raising committee was set up by officials of the four Colston commemoration societies, with Arrowsmith as honorary secretary.

The fund-raising drive commenced in April 1894 with an appeal to the four Colston societies with a combined membership of 1,550, some of the wealthiest people in the city. It was a nightmare from the very beginning, with this first subscription raising less than a quarter of the £1,000 required. A second round of subscriptions doubled this amount, but still fell way short of the target. The committee then decided to open up the fund-raising to the general public, which appears to have been a complete flop as hardly any more money was collected. In July 1894 a bitter letter of complaint (probably written by Arrowsmith himself) under the pseudonym *In Statu Quo* appeared in the *Bristol Mercury* with the concluding lines:

> There is enough wealth in Bristol to erect 400 statues, if necessary, without so much begging and praying…Why two or three gentlemen are always saddled with the making up of deficiencies, whether for church, chapel, hospital, or school, I cannot comprehend; but it is the same old tale of working a willing horse to death.[783]

By the time of the unveiling of the statue over a year later, on Colston day 13th November 1895, the fund was still hundreds of pounds short of its target.

Accounts of the unveiling emphasise that hundreds, if not thousands, of Bristolians gathered in the Centre to witness the ceremony. However, large numbers were not unusual for a typical 'Colston Day', which according to one source had been "virtually a public holiday since the 1720s" and during the Victorian revival had effectively become 'Bristol Day'.[784] It is therefore hard to judge how many members of the public were in the centre of Bristol merely because it was a public holiday, one of the few such days in the calendar year the working classes would have enjoyed.

The unveiling was led by the Mayor and Bishop of Bristol, surrounded by the business and political elite of the city. The mayor's speech concentrated on Bristol's maritime history of mercantilism and Colston's philanthropy. There was, of course, no direct mention of Colston's leading role in the slave trade through his management positions and investments in the Royal African Company. However, the Mayor made one major indirect reference in his speech in stating that Colston's "business was mainly with the West Indies"; arguably code for involvement in slavery and the slave trade.[785] It is interesting that in 1895 there was at least some clarity about this aspect, albeit indirect. This should be compared to clumsy attempts by apologists over a century later to 'airbrush the history' by portraying Colston as merely an Iberian, Mediterranean or Levant merchant with no direct connections to trans-Atlantic slavery.

The statue itself carried the messages that the Victorian re-inventors wanted to disseminate; Colston as the thoughtful and wise 'father of the city', 'merchant prince' and 'moral saint' and crucially that all of Bristol was behind the statue. It was adorned with four tablets carrying images that propagated these narratives, as described by a journalist from the *Bristol Mercury* the day after the unveiling:

> The front panel is framed with sprays of evergreens and surmounted by a shield with emblems of that wisdom and learning of which Edward Colston was such a brilliant example, and bears the inscription: "Erected by citizens of Bristol as a memorial of one of the most virtuous and wise sons of their city, AD, 1895." The back panel represents the finding of a dolphin by an officer and some of the crew in a hole in the ship's side… The city arms are at the top of the panel. The right-hand panel shows Colston distributing alms to distressed widows and orphans. His crest is at the top of the panel. The left-hand panel, or anchor panel, is symbolical of the sea.[786]

After the unveiling, Arrowsmith and the fund-raising committee, still hundreds of pounds short of paying for the statue, made another rather desperate attempt to cajole cash from the numerous wealthy members of the Colston societies. As the hundreds of diners sat down at the different banquets they were faced with "small envelopes…with a suggestion that they should contribute small sums towards the balance still wanted in connection with the Colston Statue Fund".[787] Once again the response was fairly paltry, with more than 200 members of the Liberal Anchor Society, Arrowsmith's own organisation, only donating £12 and the Tory dominated Dolphin Society producing a pitiful £1/10s.[788]

Attempts to make the "citizens of Bristol" feel guilty about their lack of financial enthusiasm for the Colston statue clearly failed and the whole fund-raising exercise ground to a halt at the end of 1795. Arrowsmith and the committee appear to have given up on the public subscription scheme at this point and one source noted that the remaining balance of "about £150 was given by an anonymous citizen who had already subscribed liberally".[789] Another source, *Arrowsmith's: Dictionary of Bristol*, which we might expect to be close to the truth in this particular matter, stated enigmatically that the 'mystery' donor was "a gentleman who had been one of the promoters of the design".[790]

The "anonymous citizen" was almost certainly Arrowsmith himself who, by this late stage, had probably had enough of trying to extract money from his fellow Bristolians. The abject failure of even the Colston societies to make a majority contribution to the statue, let alone the disastrous 'public subscription' scheme, puts to the sword the idea that this was a universally popular project as some Bristol myth-makers suggest. From a study of the published subscription

Right, John Cassidy's 1895 statue of Edward Colston.

Left, the panels that adorn the statue's plinth. From the top: the text on the front of the plinth; Colston distributing alms; the myth of a dolphin saving one of Colston's ships; and two winged horses with webbed feet, an anchor, a mermaid and a merman.

lists, it can be verified that a number of the Bristol business elite had contributed to the fund. However, at the end of the day, the statue was the vanity project of one wealthy business owner who ended up grudgingly paying for his idea. The memorial to Edward Colston was thus hardly "Erected by citizens of Bristol" as the inscription on the memorial claims so defiantly.

The apathy surrounding the funding of the statue of Colston was mirrored to some extent by the decline in the importance of the various ceremonies around the turn of the century. It appears 'Colston Day' as a full day's holiday in Bristol disappeared in 1901, another sign of the waning of the 'cult of Colston'.[791] Jordan argues that the rituals of the Colston societies in Bristol were coming under increasing pressure at the end of the Victorian period due to political infighting between Liberals and Tories and the concurrent rise of socialism and the struggle for universal suffrage. The latter was demonstrated by the creation of the new 'general unions' and mass street protests such as those surrounding the strike wave of 1889–90 and 'Black Friday' in 1892–3 and the increasing success of avowed socialists in local elections.[792] In the early twentieth century the annual banquets associated with the various Colston societies were disrupted by suffragette protests and were not revived after World War One.[793]

Slavery uncovered

The social and political changes in pre-WW1 Bristol which were undermining elite patronage, creating new organisations within the working classes and disrupting cosy civic identities created a space for critical assessments of the City's icons. In the run-up to the bi-centenary of Colston's death in 1921, the Rev H. J. Wilkins, Vicar of Westbury-on-Trym and Minister of Redland Chapel wrote a comprehensive and provocative history of Edward Colston, highlighting his leading role in the slave trade, the profits he acquired from this business and how he multiplied this wealth as a major money-lender and mortgage broker.[794] In a recent assessment of Wilkins and his book on Colston, Coates observes:

...It is a characteristic piece of Wilkins, the bulk of it being a simple chronology of the major events and publication of the key documents of Colston's life, followed by a five-page assessment of the man's character. Despite having been elected president for 1919 of one of the societies that had been financed by Colston's munificence, the Anchor Society, Wilkins does not shy away from the subject's involvement in the slave trade, and is quite blunt about his narrow-minded, partisan, overbearing, unforgiving and otherwise unpleasant personality. He comes reasonably close to saying that Colston was a nasty piece of work, judged by the standards of any age, calling him 'extremely difficult to co-operate with', 'unbending', 'narrow', and mentioning 'the distortion of his judgement by his favourite religious obsession,' his bigotry and his prejudice, while at the same time acknowledging his public generosity.[795]

As Coates notes, Wilkins came to the conclusion that Colston's character was best demonstrated by his financial dealings in Britain:

He demands his "pound of flesh" even though others must work solely and absolutely for his advantage. He refuses the invitation to take over everything [the creditors property] but demands that his unfortunate creditors shall continue to work for nothing so that he may be paid in full.

Colston forcing people to work for nothing for his benefit crudely resonated with his involvement in transatlantic slavery, though in this case, with merely destitution or debtors jail hanging over his creditors' heads rather than the lash and execution. As for his philanthropy, Wilkins was scathing in his assessment: "He condescended to use 'the power of the purse'—always a sign of littleness..."[796]

Wilkins went on to publish the names of more than seventy great Bristolians (including St Wulfstan) who he believed had been "completely overshadowed and lost sight of" by the dominating presence of the 'cult of Colston'.[797] He concluded:

I have urged (having regard to the unhistorical and ill-proportioned position Bristol has given to Edward Colston through the absence of documentary evidence and political partisanship with its charitable efforts) that Bristol should free herself from such a position, recall her heritage and rise to a true "Commemoration" on November 13th in each year of the noble galaxy of benefactors and worthies of "The Metropolis of the West"[798]

Although Wilkins's book and supplement were certainly ground-breaking in being the first texts to really open up the history of Colston's involvement in the slave trade, the reactions of both the elite defenders of Colston and civic bodies were muted. Dresser suggests that this 'silence' was perhaps a reaction in itself, noting that:

Interestingly, by the time the 1934 edition of the official guide to Bristol was published, in the year of the centenary of the implementation of the Slave Emancipation Act, all reference to Colston had been dropped.[799]

However, this did not mean that the ritual Colston commemorations and ceremonies were being openly challenged. As Jordan noted, the street events and society banquets had been declining or moving behind closed doors since WW1. Wilkins may have had a part to play in this, though it is unlikely that the Merchant Venturers or Colston charities would have admitted this publicly.

Arguably the next significant exposure of slavery in Bristol was in historical fiction with the publishing of *The Sun is My Undoing* by Marguerite Steen in 1941, a novelist from Liverpool.[800] The book was very popular both locally and nationally during the war years. The story was set in Bristol and is outlined by Dresser:

> ...this book traces the lives and fortunes of the Floods, a local family involved in the slave trade. It also looks at those whom the Floods had enslaved in both Africa and the Caribbean...Steen's willingness to confront with such a shrewd and unflinching eye the realities of interracial sexual relationships, commercial corruption and the brutalising influence of slavery earned her the unqualified admiration of many Bristol readers. The book was also praised by none other than the Marxist historian and Caribbean politician, Eric Williams, who pronounced her novel superior to academic histories of British slavery.[801]

Up until this point the only academic study of slavery and the slave trade in relation to Bristol had been written by Bristol University professor C. M. MacInnes. His *Gateway to Empire* (1939), although scholarly, is full of imperialist exhortations, attempts to portray the British slave-system as being the most humane and characterising the slave owners as 'kind despots'. The book was dedicated to:

> the Master, Wardens and commonalty of Merchant Venturers of Bristol whose fellowship has played so notable a part in the history of the Empire[802]

So it is no surprise that MacInnes should take these positions, or that Eric Williams could see through them and their like. In a later work, the pamphlet *Bristol and the Slave Trade* (1963), MacInnes even belittles the leading abolitionist Thomas Clarkson, portraying him as a naïve 'drama queen' whilst championing the British state as the 'White Knight' in the battle against global slavery. In both of MacInnes's works studied here, he makes only a very brief and indirect reference to Edward Colston; thus playing down the important role of 'Bristol's virtuous and wise son' in the slave trade in the seventeenth century.[803]

Interestingly, halfway through the latter text, MacInnes deviates from the historical narrative into a telling rhetorical defence of those in Bristol who ran and profited from slavery and the slave trade:

In the course of the eighteenth-century mayors of Bristol, sheriffs, aldermen, town councillors, Members of Parliament, the Society of Merchant Venturers and, indeed, men of the highest repute in the place were engaged in this traffic [the slave trade]. These were not wicked men but pillars of society in their own time and there seems to be little justification for that macabre self-satisfaction which some Bristolians appear to derive from the recollection of the presumed moral depravity of their forbears. If these men are to be judged then it should be by the moral standards of the time in which they lived. Since the nation as a whole at that time condoned their activities and applauded them for their enterprise, there would appear to be no special reason why they should be selected for particular condemnation. Many of them honestly believed that though negroes [sic] looked like men they were not really human.[804]

There are a number of claims and supposed 'facts' in this emotive extract which bear closer scrutiny in that they reveal more about MacInnes than the historical context. For example, his assumption that "pillars of society" cannot be "wicked men"; that role, we suppose, is reserved for the Bristolian lower orders, or perhaps enslaved Africans? He also claims that "the nation as a whole condoned their [the slave traders'] activities". This is patently false, on two grounds. First, as we have seen in this book many people actively opposed slavery, over many centuries; and, second 'condone' is a positive statement, in the sense that you have to indicate support for something. MacInnes seems unaware that the vast majority of the population of Britain were disenfranchised throughout the period of Caribbean slavery. So how could they condone it? Certainly not through the ballot box. What we do have are petitions of hundreds of thousands, even millions of British people opposing slavery and the slave trade in the eighteenth and nineteenth century. What of petitions "condoning" the business of slavery? Typically such petitions to Parliament were sent by financially self-interested groups, often "pillars of society", such as merchants, planters, mayors, aldermen and councillors or manufacturers of goods related to the triangular trade.[805] And finally, we will leave the motive behind MacInnes's concluding reference to the racism of the period for the reader to judge.

These defensive positions, that the organisers and profiteers from slavery should be judged by the moral standards of their time and MacInnes's fallacious attempt to assert 'everyone' supported them 'in any case', were to reappear during the debates about memorialisation in the early twenty-first century. In particular, spokesmen for the Society of Merchant Venturers would make similar claims that 'we were all in it together' to try to obscure their organisation's historical involvement in leading, organising and profiting from the 'vile trade'.

Professor MacInnes was clearly annoyed by the so-called 'macabrely self-satisfied Bristolians' who dared to question the morality of their illustrious 'forbears'. This is interesting secondary evidence for active criticism of the role of Bristol merchants in the transatlantic slave trade in the years prior to 1963, the date the pamphlet was originally published. Who were these dissenting Bristolians? There is some indication of critics uncovering the hidden history of Edward Colston in the early 1960s. In a comment piece entitled "There were two sides to Mr Colston", written under the pseudonym *Neptune* in the *Bristol Evening Post* of October 1961, the author, after a mild beginning stated:

Not all his [Colston's] personal qualities were wholly admirable, I read that he was obstinate, short-tempered, and intolerant, with a narrowness of outlook that bordered on bigotry in religious and political matters.

Having noted Colston's Jacobite sympathies and the riot of 1715, *Neptune* added:

Then there was the fact that much of his wealth came from the slave trade, his sympathies were narrow.[806]

The fact that the writer concealed their identity in order to make these statements suggests that criticising Colston was somewhat taboo and its novelty may explain MacInnes's angry reaction. After this defensive flannel from an 'eminent historian' at Bristol University in the 60s, somebody had to tell it straight; but we had to wait for a 'proper' Bristolian to do that in the 1970s.

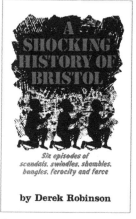

The impact of post-colonial immigration from Caribbean countries after World War II, the struggle for civil rights exemplified by the bus boycott campaign in 1963 and the student and worker radicalisation of the late 1960s led to a critical cultural and political scene in Bristol in the 1970s.[807] This was reflected to some degree in the book *A Darker History of Bristol* (originally *A Shocking History of Bristol*). Published half a century after Wilkins's original exposé of Colston, Bristolian Derek Robinson's study of hidden histories of the city was extremely popular and certainly caused a scandal when it was released. Writing in 2005 for the second edition, Robinson recalled the civic environment into which his controversial book was released and how it was received:

1973 was a big year for Bristol. It marked six hundred years as city and a county. Joy was unconfined. The thunder of self-congratulation was deafening. The city fathers danced in the streets. So many people tried to slap themselves on the back that casualty wards for miles around were full of dislocated shoulders.

Well I didn't buy it. Not all of it anyway. I'm a Bristolian, born and bred. I knew that, during the past six hundred years, the city and county had generated its fair share of blood and thunder. Also thud and blunder.

So I wrote this book, to help balance the story. I was not out to blacken Bristol's reputation. Some good things have happened here. Equally, you don't have to look hard to find bungling and swindling, cock-ups and carnage, ferocity and farce.

The book drew blood. A disgusted ratepayer, George Bodger, wrote to the Western Daily Press demanding that it be burned in the gutters. But Bristolians are a fair and level headed lot. They know their history is like their geography: full of highs and lows. The true picture is the whole picture and this New Edition aims to offer nothing less.[808]

Robinson's accessible and popular book certainly did "draw blood" in that it directly confronted the subjects of forced white labour and black chattel slavery and their connections to the Bristol merchants. Neither did it pull its punches with Edward Colston who is directly implicated along with the rest of the "slaving community" in the city:

The slave trade was a huge, roaring bandwagon and all the city fathers were on board: mayors, sheriffs, aldermen, councillors, Merchant Venturers, and last but not least Mr Edward Colston, MP, who shrewdly invested much of his considerable wealth in the slave trade and got it all back again umpteen times over, a feat which the boys and girls of Colston's Schools might ponder as they kneel in prayer on Founder's Day.[809]

Robinson was ahead of his time in drawing reference to the ceremonies that school children had to attend in order to worship slave traders such as Colston. He also provided a blunt and amoral epitaph to his story of Bristol and slavery. Referring to those Professor MacInnes's called the 'pillars of society' he stated: "They did it for the money".[810] It was a suitable riposte to MacInnes's pompous justification of the merchant and civic elite.

Further exposure of Colston came in David Foot's book *Famous Bristolians* published in 1979:

Perhaps it's just as well not to analyse too carefully how Bristol's most famous philanthropist made most of his money—the Church, after all, turned a blind eye to Slave Trade exploitation. Succeeding generations of Colston's admirers would prefer to point to the £75,000 he gave to charity...

He was Bristol's MP, a dogmatic Tory who hated Whigs as much as he hated any rival businessman who threatened him in a deal.

Colston was astute, stubborn and self-willed. He died a bachelor in 1721 at the age of 84, his private life fleetingly touched by allegations of scandal, supposedly the work of his political opponents...[811]

These populist works were tail-ended by academic historians in the 1970s and 80s who produced a trickle of local history pamphlets and books looking at the business of the slave trade, the abolition movement in the city and profiling the Bristol slaving dynasties.[812] The detailed works authored by David Richardson in the 1980s and 90s were primarily economic histories detailing the anatomy of trading activities related to the slave-system in the city and cataloguing the voyages of slave ships. Despite their importance in providing a comprehensive evidential basis for understanding the involvement of the city in the business of slavery, they lacked a social history perspective and remained outside of the mainstream of popular local history. However, whilst a few academic historians were beavering away in the archives, undermining rosy historical perspectives about Bristol's maritime past, others in the city were planning to celebrate them.

The *Matthew* and the Festival of the Sea

In preparation for the 500th anniversary of Giovanni Caboto's (John Cabot) landfall in North America in 1997, a project was initiated in Bristol to create a replica of the ship, the *Matthew,* which carried his entourage across the Atlantic. The plan was to launch the vessel in 1995, carry out sea trials and then sail it to Newfoundland to meet the Queen as part of the multi-million pound 'Cabot 500' celebrations. A few years previously in 1992, similar 'celebrations' to mark the voyage of Columbus to the 'New World' in 1497 had been met by protests of indigenous peoples and their supporters across the American continent. As one native-American journalist noted:

Columbus' Caribbean landfall in 1492 marked the beginning of the Spanish and Portuguese invasion of the Americas. In British and Canadian history, Cabot's 1497 voyage is considered more significant, because it signalled the beginning of the British and French assault on the land and Indigenous peoples of North America.[813]

The replica of the *Matthew* ferrying tourists around the Floating Harbour in 2019.

Protests would dog the 'celebrations' of Cabot on both sides of the Atlantic. In July 1995 members of the Merchant Venturers announced they were going to have an exclusive ball in central Bristol to celebrate the launching of the *Matthew*. The 1,800 wealthy guests, paying £75 a ticket, would be wined and dined in marquees in Queen Square that September.[814] Within days of the announcement the banquet was renamed the "Slave Traders Ball" by protesters from the Bristol Peoples' Party (BPP). Fronted by anarchist agitator Ian Bone, the BPP and a number of other groups planned to converge on Queen Square to demonstrate against the event. For the protestors the ball represented Bristol's wealthy elite lavishly celebrating their own version of maritime history whilst ignoring the mass suffering caused by colonialism and transatlantic slavery.[815]

As a result of the threat to "wreck the ball" Queen Square was fenced off from the general public and a large police presence including undercover officers was organised to protect the event. On the night of the ball, Police made a mass arrest of homeless people and squatters who attempted to march from St Paul's to the venue, whilst many others were detained in its vicinity. However, late into the evening, a group of demonstrators evaded police cordons, pushed the fences down and stormed into the marquees, eating food from the tables and disrupting the event. Several protestors were injured by security guards before police arrived and made numerous arrests of the interlopers.[816]

The following year saw Bristol's 'Festival of the Sea' which celebrated the city's seafaring past. It was the largest maritime festival ever hosted in Britain involving over 700 vessels, 1,000 performers, 360,000 ticket holders and, it is claimed, a TV audience of 23 million.[817] However, there was one major problem with the festival: there wasn't going to be any significant mention of Bristol's maritime role in slavery, the slave trade or colonialism.[818] This was perhaps no surprise as the organisers were not a nominally democratic body such as the City Council but a group of businessmen, property speculators and stockbrokers linked to the Merchant Venturers.[819] The four day festival was a private venture aimed at making a profit out of cordoning off Bristol city centre and selling tickets at a minimum of £20 per adult. Apart from making money, its principal objective appeared to be promoting a connection between a sanitised 'top-down' history of mercantilism in Bristol with a vision of a neo-liberal and entrepreneurial future. In practical terms the Festival:

> attempted to articulate a 'maritime' identity for Bristol which would draw tourists to the city. In the longer term, the intention was to attract national and international investment by 'place-marketing' the city as a distinctive location boasting plentiful character and history.[820]

Problematic histories, particularly 'from below', of forced labour, especially chattel slavery, or the crimes of colonisation, were going to ruin this rosy 'maritime identity'. This in turn would tarnish both the image of the city and some of its elite organisations, such as the Merchant Venturers, which retain a historical legacy to these practices. So these histories were excluded from the event which caused a series of protests:

> An 'Anti-Festival of the Sea' was staged by local multi-cultural arts groups on the eve of the event. Meanwhile, throughout the site fly-posters highlighted Bristol's historical complicity with the slave trade, and pop group Massive Attack complained on the live television coverage about the partial histories presented at the festival.[821]

In 1997 the *Matthew* made its voyage across the Atlantic, arriving in Bonavista, Newfoundland on 24th June. The Queen who had been touring Canada over the previous days in preparation for the arrival of the *Matthew* had been followed by indigenous protestors. First Nations demonstrators converged at the 'Cabot 500' event in Bonavista, where the Queen was to give a speech. A journalist recounted the 'historic' moment:

> Explorer John Cabot's landing, the queen said in a speech, "represents the geographical and intellectual beginning of modern North America."

What the queen did not say was that, less than 350 years after her pirates and thieves invaded the sovereign Beothuk territories in Newfoundland, the Beothuk nation had been exterminated. Shanawdathit, the last of her nation, died of tuberculosis in 1829. The other Indigenous populations in Newfoundland and Labrador have come perilously close to extinction since the European arrival. Innu leader Katie Riche said: "I see nothing to celebrate. Along the way a whole nation, the Beothuks, were wiped out. We don't want that to happen to us." Newfoundland and Labrador First Nations people had been invited to participate in the Cabot quincentenary. They declined. "[The First Nations of] Newfoundland and Labrador are still waiting to be 'discovered' by the federal government," said a Native spokesperson earlier this year. Many Native people thought the millions of dollars poured into the Cabot festival would be better spent settling land claims or taking care of human needs.[822]

The protests in Bristol and Canada had certainly drawn the battle lines over the representation of the city's history.[823] A year or so later, on a dark night, a protestor scrawled SLAVE TRADER on the base of Colston's statue in the city centre, the first of several actions against the monument over the succeeding years. According to an article in *The Times* which reported the attack:

Leaders of the black community in Bristol yesterday condemned Colston...as one of the worst offenders in the history of slavery and said the statue should be taken down.[824]

The disquiet generated in certain quarters by the 'Cabot 500' celebrations and the Festival of the Sea was allayed to some degree with the establishment of the *Bristol Slavery Trail*, followed in 1999 by the hugely successful *A Respectable Trade? Bristol and Transatlantic Slavery* exhibition in Bristol's Industrial Museum (now M Shed).[825] The latter was the culmination of a three year programme of public consultation and discussion that had been developed under the auspices of the Bristol Slave Trade Action Group, an organisation that had been formed in 1996 by a small group of activists, city councillors and academics, partly in reaction to the controversy surrounding the Festival of the Sea.[826] One of the black artists featured in the exhibition, Tony Forbes, summed up the anxiety amongst some Bristolians about the Festival and the launch of the *Matthew*:

I really love this city. I was born in St Paul's and grew up on a white council estate called Southmead. There are things about Bristol I'm proud of, but... The Festival of the Sea in 1996 was an example of how some of the institutions that run the city have failed to understand the people of Bristol. They celebrated Bristol's maritime history and ignored slavery.

The centrepiece was the launch of the replica of John Cabot's ship, the Matthew. His voyage in 1497 opened the way to the genocide of Native Americans and colonisation. This festival, encouraged by the Council, funded by big business and hyped by our media, was a slap in the face to the black community and an insult to the intelligence and sensitivity of many Bristolians. It was the weekend that broke my heart.[827]

At the end of 1997 the first memorial honouring the memory of enslaved Africans in the city was unveiled. It wasn't an auspicious start. It was a small plaque funded by Bristol MEP Ian White and dedicated by ex-Colston's school girl and historical novelist Philippa Gregory. It is now largely forgotten both in memory and location. In 1999, a new bascule footbridge was built across the river Frome at St Augustine's Reach in Bristol's Floating Harbour connecting Queen Square with Millennium Square. The opportunity was taken at the time to remember Bristol's slaving past when it was named after Pero Jones (1753-1798), an enslaved African servant who arrived in Bristol from the Caribbean Island of Nevis in 1783. Jones was 'owned' by the prominent merchant family, the Pinneys, who lived in the 'Georgian House'. Not without some controversy, one local politician called the naming "gesture politics".[828] The unique horned appearance of the bridge was created by Irish artist Ellis O'Connell and it was opened by Home Office minister Paul Boateng. For many, the fact that the bridge was not a dedicated memorial to the suffering of the enslaved, made the naming seem contrived and shallow; a last-minute gesture to placate critics. For many Bristolians, the name never stuck in any case, and it goes under various nicknames such as the 'Horned Bridge', 'Shrek's Bridge' and, rather unkindly, 'that Slave's Bridge'.

As Bristol entered the twenty-first century, and the memories of the divisive Festival of the Sea began to fade, the disquiet concerning the commemoration, celebration and memorialisation of those who were major players in the slave system appeared to go underground. After all, wasn't Bristol doing something about slavery now with all these exhibitions and trails? In 2001, historian Madge Dresser's social and cultural history of slavery and abolition in Bristol was published. Aptly named *Slavery Obscured*, Dresser's work showed how a class of powerful merchants, through the lucre of slavery and the slave trade, had emerged in the eighteenth century and grasped economic, political and cultural influence over the city. Ironically, it appeared that the legacy of that bourgeois seizure of power endured, represented by the continued influence of the Society of Merchant Venturers in protecting their history and traditions, despite the horrific sub-text of slavery.

A nine-day period in November 2006 saw the first public events launched by *Bristol Radical History Group* (BRHG) with more than 30 historical re-enactments, commemorations, talks, films, gigs and exhibitions across the city.

Taking the approach of 'history from below' the topics addressed in *Bristol Radical History Week* included "rioters, rebel slaves, pirates, mutineers, Jacobin plotters, radical preachers, raunchy ranters and abolitionist revolutionaries", all performed by interested volunteers with an historical bent, along with performers and academic historians. One of these volunteers was one of your humble scribes who was roped in to do a couple of talks: one on the history of the *Seven Stars* public house and another on pirates and privateers out of our fair city. The talk was attended by Professor Peter Linebaugh from the University of Toledo in Ohio, co-author of *The Many-Headed Hydra*, the book that had helped inspire BRHG. It was from these meetings that the idea for a plaque to mark the importance of the *Seven Stars* in the campaign for the abolition of the slave trade was born.

Abolition 200

In January 2006 Deputy Prime Minister John Prescott announced that Britain would mark the 200th anniversary of the abolition of the British slave trade in 2007. To this end the Labour government encouraged city councils in London, Liverpool, Bristol and Hull to stage commemorative events. The very next month, at the General Synod of the Church of England, delegates voted unanimously to apologise to the descendants of slaves for the church's involvement in the slave trade. The Bishop of Southwark went on to confirm in a speech before the vote that the Society for the Propagation of the Gospel in Foreign Parts (SPG) had indeed owned and exploited enslaved Africans on its plantations in Barbados, bequeathed to the organisation by the Codrington family.[829]

The issue of 'apology' caused a firestorm in the media with John Prescott initially saying that the Government wouldn't formally offer an apology but a 'statement of regret'.[830] In November 2006 Prime Minister Tony Blair went further:

> It is hard to believe that what would now be a crime against humanity was legal at the time. Personally I believe the bicentenary offers us a chance not just to say how profoundly shameful the slave trade was— how we condemn its existence utterly and praise those who fought for its abolition, but also to express our deep sorrow that it ever happened, that it ever could have happened and to rejoice at the different and better times we live in today.

Paul Stephenson, a black civil rights activist from Bristol, added:

> It's historic for a British Prime Minister to say this and it is to be welcomed. It shows a recognition of the importance of human rights and challenges

Codrington College (now part of the University of the West Indies) in 1905.

the deniers who don't admit that the British Empire caused so much social, physical and psychological damage.[831]

Just days later D'Arcy Parkes speaking on behalf of the Society of Merchant Venturers made the following statement to the *Bristol Evening Post*:

> We all regret that the slave trade happened. Slavery was a trade in which all of Bristol was involved in, but we believe an apology is totally meaningless.[832]

This 'we were all in it together' position was a deliberate attempt to try and lessen the important role the Society of Merchant Venturers and its members had historically played in slavery and to make all Bristolians culpable, something which was patently untrue. Also, in a climate where reparations for transatlantic slavery were being discussed, it conveniently side-stepped the issue of who benefited financially, suggesting that all Bristolians had done so, again untrue. Finally, it carried an implicit, simplistic message for modern-day Bristolians that slavery was merely a 'white versus black' issue which *we all* regret.

Funding for 'Abolition 200' was not to come from the coffers of central government but from the Heritage Lottery Funding (HLF) and the local councils themselves. In Bristol, the council set aside £200,000 to fund events and a further £2 million came from separate applications to the HLF. The latter were mainly large grants for future exhibitions about slavery such as *Breaking the Chains* at the ill-fated British Empire and Commonwealth Museum.[833]

In 2006, Bristol City Council (BCC) hastily set up a management team to coordinate the 'Abolition 200' events, which appeared to critics to be a non-inclusive, bureaucratic 'stitch up' over the representation of the history of slavery and abolition. This view was compounded in a stormy meeting in the Malcolm X Centre in St Paul's where members of the management team appeared to be offering 'Abolition 200' as a 'done deal' without wider consultation or involvement. The critics included 'Operation Truth 2007', a Bristol-based African-centric group, the Black Development Agency and the Consortium of Black Groups who argued that:

> Bristol City Council has a track record of organising and planning events that promotes the wealth and development of the city without consultation and consideration for people of Afrikan descent. The Festival of the Sea back in 1997 and the naming of 'Merchants Quarter' are examples of the lack of respect and sensitivity towards the Afrikan and Caribbean communities.[834]

After the meeting in St Paul's, these groups refused to support or participate in the Abolition 200 events on the basis that the abolition of the slave trade in 1807 was not something to celebrate as the legacy of racial oppression remained today.

Bristol Radical History Group had some sympathy with this position and retained its independence from the official events. Members of the group had become motivated to cover the history of abolition in detail after the 'apology debate' had arisen in 2006. In May of that year, BBC Points West had reported on a public meeting discussing whether 'Bristol should apologise for slavery'.[835] BRHG thought this a counter-productive gesture in that it suggested present day Bristolians (white or black) were somehow collectively responsible for slavery. Instead BRHG suggested if anyone was going to apologise then the Society of Merchant Venturers should do so, as it was their organisation that had facilitated the slave trade and their members that had been the principal profiteers from slavery in Bristol.

Slavery - The Hidden History

IS THIS MAN HOLDING A PETITION FOR ABOLITION?

BRISTOL RADICAL HISTORY GRO[]
WWW.BRH.ORG.UK
EVENTS FROM 4TH TO 15TH MARCH 2007

BRHG poster from 2007 featuri[]
Maroon leader, Leonard Parkins[]

Members of BRHG were also very concerned with how the history of British abolition would be framed by 'Abolition 200'. Their historical investigations showed that, post-abolition of the slave trade (1807) and emancipation (1838), the 'official' history had been distorted and sanitised in a number of ways. First, it concentrated on reactionary figures such as William Wilberforce to the exclusion of many other anti-slavery activists and the mass movement which sustained the abolition campaign. Second, it refused to centralise or even acknowledge the violent revolts and revolutions of the enslaved (and the defeat of British forces by them) that finished off both the trade and slavery. Instead Africans were treated as silenced victims without agency. Third, it failed to contextualise West African slavery within the systems of forced labour of early capitalism which incarcerated both black and white people on a class basis. Finally, it completely ignored the effect of the French Revolution and the impact of the 'natural rights of man' on both the enslaved and the abolition movement.[836] Instead the 'history of abolition' appeared to have become a peculiarly British institution, where apparently our enlightened rulers had led the world in a progressive campaign to 'rescue the poor African' from his fate. As Eric Williams sarcastically observed:

> British historians often wrote as if their country had only undertaken the largest branch of the Atlantic slave trade of any colonial power 'in order to have the satisfaction of suppressing it'.[837]

BRHG was determined not to let this version of the history dominate during 'Abolition 200' and in March 2007 ran its own series of events entitled *Slavery—The Hidden History* to counteract the sanitised 'official' version.[838]

The official 'Abolition 200' events went ahead, and it was claimed that "100 officially sanctioned events attracting 200,000 people were staged" during 2007, including "24 commemorative and educational projects relating to black history in general and to abolition in particular".[839] The protests and criticism continued nevertheless. In March, at a commemorative service at Bristol Cathedral to mark the Act of Parliament abolishing the slave trade, members of 'Operation Truth' who had called for a boycott demonstrated outside. One spokesperson, Jendayi Serwah, stated:

> Abolition 200 is an affront to all people of African descent. It is a propaganda tool where a revisionist history of African people is being promoted which presents the oppressor in the role of liberator.[840]

Other critics such as Ros Martin, a Bristol based poet and playwright, questioned the role of 'Abolition 200'. What was being marked by whom and for whom? Where did the Diaspora of African descent in Bristol fit in with the narrative being created about their ancestors? Were the memories and struggles of the enslaved Africans even going to feature in this narrative? She also raised the question about Colston's role in Bristol; what did he represent and why was he still feted? Martin and her supporters instigated several protests

273

outside the Colston Hall highlighting these issues and the hypocrisy of staging 'Abolition 200' events in an institution named after a major slave trader.[841] In September 2007, partly in response to these demonstrations, a debate was held at the British Empire and Commonwealth museum entitled 'Who was Edward Colston—Merchant, Philanthropist or Criminal?'[842] Martin argued passionately for change, that it was time to deal with icons such as Colston and that their 'sacred' status was over.

A measure of this 'sacred' status was the failure of the 'Two Coins Project' launched by artist Graeme Mortimer Evelyn during the 'Abolition 200' year. The idea was to erect an installation around the Colston statue and to project a silent subtitled film about slavery, using images from Bristol, West Africa and the Caribbean.[843] Although the films were made, and the project received development funding from the Arts Council and Bristol City Council, it was never realised after it appears the latter body got 'cold feet'. It was interesting that of all the 'Abolition 200' official projects and events, the only one that aimed at actually confronting a physical legacy of the slave-trading dynasties in Bristol was blocked without explanation.

Several critics, including BRHG, made the point that 'Abolition 200' had not challenged the existing 'infra-structure' of memorials, celebrations and organisations that were connected to the history of slavery and the slave trade in the city. In a televised BBC debate in March 2007 in the Arnolfini Arts Centre, the question was asked "what should be the legacy of the 'Abolition 200' year in Bristol?" To rapturous applause, BRHG member Christina Heatherton replied that the best legacy would be to disband the archaic Society of Merchant Venturers and donate their money to schools and hospital projects in the Caribbean.[844] Another troubling aspect of the 'Abolition 200' legacy was the embarrassing fact, that despite the hundreds of thousands of pounds committed to the project in Bristol, no attempt had been made to physically memorialise the enslaved Africans or commemorate those who had fought against slavery. From this perspective, all that had been achieved was a vague 'declaration of regret' for the transatlantic slave trade, signed by the Lord Mayor and leading Councillors in January 2007.[845] In terms of memorialisation this now forgotten 'piece of paper' was all that emerged from 'Abolition 200'. In retrospect, a huge opportunity had been missed by local government to correct this glaring omission in Bristol's landscape.

Memorialisation

On 1st May 2009, historian of Caribbean slave rebellions, Richard Hart unveiled a plaque on the *Seven Stars* in Thomas Lane, the 'Pub that changed the World'.[846] Created by Mike Baker and erected by BRHG to augment an older Bristol Civic Society blue plaque, its primary purpose was to raise the profile of the pub in terms of its worldwide importance in the abolition of the British slave trade. This plaque, to remember Thomas Clarkson, Landlord Thompson and the whistle-blowing slave-ship sailors, was the only physical memorial to come out of the anniversary of the abolition of the slave trade in Bristol. The bulk of the project was financed by public subscription—gigs in the pub, donations, talks, poetry slams and the proceeds from BRHG's first pamphlet *Cry Freedom, Cry Seven Stars*.[847] The total cost was a not insignificant £3,800.

Another 'unofficial' project that came out of the BRHG events in 2006–7 was a brand new 'Wulfstan Window' in St Mary's Church in Hawkesbury, the very same church in which Wulfstan had started his career as a lowly Priest. Amazingly it took a thousand years after his birth to get the memorial put in place and it was the 'can do' actions of BRHG activists that helped inspire it. Various events were held in the Church and in a nearby pub, culminating in subscriptions from a number of people that helped raise the £4,000 needed. Local stained-glass artist Caroline Pederick won a competition for the design and chose fragmented episodes from Wulfstan's life, presenting them uniquely in three roundels. To much acclaim, the new windows were unveiled in 2011, with a dedication by the then Bishop of Gloucester, Michael Perham. Perham also suggested adding Wulfstan's name to St Mary's Church and it is still hoped that one day this might yet happen. In contrast not one of the central Bristol churches refers to Saint Wulfstan in any way, shape or form to this very day,[848] whilst slave-trader Edward Colston is feted and celebrated. Was Wulfstan ignored by the Bristol merchants and their allies in the church because he represented an unacceptable truth, or because he exposed one?

Despite these small but important interventions in Bristol, as of 2019, there is still no proper memorial to the more than 500,000 enslaved Africans transported across the Atlantic by Bristol slave traders, nor the millions who suffered the misery of forced labour in the plantations.[849] There is nothing that explicitly marks these horrific events in the city and nowhere for Bristolians, black and white, to pay their respects to these people. Instead, the landscape is still dominated by statues, buildings and roads memorialising those who undertook for profit these crimes against humanity.

In contrast, one of Bristol's continental rivals in terms of the slave trade, the French city of Nantes is light years ahead with a fantastic memorial on the quayside of the river Loire. In the eighteenth century, Nantes became France's largest slaving port, and it wasn't until 1848, after a long campaign led by French writer and activist Victor Schoelcher, that the abolition of slavery was achieved. Nantes moved on, but between cynicism and a guilty conscience, a cloak of silence fell over the subject and it was forgotten. It wasn't until the 1990s that the people of Nantes, together with their City Council, began a conscious process of facing up to the city's history. In 1992 the *Shackles of Memory* exhibition, attracting more than 400,000 visitors, enabled people to understand and analyse the reality of that history. Since then, Nantes has continued to move along this path by initiating local and international projects: cooperation and twinning with towns in Africa and South America; the organisation of the Global Forum on Human Rights; and the opening of rooms dedicated to the history of slave trading at the Nantes Museum and the Institute for Advanced Studies. Finally, in 2011, a memorial was constructed:

> in homage to all those who have fought, fight and will fight against slavery... [marking] the close of one cycle and the beginning of the next: that of the present and the future.[850]

The memorial was complemented by more than 2,000 plaques set into the pavements surrounding the memorial. Each marks a slave-ship voyage that left from Nantes and remembers the enslaved Africans that suffered and died on that ship during the transatlantic crossing.

Challenging the 'cult of Colston'

The annual 'Charter Day' ceremony held in Bristol Cathedral in November marks the official founding of the Society of Merchant Venturers in 1552. Each year, hundreds of pupils at the schools the Merchant Venturers control are bussed in to listen to a sermon given by the Bishop of Bristol. At the end of the ceremony the pupils are presented with Colston buns whilst the Merchant Venturers make their way to their HQ at Merchants' Hall in Clifton for their annual dinner where they appoint their new master for the coming year. In 2014 independent radio journalist Tony Gosling managed to gain entrance to the cathedral and secretly filmed Bishop Mike Hill's speech to the pupils. Preaching on Edward Colston, the Bishop said:

> I think he was a man who lived a life of significance, and I've found there may be still some speculation however, on some of the circumstances around his business roots right here [in Bristol]. It is speculation.[851]

Once the video was shared on social media it soon gained local press coverage. Responding to accusations that his sermon had said Colston's slave-trade connections were speculation, the Bishop claimed his words had been misinterpreted.[852] For many observers, this was a classic example of the clumsy airbrushing of the history surrounding Colston. For others it was the last straw. A Bishop, preaching to school children that Colston was a man of "significance" whilst apparently denying his role in the slave trade was going too far. Teacher Christine Townsend made a written complaint to the Archbishop of Canterbury via Lancaster House, accusing Bishop Hill of preaching falsities. In the meantime, Townsend made contact with BRHG and encouraged them to investigate Edward Colston's involvement in the slave trade. Although her complaint to the ruling body of the Church of England was not upheld, the Bishop's sermon initiated a chain of events that would begin a significant challenge to the 'cult of Colston'.

On 7th November 2015 a small group of protestors gathered outside Bristol Cathedral, they included a retired teacher, a security guard, an historian, a grandparent, an educator, three artists, a mother with a toddler in a buggy and a former student of Colston Girls.[853] They handed leaflets out to teachers and pupils from Colston Girls' School who were attending the annual Commemoration Day, a ceremony that celebrated the so-called 'founder' of the school Edward Colston. The leaflets entitled *Colston and Slavery still obscured?* (for adults) and *Why we are protesting outside today* (for pupils) contained historical facts about Edward Colston's involvement in the slave trade. The former ended with a question and a demand:

> For how much longer are school children expected to commemorate Colston in the city's cathedral whilst conveniently disregarding the memory of enslaved Africans whose lives were brutalised and cheapened by the trade in human cargo? The Bishop of Bristol needs to inform school children of the truth, to restore humanity dignity to the memory of those whose lives were commodified. After all it is he that presides over these commemorations. The ball is in his court…[854]

Six days after the protest, on Friday 13th November, Alistair Perry, Principal of the school wrote a letter to parents which began:

> At this time of year, celebrations and events commemorating the life of Edward Colston sometimes provoke strong reactions from some members of the community of Bristol. We have noted this in particular this year, and have had incidents reported to us where members of the public have approached students to engage them in conversation about the history of the school, sometimes in a forthright manner. One such incident occurred at lunchtime today.[855]

Within days this had become a local and then national media story with headlines: "Protesters target girls' and 'accost' them in the street" (*The Times*), "Schoolgirls are being warned about wearing their uniforms in public" (*The Daily Mail*, *The Sun*) and "Campaigners have also mounted demonstrations outside the school" (*Bristol Post*).[856] Perry made no attempt to refute this tissue of lies or to disassociate the Colston protestors from the clear confusion about quite separate incidents. This led to suspicions that the story had been leaked by CGS in the first place. It was a terrible start for a campaign, but the protestors would not be deterred. They issued a press release in response to the media stories (see Appendix 8) and organised to meet with representatives of the Cathedral and CGS to discuss the annual 'celebrations' of Edward Colston. Despite contacting the Society of Merchant Venturers several times it appeared they were reluctant to meet the protestors face-to-face.

The two meetings in December 2015 between the protestors and the Dean of the Cathedral, David Hoyle and Principal of CGS, Alistair Perry were essentially fact-finding exercises. The protestors wanted to hear what these institutions believed the Commemoration Day and Charter Day ceremonies actually were. Through the discussions, the content of the events was explained and the meaning of the various symbols of Edward Colston, the chrysanthemum worn by the CGS pupils and the Colston buns and coins that were handed out at both events, were revealed. An historian from BRHG outlined the evidence for Edward Colston's significant role within the seventeenth century slave trade. This was acknowledged by CGS history teacher, John Whitehead, who added that the "students often want to pull the statue down" when they learned about Colston's role in the slave trade.[857]

From the protestors' perspective, the most interesting aspect of the discussions was the difference in what both institutions thought the ceremonies were. The Dean claimed that both events were not 'celebrations' of Edward Colston and said the Cathedral should not be 'celebrating' a slave trader and he was deeply concerned if this was the case. Whereas the Principal of CGS had already stated in the letter to parents that they were "celebrations and events commemorating the life of Edward Colston".[858] This contradiction would dog both institutions and eventually lead to a split between the Society of Merchant Venturers and the Diocese.

During spring 2016, the group of protestors attracted more active members and supporters, named themselves *Countering Colston* (CC) and launched a website.[859] By August CC had completed much of the research into Edward Colston and the various ceremonies of remembrance to him, and had collated the statements from the discussion with both institutions. CC then decided to invite the head of CGS and the Dean to a joint meeting at the Cathedral to present its findings. However, both organisations declined to meet the protestors and broke off negotiations. Anthony Brown, Chair of the CGS Trustees, reversed their previous stance, claiming in a letter to CC that the Commemoration Day Service was not a celebration "of a single life" and that the Charter Day "has no relationship to any individual". Significantly, the 'elephant in the room', Edward Colston, was not mentioned in the letter.[860] The Cathedral in stark contrast stated:

We acknowledge Edward Colston's involvement in the slave trade and recognise that it is entirely inappropriate to celebrate his life.

The Dean went on to accept that Edward Colston was (of course) referred to in the ceremonies and that his will was read out on Commemoration Day. He claimed that in future:

I will instruct preachers that if they are going to mention Colston they must include, at the very least, an accurate account of his life and legacy... Steps have already been taken to ensure that the quotation from Colston's will (describing the foundation of the Girls' School) will be balanced with a statement about his involvement in the slave trade.[861]

This statement marked the first time in several hundred years that Colston's real history in terms of his involvement in the slave trade was to be referred to in any of the ceremonies taking place in Bristol. Despite the refusal of both the Cathedral and CGS to negotiate or even communicate with CC any further, this was a step forward. It appears that the "detailed discussion in the Cathedral chapter" that had been prompted by the intervention of CC, had recognised the contradiction of commemorating a philanthropist whilst hiding the fact that he was a major organiser and profiteer from the slave trade. After studying the Dean's letter one CC member wryly noted that the original meaning of 'philanthropist' was a 'lover of humanity' and they weren't sure how you could actually 'balance' the deaths of 20,000 men, women and children with charitable donations. After all, the same logic of 'balancing' could be applied to commemorating Jimmy Saville, couldn't it?[862]

As a result of the cessation of dialogue and the refusal of the Merchant Venturers to discuss the issues around the celebrations of Edward Colston, the protests continued in November 2016. The ceremonies at the Cathedral weren't the only commemorations of Edward Colston that were being hosted in the Diocese's churches. Every year on 13th November, 'Colston Day', members of three Colston charities, the Anchor, Dolphin and Grateful, march along Corn Street to St Stephen's church in the centre of Bristol to celebrate his birthday.[863] In 2016, the parade of about 40 men in Edwardian style top hat and tails, many of them members of the Merchant Venturers, was confronted by demonstrators with placards reading "Colston was a slave trader", "Stop celebrating slave traders" and "Reparations not celebrations". At the end of the service of 'thanksgiving' several clergymen came out to discuss the protest with demonstrators. Whilst this was happening some members of the Merchant Venturers angrily confronted protestors in an attempt to intimidate them.[864] The historic impact of this event would only become apparent a year later.

Victories

On 3rd April 2017, the Bristol Music Trust (BMT) took the brave and momentous decision to change the name of the Colston Hall. The *Bristol Post* gave over more print inches to this topic than any other; it made national and international news and is still bubbling away in the letters pages of the *Post* to this day. 2017 marked the 150th anniversary of the opening of the Colston Hall, which had been tainted with its connections to slavery for many years. There had been an unofficial boycott by some Bristolians, the highest profile being the internationally famous and influential Bristol band *Massive Attack* who said they would never play there whilst the Hall retained its name. In early 2017, in response to the 150th anniversary 'celebrations' and armed with knowledge of dissent within the BMT, Countering Colston mounted several protests outside the hall calling for a name change.[865]

'Colston Hall 150'
pop-up banner

One of the Bristol Music Trustees was campaigner Marti Burgess who had lobbied for a name change as part of the planned refurbishment of the hall. Burgess's heartfelt letter to her fellow trustees, which included research from Countering Colston's historians and activists, helped win the argument (see Appendix 9). In April the board of the BMT voted unanimously for the name of the Hall to be changed. In a public announcement, Chief Executive, Louise Mitchell, stated that the Colston Hall had originally taken its name from Colston Street and that the hall had not benefited from Colston's money. She summed up by saying:

> We really don't feel that an association with Edward Colston, however tenuous, is something we want…The name Colston does not reflect the trust's values as a progressive, forward thinking and open arts organisation…We want to look to the future and ensure the whole city is proud of its transformed concert hall and so, when we reopen the new building in 2020, it will be with a new name.[866]

Mitchell added in a later statement, after claims that the decision had been motivated for financial reasons, that it had been "entirely moral", rather than financial and referred to Colston as a "toxic brand".[867]

The Colston Hall name change sparked a hugely negative reaction amongst some *Bristol Post* letter writers and BBC Radio Bristol listeners, many feeling that an attack on Colston was an attack on 'Bristol', all the while revealing an alarming lack of empathy for other viewpoints. A particular accusation of critics was that changing the name of the hall was 'erasing', 'whitewashing' (sic), 'airbrushing' or 're-writing history' and some even claimed that removing memorials to Colston would hide associations Bristol had with the transatlantic slave trade. Historians from CC (the authors of this book) responded in an article in the *Bristol Post* entitled "Renaming Colston Hall is an opportunity to rediscover the hidden history of Bristol" arguing:

> The idea that renaming the Colston Hall is somehow 'rewriting' or 'erasing' history just does not make sense. History is written in history books and it is from these sources that we learn about historical figures and events. From this written history decisions are made to celebrate, commemorate or memorialise certain people or events. The campaigners who want to change the name of the Colston Hall are not burning books, in fact the complete opposite. They are asking Bristolians: who do you want to celebrate? What do you want to call your public buildings? After all, the Colston Hall has been 'our' building for nearly a century and we need to make it a place which is welcoming to all in the 21st Century.

We went on to issue a challenge:

> This is also a great opportunity for us to uncover those people and events which have been obscured by the 'cult of Colston', to celebrate some things we can all be proud of. Edward Colston should be consigned to the museums and history books where he belongs.[868]

The associated idea, that many critics of the name-change were echoing, was that memorials had to be kept in order to remind us of the slave trade, also seemed pretty nonsensical. After all, did we need statues celebrating Adolf Hitler to remind us of the horrors of fascism? This somewhat ridiculous position seemed even more unsavoury in the context of there being no significant memorial in the city to remember the suffering of the enslaved.

Several vociferous critics, including the Conservative councillor Richard Eddy, trotted out the misinformation generated by CGS and the national media in 2015 by claiming that renaming the hall:

...panders to a tiny minority who conveniently remain silent over such outrages as protestors harassing school children for simply attending Colston's Girls' School.[869]

Our response was to point out:

> We guess the irony is lost on Richard Eddy when he claims that "Renaming the Colston Hall is pandering to a 'tiny minority'". It was actually a tiny minority of powerful merchants and politicians that put Colston on the pedestal that he sits on today. The majority of Bristolians never had a say in the naming of buildings, statues or streets. The tiny minority that the city should stop pandering to are the Society of Merchant Venturers who, since their Royal Charter of 1552, have been dictating who should or should not be memorialised—it's for the people of Bristol to decide who is remembered and why—and there are plenty of great candidates.[870]

In fact, a number of suggestions for a new name for the public building were put forward almost immediately. The authors of this book suggested 'Wulfstan Hall'; well-known Bristol civil rights campaigner Paul Stephenson proposed 'Clarkson Hall'; whilst other ideas included 'Hannah More Hall', 'Freedom Hall' or the less controversial 'Bristol Music Hall'. The interim name chosen by the BMT was 'Bristol Concert Hall' to be replaced in 2020 after consultation and refurbishment of the building.[871]

The decision of the BMT to change the name of the Colston Hall sent a shockwave through the city and beyond. In particular it incensed the defenders of Colston's legacy such as the Merchant Venturers and their allies. It was true that many Bristolians were affected by the change as they had memories and thus emotional attachments to the Hall through visiting or appearing in concerts and shows as children, teenagers and adults. Though this did not mean they necessarily shared the same views as the 'Colston loyalists' or were willing to boycott the new hall as Richard Eddy and others suggested.[872] And, despite the attempts of some 'loyalist' correspondents to vainly challenge the history of Colston's major involvement in the slave trade in the letters page of the *Bristol Post*, the evidence seemed incontrovertible.[873] Even a journalist from the vitriolic, right-wing national periodical *The Spectator* had been convinced by the historical knowledge and arguments of CC activists. He commented:

> I went to Bristol recently, thinking that Colston probably shouldn't fall, and that this story was just another example of juvenile activism. To my surprise, though, I'm now not quite sure that the protestors against Colston don't have a point.[874]

By November 2017 there seemed to be a general acceptance in Bristol that the history of Colston was deeply problematic, whatever your views on what should be done about it. The fig leaf of philanthropy that had been employed to hide much of the unpalatable history of Edward Colston was now significantly diminished, creating explicit contradictions for those who continued to celebrate his memory.

The new landscape of debate that CC helped create through exposure of the history of Colston in the public domain (rather than in the ivory towers of academia) was reflected in the actions of institutions such as the church and schools as well as in the Society of Merchant Venturers. Whilst the arguments over the Colston Hall raged in the spring of 2017, less obvious but crucially important manoeuvres were occurring in the Diocese of Bristol. Buried in the *2016 Annual Reports & Accounts* for St Stephen's Church was the following minute:

> The annual Colston Day service took place in the church in November, and as anticipated, attracted a significant amount of protest, both in person on the day and subsequently via social media. This led to a questioning over what our involvement should be in future years, given the feelings in the city as a whole about the historical slavery issue and Edward Colston's part in it. We are now as a result, embarking on discussions with the charities involved, regarding future arrangements for the service and Saint Stephen's involvement.[875]

Clearly one or more of the clergy who had met the protestors the previous November were unhappy about hosting the Colston celebrations and were prepared to do something about it. On Colston Day in 2017, members and supporters of CC headed down to the ritual at St Stephens to demonstrate once again. When they arrived:

> ...someone from the church came out and explained that St Stephen's wants "nothing more to do with Colston". A little later the church administrator appeared and confirmed that "the ceremony was cancelled, not postponed"[876]

The gravity of this historic moment was captured in a headline in the *Bristol Post*:

> Bristol church refuses to host most important thanksgiving service to honour slave trader Edward Colston for the first time in almost 300 years

A spokesperson for the Parochial Church Council (PCC) at St Stephen's Church said they "had taken the decision after much thought". He added:

Following focused discussions at the PCC and general conversations within the wider Saint Stephen's community over recent years, there has been a growing concern about the thanksgiving service's connection to Edward Colston…Colston is a divisive figure within the city of Bristol and the PCC has made the decision that it no longer wishes to hold a thanksgiving service at Saint Stephen's on or around the birthday, or to the memory, of Edward Colston…Rather than celebrating the past the PCC wishes to focus on learning from the past, reconciliation and positively shaping the future. [877]

One protestor joked "that was the best demo I've ever been on…we had won months before we even got there".

There had already been signs that there was change in the air prior to the annual celebrations of Colston in 2017. In October, John Whitehead the new Principal of Colston's Girls' School announced, in reference to the annual Commemoration Day service at the Cathedral:

After consultation with students from all year groups we have decided to remove all reference to Edward Colston from the service and we will no longer be asking the students to wear a chrysanthemum in his memory. The focus of the service will be on the values of CGS throughout its existence and a clear acknowledgement of the damage done by slavery in the past and the present.[878]

The intervention of the students was a welcome step forward and it is clear they certainly could see the contradiction in celebrating a slave trader. *The Spectator*, however, did point one significant problem with the revamped Commemoration Day:

Next month, as they have done for more than a century, the pupils of Colston's Girls' School will troop into Bristol cathedral for a special service in honour of the man who gave their school its name. There's just a little snag: Edward Colston (1636–1721) will not be named, not even once, because of a heated controversy over his involvement in the transatlantic slave trade. It will be a commemoration service for… well, it's not entirely clear.[879]

The ripples of dissent that had spread from the original protests in 2015 were now affecting almost all of the Colston celebrations in the city. In October 2017, another Colston ceremony was 'discovered' by CC at St Mary Redcliffe, a huge church that is the equal of Bristol Cathedral. The Colston Society holds its annual commemoration of the slave trader on the 18th October, ironically

'World Anti-slavery Day'. The event had not been advertised on the church's website and when two protestors from CC arrived they were met by five police and PCSO officers who were apparently 'guarding' the entrance. The Vicar of St Mary Redcliffe led the service, which included members of the Colston Society and pupils from both St Mary Redcliffe CE Primary School and St Mary Redcliffe and Temple School (secondary). A local newspaper journalist who was allowed past the police guard recounted the Vicar's awkward attempt to balance Colston's philanthropy with the deaths of thousands in Royal African Company ships:

> They had gathered, he said, to give thanks for 'Edward Colston's generosity', before following it with words spoken slowly that clanged like bells around the children's ears. They were words that obviously had been very carefully thought through indeed, perhaps even decided on by a committee. He was, the vicar said, a man of his time who 'like all of us, did what he thought was right at the time'. Colston was, also a man who, 'like all of us, with the benefit of hindsight, may have done things differently'.

Dean of the Cathedral, David Hoyle, who spoke after the Vicar, made more direct reference to the slave trade in his sermon, as did Nick Hutchen, the President of the Colston Society. However, as the school pupils collected their 'Colston Buns' and were marshalled out of the church, one CC protestor held up a white board with a more direct message "How is worshipping mass-murderers outstanding education?".[880]

Just over a year later, in January 2019, St Mary Redcliffe and Temple School announced they were changing the names of the pupils' Houses from James, Canynges, Francombe, Cartwright and Colston to Müller, Liddell, Equiano, Franklin and Johnson.[881] The headteacher explained the reason for the change:

> Role models matter to people when they are growing up. The hidden messages that a school gives about what is 'normal' and what we can aspire to be are really important. Our society has not always provided the best role models that empower every young person. We cannot change the past, but we can change the future!

Edward Colston was not explicitly named in the article, but the reference and message were clearly implicit. And, as far as we are aware, after this change, the sky still hasn't fallen in...

Conclusion

The word 'abolition' in the context of the overthrow of the system of slavery is understood in different ways. As school children in the 1960s and 70s we were brought up with the idea that abolition was the work of 'great men' such as William Wilberforce, who worked in isolation through the democratic process in Parliament to achieve change. It appeared from this narrative that all Wilberforce had done was to convince some powerful government figures that slavery was wrong and then they simply 'saw the light'. The abolition movement was thus effectively reduced to the efforts of just one man. This narrative continued by placing Britain as the most progressive nation in the world, bringing the 'rule of law' and justice to the uncivilised and moral guidance to their European peers. After abolition of the slave trade in 1807 and then the emancipation in 1834, Britain and its powerful navy apparently headed off to carry on the fight against less enlightened nations who continued to support the slave system. Britain as an imperial power took the moral high-ground and partially justified its existence by being the first to ban the slave trade and slavery.

In this nationalist narrative of abolition there are a number of huge omissions and several major distortions. The most obvious oversight is the millions of enslaved Africans who barely feature in the story and when they do, it is merely as victims or, ultimately, grateful recipients of manumission. The numerous examples of rebellion, revolt and insurrection by the enslaved that we have covered in this book are only a fraction of the resistance that took place. We have not covered in any detail the everyday forms of struggle that the enslaved used to ameliorate their conditions, reduce their labour and retain their basic human dignity. All these forms of resistance made slavery more difficult and less profitable for their owners, less palatable for the British public and

286

provided hope for the enslaved. Crucially, however, the revolts and revolutions, in particular those in Saint-Domingue in the 1790s and Jamaica in 1831, had a wider geo-political effect and hastened the end of the slave trade and slavery. As the late Caribbean historian Richard Hart proclaimed so succinctly, these were "the slaves that abolished slavery".

A second glaring omission from the 'British narrative' concerns the abolition movement which, as we have seen, ebbed and flowed in relation to the presence of slavery over centuries. It was never *just* a collection of a few enlightened, educated men. From the very beginnings of opposition to slavery in the eleventh century we see that the protestations of Wulfstan were complemented by the actions of the Bristol 'mob' against the slave traders. Their names will never be known, along with millions of others who participated in the overthrow of slavery through the centuries. The abolition movement that developed in the eighteenth and nineteenth centuries was arguably the first modern, mass human rights campaign. It involved gathering of data, testimonies of participants, statistical analysis, national networks based on local organisations, lobbying, mass commodity boycotts, propaganda, pamphleteering, petitioning, meetings, demonstrations, cultural forms such as books, plays and poems as well as the use of campaigning symbols, some of which survive to this day. A major feature of this movement was the mass participation and leadership of women both in the local organisation of abolition groups, petitioning and consumer boycotts, as well as being the authors of important political tracts, poems and plays.

A final 'elephant in the room' for the nationalist narrative is the relationship between the abolition movement and the struggle for democracy. It can be argued that where there was reform there was abolition. The two movements were intertwined; the English Revolution of the 1640s produced some of the first organised groups who stood against bondage and slavery. The Levellers, Quakers, Anabaptists and others laid the practical and theoretical foundations for the anti-slavery movements that were to come. In the late eighteenth and early nineteenth centuries the movements for parliamentary reform and the expansion of the franchise were linked again to the abolition of the slave trade and then emancipation. Ironically, one of the exceptions was the 'great man' William Wilberforce whose conscience about the evils of slavery did not extend to giving working people (or the freed enslaved) the vote. The opening up of the franchise in the 1830s through mass popular protest and riot had a dual effect, it increased the representation of those who opposed slavery and reduced the influence of the slave-holding elite. This was vital in the parliamentary struggle to abolish slavery.

Nevertheless, the British model of 'reform' within the existing parliamentary system did not extend to the concept of 'human rights'. It was in revolutionary France that the idea of the 'natural rights of man and the citizen' was established.

By its very nature the declaration of 1789 presented the revolutionaries with a dilemma. If all French people were to gain the rights of being 'citizens' then this necessarily involved the immediate abolition of slavery and the granting of these rights to the enslaved in the colonies. This question would divide the revolutionary government. The reformists who wanted 'rights' to be attached to property, effectively creating a two-tier system of citizens and non-citizens, opposed 'natural rights' and by default the emancipation of the enslaved. Despite this, the revolutionaries initially triumphed over these elements and emancipation was achieved in 1794, partly as a result of the struggle in Saint-Domingue. Although fleeting, as a counter-revolution led to the overthrow of the revolutionaries and Napoleon eventually re-established the legality slavery in 1802, this was an influential and momentous period of history. The British Empire propagandists may have claimed the moral high-ground for their tactical withdrawal from the slave-system, but it was the French revolutionaries that laid the basis of 'human rights' as we understand them today.

These omissions, from the predominant 'British narrative' of abolition, strip the history of precisely the elements that made abolition of the slave trade and emancipation a possibility. Historian Adam Hochschild in *Bury the Chains* argues that the three main factors that ended British slavery were the 1832 Electoral Reform Bill, which dramatically reduced the MPs who represented West Indian interests, the revived anti-slavery movement and, crucially, the final massive insurrection in Jamaica.[882] We agree with this assessment and would extend it to the process which led to the abolition of the slave trade in 1807. In this case, playing their respective parts were: the effects of the disastrous British military campaign to restore slavery to rebellious French colonies in the Caribbean, combined with the fear of slave revolts spreading to British possessions; the mass movement that had put the abolition of the slave trade on the agenda several years before; and the changes in the balance of power in Parliament due to the union with Ireland in 1801. In each case the inter-play of these three factors was crucial, though to varying degrees.

In considering the nature of the British abolition movement, it would be wrong to imagine that the participants were unified in thought or action. Our researches have demonstrated that there were serious political differences, tensions and arguments amongst them. Primarily, these revolved around tactical approaches to achieving abolition, the first sign of which was focusing the initial campaign upon the slave trade rather than slavery as such. For the latter there were several schools of thought; a laissez faire Burkean approach which assumed slavery would die out naturally, ameliorists who naively thought that regulation and improving the conditions of the enslaved by law would gradually bring slavery to an end and the immediatists who realised that the only course of action was to bring about its demise as soon as possible.

Central to the popularity of the last position was the hugely influential writing of Elizabeth Heyrick in the 1820s who has been largely forgotten and is yet to be memorialised.

Heyrick is not alone; most abolitionists (with the exception of the movement grandees such as Wilberforce, Clarkson and Buxton) have been excluded from public memorialisation. In particular, female abolitionists are almost invisible in terms of representation across the country. This is mirrored in Bristol where there are no monuments to commemorate any abolitionists, whilst slave-trader Edward Colston dominates the city-scape. This vista, which celebrates slavers rather than abolitionists, has been read by apologists as representative of the will of Bristolians. Instead, as the historical evidence demonstrates, the memorial landscape was the product of a wealthy elite who controlled the economic, political, legal and civic environment in the city. When you look at the streets, buildings and statues named after and representing slavers, colonial invaders and other ne'er do wells, you are looking at the perspective and will of this elite expressed concretely. It is not a Bristolian vista; it is the vista of organisations such as the Society of Merchant Venturers. This pattern is repeated across many towns and cities in the UK.

The British abolitionists may have been largely excluded from memorialisation but another group of 'abolitionists' who were far braver, resourceful and gave their lives for freedom are completely excluded from commemoration in Britain and will apparently remain so for some time to come. These were the enslaved Africans who rose up against their oppressors, most of whom were martyred in the cause of freedom, suffering rape, torture, hanging, beheading and being burned alive at the hands of their British 'masters'. We do know some names, Cudjoe, Tacky and Sam Sharpe in Jamaica, Nanny Grigg and Bussa in Barbados, Quamina and Damon in Guyana and Prince Klaas in Antigua. These brave rebels have been completely ignored in Britain and have only been memorialised in Caribbean colonies since independence. The names and characters of the many tens of thousands of enslaved Africans who revolted on the plantations, ran away to become maroons or rose up in desperate circumstances on board slave ships, will probably never be known. Only when these people are remembered in Britain will significant change finally be on the cards.

Another aspect of the memorialisation of slave traders and slave holders, whether philanthropists, city fathers or civic leaders are the historical silences that surround their wealth. We speak of these merchants, planters, bankers and manufacturers 'making money' as if it was they alone who created their riches. This excludes those who *actually* created the wealth: the mass of enslaved Africans, penal labourers and indentured servants who literally toiled their lives away on the plantations; the sailors, often coerced on to slave ships, who suffered and died in their thousands; and the workers in the factories, often child labourers, who produced the commodities from and for the business of slavery. These are the people who *really* built Bristol and they deserve to be memorialised. Whilst they laboured in miserable and dangerous conditions the majority of slave traders and slave owners accumulated wealth, lived a life of opulence in Bristol, built mansions and bought land, created a fake culture of gentility and threw some crumbs of charity at their whim. Many never got near a plantation or even stepped onto a ship, despite their conceited claims to be 'Merchant Venturers'. So why should they be memorialised?

During the campaign to change the name of the Colston Hall in Bristol the authors of this book were accused by opponents of wanting to 'erase history', some even claimed that we were covering up the history of slavery in Bristol. This is far from the truth. In fact, we wanted to do the opposite, to open up the history of the forgotten: the enslaved African, the indentured servant, the pressed sailor, the child labourer and the abolitionist, who were all part of the history of forced labour and chattel slavery. This richer and deeper history of the city has been smothered by monolithic figures such as Edward Colston and his ilk, icons chosen by a wealthy Clifton elite whose organisations such as the Society of Merchant Venturers have largely propagated *their* history and continue to do so today. Thus, the question is not about 'erasing history' when it comes to challenging celebrations, commemorations and memorialisation of slave traders such as Edward Colston. After all, history is in history books; no-one is erasing them. The key question is what events and which people should we commemorate from Bristol's past? History is not merely what happened, but how we remember it. As one participant on a recent history walk succinctly stated "there's a difference between denying history and not honouring it."

The fact is, Bristol has been cursed by slavery, along with a host of other cities in Britain, and not only London and Liverpool: Bath's Georgian splendour was built on money obtained through slavery; Chester was as prominent as Bristol in the days of Wulfstan; Glasgow's Merchant City is based on its Tobacco Lords; Lancaster's fine reputation for furniture manufacture resulted from its importation of West Indian and Cuban mahogany; while two of Plymouth's favourite sons, Hawkins and Drake, were pioneers in the African slave trade.

Repeated recent respondents in the *Bristol Post* have argued that because the slave trade was 'legal' that this somehow exonerates those who were involved. This argument was used to justify the continued memorialisation of slave traders such as Edward Colston. As we have seen in this book, slavery was never consistently condoned or 'legal', there were periods when it was banned and when it resumed there was always some opposition. Wulfstan and his supporters were able to get the trade stopped in 1090 and if it was so wrong in the early middle-ages then it was certainly morally wrong in 1590, 1690 and 1790. It is likely the educated elite in Bristol would have known this history and, perhaps, this is the reason the legacy of Wulfstan has been obscured. These correspondents also point to the Egyptians, Romans and Vikings as having all used slave labour, peoples who, they say, apparently have no hang-ups about their own past, suggesting Bristol should be the same.

The truth is different. Bristol desperately needs to address this aspect of its past and with its current mix of cultures and nationalities the topic is divisive and indeed sometimes toxic. By reappraising who we memorialise and adding balance by creating a meaningful landmark memorial to remember the victims of the slave trade, the city could show the way forward, in a similar manner to Nantes in France. Bristol also has a lot to be proud of: its part in abolition, political, social and religious reform. Surely, in the twenty-first century, it is finally time to reconcile, remember and reflect this crucial aspect of Bristol and the nation's past. Now is the time to tell the world.

Postscript

Our history of the Atlantic slave trade began with fish, and it will end with fish. It is often thought that the everyday lives of Bristolians and the peoples of the Caribbean were worlds apart. This was not wholly true. In his brutal autobiographical novel *Running!* Author Maxie Lane describes the cuisine in the Bristol working-class districts of St Phillips Marsh and Barton Hill between the wars:

> ...Yes, it was one-meal-a-day existence, except on Sunday, day of fiesta and 'T. Fish' for breakfast.

> 'T. Fish' could be seen, shaped like kites, lying in the piled shop windows, lying amongst the sweets, swedes, cough mixtures, etc., flat stiff and briny, piled behind the dirty hot glass. Big flies fornicated over them and shit at random. Finny ends curled up; they dropped on shop floors, trampled by customers and contemptuously kicked into dark corners to lie unnoticed, unwanted, until purchased on Saturday, soaked in a bucket of water all night and boiled madly on the Sabbath morning. Bells pealing triumphant, pigeons crooning cool from a million lofts, and over slumland the smell of fish emerging from the long sleep. Bones a-heaping, a-sucking, frantic cats prowling voracious, and dry bread in the watery gravy, eyes down and 'All Things Bright and Beautiful' over the Marsh. Even the vagrants who kipped on the warm ashes of the electric light works, even they had 'T. Fish' on Sunday.[883]

In the 1930s, in terms of culinary delights, it appears not much separated the impoverished from East Bristol with the impoverished of the West Indies, who shared the national dish of saltfish. As we have learned, part of understanding the complex history of the movements of people and commodities across the Atlantic involves recognising the differences and the intersections between the oppressed, rather than merely recounting the narrative of the oppressors.

Colston's coat of arms in the entrance lobby of the Red Lodge Museum, despite the fact that Edward Colston never owned the building.

A daughter of Florence Poulett and Thomas Smyth of Ashton Court, with her Black Page (c. 1640) by circle of Gilbert Jackson. Red Lodge Museum. Thomas 'Honest Tom' Smyth was the son of Lady Gorges, widow of Sir Hugh Smyth and the fourth wife of colonialist Fernando Gorges.

The Death of Edward Colston by Richard Jeffreys Lewis (c. 1844).

Late nineteenth Century *Wills Three Castles* cigarette advertisement with St Mary Redcliffe church in the background.

Sold Down the River by Tony Forbes (1999), currently exhibited in M Shed in juxtaposition with *Some Who Have Made Bristol Famous* by Ernest Board, where Colston is talking to Carpenter...

Appendices

Appendix 1: Colston Casebook (ad nauseam)

A list of Colston related statues, buildings, schools, streets, organisations, pubs, symbols and food:

Colston's Almshouses—St Michael's Hill, BS2

Colston Arms Public House—(two originally, one remains in 2018)

Colston's Arms Public House—(four originally, none remain in 2018)

Colston Avenue—Centre BS1

Colston Badge—Bronze Chrysanthemum

Colston Bun—Distributed on Colston Day; sweet bun made of yeast dough and flavoured with dried fruit

Colston Bust—(2 x) Armoury Square, Easton, BS5 and Bristol City Museum and Art Gallery; latter by John Michael Rysbrack [terracotta bust of Edward Colston]

Colston Charities or Societies—Various, including Dolphin, Anchor, Grateful and, of course, Colston.

Colston Close—Winterbourne, recent housing

Colston Colossus—Proposed for Brandon Hill (prior to Cabot memorial) in 1839

Colston Day—various including November 13th [Cathedral, St. Stephens and St. Mary Redcliffe, Red Lodge etc.]

Colston Girls School—Cheltenham Road, BS6 and Henleaze Road, BS9

Colston Hall—Colston Street, Centre, BS1 [to be changed 2020]

Colston House—Colston Street, Centre, BS1

Colston House and Dolphin House—27 & 25 Effingham Road, Bishopston, BS7

Colston Lodge(s)—Freemasons Hall, Park Street, BS1
Colston Parade—Redcliffe, BS1
Colston Portraits—at least two
Colston Primary School—16-18 Cotham Grove, BS6 [changed 2018]
Colston Road—Easton, BS5
Colston Research Society—Bristol University, BS8
Colston's School and Collegiate—Stapleton, BS16
Colston Stained Glass Window—(2 x) Bristol Cathedral, College Green, BS1 and St. Mary Redcliffe Church, BS1
Colston Statue—(2 x) by John Cassidy, Colston Avenue, Centre BS1, copy at Colston Girls School
Colston Statue and Tomb—by John Michael Rysbrack, All Saints Church, Corn Street, BS1
Colston Street—Centre, BS1
Colston Street Bar and Kitchen—Centre, BS1
Colston Tower and Colston Centre—Centre, BS1
Colston Yard Pub—Former Smiles Brewery Tap, off Colston Street [changed 2017]

Appendix 2: The Charge of Immorality against Edward Colston

BRISTOL,
Friday, Novemb. 26, 1714
"SIR,

I am resolv'd to perform my Promise to you before I left *London*, to give you an account of what we went about, the Riot at this Place; but my constant attendance on my Lord, as it has given me an opportunity to be well inform'd of every Particular, so it obliges me to shorten my Relation by leaving out several things that would have been entertaining… You will do well to let Mr. R——— [James Roberts] have my Account of Fact, to be put in Order by some Friend of his, that the World may not be impos'd upon by false and trifling Relation… There are some things previous to this Business, which 'tis requisite you should know, to let you into the Temper and Spirit of the Citizens of this Place.

They have among them a sort of Club, which call themselves the *Loyal Society*, and have under that Name sent up several foolish addresses, in favour of *Arbitrary Power*, Hereditary Right and Sacheverel, they are very officious on all *High Church* Festivals, and make more Noise, drink more Beer, and sweer more Oaths than half the rest of their Fellow Citizens. These Wretches, 'tis thought, fomented the late Riot, which they durst not do, if they were not satisfy'd of the peacable and dutiful Disposition of their opponents, for four in five of the sober, Honest, Thriving part of the Magistrates and Citizens of *Bristol* are *Whigs*. And the *Tories* cou'd never have carry'd any Point here, but by the Interest of a very great *Tory*, and till lately a *Noonjuror*, Mr. C——— [Colston], who has shewn how far he prefers good Works to Purity of Life, by laying out some Thousands of Pounds in building Hospitals here, while himself liv'd very much at his ease with a *Tory*, tho' of a different Sex at M——-ke [Mortlake]. The appearance of such good Deeds acquir'd him so general Name here, that the People forgot he was a Jacobite, and everyone agreed that Mr C——— [Colston] was the best man to represent them, and his countenancing the Jacobite Interest, made the Faction rampant in a Place to which he had been so great a benefactor.

This 'tis necessary you should be acquainted with, to remove any wrong opinion you may conceive of the Citizens of *Bristol*, who I find are very Loyal to His Majesty, and very thankful to Providence for having the Protestant Succession secured to them…"

Appendix 3: Edward Colston's charitable donations

Target of donation	Date	Type of donation	Sum (£)	Sub-tot.
Bristol	1691	Almshouses	9,100	
	1696	Temple Street School	8,000	
	1702	Workhouses, farm and rebuilding Boys' hospital	2,400	
	1708	Colston's School	40,000	
	Will (1720)	Apprentices (Colston's and Temple Schools)	1,200	
	Will (1720)	Charity schools 4 x £10 x 12 years	480	
	Will (1720)	Repairing St Mary Recliffe church	100	
	?	Repairing churches (general)	1,130	
	Will (1720)	Sermons (Lent, Newgate, All Saints) x 20 years?	660	£63,0
London	Will (1720)	Workhouses, hospitals	2,600	
	Will (1720)	Society for Propagating the Gospel	300	
	Will (1720)	Mercers	100	
	1684	St Bartholomews, Christ Church, Bishopsgate	3,100	
	1708-9	Relief to London poor	20,000	£26,1
Surrey	Will (1720)	Almshouses	?	
	Will (1720)	Education (£25 + £20) x 12 years	540	
	Will (1720)	85 poor people x £1 on his death	85	£62
Devonshire	?	Church at Tiverton	50	£5
Lancashire	?	Church	20	£2
England	Will (1720)	Small livings, 60 x £100	6,000	
	Will (1720)	Schools (18) x £5 x 12 years	1,080	£7,0
			Total	£96,

Total amount donated in Will: £13,

Total amount donated during lifetime: £83,

Total amount left to Bristol in Will: £2,4

Total amount left to London in Will: £3,0

Source and page [xx]	Notes
Wilkins [86]; Bib. Dic. [49]	
Wilkins [87]; Bib. Dic. [49]	
Wilkins [87]; Bib. Dic. [49]	
Wilkins [87]; Bib. Dic. [50]	Bib. Dic. states this was £11,000
Wilkins [87, 148]; Bib. Dic. [51]	
Wilkins [87, 148]	
Wilkins [147]	
Wilkins [88]	
Wilkins [88, 139-140]; Bib. Dic. [50]	
Wilkins [88, 136, 146]	
Wilkins [88, 136]	
Wilkins [88, 146]	
Wilkins [88]; Bib. Dic. [50]	
Wilkins [61]	No other evidence found
Wilkins [88, 143]; Bib. Dic. [50]	
Wilkins [88, 143]; Bib. Dic. [50]	
Wilkins [88, 143]; Bib. Dic. [50]	
Wilkins [88]; Bib. Dic. [51]	
Wilkins [89]; Bib. Dic. [51]	
Wilkins [89, 145]; Bib. Dic. [50]	
Wilkins [89, 149, 154-155]; Bib. Dic. [50]	

Sources

Wilkins, H. J. *Edward Colston [1636-1720 AD]* (Bristol: Arrowsmith, 1920) pp. 86-89, 139-155.
A new and general biographical dictionary Vol. 4 (London: W. Strahan et al., 1784) pp. 49-52.

Appendix 4: Leading agents of slave-ship voyages from Bristol (1698-1807).

Name	Source 1 (TASTDB)			Source 2 (Richardson)		
	Voyages	Dates	Rank	Voyages	Dates	Rank
Laroche, James	104	1727-1766	1	132	1728-1769	1
Hobhouse, Isaac	68	1721-1746	2	44	1722-1747	9
Fowler, John	63	1751-1778	3	77	1758-1777	2
Jones, James	63	1783-1794	4	68	1783-1795	3
Day, James	57	1711-1742	5	56	1711-1742	6
Rogers, James	57	1774-1793	6	51	1783-1792	7
Farr, Richard	53	1726-1772	7	37	1726-1745	14
Anderson, John	52	1764-1797	8	66	1764-1797	4
Powell, John	49	1755-1789	9	58	1755-1776	5
Deane, Thomas	47	1747-1795	10	40	1747-1764	11
Saunders, Edmund	38	1706-1739	11	32	1723-1739	18
Lougher, Walter	37	1725-1764	12	49	1732-1760	8
Ruddock, Noblet	37	1712-1730	13	30	1712-1725	20
Jones, Thomas	34	1767-1795	14	34	1767-1794	17
Tonge, Henry	33	1728-1753	15	42	1730-1753	10
Jacob, Samuel	32	1716-1745	16	40	1716-1747	12
Jefferis, William	28	1713-1746	17	34	1713-1747	16
Henvill, Richard	28	1709-1735	18	30	1709-1744	19
Becher, John	28	1712-1733	19	28	1711-1732	21
Hare, William	27	1729-1752	20	38	1729-1752	13
Hooke, Abraham	27	1702-1735	21	23	1702-1727	27
Dampier, Henry	26	1728-1742	22	34	1727-1744	15
Day, Peter	26	1711-1734	23	20	1711-1734	30
Duckinfield, John	23	1712-1731	24	23	1714-1730	26
Way, Joseph	22	1702-1720	25	17	1702-1720	35
Anderson, né Young, Charles	22	1793-1807	26	16	1797-1805	36
Bright, Henry	21	1747-1766	27	21	1749-1766	29
Becher, Michael	20	1711-1752	28	25	1727-1752	23
Rumsey, James	20	1753-1762	29	20	1753-1762	32
Challoner, William	20	1714-1734	30	13	1714-1726	44

Name	Source 1 (TASTDB)			Source 2 (Richardson)		
	Voyages	Dates	Rank	Voyages	Dates	Rank
Gordon, William	19	1729-1757	31	25	1729-1757	24
Lougher, Richard	19	1721-1747	32	23	1722-1745	28
Farr, Richard (jnr)	19	1736-1772	33	20	1747-1772	31
Gordon, Robert	19	1751-1767	34	14	1751-1767	41
Sims, Thomas	18	1763-1772	35	25	1763-1772	25
Tunbridge, Robert	18	1708-1721	36	18	1708-1721	34
Hamilton, David	17	1766-1778	37	28	1766-1778	22
Iles, Joseph	17	1720-1749	38	19	1720-1750	33
Grant, Abel	17	1719-1743	39	14	1721-1743	42
Scandret(t), Charles	16	1721-1737	40	16	1721-1738	39
Freke, Thomas	15	1716-1731	41	14	1716-1731	40
Jefferis, Joseph	14	1717-1732	42	12	1717-1734	47
Rogers, Francis	13	1700-1714	43	10	1700-1714	51
Chilcott, John	11	1770-1777	44	12	1770-1777	46
Dolman, Thomas	11	1714-1730	45	11	1714-1730	48
Coghlan, John	11	1759-1781	46	10	1759-1781	50
Cross(e), John	10	1737-1747	47	16	1737-1747	37
McTaggart, James	10	1772-1787	48	14	1771-1787	43
Power, Thomas	10	1734-1747	49	13	1734-1748	45
Jenkins, Walter	10	1732-1741	50	11	1732-1741	49
Harris, Phillip	9	1711-1726	51	16	1715-1726	38
Scandret(t), Christopher	9	1729-1737	52	10	1729-1738	52
Total	1474			1549		

Sources

Source 1: Voyages: The Trans-Atlantic Slave Trade Database. https://www.slavevoyages.org (accessed 2019).

Source 2: Richardson, D. *The Bristol Slave Traders: A Collective Portrait* (Bristol: Bristol Historical Association, 1985) pp. 29-30.

Appendix 5: African resistance on Bristol ships during the middle passage (1698-1807)

Departure date	Ship name	Owner	Captain
1721-02-23	Robert	Arding, Richard*	Harding, Richard
1727-11-??	Queen Caroline	Matthews	Halladay, Anselm
1727-??-??	Loyal George	Swayne, Joseph*	Tucker, Timothy
1729-??-??	Scipio	NK	Roach, Edward; Seabons, James
1733-10-23	Juba	Heylyn; Rogers*	Alleyn, Christopher
1734-01-07	Scipio	Heylyn, Edward; Rogers, Robert*	Gordon, William; Cartnell, Robert
1735-09-19	Prince of Orange	Farr, Richard*; Heylin, Edward	Bird, Japhet
1736-05-21	Manchester	NK	Watkins, John
1736-08-31	Prince of Orange	NK	Bird, Japhet
1746-07-21	Vine	NK	Jenkins, Richard
1749-12-05	Earl of Radnor	NK	Williams, William
1749-06-23	King David	NK	Holland, Edmund; Montgomery, Hamilton
1750-10-25	Chard	NK	Leach, James
1750-05-12	Jamaica Packet	NK	Merrick, George

Form of African resistance	Fate of voyage	No. enslaved embarked	disembarked	Source
Slave insurrection	Voyage completed as intended	220	190	[1]
Slave insurrection	Captured by slaves: ship did not reach the Americas	20	0	[1]
Slave insurrection	Voyage completed as intended	271	217	[1]
Slave insurrection	Shipwrecked or destroyed after disembarkation	276	209	[1]
Slave insurrection	Shipwrecked or destroyed after embarkation of slaves or during slaving	367	313	[1]
Slave insurrection	Voyage completed as intended	222	197	[1]
Vessel's boats attacked from shore	Voyage completed as intended	306	251	[1]
Slave insurrection	Voyage completed as intended	271	217	[1]
Slave insurrection	Voyage completed as intended	360	273	[1]
Slave insurrection	Taken by Africans off the Windward Coast of Africa, fate of ship unknown	196	0	[1], [2] p. 5
Vessel attacked from shore	Cut off by Africans from shore, ship did not reach the Americas	276	0	[1]
Slave insurrection	Voyage completed as intended	276	209	[1]
Vessel attacked from shore	Cut off by Africans from shore, ship did not reach the Americas	276	0	[1]
Slave insurrection	Voyage completed as intended	400	260	[1]

Departure date	Ship name	Owner	Captain
1752-02-28	Juba	Curtis, John*	Smith, Charles
1752-03-24	Marlborough	Lougher, Walter*	Codd, Robert
1753-08-12	Matilda	Wraxall, Nathanial*	Bird, Japhet; Davis, Henry
1757-10-13	Two Sisters	Bull, William*	Cowie, Robert
1760-10-09	Hope	Fowler, John*	Owens, Thomas
1762-05-05	Black Prince	Laroche, James*	Miller, William
1764-05-17	Jolly Prince	Laroche, James (Jr)*	Holloran, Patrick
1767-04-17	Africa	Sims, Thomas*; Morgan, John*	Morgan, John
1768-02-06	Africa	Fowler, John*	Watkins, William
1768-03-03	Andrews	Hamilton, David	Robe, Archibald
1768-01-09	Indian Prince	Jones, Thomas	Lambert, John
1768-05-07	King David	NK	Patey, Benjamin; Broad
1775-07-20	Phoenix	Powell, J; Powell (Son)*	Taylor, Charles; Smith, John
1782-10-13	Wasp	Jones, Thomas*	Bowen, Richard
1784-08-03	Wasp	Jones, Thomas; Champlain, John	Bowen, Richard

Form of African resistance	Fate of voyage	No. enslaved		Source
		embarked	disembarked	
Slave insurrection	Voyage completed as intended	339	277	[1]
Slave insurrection	Captured by slaves off Bonny coast, 270 escaped to shore, fate of ship and remaining slaves unknown	420	0	[1], [2] p. 62
Slave insurrection	Voyage completed as intended	198	150	[1]
Slave insurrection	Voyage completed as intended	220	240	[1]
Vessel attacked from shore	Cut off by Africans from shore, ship did not reach the Americas	367	0	[1]
Slave insurrection	Voyage completed as intended	438	394	[1]
Slave insurrection	Captain and crew massacred by slaves off Cape Mount, fate of ship unknown	196	0	[1], [2] p. 179
Slave insurrection	Voyage completed as intended	230	197	[1]
Slave insurrection	Shipwrecked or destroyed - unspecified	310	262	[1]
Vessel's boats attacked from shore	Voyage completed as intended	352	287	[1]
Vessel attacked from shore	Cut off by Africans from shore, ship did not reach the Americas	276	0	[1]
Vessel attacked from shore	Shipwrecked or destroyed after disembarkation	207	157	[1]
Slave insurrection	Voyage completed as intended	359	328	[1]
Slave insurrection	Voyage completed as intended	225	130	[1]
Slave insurrection	Voyage completed as intended	214	197	[1]

Departure date	Ship name	Owner	Captain
1787-08-10	Ruby	Tapscott, William*; Rogers, James*	Williams, Joseph
1789-10-04	Crescent	Rogers, James*; Laroche, James (Sir); Fydell, Richard; Walker, Thomas	Roper, William
1790-04-14	Albion	Jones, James	Wade, John Robinson
1791-01-27	Favourite	Fitzhenry, Patrick	Fitzhenry, John
1792-04-10	Mermaid	Rogers, James	Mulling, James; Taylor, Edward
1795-07-20	Isabella	Jones, Thomas*; Dorvell, William; Jones, Esther	Given, Thomas

Form of African resistance	Fate of voyage	No. enslaved embarked	No. enslaved disembarked	Source
Slave insurrection	Voyage completed as intended	105	97	[1]
Slave insurrection	Voyage completed as intended	270	263	[1]
Slave insurrection	Voyage completed as intended	262	262	[1]
Slave insurrection	Voyage completed as intended	243	223	[1]
Slave insurrection	Voyage completed as intended	159	129	[1]
Vessel attacked from shore	Captured by the French - before slaves embarked	0	0	[1]

Sources

[1] Voyages: The Trans-Atlantic Slave Trade Database. https://www.slavevoyages.org (accessed 2019).

[2] Richardson, D. *Bristol, Africa and the Eighteenth-Century Slave Trade to America Vol. 3 The Years of Decline 1746-1769*. Bristol: The Bristol Record Society, 1991.

* Designates leading agent

NK = Not Known

Appendix 6: Distribution of compensation money to slave owners in Bristol (1834)

Rank	Awardee	Address in Bristol	Sex
1	Thomas Daniel	Berkeley Square, Bristol	M
2	James Evan Baillie	Rodney House, Clifton, Bristol	M
3	Philip John Miles	Kings Weston House, Kings Weston Lane, Bristol	M
4	Hugh Duncan Baillie	Park Row, Bristol	M
5	George Henry Ames	Cote House, Westbury-upon-Trym, Bristol	M
6	James Cunningham	Clifton, Bristol	M
7	Thomas Kington the younger	Charlton House, Somerset [Shepton Mallet]	M
8	Benjamin Bickley	Meridian Place, Clifton, Bristol	M
9	Charles Pinney	Camp House, Clifton, Bristol	M
10	Richard Bright of Ham Green	Queen Square, Bristol	M
11	William Hudson Heaven	Bristol	M
12	Charles Thomas Alleyne	2 Litfield Place, Clifton, Bristol	M
13	John Frederick Pinney	Berkeley Square, Bristol	M
14	James Cunningham	8 Queen Square, Bristol	M
15	Arthur Foulks	Redland House, Bristol	M
16	George Cunningham	Rodney Place, Clifton, Bristol	M
17	Robert Edward Case	Clifton, Bristol	M
18	Richard Haynes	Ashley Villa, Richmond Road, Clifton, Bristol	M
19	Philip Protheroe the younger	Richmond Hill, Clifton, Bristol	M
20	Charles Edward Bernard M.D.	14 Manchester Buildings, Parliament Street, Bristol	M
21	Michael Hinton Castle	Stapleton Grove, Stapleton, Gloucestershire	M
22	Thomas Sealy	4 Saville Place, Clifton, Bristol	M
23	William Chrystie	Clifton, Bristol	M
24	Philip Vaughan	Redland, Bristol	M
25	James Lewis III	Clifton, Bristol	M
26	John Gordon of Bristol		M

Compensation (£)	Number of enslaved	Cumulative (£)	Share of wealth (%)	Cumulative (%)	Notes
71,562	2,523	71,562	16.63	16.63	
34,253	1,015	105,815	7.96	24.60	
30,131	1,381	135,946	7.00	31.60	
21,747	613	157,693	5.05	36.66	
18,322	476	176,015	4.26	40.91	
15,814	760	191,829	3.68	44.59	
15,338	606	207,167	3.57	48.16	
14,845	537	222,012	3.45	51.61	50% of compensation
12,515	680	234,527	2.91	54.51	
11,972	640	246,499	2.78	57.30	
11,739	638	258,238	2.73	60.03	
11,230	519	269,468	2.61	62.64	
10,695	540	280,163	2.49	65.12	
10,324	515	290,487	2.40	67.52	
8,911	426	299,398	2.07	69.59	
8,433	417	307,831	1.96	71.55	
8,140	476	315,970	1.89	73.45	
7,293	319	323,263	1.70	75.14	
6,704	339	329,967	1.56	76.70	
6,491	346	336,458	1.51	78.21	
5,646	122	342,104	1.31	79.52	
5,117	228	347,221	1.19	80.71	
4,878	262	352,099	1.13	81.84	
4,616	229	356,715	1.07	82.92	
4,399	263	361,114	1.02	83.94	
3,963	208	365,077	0.92	84.86	

Rank	Awardee	Address in Bristol	Sex
27	Nathaniel Cave of Stirling Plantation	31 Caledonia Place, Clifton, Bristol	M
28	Robert Bright	Abbots Leigh, Somerset	M
29	John Gordon of Wincombe Park		M
30	Ann Trotman (née Hamilton)	7 York Place, Clifton, Bristol	F
31	Rev. Robert Allwood	3 York Place, Clifton, Bristol	M
32	Stephen Cave	Cleve Hill House, Bristol	M
33	Henry Bush	Litfield House, 1 Litfield Place, Clifton, Bristol	M
34	George Hilhouse	Clifton, Bristol	M
35	Langford Redwood Esq.	33 Royal York Crescent, Clifton, Bristol	M
36	Jane Elizabeth Nusum	10 Park Place, Clifton, Bristol	F
37	Susanna James Mountague	7 Charlotte Street, St Augustine, Bristol	F
38	Richard Honnywill junior	Bristol	M
39	Anne Grant	Clifton, Bristol	F
40	Henrietta Grant	Clifton, Bristol	F
41	Charles Edward Bernard junior	Bristol	M
42	Walter Craufuird Bernard	33 Cornwallis Crescent, Bristol	M
43	William Tabbernor	69 Castle Street, Bristol	M
44	Mary Dehany Mountague	Bristol	F
45	Charlotte Augusta Lyall (née Bayley)		F
46	George Protheroe	Bristol	M
47	Thomas Jones	Bristol	M
48	Jeremiah Osborne	Henbury, Bristol	M
49	Richard Brickdale Ward	Down Side House, Downside Road, Westbury, Clifton, Bristol	M
50	Rev. William Drake Sealy	15 Richmond Terrace, Clifton, Bristol	M
51	Evan Baillie	Bristol	M

Compensation (£)	Number of enslaved	Cumulative (£)	Share of wealth (%)	Cumulative (%)	Notes
3,615	162	368,692	0.84	85.70	
3,291	161	371,983	0.76	86.47	
3,181	174	375,164	0.74	87.21	
3,097	142	378,261	0.72	87.93	
2,636	51	380,897	0.61	88.54	
2,442	125	383,339	0.57	89.11	
2,416	114	385,754	0.56	89.67	
2,416	114	388,170	0.56	90.23	90% of compensation
2,064	132	390,234	0.48	90.71	
1,920	88	392,154	0.45	91.15	
1,903	95	394,057	0.44	91.60	
1,824	94	395,881	0.42	92.02	
1,680	62	397,561	0.39	92.41	
1,680	62	399,241	0.39	92.80	
1,673	90	400,914	0.39	93.19	
1,673	90	402,586	0.39	93.58	
1,660	78	404,246	0.39	93.97	
1,641	81	405,887	0.38	94.35	
1,636	81	407,523	0.38	94.73	
1,622	87	409,145	0.38	95.10	
1,284	69	410,429	0.30	95.40	
1,213	44	411,641	0.28	95.68	
1,213	44	412,854	0.28	95.97	
1,105	54	413,958	0.26	96.22	
1,008	37	414,966	0.23	96.46	

Rank	Awardee	Address in Bristol	Sex
52	George Weare Braikenridge	21 Queen Square, Bristol	M
53	John Braikenridge	Brislington	M
54	George Gibbs	Bristol	M
55	Elizabeth Lawrence Hay (née Allen)	Bristol	F
56	William Claxton	1 Nursery Villas, Chantry Road, Clifton, Bristol	M
57	Robert Podmore Clark	5 Ellenborough Buildings, Redland, Bristol	M
58	John Cave of Brentry	Brentry House, Westbury-upon-Trym, Bristol	M
59	Charles Anthony Partridge	Cotham Lodge, Bristol	M
60	Lucy Tobin (née Oliver)	3 Vyvyan Terrace , Clifton, Bristol	F
61	Elizabeth Corne Bennett then Mais (née Pownall)	Redland, Bristol	F
62	Herbert Jarrett James	Clifton, Bristol	M
63	William Weare	Great George Street, Bristol	M
64	Elizabeth Hale	Bristol	F
65	Robert James Hale	1 Brownham Place, Hotwells, Bristol	M
66	Rachel Claxton (née Mardenbrough)	Clifton, Bristol	F
67	Henry Sealy	29 Berkeley Square, Bristol	M
68	Elizabeth Giles	28 Clare Street, Bristol	F
69	Catherine Gordon (née Hering)	Bristol	F
70	Dorothy Little	3 Lower Park Row, Bristol	M
71	Charles Payne of Bristol the younger	Freeman House, Clifton, Bristol	M
72	Elizabeth Henderson (née Anderson)	12 Catherine Place, Clifton, Bristol	F
73	Sydney Mary Anderson	12 Catherine Place, Clifton, Bristol	F
74	Martha Delaroche (née Shapland)	32 Catherine Place, Bristol	F
75	Mary Tucker	7 Meridian Place, Bristol	F
76	John Henry Cutting	Bristol	M

Compensation (£)	Number of enslaved	Cumulative (£)	Share of wealth (%)	Cumulative (%)	Notes
970	52	415,936	0.23	96.68	
970	52	416,906	0.23	96.91	
875	47	417,781	0.20	97.11	
814	50	418,595	0.19	97.30	
751	44	419,346	0.17	97.48	
666	33	420,012	0.15	97.63	
661	46	420,673	0.15	97.78	
661	46	421,335	0.15	97.94	
661	46	421,996	0.15	98.09	
637	30	422,633	0.15	98.24	
580	25	423,213	0.13	98.37	
522	28	423,735	0.12	98.50	
433	18	424,168	0.10	98.60	
433	18	424,601	0.10	98.70	
428	24	425,028	0.10	98.80	
391	17	425,419	0.09	98.89	
340	13	425,759	0.08	98.97	
325	18	426,084	0.08	99.04	
297	13	426,381	0.07	99.11	
266	15	426,647	0.06	99.17	
251	14	426,898	0.06	99.23	
251	14	427,148	0.06	99.29	
244	13	427,392	0.06	99.35	
241	11	427,633	0.06	99.40	
233	9	427,866	0.05	99.46	

Rank	Awardee	Address in Bristol	Sex
77	Christopher Henry Massiah	8 Bellevue, Clifton, Bristol	M
78	Thomas Osborn	Frenchay, Bristol	M
79	William Derrickson Beard	13 Harford Street, Bristol	M
80	John Lyons Nixon		M
81	Heriot Pearce Hall	Richmond Terrace, Clifton, Bristol	F
82	Lucretia Pearce Hall	Richmond Terrace, Clifton, Bristol	F
83	Maria Pearce Hall	Richmond Terrace, Clifton, Bristol	F
84	John M. Tucker	Bristol	M
85	Ann Trotman junior	7 York Place, Clifton, Bristol	F
86	Samuel Flook	Gloucester Lane, Bristol	M
87	Thomas Flook		M
88	William Munro	Druid Stoke House, Westbury-on-Trym, Gloucestershire	M
89	Henry Samuel Beer	Clifton Villa, Clifton, Bristol	M
90	Charlotte Cunningham	Clifton, Bristol	F
91	Eliza Cunningham		F
92	Jane Cunningham	9 Buckingham Vale, Clifton, Bristol	F
93	John Grant Wilson	17 Richmond Terrace, Clifton, Bristol	M
94	Henry Adams Mayers	Redland, Bristol	M
95	Rachel Allen James	Hotwells, Bristol	F
96	Lt-Col Christian Frederick Lardy	4 West Park, Westbury-upon-Trym, Bristol	M
97	Sarah Elizabeth Johnson	1 York Place, Clifton, Bristol	F

Notes on claims

1. Only successful claimants were considered.
2. Only cases where money was directly awarded were included (e.g. Chancery cases excluded).
3. Successful claimants were only counted if they lived in Bristol or its immediate environs in the period of compensation payouts (1834-37).
4. In cases of multiple successful claimants, equal splits were assumed unless other information was available.
5. The numbers of enslaved Africans 'owned' by each claimant are estimates.
6. The figures in this table are conservative as they only include those claimants who have addresses in Bristol stated in the UCL database.

Compensation (£)	Number of enslaved	Cumulative (£)	Share of wealth (%)	Cumulative (%)	Notes
229	12	428,095	0.05	99.51	
208	9	428,303	0.05	99.56	
191	11	428,494	0.04	99.60	
191	5	428,685	0.04	99.65	
167	10	428,852	0.04	99.68	
167	10	429,018	0.04	99.72	
167	10	429,185	0.04	99.76	
164	8	429,349	0.04	99.80	
116	3	429,465	0.03	99.83	
103	4	429,567	0.02	99.85	
103	4	429,670	0.02	99.87	
94	7	429,764	0.02	99.90	
73	4	429,837	0.02	99.91	
67	3	429,904	0.02	99.93	
67	3	429,972	0.02	99.95	
67	3	430,039	0.02	99.96	
58	2	430,097	0.01	99.97	
34	3	430,131	0.01	99.98	
29	1	430,160	0.01	99.99	
29	3	430,189	0.01	100.00	
19	1	430,208	0.00	100.00	
430, 208	18,212				

Source

Legacies of British Slave-ownership database, https://www.ucl.ac.uk/lbs/ [accessed 2019].

Appendix 7: Reinvestment of compensation in emerging industries

Table of those compensated for ownership of enslaved Africans with significant investments in Bristol industries and construction projects (post-1834)

Key

= Rank in list of successful claimants from Bristol for emancipation compensation (See Appendix 6).

£ Then = Share of emancipation compensation monies (£).

£ Now = Equivalent in 2016 by GDP per capita (£ Millions).

MV = Member of Society of Merchant Venturers.

SB = Clifton Suspension Bridge (1831).

R = Great Western Railway Company (1835)[1].

S = Great Western Steamship Company (1836).

C = Great Western Cotton Company (1837).

Notes

1. A number of successful claimants of compensation money invested in railways outside of Bristol and so do not appear on this table. These include (with rank in brackets): James Evan Baillie (2)—Welsh Midland Railway; James Cunningham (6)—Bath and Weymouth Great Western Union Railway; William Chrystie (23)—Southampton Railway; and Nathaniel Cave (27)—Caledonian Railway.

2. Phillip John Miles did not directly invest in the Great Western Cotton Factory, it was actually his son Phillip William Skynner Miles, though it is likely that the compensation money stimulated this financial interest. PWS Miles, also an MP for Bristol, invested in the Avonmouth railway and docks. Phillip John Miles's younger son, Edward Peach William Miles, helped switch the family's Caribbean trading interests to Australasia. EPW Miles held several prominent directorships across the imperial world, including the New Zealand Shipping Company, The Union Bank of Australia, The London and Westminster Bank, The Panama, New Zealand and Australian Royal Mail Company and remained a member of the Society of Merchant Venturers in Bristol.

Sources

This table was derived from the following sources: Legacies of British Slave-ownership database https://www.ucl.ac.uk/lbs/; *An Account of the Proceedings of the Great Western Railway Company: With extracts from the evidence in support of the bill before the committee of the House of Commons in the session of 1834.* (London: Smith & Ebbs, 1834) p. 21; Grace's Guide to British Industrial History: Great Western Steamship Co https://www.gracesguide.co.uk/Great_Western_Steamship_Co; Portman, D. "A business history of the Clifton Suspension Bridge." *Construction History* 18 (2002); "Advertisements & Notices" *Bristol Mercury*, 2 February 1830; Richardson, *The Maltreated and the Malcontents* pp. 9-11; Marshall, *Bristol and the Abolition of Slavery* p. 27; Latimer, J. *The History of the Society of Merchant Venturers*; From Slaves to Sleepers: The dark saga behind the Steamship Great Britain, Nonesuch Expeditions http://www.nonesuchexpeditions.com/ss-great-britain/slaves-to-sleepers/the-dark-saga.htm.

Name	#	£ Then	£ Now	MV	SB	Great Western R	S	C	Notes
Thomas Daniel	1	71,562	86.2	•	•	•			Sheriff, Mayor, Alderman and Master SMV, previous partner in the banking business of Ames, Cave & Co, sugar merchant, original trustee of Clifton Suspension Bridge.
Phillip John Miles	3	36,573	43.4	•				•[2]	Bristol MP, financial interests in banking, haberdashery, rope-making, gunpowder, brass and glass manufacture; business partner of Thomas Kington (jnr).
George Ames	5	18,322	22.1					•	Business partner of the Baillie, Daniel and Cave families.
Thomas Kington (jnr)	7	15,338	18.5	•			•	•	Business partner of Philip Miles, Bristol Brass Wire and Copper Co., Chairman of Clifton Suspension Bridge Trustees.
Charles Pinney	9	12,515	15.1	•				•	Mayor, Councillor, Alderman, Sheriff, Master of SMV, President of Anchor Society, business partner of George Ames and Robert Case. Invested in Canadian bonds and Indian railways.
Robert Case	17	8,140	9.8					•	Business partner of Charles Pinney.
Phillip Protheroe (jnr)	19	6,704	8.1	•	•				Master of SMV, Chairman of Clifton Suspension Bridge Committee.
Robert Bright	28	3,291	4.0	•	•	•	•	•	Deputy chairman of GWR, business partner of George Gibbs.
Henry Bush	33	2,416	2.9	•	•	•	•	•	Investor in Bristol & Gloucestershire Extension (Railway), Master of SMV.
George Gibbs	54	875	1.1	•	•	•	•	•	Investor in the Portbury Pier and Railway, business partner of Robert Bright, director of GWR, Master of SMV.
John Cave	58	661	0.8	•	•	•			Glass and vitriol manufacturer; Sheriff, Mayor and Master of SMV.

Appendix 8: Press release regarding protests on 7th November 2015

PROTEST OUTSIDE BRISTOL CATHEDRAL AT COLSTON COMMEMORATIONS INSIDE THE CATHEDRAL

Several newspapers published articles on 17 November about children from a Colston school in Bristol, being accosted. This may relate to events 10 days earlier, where there was a public protest outside Bristol Cathedral on 7 November, aimed at the Colston commemorations going on inside the cathedral.

We refute strongly that children were accosted on 7 November. We believe the school have overreacted to events of 7 November 2015 by unduly alarming parents and children and being economical with the truth. Inside the Cathedral, whilst preparations were being undertaken to mark Colston's Founder's Day attended by Colston's Girls' School, we were protesting outside.

At the time of my arrival there were 6 of us. Our protest entailed distributing leaflets headed: 'WHY WE ARE PROTESTING OUTSIDE TODAY' that explained our presence, one of us holding a lighted candle. Our presence and activities were always in a visible public space with staff present.

Shortly, another 6 joined us. Among us: a retired teacher, a security guard, a historian, a grandparent who had dropped off a child to the ceremony, a teacher, three artists, a mother with a toddler in a buggy and a former student of Colston Girls. We are representative of the Bristol population whom the children live among.

We believe the teachers only panicked because they did not have a risk assessment in place that anticipated protest. Had the staff that were present with the children read the leaflets, that they were so quick to take off the children, they would have realised, it was the Merchant Venturers' commemoration of Charter day and the Bishop's comments in the Cathedral in 2014 that brought us as individuals to protest outside the Cathedral.

We found students bright, attentive and curious. Many were entering the Cathedral with little understanding of who Colston was or indeed why they were there. Others were keen to learn more and asked for leaflets.

Education takes place everywhere. We were not outside any school or in the street harassing children. Our aim was to protest at a ceremony in a significant religious and spiritual place of worship, 'celebrating' a controversial historical figure without acknowledging his direct involvement in the propagation of slavery and his amassed wealth from slave trading activities.

Neither did the ceremony seek to honour the memory and suffering of Africans and others exploited by the slave trade, creating memorialisation dissent in the Bristol community. This is what we are seeking to publicly highlight and change.

Why is this controversial?

The spreading of panic and fear in children and parents through the media glosses over public dissent and smothers the truth.

We are open to meeting with the Colston's School, the Bishop and the Cathedral for discussion on a way forward.

Appendix 9: Letter from Marti Burgess
to Bristol Music Trust

I would like to vote to approve of the name change and announcing it as proposed by the executive team. As this is really important to me, I have decided to let you have my thoughts and reasons why I consider a name change is the right thing to do.

As a young person I attended the hall often and in fact saw my first concert there. Like most people I was not aware that Colston had any connection to slavery. I first became aware of the fact that Colston had been involved in the slave trade in the 1990s and like many within the black community I decided that I would join the boycott and signed a number of petitions.

When the Hall reopened after the Foyer was built I was invited but chose not to attend because of the retention of the name. The first time I attended was in 2009/2010 after I was asked by Paul Stephenson, as Chair of the Legacy Commission, to help organise a slavery remembrance event at the Hall. Whilst at the event, someone suggested that I apply to join the board of the new company being set up to take over the hall. My initial reaction was negative but it was pointed out to me that by joining the board I could impact the name change agenda. I have always made it clear that my view is that the hall should change its name and that was one of my reasons for joining the board as well as a desire to be involved in a new era of the premiere music venue in my home town.

I would like to now turn to Colston and why he should not be someone who is perceived to be honoured by having the hall named after him. I know as do many others that the hall only bears Colston's name because of the location however many others (including the majority of his defenders) do not see it that way and consider the hall like the statue as part of memorialisation of him as a 'great son' of the city.

I understand that researchers have discovered that 85,000 African men, women and children were enslaved and transported on Royal African Company ships under Colston's leadership, he was effectively the CEO of that company not a simple shareholder or bystander in the trade. Nearly a quarter of the enslaved Africans on Colston's ships died before even reaching the Americas. The vast majority of the rest went on to a life of hardship throughout the Americas.

When the subject of Colston is brought up he is often defended and campaigners are accused of trying to obscure history or changing it. My view is that it is the defenders of Colston who are really obscuring and airbrushing the city's history by failing to honestly convey the scale of suffering caused by Colston's actions. It makes no sense to say the campaigners are trying to change the past. Instead, they are trying to change how the past is recounted.

The campaigners want to tell the true history of men like Colston, not the fake history that presents him as a hero. I have also heard the argument that we should extend a principle of charity and sympathy to Colston, who had the moral misfortune of living in a social environment where slavery was seen as acceptable. It is one thing to extend reasonable understanding but it quite another to pretend that he was a great philanthropist, while downplaying the extent of his involvement in slavery. It would be perverse to say that charity required us to continue to be perceived as honouring Colston as a hero. That would not be respectful towards the memory of the people whose lives were destroyed by slavery or his contemporaries who recognised the evil of the slave trade at the time of Colston.

Most of the above are my moral reasons for supporting the name change. However I also consider that there are strong commercial reasons to do so in furtherance of our duties to act in the best interest of the charity. It cannot be in the best interest of the charity to continue to cling on to a name which impacts on our ability to operate commercially. Our 150th birthday celebrations and campaign to raise funds for the refurbishment have been impacted by this argument and each time we do anything or put out a press release our objectives are obscured by the controversy over the name. In addition, there is still a proportion of the public who do still continue to boycott the venue.

The whole argument is bigger than the hall and is about the city and how we recognise that we can all have different perceptions on our shared history. I strongly hold the view that as a board of trustees we now have the opportunity to seize hold of the argument and shape the history of our city and personally I would rather be seen to be part of the movement to effect this change.

I do hope you all agree and support the motion put forward by the executive team.

Maps

This section contains details of maps taken from *Atlas minimus universalis, or, A geographical abridgement ancient and modern of the several parts of the earth: in fifty-five maps composed principally for the use of schools* by William Faden, published in London in 1798. A copy of this work can be found on Archive.org.

For more information about place names, see the Glossary of Locations. on page 330.

Map 1: The Caribbean
Map 2: Eastern seaboard of North America
Map 3: South America
Map 4: West Africa

Map 1: The Caribbean

TROPIC OF CANCER

Longitude W. from London

O C E A N

A T L A N T I C

LEEWARD ISLES

St. Bartholomew
St. Martin
Anguilla
Barbuda
Antigua
Saba
St. Eustatia
St. Christophers
Nevis
Montserrat
Guadeloupe
Marigalante
Desirade
Dominique
Martinique
St. Lucia
Barbadoes
St. Vincent
Bequia
Grenadilles
Grenada
Tobago
Trinidad

St. Thomas
Tortola
Virgin Gorda
St. John
St. Croix
Mona
Santa Cruz

CARIBBEE SEA ISLES

Porto Rico
Puerto Rico
Cape Raphael
Aguada
Puerto del Juan
Cape Roxo
Mona

Margarita
Tortuga
Blanca
Orchilla
Aves
Roca
Aves
Bonair
Curaçao
Aruba
Monges
C. Roman
C. San Roman
G. of Venezuela
Leon de Caracas
Cumana

Silver Keys
Old Cape Français
Samana
Monte Christe
Square Handkerchief
Turks Is.
Caicos
Mayaguana
Crooked
Fortune
Mariguana

BAHAMA ISLANDS

Samana
C. St. Carlos
C. St. Antonio
Colorados
Isla de Pinos
Jardines
Bahama Bank
Old Bahama Channel

Abaco
Abra de la Key
P. del Principe
Jagua
Midas Pt.
Inagua
C. de Cruz
St. Iago
St. Martha
Windward Passage
St. Nicholas

HISPANIOLA or St. DOMINGO

S. Domingo
St. Domingo
Samana
Jacmel
Cape Tiburon
Leogane
Port au Prince
Les Cayes
Altavela
Yaquimo

JAMAICA
Pt. Negril
Spanish Town
Kingston
Port Royal
Morant
Port Morant
Pedro Shoals
Serena
Serrana
Pracel

C. de la Vela
C. Aguja
C. Galera
Rio Hacha
St. Martha
Carthagena
Tolu
C. Blanco

S O U T H   A M E R I C A

Lake of Maracaybo
Maracaybo

Porto Bello
Almirante Bay
Bocca toro
Bluefields Lagoon
Chagre
Nicaragua
Dios
the Habbies
Pearl Keys
Corn Is.
St. Andres
St. Catalina or Old Providence
Albuquerque
Romador
Vela
Cisanbel
Serranilla
Bajo Nuevo
Bajo del Comboi
Vivoras

C A R I B B E A N   S E A

Gr. Cayman
L. Cayman

Map 2: Eastern seaboard of North America

British Statute Miles

1   2   3   400

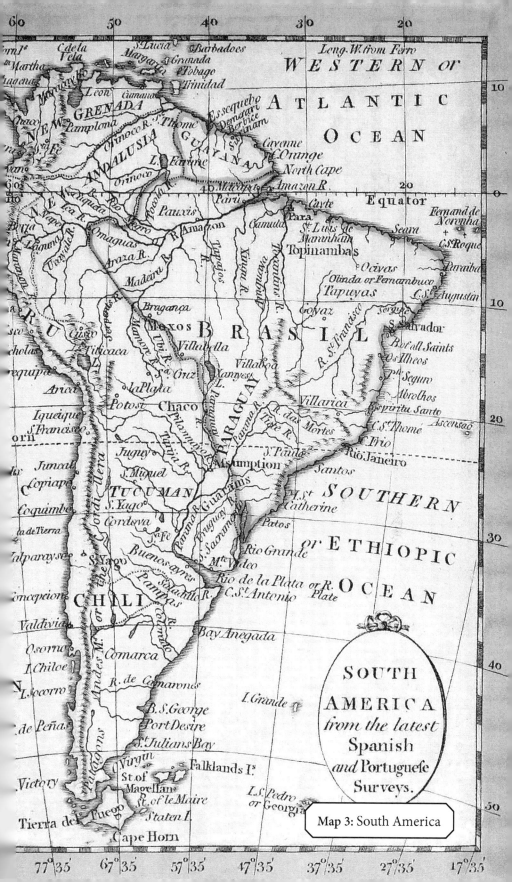

Map 3: South America

ATLANTIC

30

Str. of Gibraltar
Madeira   Porto   Tangier   Sicily   Mo
Santo   Sale   Oran   Algier   Tunis   sal   MEDITERR
Canary Is.   Morocco   Fez   BARBARY   Malta   Ca
Palma   MOROCCO   M.Atlas   Land   Tripoli   Ba
Ferro   Ifren   of Dates   Fezzan   Sant
Tenerife   Canary   C.Bojador   Tesset   Zuenziga   Morzouk   Ghie
Zanhaga   Lempta
20   Tegaza   Terga
C.Blanco   Guaden   SAHRA or the Desert   Tropic of   Cancer   K

Cape Verd Is.   Tocrur   Niger R.   Gaze
Sal   Tombut   N I G R I T I A
St.Lucia   Bonavista   Pt.S.Louis   Gago   Secm
S.t Yago C.   Grounel   Ghanarg   Rh
Fogo   Verd   Red R.   Gomba
10   James Fort   Senegal R.   Bambook   Ayos
Bissao F.   R.Gambia   Songo
C.Verga   Mandinga
Sierra Leona   G U I N E A
C.Mount   Axim   Gold Coast   Benin
C.Palmas   Cape Coast   Calbary
Castle   Biafra
Gulf of Guinea   R. Gabon   A
0   I.S.t Thomas

Equator   C. Lopo Gonsal
St.Matthew   Arnobon   Loango
Cacongo   S.t s
Zaire R.   CONGO
E T H I O P I C   C. Ledo   LOANDA
ANGOL
Ascencion   Benguela   Co

10   or   Cumeni R.
St.Helena   C. Negro   Cimbeb
to the
Matam
SOUTHERN   Angra Fria

20   Tropic of Capricorn   Angra
do Ilheo

Meridian of Ferro
Meridian of London

C. dos Voltas   Nan

O C E A N   Table Bay
C. of Good Hope

Map 4: West Africa

Long. W. from London.

17 35   7 35   2 25   12 25

Glossaries

Glossary of abbreviations

AAS   American Anti-Slavery Society
BA   Bristol Archives
BBC   British Broadcasting Corporation
BCC   Bristol City Council
BCRL   Bristol Central Reference Library
BDC   Bristol Dock and Canal Company
BMT   Bristol Music Trust
BPP   Bristol Peoples' Party
BRHG   Bristol Radical History Group
BUC   Bristol University College
CC   Countering Colston
CGS   Colston's Girls' School
DD   Doctor of Divinity
FOS   Festival of the Sea
GC   Guinea Company
GWCF   Great Western Cotton Factory
GWR   Great Western Railway
GWSC   Great Western Steamship Company
HLF   Heritage Lottery Fund
MVTC   Merchant Venturers' Technical College
PCC   Parochial Church Council
PCSO   Police Community Support Officer
PIC   Providence Island Company
RAC   Royal African Company
SMV   The Society of Merchant Venturers
SPCK   Society for the Promotion of Christian Knowledge
SPG   Society for the Propagation of the Gospel in Foreign Parts
SSC   South Sea Company
UCL   University College London
UB   University of Bristol
UWE   University of the West of England
WAS   West Africa Squadron

Glossary of locations

Europe and North Africa
Algeria (Argiere)—Atlantic Coast, North Africa.
Canary Islands—Spanish from fifteenth century, 60 miles west of Morocco in the Atlantic.
Gascony—South-western coast of France.
Iberian Peninsula—Principally divided between Spain and Portugal, encompasses Andorra in the north to Gibraltar in the south.
Levant—Eastern Mediterranean, historical region of Syria, from Egypt to Turkey including Palestine and Cyprus.
Lisbon—Capital of Portugal.
Madeira—Portuguese island settled 1412, west of Africa in north Atlantic, 200 miles north of Canaries.
Sallee—Morocco, Atlantic Coast, North Africa.
Turkey—Eastern Mediterranean.

West Africa
In the eighteenth Century comprised the Guinea Coast, Pepper (Grain) Coast, Ivory Coast, Gold Coast and Slave Coast, originally explored by the Portuguese in the fifteenth and sixteenth centuries.

Angola—Lies on the west coast of south-central Africa, below the Congo, first reached by the Portuguese in 1484 and settled a century later.
Ashanti, Empire on the Gold Coast—Capital Accra, part of modern-day Ghana.
Bonny—Island town in Niger delta on River Bonny, originally part of the homeland of Ibani people, name corrupted to Bonny, it then belonged to the Igbo people, modern day Southern Nigeria.
Bar of Bonny—A sand bar at the mouth of the River Bonny.
Bence Island—Situated in the middle of the River Sierra Leone in Freetown Harbour, 20 miles from the capital Freetown.
Benin—French speaking Kingdom on the Slave Coast, modern day Republic of Benin.
Bight of Benin (Bay of Benin)—In which the Slave Coast sits, part of larger Guinea Gulf.
Cape Corso Castle—'Slave' fort on the Gold Coast, modern day Ghana.
Cape Verde Islands—Island country in the Atlantic, 350 miles west of Cape Verde Peninsula off the Northwest coast of Africa, uninhabited until settled by the Portuguese in the fifteenth century.
Lagos—Commercial centre of Nigeria.
Liberia, Cape Mount (Grand Cape Mount)—In modern day Liberia situated between Sierra Leone and Cote d'Ivorie (Ivory Coast).
Old Calabar—Port city and capital of Cross River State, belonging to Igbo people, modern day Southern Nigeria.
Sierra Leone—Situated on the southwest Atlantic coast of West Africa.
Whydah (Ouidah)—Former kingdom and coastal city in Southern Benin, Slave Coast.
Windward coast of Africa—Stretches from Senegal and Gambia to Benin.

North American Mainland, Eastern Seaboard
Bermuda—British island colony in North Atlantic, 700 miles east of Carolina, settled by English in 1612 in order to help develop Virginia.
Boston—Capital of Massachusetts.
Bonavista—Town on the coast of Newfoundland, Canada.
Carolina—Capital Charles Town (Charles II) now Charleston, originally claimed for Spain, became an English colony after 1663, divided into North and South Carolina around 1729.

Delaware—First settled by the Swedish in 1631, then the Dutch, followed by the English under William Penn. Separated from Pennsylvania in the eighteenth century.

Georgia—Named after George II, last and southernmost of Britain's original 13 colonies, settled 1733.

Harper's Ferry—West Virginia, United States.

Kentucky—Formally part of Virginia, the Commonwealth of Kentucky was admitted to the Union in 1792.

Kansas—US State, first settled by European Americans in 1827.

Lake Erie—Fourth largest of the Great Lakes, situated on the border between Canada and the United States.

Louisiana—First settled by the Spanish then the French, formed French America, bordered between Florida and Texas (east to west) and from the Gulf of Mexico to Canada (south to north). Purchased by the United States for five cents an acre in 1803.

Maryland—Named after Charles I's wife Mary, capital Baltimore.

New England—Area comprising six former English colonies now US states: Connecticut, Maine, Massachusetts, New Hampshire, Rhode Island and Vermont.

Newfoundland—Island off the east coast of the North American mainland. First recorded in 1497 by John Cabot after originally being briefly settled by the Vikings around 1000. English colony founded by Humphrey Gilbert in 1585, followed by John Guy in 1610; initially shared with the French until Treaty of Utrecht 1713. Became part of Canada in 1949.

New York—City and state. The city was originally Dutch and called Peter Stuyvesant, renamed after Duke of York (James II).

Pennsylvania—First settlers were Swedish in 1643, followed by the Dutch, then English. Charles II gave the land to William Penn in 1681 to provide a home for Quakers. Capital Philadelphia.

Tennessee—Landlocked state initially part of North Carolina.

Virginia—Named after the 'virgin queen' (Elizabeth I). Original settlement Jamestown (James I) settled 1607. England's first established colony, becoming 'Commonwealth of Virginia', nickname 'Old Dominion'.

Washington—Capital city of the United States, District of Columbia (D.C.)

The Spanish Main

Part of Spain's New World Empire, it comprised mainland coastal possessions surrounding the Caribbean Sea and the Gulf of Mexico, known collectively as the Spanish Main. During the sixteenth and seventeenth centuries, the southern portion of these coastal possessions was known as the Province of Tierra Firme, or the "mainland province" (as opposed to Spain's nearby insular colonies such as Cuba, Hispaniola, Jamaica and Puerto Rico in the Caribbean). Anti-clockwise from Florida this included the western shore of the Gulf of Mexico which contained Texas and Mexico (North-east to California), Central America with Nicaragua, Costa Rica and Panama and the north coast of South America including, Columbia, Venezuela and Guyana.

Berbice—Region along the Berbice River in eastern Guyana.

British Guyana—On the north coast of South America, originally Dutch, became British Guyana in 1814. Comprised Demerara (Demerary), Essequibo and Berbice. Now modern-day Guyana.

Brazil—Originally Portuguese South America, first explored 1500, settled 1532.

Demerara (Demerary)—Between the Essequibo and Berbice rivers in central Guyana.

Essequibo—Western coastal region of Guyana.

Pernambuco—Coastal state in northern Brazil.

West Indies

Bahamas—South west of Florida, north east of Cuba.

Greater Antilles—A grouping of the larger islands in the northern part of the Caribbean Sea.

Cuba—Largest of all the Caribbean islands. Settled by the Spanish late fifteenth century, originally inhabited by the Taino people. Located in the northern Caribbean where the Caribbean Sea, Gulf of Mexico and Atlantic meet. Capital Havana.

Hispaniola—First European colony in the Americas, settled by Christopher Columbus in 1492/3. In 1655 the French conquered the western third of the island and called it Saint-Domingue (St Dominique – Spanish Santo Domingo anglicised to St Domingo or San Domingo). The 1697 Treaty of Ryswick formally ceded it from Spain to France, becoming the independent Republic of Haiti on 1st January 1804. Capital is Port-au-Prince. The remaining French speaking (western) part of the island stayed as Haiti while the Spanish (eastern) part of the island became the Dominican Republic

Jamaica—Third largest island in the Greater Antilles, settled by the Arawak and Taino indigenous peoples. Taken by the Spanish in 1509 and then the British in 1655. Capital Kingston (originally Port Royal, destroyed by earthquake).

Lesser Antilles—A long island arc between the Greater Antilles to the north-west and the continent of South America, forming the eastern boundary of the Caribbean Sea. The Lesser Antilles comprise the Windward Islands in the south, Leeward Islands in the north and the Leeward Antilles in the west.

Leeward Islands—Island chain to the north of the Lesser Antilles, so named as they point away from the prevailing winds.

Antigua and Barbuda—Capital St John's.

Anguilla

Guadeloupe archipelago—French

Montserrat

Santa Catalina—Providencia group of islands off of Nicaragua, eastern Caribbean

Saint Croix—French

Saint Kitts and Nevis—Capital Basseterre

St Martin—French, north of island, Sint Maarten (Dutch), south of island St Barths, also Saint Barthélemy (French)

Tortola—British Virgin Islands

Windward Islands—Island chain to the south of the Lesser Antilles, so named as they point towards the prevailing winds.

Barbados—In the North Atlantic, just east of the Caribbean Sea; capital Bridgetown.

Grenada

Martinique—French

Saint Lucia—French/British

Saint Vincent and the Grenadines

Trinidad and Tobago

Notes

Introduction (pp. i-xiv)

1 Evans was born in Ellbroad Street, Bristol in 1773 and died tragically whilst entering the Brunswick Theatre in London – "the building fell and he perished in the ruins in his fifty-fifth year of his age" in 1828. Nicholls, J. F. and Taylor, J. *Bristol Past and Present*. Vols. I, II and III (Bristol: J. W. Arrowsmith, 1882) p. 282.

2 Evans, J. *A Chronological Outline of the History of Bristol, and the Stranger's Guide Through its Streets and Neighbourhood* (Bristol: Printed at the Office of the late 'Bristol Observer', 1824).

3 Chronology of Slavery from Dresser, M. and Giles, S. (Eds.) *Bristol and Transatlantic Slavery* [Catalogue of the exhibition 'A Respectable Trade? Bristol and Transatlantic Slavery', 1999] (Bristol: Bristol Museum and Art Gallery, 2000).

4 Primary sources are written, visual, oral and physical materials from the period of study such as original documents, letters, newspapers, photographs, songs, paintings, recordings, transcripts and artefacts. Secondary sources are articles, papers and books that construct the history of the period using primary sources.

5 *Trans-Atlantic Slave Trade Database* http://www.slavevoyages.org/; *Legacies of British Slave-ownership* https://www.ucl.ac.uk/lbs/.

6 *Trans-Atlantic Slave Trade Database* http://www.slavevoyages.org/

7 In this text to we refer to chattel slavery as 'slavery'. The term 'modern day slavery', which is currently in vogue, is very misleading as it conflates mostly non-chattel types of forced labour with 'slavery', probably for shock value.

8 MeasuringWorth. "Five Ways to Compute the Relative Value of a U.K. Pound Amount, 1270 to present." https://www.measuringworth.com/calculators/ukcompare/ (accessed January, 2019).

9 Peile, J. H. F. (Trans.) *William of Malmesbury's Life of Saint Wulfstan: Bishop of Worcester* Original version, 1934 (Burnham-on-Sea: Llanerch Press, 1996).

Saint Wulfstan (pp. 1-11)

10 Coleman was Wulfstan's friend and chaplain and he wrote *English Life* immediately after Wulfstan's death in 1095.

11 Wulfstan (d.1095) was the second Bishop of Worcester of that name and should not be confused with the first (d. 1023), his maternal uncle. The first Archbishop of York (d. 956) also shared the name Wulfstan.

12 Saint Wulfstan was probably named after his maternal uncle who was Bishop of London and

Worcester and became Archbishop of York (1002-1023, d.1023). Saint Wulfstan's relative and namesake is an interesting figure as he was also an early opponent of slavery in Anglo-Saxon England. Historian David Pelteret argues that Saint Wulftsan's predecessor "took it for granted that slaves *did* possess rights; he in no wise regarded them as privileges dependent on the charity of the free". He argued in his writings that slaves deserved "humane and just treatment" and used "his power in Church and State to seek acceptance of his views". This earlier Wulfstan "attacked the trading of slaves and their sale abroad" and materially improved the conditions of slaves at home. Pelteret, D. A. E. *Slavery in Early Medieval England: From the Reign of Alfred Until the Twelfth Century* (Suffolk: Boydell & Brewer, 2001) p. 101.

13 An alternative spelling is Beorhtheah.

14 In Evans' original chronicle he mistakenly gave the date of 1080 for the beginning of the survey which became the Domesday Book. The actual date is 1085.

15 This claim was made by writer and broadcaster Stephen Fry on QI (Quite Intelligent), the fact-based game show on BBC TV.

16 A chattel slave is an enslaved person who is owned forever and whose children and children's children are automatically enslaved. Chattel slaves are individuals treated as complete property, to be bought and sold. *The Abolition Project* http://abolition.e2bn.org/slavery_40.html.

17 *Bristol Past: The Saxon Slave Market* http://www.buildinghistory.org/bristol/saxonslaves. shtml.

18 Rodgers, N. *Ireland, Slavery and Anti-Slavery: 1612-1865* (London: Palgrave Macmillan, 2007) pp. 19-20.

19 Jones, P. *Satan's Kingdom: Bristol and the Transatlantic Slave Trade* (Bristol: Past & Present Press, 2007) p. 2.

20 Robinson, D. *A Darker History of Bristol* (Bristol: Countryside Books, 2005) p. 11.

21 Evans is quoting Leland, who was an earlier Bristol Chronicler.

The Carmelite Priory (pp. 12-21)

22 Little, B. *The City and County of Bristol–A Study of Atlantic Civilisation* (Wakefield: S. R. Publishers Limited, 1967) p. 46.

23 Weare, G. E. *A Collectanea Relating to the Bristol Friars Minors (Gray Friars) and Their Convent: Together with a Concise History of the Dissolution of the Houses of the Four Orders of Mendicant Friars in Bristol* (Bristol: W. Bennett, 1893) p. 98.

24 Jones, *Satan's Kingdom* p. 2.

25 John Wycliffe, 'The Morning Star of the Reformation,' was Canon and Prebendary of Aust in the Collegiate of Westbury-on-Trym from 1362-1384, and whose followers had great influence in these parts. Wilkins, H. J. *Edward Colston (1636-1721 A.D.), Supplement to a Chronological Account of His Life and Work Together with an Account of the Colston Societies and Memorials in Bristol* (Bristol: Arrowsmith, 1925) p. 33.

26 Dresser, M. and Fleming, P. *Bristol: Ethnic Minorities and the City 1000–2001* (London: Phillimore, 2007) pp. 30-31.

27 Other eminent characters that belonged to this priory: John Stow, an ingenious poet, soon after the time of Chaucer; John Walton, DD, prior in Henry VI.'s time; Nicholas Cantilupe, DD, of Cambridge. Eleanor, Duchess of Buckingham, 1530, bequeathed her heart to Greyfriars' Church, London, and her body is in the White Friars' Church in Bristol. Chilcott, J. *Chilcott's descriptive history of Bristol, ancient and modern: or, A guide to Bristol, Clifton, & the Hotwell: including an account of the Bristol riots: with topographical notices of the neighbouring villages, etc.* 3rd ed., improved. (Bristol: J. Chilcott, 1835) p. 139.

28 "Milverton was a great anti-Wycliffist and champion of his order, both by his writing and preaching. He laboured to make all believe that Christ Himself was a Carmelite (professor of wilful poverty), and his high commending of the poverty of Friers tacitly condemned the pomp of the Prelates—the Bishop of London had him cast in jaile." Nicholls and Taylor, *Bristol Past and Present* p. 113.

29 Merritt, D. *Sculpture in Bristol* (Bristol: Redcliffe Press, 2002) p. 105.

30 As Steve Poole notes "Cabot was not the first choice of the elite; an earlier proposal [1839] was for 'a colossal statue of Edward Colston...overlooking the city which contains so many records of his worth'" Poole, S. "'Till our liberties be secure': popular sovereignty and public space in Bristol, 1780-1850" *Urban History*, 26, no. 1 (1999), p. 53, n. 41.

31 Kurlansky, M. *Cod: A Biography of the Fish That Changed the World* (London: Vintage, 1999) p. 27.

32 A sculpture of William Tyndale by Laurence Holofcener was placed in Millennium Square in 2000. Merritt, *Sculpture in Bristol* p. 60. Bristol Baptist College acquired one of only three surviving Tyndale bibles in 1776 for 20 guineas and sold it recently to the British Library for over one million pounds.

33 Weare, *Collectanea Relating to the Bristol Friars* p. 54, 74.

34 Ibid. pp. 98-100.

35 Ibid. p. 94. The Corporation was Bristol Corporation which was effectively the city council.

36 Ibid. p. 97.

37 Nicholls and Taylor, *Bristol Past and Present* p. 113.

38 Fleming, P. and Costello, K. *(Discovering) Cabot's Bristol* (Bristol: Redcliffe Press, 1998) p. 65.

39 Little, *The City and County of Bristol* p. 103. St Mark's church survived as the Lord Mayor's chapel on College Green.

40 Wilkins, H. J. *Some Chapters on the Ecclesiastical History of Westbury-on-Trym* (Bristol: Arrowsmith, 1909) p. 17.

41 Ibid. p. 36.

42 The La Plata (River Plate) estuary lies between modern-day Uruguay and Argentina. Dresser, M. *Slavery Obscured: The Social History of the Slave Trade in Bristol* (Bristol: Redcliffe Press, 2007) p. 8.

43 Griffiths, K. and Steeds, M. *Pirates and Privateers out of Bristol* (Bristol: Fiducia Press, 2010) p. 36.

44 A tablet was erected in their memory. The inscription reads thus: In memory of the undernamed Martyrs, who, during the reign of Queen Mary, for the avowal of their Christian faith, were burnt to death on the ground upon which this Chapel is erected. William Shapton, suffered October 17th, 1555. Edward Sharp, September 18th, 1556. Richard Sharp, May 17th, 1557. Thomas Hale, May 17th, 1557. Thomas Banion, August 17th 1557. Be not afraid of them that kill the body and after that have no more that they can do. Brown, H. and Harris, P. J. *Bristol, England* Revised edition (Bristol: Burleigh Press, 1971) pp. 72-73.

45 Chilcott, *Chilcott's descriptive history of Bristol* p. 139.

The Great House (pp. 22-48)

46 This was equivalent in 2016 to a staggering £9 million by GDP per capita conversion.

47 Dresser and Fleming, *Bristol: ethnic minorities* p. 46.

48 Bettey, J. H. "Feuding Gentry and an Affray on College Green, Bristol, in 1579" *Transactions of the Bristol and Gloucestershire Archaeological Society* 122 (2004): 153-159.

49 A prebendary is a canon of a cathedral or collegiate church whose income originally came from a prebend, effectively a salaried position in the diocese.

50 Hutton, S. *Bristol and its Famous Associations* (Bristol: J. W. Arrowsmith, 1907) pp. 349-350.

51 Macinnes, C. M., *Bristol: A Gateway of Empire* (Newton Abbot: David & Charles (Holdings), 1968) pp. 64-65.

52 Linebaugh, P. and Rediker, M. *The Many-Headed Hydra: Sailors, slaves, commoners, and the hidden history of the revolutionary Atlantic* (London: Verso, 2000) p. 16, 20 and 56.

53 Jackson, M. *Let This Voice Be Heard: Anthony Benezet, Father of Atlantic Abolitionism* (Pennsylvania: Penn Press, 2009) p. 73.

54 Bettey, "Feuding Gentry and an Affray on College Green, Bristol, in 1579" p. 159.

55 Hudleston, C. R., *How to see Bristol, A Complete and Well Illustrated Guide to the City of Bristol* (Bristol: J. W. Arrowsmith, 1931) p. 10.

56 Griffiths and Steeds, *Pirates and Privateers out of Bristol* p. 38.

57 Wilkins, *Some Chapters on the Ecclesiastical History of Westbury-on-Trym* p. 34.

58 Confusingly, William Colston's cousin, another William Colston, was involved in Guy's 'Sea Forest Colony'. He was a brother-in-law to John Guy. Ibid p. 34.

59 In an article in *The Times*, under the heading 'Black servant wielded the whip in Tudor England', an account is given of a court case in 1597 where John Guy complains that he is 'mistreated' by Sir Edward Wynter's black porter Swarthye, who had been ordered by Wynter to whip him. *The Times* 22 March 2018.

60 English, C. "Guy, John (c.1575 – 1628), colonial governor." *Oxford Dictionary of National Biography*. Accessed July 2018.

61 Blackburn, R. *The American Crucible: Slavery, Emancipation and Human Rights* (London: Verso, 2011) p. 61.

62 Sluiter, E. "New Light on the '20 and Odd Negroes' Arriving in Virginia, August, 1619," *William and Mary Quarterly*, 54 (1997): 396-98.

63 McCartney, M. Virginia's First Africans. In *Encyclopedia Virginia*. (accessed 23 December 2018) http://www.EncyclopediaVirginia.org/Virginia_s_First_Africans.

64 Parker, M. *The Sugar Barons: Family, Corruption, Empire and War* (London: Hutchinson, 2011) p. 21.

65 Ibid. p. 15.

66 Porter, R. "The Crispe Family and the African Trade in the Seventeenth Century." *The Journal of African History* 9, no. 1 (1968) pp. 57-62.

67 Ibid. p. 62.

68 Ibid. p. 74.

69 Kupperman, K. O. "Errand to the Indies: Puritan Colonization from Providence Island through the Western Design." *The William and Mary Quarterly* 45, no. 1 (1988) p. 75.

70 Blackburn, R. *The Making of New World Slavery: From the Baroque to the Modern 1492-1800* (London: Verso, 1998) pp. 225-226.

71 Kupperman, K. O. *Providence Island, 1630-1641: the other Puritan colony.* (London: Cambridge University Press, 1995) pp. 170-172.

72 Parker, *The Sugar Barons* p. 119.

73 See for example Farr, J. "Locke, Natural Law, and New World Slavery." *Political Theory* Vol. 36, no. 4 (2008). And as George Caffentzis notes in *John Locke: The Philosopher of Primitive Accumulation* Bristol Radical Pamphleteer #5 (Bristol: Bristol Radical History Group, 2008) "Locke is also not only the main intellectual founder of liberalism, but also of neoliberalism, the "ruling idea" of the ruling class of today".

74 Griffiths and Steeds, *Pirates and Privateers* p. 40.

75 Hall, I. V. *A history of the sugar trade in England with special attention to the sugar trade of Bristol* (Unpublished MA thesis, University of Bristol, 1925). Part I p. 17. and Part II p. 9.

76 Ibid, p. 38.

77 Little, *The City and County of Bristol* p. 182.

78 Sacks, D. H. *The Widening Gate–Bristol and the Atlantic Economy, 1450-1700* (Berkley: University of California Press, 1991) p. 54.

79 According to Sacks this figure remained fairly constant into the seventeenth century and equated to approximately 1 per cent of the population of Bristol. Ibid. p. 60.

80 Ibid. p. 83.

81 Buchholdt, M. "The Wider Family of Colston," *The Bristol Templar* (1992) pp. 33-34.

82 Wilkins, H. J. *Edward Colston (1636-1721 A.D.), a Chronological Account of His Life and Work Together with an Account of the Colston Societies and Memorials in Bristol* (Bristol: Arrowsmith, 1920) p. 9.

83 Sacks, *The Widening Gate* p. 68.

84 Giles Penn was father of Bristol-born Admiral Sir William Penn and grandfather of Quaker William Penn founder of Pennsylvania.

85 Griffiths and Steeds, *Pirates and Privateers* p. 42.

86 Buchholdt, "The Wider Family of Colston" p. 35.

87 Wilkins, *Edward Colston* p. 9.

88 Brown and Harris, *Bristol, England* p. 77.

89 Sugar boiling was highly skilled and dangerous: "'If a Boyler [Boiler] get any part into the scalding sugar' said a contemporary, 'it sticks like Glew [glue], or Birdlime [bird faeces], and 'tis hard to save either Limb or Life.'" 'Sugar Factory' by Noël Deerr, picture caption in Section one of Parker, *The Sugar Barons*.

90 Linebaugh and Rediker, *The Many-Headed Hydra* pp. 124-125.

91 Parker, *The Sugar Barons* p. 50.

92 £20 in 1649 was equivalent to £73,000 in 2016 by GDP per capita conversion.

93 In later life Downing laid out the street that bears his name in London, home of successive Prime Ministers since William Pitt the younger.

94 Ibid. pp. 57-58.

95 Linebaugh and Rediker, *The Many-Headed Hydra* p.124.

96 Ibid. p. 71.

97 Evans's footnote states "On this mount Mr Carden, in 1823, built a neat residence, which is called Colston's Fort House".

98 Evans's footnote states "Sir Fernando Gorges at this time occupied Sir John Young's lower house, now Colston's School".

99 Little, *The City and County of Bristol* pp. 125-127.

100 Wilkins, *Some Chapters on the Ecclesiastical History of Westbury-on-Trym* pp. 17-19.

101 Little, *The City and County of Bristol* p. 129.

102 Linebaugh and Rediker, *The Many-Headed Hydra* pp. 76- 79.

103 Wilkins, *Edward Colston* p. 9.

104 Buchholdt, "The Wider Family of Colston" p. 34.

105 Neither of these forts remains today. Prior's Hill Fort was located at the top of Nine Tree Hill in Freemantle Square, Kingsdown. Colston's Fort was located near Montague Place, Kingsdown.

106 Thomas Rainsborough was the son of Captain William Rainsborough (see entry for 1635).

107 Evans, *Chronological Outline of the History of Bristol* p. 206.

108 Little, *The City and County of Bristol* p. 129.

109 Buchholdt, "The Wider Family of Colston" p. 34.

110 Wilkins, *Edward Colston* p. 11.

111 Morgan K., *Edward Colston and Bristol* (Bristol: Bristol Branch of the Historical Association, 1999) p. 2.

112 Hunt, T. "A jewel of democracy", *The Guardian* 26 October 2007.

113 Linebaugh and Rediker, *The Many-Headed Hydra* p. 111.

114 For details of his grandson Baron John Scrope see the entries for 1727 and 1728.

115 Robinson, *A Darker History of Bristol* pp. 11-12.

116 Parker, *The Sugar Barons* p. 74.

117 Dresser, *Slavery Obscured* p. 20.

118 Latimer, J. *The Annals of Bristol in the Seventeenth Century* (Bristol: William George's Sons., 1900) p. 252.

119 Hall, *A history of the sugar trade* part II pp. 9-10.

120 Wilkins, *Edward Colston* p. 12.

121 Linebaugh and Rediker, *The Many-Headed Hydra* p. 126.

122 Ibid. p. 319.

123 Nicholls and Taylor, *Bristol Past and Present* Vol III p. 94.

124 Quoted from *The Lambs Warre*, 1657 in Linebaugh and Rediker, *The Many-Headed Hydra* pp. 94- 96.

125 Jackson, *Let This Voice Be Heard* p. 35.

126 Brown and Harris, *Bristol, England* p. 77.

127 Sacks estimates that at least 11 per cent of the city of Bristol's population were non-conformists in 1676. *The Widening Gate*, p. 376.

128 Quoted from Sacks, *The Widening Gate,* p. 290.

129 Parker, *The Sugar Barons* p. 130 – see 1754.

130 Linebaugh and Rediker, *The Many-Headed Hydra* p. 125.

131 Ibid. p. 127.

132 Wilkins, *Edward Colston* pp. 9, 12 and 13. Nicholl's in *Bristol Past and Present* speculates that Roman Catholics of Colston's acquaintance in Portugal jibed him about the lack of benefactors in the Protestant faith, spurring him on to his philanthropic actions later in life.

133 Sacks, *The Widening Gate* pp. 295-296.

134 For a full appraisal of the Penn family's association with slavery and the Duke of York see Jim McNeill's *The Life and Family of William Penn*. Bristol Radical Pamphleteer #18 (Bristol: Bristol Radical History Group, 2012).

135 Thomas, H. *The Slave Trade: The Story of the Atlantic Slave Trade, 1440-1870* (London: Picador, 1997) p. 203.

Edward Colston (pp. 49-84)

136 Worsted hose is stockings, socks, or tights made from a fabric derived from a fine smooth yarn spun from combed long-staple wool.

137 Wilkins, *Edward Colston* p. 12.

138 Thomas, *The Slave Trade* p. 197.

139 TNA *The Royal African Company Trades for Commodities along the West African Coast* [Transcript] (1672) CO 268/1,ff. 5-6.

140 These figures come from a study by the authors of a database for transatlantic slave-ship voyages in the period 1672-1713. They demonstrate that RAC ships embarked 170,987 enslaved Africans and disembarked 134,817, suggesting that 36,170 people died during the crossing (an average mortality rate of 21 per cent per voyage) *Trans-Atlantic Slave Trade Database*. Previous figures were conservative, mainly due to lack of the comprehensive data which is now available and underestimated the numbers of enslaved Africans transported. The factors and methods for their correction are explained in Ball, R. Edward Colston Research Paper #1: *Calculating the number of enslaved Africans transported by the Royal African Company during Edward Colston's involvement (1680-92)* (Bristol: Bristol Radical History Group, 2017). Previous estimates include 125,000 Africans transported with 25,000 dying en route from Blackburn, *The Making of New World Slavery* p. 255. They are supported by Richardson, who states that, between 1672 and 1711, more than 120,000 Africans were transported, with about 100,000 surviving the crossing. Richardson, D. *Bristol, Africa and the Eighteenth-Century Slave Trade to America Vol.1 The Years of Expansion 1698-1729* (Bristol: The Bristol Record Society, 1986) p. xxiv. These earlier figures from Blackburn and Richardson tie up closely with those from the *Trans-Atlantic Slave Trade Database* if the correction factors used by Ball are applied.

141 Another founding member was George Berkeley, 8th Baron and 1st Earl of Berkeley (Gloucestershire) "the first peer ... to collect directorships." Thomas, *The Slave Trade*, p. 201.

142 Sletias are a textile from Silesia in Germany; in 1683 "three fine sletias" (three rolls) could buy a person. Davies, K. G. *The Royal African Company* (London: Longmans, Green & Co., 1957) pp. 234-236.

143 In 2016 by GDP per capita conversion this equates to £10 million. Ball, R. Edward Colston Research Paper #2: *The Royal African Company and Edward Colston (1680-92)*. (Bristol: Bristol Radical History Group, 2017).

144 Wilkins, *Edward Colston* p. 21.

145 Ibid. p. 13.

146 Mintz, S. W. *Sweetness and Power: The place of sugar in modern history* (New York: Viking Penguin, 1985) p. 148.

147 Ibid. p. 20. £500 was worth the equivalent of £1.5 million in 2016 by GDP per capita conversion.

148 Edward Colston became one of the 24 'assistants' in the RAC a year after he joined and then deputy-governor in 1689. *The History of Parliament: COLSTON, Edward II (1636-1721), of*

Mortlake, Surr. http://www.historyofparliamentonline.org/volume/1690-1715/member/colston-edward-ii-1636-1721.

149 This may have been one of the reasons Edward Colston spent hardly any time in Bristol in the 1680s; a trip there and back to London by carriage took at least six days in good weather.

150 Wilkins, *Edward Colston* p. 24.

151 Scott provides a useful summary of the organisation and financing of the RAC: "A considerable portion of the [RAC] charter [1672] is occupied with provisions as to the internal government of the company. The stock-holders were to elect annually one governor, one sub-governor, one deputy-governor and twenty-four assistants. This part of the constitution is similar to that of the East India Company at this date, except that the twenty-four officials are here called assistants instead of committees, and that a new office–that of sub-governor–is created. The latter difference is accounted for by the fact that the governorship of the African Company was an honorary appointment filled by members of the royal family. The quorum at the court meeting was seven, of whom either the governor, sub-governor or deputy-governor must be one. In 1714 the qualification for an assistant was £2,000. Each £500 of stock commanded one vote up to a maximum of five votes. In 1680 the stock-holders numbered 198." Scott, W. R. "The Constitution and Finance of the Royal African Company of England from Its Foundation Till 1720." *The American Historical Review* 8, no. 2 (1903) p. 245.

152 In 2016 around £5 million (by GDP per capita) and £26.5 million (as a share of GDP)

153 Ball, Edward Colston Research Paper #2: *The Royal African Company and Edward Colston (1680-92)*.

154 Wilkins, *Edward Colston* pp. 13 and 23.

155 Ibid. pp. 25-27.

156 Ibid. p. 29.

157 Hall, *A history of the sugar trade* Part II p. 9.

158 Wilkins, *Edward Colston* p. 49.

159 There were exceptions though. In 1688 the Bristol ship *Society,* laden with enslaved Africans and 'elephants' teeth' from Guinea was seized and condemned in Virginia, as was the *Betty,* also of Bristol, for breaking the monopoly of the Royal African Company.

160 Spiriting was that "form of treachery through which…countless men and women in the mid-seventeenth century were 'enticed' or 'seduced' into bonds of servitude in the plantations… 'spirits' gulled their victims into voluntarily sailing to Virginia or the West Indies with false tales of rich prospects upon completion of their service. In all these instances the hapless person found himself bound in a contract for labour which he had entered without his informed consent" Sacks, *The Widening Gate* p. 253.

161 Chilcott, J. *Chilcott's descriptive history of Bristol* p. 47.

162 Lading is an old term for a ship's contents or load.

163 Griffiths and Steeds, *Pirates and Privateers* p. 41.

164 £15 was worth the equivalent of £44,000 in 2016 by GDP per capita conversion.

165 £15,000 was equivalent to £44 million in 2016 by GDP per capita conversion. Robinson, *A Darker History of Bristol* pp. 13-16.

166 Nicholls and Taylor, *Bristol Past and Present* Vol III p. 114.

167 Coules, V. *The Trade: Bristol and the Transatlantic Slave Trade* (Edinburgh: Birlinn, 2007) p. 133.

168 Robinson, *A Darker History of Bristol* p. 34.

169 Wilkins, *Edward Colston* p. 33.

170 Ibid. p. 32.

171 Edwards senior looked after Colston's financial affairs in Bristol (see 1702). Nicholls and Taylor, *Bristol Past and Present* Vol III pp. 122-123.

172 Wilkins, *Edward Colston Supplement* pp. 5-17.

173 £1,000 of stock in 1690 was worth in 2016 the equivalent of £2.9 million (by GDP per capita conversion) and nearly £30 million as a share of GDP.

174 Wilkins, *Edward Colston* p. 39.

175 Davies, *The Royal African Company* pp. 329-331.

176 Hanham, A. A. "Colston, Edward II (1636-1721), of Mortlake, Surr." in *The History of Parliament: the House of Commons 1690-1715*, eds. Hayton, D., Cruickshanks, E. and Handley, S. (London: Boydell and Brewer, 2002). Accessed 2017. http://www.historyofparliamentonline.org/volume/1690-1715/member/colston-edward-ii-1636-1721.

177 Buchholdt, "The Wider Family of Colston" p. 35.

178 Wilkins, *Edward Colston*, p. 66.

179 Patterson, O. "Slavery and slave revolts: A socio-historical analysis of the first Maroon War Jamaica, 1655-1740." *Social and Economic Studies* 19, no. 3 (1970) p. 297.

180 Ibid. p. 299.

181 Ball, Edward Colston Research Paper #2.

182 Ball, Edward Colston Research Paper #1.

183 Wilkins, *Edward Colston*, p. 89.

184 Thomas, *The Slave Trade* p. 202.

185 For more on this see Simpson, W. and McNeill, J. *Nicotiana Brittanica: The Cotswolds' Illicit Tobacco Cultivation in the 17th Century* Bristol Radical Pamphleteer #9 (Bristol: Bristol Radical History Group, 2009).

186 Clarke, C. C. *The Society of Merchant Venturers of Bristol—by Charles Cyril Clarke (Master 1920-21) being a Lecture given at the Royal Colonial Institute, Bristol, on Jan 2nd, 1922* (Bristol: J. W. Arrowsmith 1922).

187 It is unclear how Edward Colston reconciled being simultaneously, deputy-governor of the Royal African Company and a member of The Society of Merchant Venturers, one of the RAC's arch-opponents in the struggle to control the West African slave trade. Colston left the RAC in 1692 and appears to back the winning side (the Merchant Venturers) after this point. Colston's knowledge of the RAC and its campaign to retain the monopoly would have been very valuable to the Merchant Venturers in the 1690s. Other than his 'philanthropy' this was perhaps the reason he was so feted by the Bristol elite of the period; he had helped to make them fabulously wealthy.

188 Pettigrew, W. A. "Free to Enslave: Politics and the Escalation of Britain's Transatlantic Slave Trade, 1688-1714" *The William and Mary Quarterly*, Third Series, Vol. 64, No. 1, (2007) p. 33.

189 Horne, G. *The Counter-Revolution of 1776: Slave resistance and the origins of the United States of America* (New York: NYU Press, 2014), p. 46.

190 Linebaugh and Rediker, *The Many-Headed Hydra* pp. 57-58. For further information about these practices in Bristol see Button, A. *Bristol's White Slave Trade: Indentured and Enforced Labour in the 17th Century*. Bristol Radical Pamphleteer #13 (Bristol: Bristol Radical History Group, 2010) and Sacks, *The Widening Gate* Part 3.

191 Sacks, *The Widening Gate* p. 296. Indentured Servitude from Britain and Ireland to the Americas didn't end until the end of the 18th Century when the American Revolutionary War hastened its demise. Not many discovered the "mountains of roast beef and rivers of rum" promised. Mayer, H. *All on Fire*, (New York: St. Martin's Press, 1998) p. 4.

192 Nicholls and Taylor, *Bristol: Past and Present* Vol. III p. 165.

193 Wilkins, *Edward Colston*, p. 43. Wilkins quotes Silas Told, a Methodist chaplain who had written his memoirs in 1775. Born in 1711 he had attended Colston's Hospital School and went to sea at the age of 14 on a Bristol slave ship. He witnessed Colston's funeral and many horrors of the slave trade, including the barbarity of some of the slave-ship captains. His memoirs were published in 1786, John Wesley wrote a note in it to the Reader advising Told was "not much indebted to education". Told, S. *The Life of Silas Told Written by Himself With a Note to the Serious Reader by John Wesley, AM* (1786).

194 Wilkins, *Edward Colston*, pp. 86-89, 143.

195 Evans mistakenly claimed it to be 1703. Little gives the date of 1702 and claims that Colston was refused again in 1706. Little, *The City and County of Bristol* p. 184.

196 Wilkins, *Edward Colston* p. 44.

197 Latimer, J. *The Annals of Bristol in the Eighteenth Century* (Bristol: W. & F. Morgan, 1898) p. 46

198 See for example Macmillan, R. *Bristol Post Your Say* "Colston: Main concern was for those in

charities" 11 August 2017.

199 See for example Whittern, D. *Bristol Post Your Say* "There's just no evidence to stack up" 24 October 2017 and *Bristol Post* 11 July 2017 Rogers, G "Keep the name and use it to teach pupils".

200 Hanham, "Colston, Edward II (1636-1721), of Mortlake, Surr.".

201 Hanham, A. A. "EDWARDS, Thomas (c.1673-by 1743), of the Middle Temple and Filkins Hall, Oxon." in *The History of Parliament: The House of Commons 1690-1715*, eds. Hayton, D., Cruickshanks, E. and Handley, S. London: Boydell and Brewer, 2002. Accessed 2018. http://www.historyofparliamentonline.org/volume/1690-1715/member/edwards-thomas-1673-1743.

202 *Bristol Post* 11 August 2017 Macmillan, R. "Main concern was for those in charities"; Wilkins, *Edward Colston*, p. 55.

203 Arthur Bedford was an interesting fellow. He wrote to the SPCK on 13th September 1708 to say the players (actors) had been driven out of the liberties of the city, the justices of Gloucestershire having made an order that no plays should be acted in the county. In 1710 he was one of the chief subscribers to pay for a monthly sermon at the Marshalsea debtor's prison in London. Lowther Clarke, W. K. *A History of the S.P.C.K* (London: SPCK, 1959) pp. 95, 100.

204 Wilkins, *Edward Colston* pp. 58, 92.

205 Little, *The City and County of Bristol* pp. 182-3. A cursory look on the website of the *Society for Promoting Christian Knowledge* has Edward Colston expunged from their history http://spckpublishing.co.uk/. He is mentioned on the *Wikipedia Mortlake* website, where his house is featured and that he was great benefactor to the port city of Bristol—but not Mortlake https://en.wikipedia.org/wiki/Mortlake. The *Christ's Hospital School* website has him down as an 'Old Boy' but not as a benefactor—see entry for 1654 https://www.christs-hospital.org.uk/.

206 Perpetuana (or 'Perpett') was a durable, usually wool or worsted fabric, made in England from the late sixteenth through the eighteenth centuries

207 Wilkins, *Edward Colston*, p. 48.

208 Hall, *A history of the sugar trade* Part II p. 16.

209 Barrett, W. *The History and Antiquities of the City of Bristol* (Bristol: William Pine, 1789) p. 655.

210 Brown and Harris, *Bristol, England* p. 133.

211 Hanham, "Colston, Edward II (1636-1721), of Mortlake, Surr.".

212 Codrington's plantations were in Antigua and Barbuda as well as Barbados. Codrington III wanted his bequest to support a college in Barbados, including educating Africans; however the latter idea was quashed by his fellow plantation owners. Codrington College is now affiliated to the University of the West Indies. The Codringtons are infamous for another reason. Due to low birth rates in the West Indies, replenishing the enslaved was essential for the planters. Pro-slavery MP Christopher Bethell Codrington courted controversy in the early 1800s by suggesting Barbuda would make a 'fine Nursery for Negroes'. The Codrington's richly endowed pile in south Gloucestershire, just north east of Bristol, was Dodington House and Park, currently home to multi-millionaire vacuum cleaner salesman Sir James Dyson. Parker, *The Sugar Barons* Chapter 13 and pp. 206-207.

213 Robinson, *A Darker History of Bristol* p. 70.

214 *Barbados 4215 (Codrington)*, Legacies of British Slave-ownership database https://www.ucl.ac.uk/lbs/claim/view/6568.

215 Colston was classified as a Tory in the 'Hanover List' of 1710 which defined "Tories, Whigs, and those doubtful": Appendix XXVI: Contemporary lists of Members. Published in *The History of Parliament: the House of Commons 1690-1715*, ed. D. Hayton, E. Cruickshanks, S. Handley, 2002; Hanham, A. COLSTON, Edward II (1636-1721), of Mortlake, Surr. Published in *The History of Parliament: the House of Commons 1690-1715*, ed. D. Hayton, E. Cruickshanks, S. Handley, 2002

216 Latimer, *The Annals of Bristol in the Eighteenth Century* p. 86, 111.

217 Francis Colston owned the Sloop *Content* a slave ship that was lost between Jamaica and Britain in 1707. *Trans-Atlantic Slave Trade Database* http://www.slavevoyages.org/.

218 Hanham, A. A. "Bristol (Constituencies)" in *The History of Parliament: The House of Commons 1690-1715*, eds. Hayton, D., Cruickshanks, E. and Handley, S. London: Boydell and

Brewer, 2002. Accessed 2018: https://www.historyofparliamentonline.org/volume/1690-1715/constituencies/bristol.

219 According to historian Andrew Swift the situation in Bath was far worse: "Bath was the biggest of the English boroughs where the right to vote was restricted to the corporation, and as such was roundly condemned by Tom Paine in his *Rights of Man*. The corporation was essentially a self-perpetuating oligarchy of around 30 men, who ran the city and sent two MPs to Parliament. As members of the corporation retired or died, others were co-opted on. The corporation was basically answerable only to itself. They controlled every aspect of life in Bath—and held the reins of economic power. It was probably the most undemocratic place in the country. By the early nineteenth century Bath's population was over 30,000, which meant that only around 0.1 per cent of the population were entitled to vote. The freemen of the city challenged this twice—in 1661 and in 1705 – but both times the House of Commons decided against them. There were also mass demonstrations and riots in the early nineteenth century, but the system only changed with the Reform Act of 1832." E-mail to authors 21 July 2017.

220 Manson, M. *"Riot!" The Bristol Bridge Massacre of 1793* (Bristol: Bristol Books 2013) pp. 42-45.

221 Wilkins, *Edward Colston* p. 72.

222 Morgan, *Edward Colston and Bristol* p. 13.

223 Jenks, L. H. *The Origin of the South Sea Company 1710–1714*. Unpublished M.A. Thesis University of Kansas 1914 pp. 55-56.

224 Hanham, "Colston, Edward II (1636-1721), of Mortlake, Surr.".

225 Latimer, *The Annals of Bristol in the Seventeenth Century* p. 409.

226 Wilkins, *Ecclesiastical History of Westbury-on-Trym* pp. 44-45.

227 Britain gained Gibraltar and Menorca from Spain and France gave up its claims to Newfoundland, the Hudson's Bay Company territories, the island of Saint Kitts and the colony of Nova Scotia in the Americas. Nova Scotia Place, and subsequently the Nova Scotia Public House, in Bristol are named after this deed. Eason, H. *Bristol's Historic Inns* (Bristol: Redcliffe Press, 1982) p. 47.

228 Barrett, *The History and Antiquities of the City of Bristol* p. 333. For two centuries after it was formed, Bristol Cathedral was seen as a 'promotion billet', whence Bishops might go on to fatter pastures, rather than a long abiding place for a shepherd of Bristol souls. Little, *The City and County of Bristol* p. 103 and Hutton, *Bristol and its Famous Associations* p. 352.

229 Benjamin Raule of Zeeland to the Elector of Brandenburg, 1680. Thomas, *The Slave Trade* p. 210.

230 Ibid. p. 236.

231 Wilkins, *Edward Colston* p. 39.

232 Latimer, *The Annals of Bristol in the Eighteenth Century* p. 100.

233 Dresser, *Slavery Obscured* p. 30.

234 Nicholls and Taylor, *Bristol: Past and Present* Vol III. p.165.

235 Lea, R. S. "EDWARDS, Thomas (?1673-1743), of the Middle Temple, London, and Filkins Hall, Oxon." in *The History of Parliament: the House of Commons 1715-1754*, ed. R. Sedgwick (London: Boydell and Brewer, 1970). Accessed 2017. http://www.historyofparliamentonline.org/volume/1715-1754/member/edwards-thomas-1673-1743; Latimer, *Annals of Bristol in the 18th Century* p. 111.

236 Wilkins. *Edward Colston* p. 75. The pineapple, which came from South America, was a symbol of wealth, hospitality and exclusivity.

237 Wilkins, *Edward Colston Supplement* pp. 19-23.

238 Hanham, A. A. "Bristol" in *The History of Parliament: The House of Commons 1690-1715*, eds. Hayton, D., Cruickshanks, E. and Handley, S. (London: Boydell and Brewer, 2002). Accessed 2018: https://www.historyofparliamentonline.org/volume/1690-1715/constituencies/bristol.

239 Hanham, "EDWARDS, Thomas (c.1673-by 1743), of the Middle Temple and Filkins Hall, Oxon." and Lea, R. S. "EDWARDS, Thomas (?1673-1743), of the Middle Temple, London, and Filkins Hall, Oxon." in *The History of Parliament: The House of Commons 1715-1754*, ed. Sedgwick R. London: Boydell and Brewer, 1970. Accessed 2017. http://www.historyofparliamentonline

org/volume/1715-1754/member/edwards-thomas-1673-1743.

240 Latimer, *Annals of Bristol in the Eighteenth Century* pp. 110-112.

241 Taylor, J. *Bristol and its Environs 1875* p. 49.

242 The history of Hoare's Bank can be found here: https://www.hoaresbank.co.uk/.

243 Other members of the Colston 'family' such as Edward's nephews Francis and his namesake Edward also had accounts at the bank in the early eighteenth century. E-mail to author from Pamela Hunter (Archivist at Hoare and Co.) 24 October 2018.

244 Laurence, A. "The Emergence of a Private Clientele for Banks in the Early Eighteenth Century: Hoare's Bank and Some Women Customers" *The Economic History Review*, New Series, 61, no. 3 (August, 2008) p. 568.

245 Ibid. pp. 569-570.

246 Two manuscript authorisations from Edward Colston to make payments from the dividends on £7,000 stock held in the South Sea Company can be found in the Bristol Archives Ref. 42198/6/1.

247 C. Hoare & Co Archive, Edward Colston (1719), Customer ledger/folio no. F369.

248 Laurence, "The Emergence of a Private Clientele for Banks in the Early Eighteenth Century" pp. 571-574.

249 Using the GDP per capita conversion this equates to nearly £62 million in 2016.

250 Stourhead House was noted for its stunning gardens, embellished with icons from Old Bristol, not least the controversial acquisition of the city's High Cross.

251 These figures were calculated using the *Trans-Atlantic Slave Trade Database* for the years 1711-1721: http://www.slavevoyages.org/.

252 Many people who recount the 'Bubble' story believe the SSC went bankrupt as a result. They are quite wrong. In fact the company's most successful trading period was 1725, five years after the 'Bubble' and it was finally wound up over a century later in 1853. Over the period of its slave trading (1714-1740) the SSC transported 41,852 enslaved Africans, of which 6,987 died during the Atlantic crossing. *Trans-Atlantic Slave Trade Database* http://www.slavevoyages.org/.

253 Wilkins, *Edward Colston Supplement* p. 17.

254 For example, Morgan implies that £71,000 was left to public charities in Colston's Will and that he gave £63,940 of benefactions during his lifetime. This does not concur with our research. Morgan, *Edward Colston and Bristol* p. 16.

255 Wilkins, *Edward Colston* p. 147.

256 Morgan, *Edward Colston and Bristol* p. 16.

257 Wilkins, *Edward Colston* p. 148.

258 This is the origin of 'Colston Day' but put back 11 days in 1752 to 13th November by the change from the Julian to Gregorian calendars. *From apprentices to the elderly: Celebrating 250 years of the Grateful Society* (Bristol: Grateful Society, 2008) p. 8.

259 Wilkins, *Edward Colston* pp. 139-140.

260 Ibid. p. 148.

261 Wilkins, *Edward Colston* p. 87; *A new and general biographical dictionary* p. 50.

262 Wilkins, *Edward Colston* pp. 81-84.

263 Nicholls and Taylor. *Bristol Past and Present*, Vol. III p. 136.

264 Nicholls and Taylor, *Bristol: Past and Present* Vol. III p. 137. Told was at that time a Colston's schoolboy at St Augustine's Back. The 90th Psalm, written by Moses, concerned life expectancy – "if by reason of strength... four score years".

265 Wilkins, *Edward Colston* pp. 155-156.

266 Foyle, A. *Bristol, Pevsner Architectural Guides* (New Haven and London: Yale University Press, 2004) pp. 93-94. Foyle claims this connection, though we have been unable to locate any evidence to verify this.

267 The portrait was removed in May 2018 to reflect the wishes of the new Lord Mayor, Cleo Lake.

268 Foyle, *Bristol, Pevsner Architectural Guides* pp. 93-94.

269 Morgan, *Edward Colston and Bristol* p. 16.

270 Wilkins, *Edward Colston* p. 96.

Slavery, Rebellion and Abolition (pp. 85-153)

271 Pettigrew, W. A. *Freedom's Debt: The Royal African Company and the politics of the Atlantic Slave Trade, 1672-1752* (Chapel Hill: University of North Carolina, 2013) p. 14 Fig. 3.

272 Richardson, D. *Bristol, Africa and the Eighteenth-Century Slave Trade to America Vol. 1 The Years of Expansion 1698-1729* (Bristol: The Bristol Record Society, 1986) p. xxviii.

273 Richardson, D. *The Bristol Slave Traders: A collective portrait* (Bristol: Bristol Branch of the Historical Association, 1985) pp. 14-21.

274 Betty, *Bristol Observed* pp. 63-64.

275 This contradiction is covered in detail in Pettigrew, *Freedom's Debt.*

276 Hanham, A. A. "DAINES, Sir William (1647-1724), of St. Leonard's, Bristol" in *The History of Parliament: the House of Commons 1690-1715*, eds. Hayton, D., Cruickshanks, E. and Handley, S. (London: Boydell and Brewer, 2002). Accessed 2017. http://www.historyofparliamentonline.org/volume/1690-1715/member/daines-sir-william-1647-1724 Matthews, S. "DAINES, Sir William (c.1656-1724), of Bristol, Glos" in *The History of Parliament: the House of Commons 1715-1754*, ed. R. Sedgwick (London: Boydell and Brewer, 1970). Accessed 2017. http://www.historyofparliamentonline. org/volume/1715-1754/member/daines-sir-william-1656-1724. See the note for 1774 in this text for his grandson Lord Barrington's banal comment on the slave trade.

277 Sloane, H. *A Voyage to the Islands Madera, Barbados, Nieves, S. Christophers and Jamaica with the Natural History of the Herbs and Trees, Four-footed Beasts, Fishes, Birds, Insects, Reptiles, Etc., of the Last of Those Islands... Illustrated with the Figures of the Things Describd... by Hans Sloane...* Vols. I and II (London: Benjamin Motte, 1707, 1725).

278 Jackson, *Let This Voice Be Heard* p. 197. Gelding is normally used to describe the castration of horses.

279 Sedgwick, R. R. "Bristol (Constituencies)" in *The History of Parliament: The House of Commons 1715-1754,* Sedgwick, R. R. ed. London: Boydell and Brewer, 1970. Accessed 2018: https://www.historyofparliamentonline.org/volume/1715-1754/constituencies/bristol

280 Dresser and Giles, *Bristol and Transatlantic Slavery* p. 98.

281 Hudleston, *How to see Bristol,* p. 10.

282 Quoted from Wilkins, *Some Chapters on the Ecclesiastical History of Westbury-on-Trym* pp. 66-67.

283 Ibid. p. 166.

284 The nursery rhyme, *Who Killed Cock Robin?* may allude to the fall of Walpole's government in 1742. Walpole carried the popular nickname 'Cock Robin'.

285 Patterson, O. "Slavery and slave revolts" pp. 304-311.

286 Hutton, *Bristol and its Famous Associations* p. 47.

287 Dresser, *Slavery Obscured* p.107.

288 Quoted from Horne, *The Counter-Revolution of 1776* p. 8.

289 Coromantee (derived from the name of the Ghanaian slave fort of Fort Kormantine in Koromanti, Ghana) was the English name for enslaved people of Akan ethnicities from the Gold Coast in modern Ghana.

290 Two roads in St John's that have a clear Bristol influence are St Mary Street and Redcliffe Street. Redcliffe Street led to Redcliffe Dock where local legend has it that the Antiguan slave market was sited. Redcliffe Dock is now a swanky shopping centre renamed 'Redcliffe Quay' – the recipient of modern-day cruise liners.

291 Sedgwick, "Bristol" in *The History of Parliament: The House of Commons 1715-1754.*

292 Foyle, *Bristol: Pevsner Architectural Guides* p. 78.

293 Patterson, "Slavery and slave revolts" pp. 310-313.

294 Horne, *The Counter-Revolution of 1776* Chap. 5 and https://en.wikipedia.org/wiki/Stono_Rebellion.

295 Best, G. M. *Cradle of Methodism 1739 – 2017* (Bristol: New Room Publications, 2017) p. 413.

296 Best, G. M. *In Their Words, the Story of Early Methodism,* (Bristol: New Room Publications, 2018) pp. 150-151.

297 Mills, S. *A Barbarous and Ungovernable People!* Bristol Radical Pamphleteer #11 (Bristol

Bristol Radical History Group, 2009) pp. 7-8.

298 Jones, *Satan's Kingdom* p. 112.

299 Best, *Cradle of Methodism* p. 414.

300 Told, *The Life of Silas Told.*

301 Best, *Cradle of Methodism* p. 418.

302 Best, *In Their Words,* p. 151.

303 Abraham Darby was the leading innovator at the Baptist Mills brass works in Bristol and in 1712 moved to Coalbrookdale in Shropshire to pioneer methods of iron manufacture.

304 Burroughs, E. A. *Bristol Cathedral—Its History, Architecture, Associations and Mission* (Bristol: Partridge and Love Ltd, 1924) pp. 28-29.

305 Best, *Cradle of Methodism* pp. 66-67.

306 Wilkins, *Edward Colston Supplement* p. 33.

307 Hutton, *Bristol and its Famous Associations* p. 373.

308 Best, *Cradle of Methodism* pp. 91, 95 and 110.

309 In contrast to Bristol, the number of slave ships leaving London increased slowly towards the end of the century, with 10-40 vessels departing for most of the years from 1760-1800. These figures were derived from the *Trans-Atlantic Slave Trade Database* http://www.slavevoyages.org/ [Accessed 31 December 2018].

310 Fryer, P. *Staying Power—The History of Black People in Britain* (London: Pluto Press, 1984) pp. 150-153.

311 Jackson, *Let This Voice Be Heard* p. 244.

312 Pettigrew, *Freedom's Debt* p. 205.

313 The second entity was launched by Messrs Goldney, Smith, Miller, Champion, Reed and Vaughan and later became known as the 'Miles Bank'. National Westminster Bank, *Three Banks in Bristol: The National Westminster Bank in Corn Street 1750-1980* (National Westminster Bank Stationery and Purchasing Department, n.d.) p. 2.

314 *Bristol Past: The Beginning of Banks in Bristol* http://www.buildinghistory.org/bristol/banks.shtml.

315 Wilkins, *Some Chapters on the Ecclesiastical History of Westbury-on-Trym* p. 25.

316 Hague, W. *William Pitt the Younger* (London: HarperCollins, 2004) p. 292.

317 Aitken, J. *John Newton—from Disgrace to Amazing Grace* (London: Continuum, 2000) p. 75. John Newton was a headstrong youth who went to sea at an early age. After many highs and lows he became a slave-ship captain before cheating death and turning to God. He went on to be an evangelical minister mentoring abolitionists William Wilberforce, Hannah More and William Cowper, and with the last he co-wrote *Amazing Grace*, the anthem of the abolitionist movement.

318 Taylor, E. R. *If we must die: Shipboard insurrections in the era of the Atlantic slave trade* (Baton Rouge: Louisiana State University Press, 2006) p. 43.

319 Voyage ID 17423 *Trans-Atlantic Slave Trade Database* [Accessed February 2019].

320 Taylor, *If we must die* pp. 41-2.

321 Taylor notes: "Pirate ships displayed a racial egalitarianism unmatched in most other spheres of existence at the time". Ibid. p. 50.

322 Ibid. p. 70.

323 Ibid, p. 129.

324 Ibid. pp. 119-121. A full account of the revolt on the *Marlborough* based on primary sources can be found in four parts on the following website: Dalton, K. "Revolt of the Marlborough" British Tars 1740-1790 https://www.britishtars.com/2016/08/revolt-of-marlborough-toll-of-captain.html [accessed February 2019].

325 Behrendt, S. D., Eltis, D. and Richardson, D., "The Costs of Coercion: African Agency in the Pre-Modern Atlantic World". *The Economic History Review*, 54 (2001) pp. 456-464.

326 Ibid. p. 473.

327 Dresser and Giles, *Bristol and Transatlantic Slavery* pp. 126, 129. Voyage IDs 17522 and 17691 *Trans-Atlantic Slave Trade Database* [Accessed February 2019].

328 Parker, *The Sugar Barons,* p. 334.

329 Ibid. p. 339.

330 Clark, W. E., *Josiah Tucker, Economist: A Study in the History of Economics*. (New York: Columbia University Press, 1903) and Hutton, *Bristol and its Famous Associations* p. 355.

331 James Nayler (or Naylor, 1618–1660).

332 Dresser and Giles, *Bristol and Transatlantic Slavery*, p. 97.

333 *Slave Revolt in Jamaica, 1760-1761: A Cartographic Narrative* http://revolt.axismaps.com/. This excellent website provides an interactive map of the 1760-61 rebellion in Jamaica.

334 Hochschild, A. *Bury the Chains: The British Struggle to Abolish Slavery* (London: Macmillan, 2005) pp. 43-44.

335 Sharp, G. *A Representation of the Injustice and Dangerous Tendency of Tolerating Slavery* (Cambridge: Cambridge University Press, 2014).

336 Clarkson, T. *The history of the rise, progress, and accomplishment of the abolition of the African slave-trade, by the British Parliament Vol. I* (New York: John S. Taylor, 1836) p. 230.

337 Best, *Cradle of Methodism*, p. 423.

338 Dresser, *Slavery Obscured*, pp. 135-136.

339 Benezet, A. *Some Historical Account of Guinea...with an Inquiry into the Rise and Progress of the Slave Trade...: Also a Republication of the Sentiments of Several Authors...Particularly an Extract of a Treatise Written by Granville Sharpe* (London: W. Owen, E. and C. Dilly, 1772).

340 Wesley, J. *Thoughts upon Slavery* (London: R. Hawes, 1774).

341 Best, *Cradle of Methodism* p. 428.

342 Jackson *Let his Voice be Heard* p. 158.

343 Wesley, *Thoughts upon Slavery* pp. 12-13.

344 Poole, S. and Rogers, N. *Bristol from Below: Law, Authority and Protest in a Georgian City*. (Woodbridge: Boydell & Brewer, 2017) p. 265.

345 Hochschild, *Bury the Chains* p. 220.

346 Poole and Rogers, *Bristol from Below* pp. 265-266.

347 Cruger's portrait, by Gilbert Stuart, is one of Bristol's civic treasures.

348 Best, *The Cradle of Methodism* p. 435.

349 See for example https://rationalwiki.org/wiki/Edmund_Burke.

350 Burke, E. "Sketch of the Negro code" in *The Works of the Right Honourable Edmund Burke, Vol. 5* (New York: Eastburn, Kirk and Co. and West and Richardson, and Oliver C. Greenleaf, 1813).

351 Davis, D. B. *The Problem of Slavery in Western Culture* (New York: Oxford University Press, 1966) p. 398.

352 Thomas, *The Slave Trade* p. 529.

353 Parker, *The Sugar Barons* p. 343.

354 Ibid. p. 331.

355 Hochschild, *Bury the Chains* p. 55.

356 Gifford, Z. *Thomas Clarkson and the Campaign Against Slavery*, (London: Anti-Slavery International 1996) p. 29.

357 Hague, *William Pitt the Younger* p. 302.

358 Richard Bright, son of the leading Bristol merchant and slave trader Henry Bright (1715-1777), is an interesting figure in that he was a Whig, Unitarian and leading Bristol Dissenter throughout his involvement in the West India Association. Bright's acceptance in the organisation is a good example of how significant political and religious divides were overcome in collective defence of the slave system amongst those with major financial interests. 'Richard Bright of Ham Green', Legacies of British Slave-ownership database, http://wwwdepts-live.ucl.ac.uk/lbs/person/view/15207 [accessed 4 March 2018].

359 *Records of the Society of Merchant Venturers–Associated Clubs & Societies–West India Association–Administrative–West India Association Minute book (1782-1804)* BA SMV/8/3/2/1.

360 Drummond, M. M. "LAROCHE, James (1734-1804), of Over, nr. Bristol, Glos." In *The History of Parliament: the House of Commons 1754-1790*, ed. Namier, L. and Brooke J. (London: Boydell and Brewer, 1964). Accessed 2019. https://www.historyofparliamentonline.org/volume/1754-1790/member/laroche-james-1734-1804; Jones, *Satan's Kingdom* p. 76.

361 'Paddy' and 'the vain' were contemporary election nicknames. Manson, *"Riot!"* pp. 55, 57-58

362 Ibid. p. 43.

363 Schama, S. *Simon Schama's Power of Art* (London: BBC Books, 2006) pp. 286-287.

364 Jackson, *Let This Voice Be Heard* p. 227.

365 Best, *The Cradle of Methodism* p. 516 and Jones, *Satan's Kingdom* p. 79.

366 Thomas, P. D. G. "BRICKDALE, Matthew (1735-1831), of Clifton, Glos. and Taunton, Som." in *The History of Parliament: The House of Commons 1754-1790*, ed. L. Namier, J. Brooke (London: Boydell and Brewer, 1964). Accessed 2018. http://historyofparliamentonline.org/volume/1754-1790/member/brickdale-matthew-1735-1831.

367 Clarkson, *The history of the rise, progress...* Vol. I pp. 161-162.

368 Hochschild, *Bury the Chains* p. 89.

369 Clarkson, T. *An Essay on the Slavery and Commerce of the Human Species, Particularly the African, Translated from a Latin Dissertation, Which Was Honoured With the First Prize in the University of Cambridge, for the Year 1785, With Additions.* London: J. Phillips, 1786. Accessed 2018. http://www.gutenberg.org/ebooks/10611.

370 Latimer, *Annals of Bristol in the Eighteenth Century* p. 455 and 480; Dresser, M. "Daniel, Thomas (1762–1854), Merchant." *Oxford Dictionary of National Biography.* (2016) Accessed July 2018. http://www.oxforddnb.com.ezproxy.sussex.ac.uk/view/10.1093/ref:odnb/9780198614128.001.0001/odnb-9780198614128-e-107411.

371 John Cave's daughter Susanna married Thomas Daniel junior in 1789. 'Cave, Ames & Cave' Legacies of British Slave-ownership database https://www.ucl.ac.uk/lbs/firm/view/2144928751.

372 Dresser, *Slavery Obscured* p. 132.

373 Best, *Cradle of Methodism* p. 510.

374 Hochschild, *Bury the Chains,* p. 124.

375 Bettey, J. H. *Bristol Observed: Visitors' Impressions of the City from Domesday to the Blitz* (Bristol: Redcliffe Press, 1986) p. 85.

376 Clarkson, *The history of the rise, progress...* Vol. I. p. 229.

377 The *Trans-Atlantic Slave Trade Database* states that the *Brothers* had a crew of 40. MacInnes claims that only 10 of a complement of 56 returned home. MacInnes, C. M. *Bristol and the Slave Trade.* (Bristol: Bristol Branch of the Historical Association, 1963) p. 11.

378 Clarkson, *The history of the rise, progress...* Vol. I. p. 229.

379 MacInnes, *Bristol and the Slave Trade* p. 11. A recent study by Breward of 2,202 sailors who embarked on slaving voyages from Bristol between 1790 and 1795 demonstrated that only 911 (41 percent) returned to Bristol. 430 (20 per cent) died on the voyages with the remainder pressed, discharged or having deserted. Based on these conservative estimates Breward argues that Clarkson's figures were reasonably accurate. Breward, M. "Crewing the Slave Trade: The Bristol Ships' Muster Rolls, 1790-1795" in Poole, S. (Ed.) *A City Built Upon the Water—Maritime Bristol 1750-1900* (Bristol: Redcliffe/Regional History Centre UWE, 2013) pp. 109-111.

380 Hochschild, *Bury the Chains* p. 113.

381 Clarkson, *History of the rise, progress...* pp. 230-232.

382 Ibid. pp. 234-240.

383 Other landmark locations that were important to the abolition movement include: Wades Hill, Herts, where Clarkson decided to put himself forward to try and end the trade; the Quaker print shop in the City of London, where the Abolition Committee met for the first time; and the Wilberforce Oak in Bromley, London where William Pitt the Younger finally persuaded William Wilberforce to stay in politics and make abolition of the slave trade his life's work.

384 Breward, "Crewing the Slave Trade", pp. 103-104.

385 Ibid. p. 103.

386 Clarkson, *History of the rise, progress...* pp. 247-248.

387 Clarkson, T. *The history of the rise, progress and accomplishment of the abolition of the African slave-trade, by the British Parliament Vol. II.* (London: Longman, Hurst, Rees, and Orme, 1808) p. 19. *Trans-Atlantic Slave Trade Database.*

388 Clarkson, *The history of the rise, progress...* Vol. I. pp. 205-206.

389 Breward notes in his study of slave-ship crews leaving Bristol from 1790-1795 that the

masters and first mates made repeat voyages, unlike the lower ratings. This suggests ordinary sailors avoided slave ships if at all possible. Breward, "Crewing the Slave Trade" p.111.

390 Falconbridge went on to accompany Clarkson to Liverpool early in 1788 where merchants, on finding out about his mission, attempted to have Clarkson assassinated.

391 Clarkson, *The history of the rise, progress... Vol. I.* p. 262.

392 Years later when relating this episode Clarkson's anger was still prevalent as he made clear in this footnote: "We may well imagine what this person's notion of another man's honour was; for he was the purser of the *Brothers* and of the *Alfred*, who, as before mentioned, sent the captains of those ships out on a second voyage, after knowing their barbarities in the former. And he was also purser of this very ship *Thomas*, where the murder had been committed".

393 Clarkson, *The history of the rise, progress... Vol, I,* pp. 269-273; Lamoine, G. *Bristol Gaol Delivery Fiats 1741-1799.* (Bristol: Bristol Record Society, 1989).

394 Ibid. p. 274.

395 Ibid. p. 275.

396 Clarkson had worked with Tucker, Camplin, Gandy, Fox, Joseph Harford, Matthew Wright and Daubeny, all of whom appear on the original list of members of the Bristol Abolition Committee. Dresser, *Slavery Obscured* Table 7, p. 139.

397 The Bluestockings, formed in the 1750s, were a group of intellectual women led by Lady Elizabeth Montagu a 'salonist', social reformer, literary critic and writer.

398 For example, William Wilberforce did not believe in universal suffrage. Brierley, L. and Reid, H. *Go Home and Do the Washing! Three Centuries of Pioneering Bristol Women.* (Bristol: Broadcast Books, 2000) p. 53.

399 Dresser, *Slavery Obscured* p. 142.

400 James, C. L. R., *The Black Jacobins*, (London: Penguin, 2001) pp 41-43.

401 Aitken, *John Newton* p. 234.

402 Hochschild, *Bury the Chains* p. 124.

403 Best, *Cradle of Methodism* pp. 438-439.

404 Dresser, *Slavery Obscured* p. 139. Joseph Harford was disowned by the Quakers after taking an oath to become a member of Bristol Corporation in 1779 – he then became an Anglican.

405 Dresser, *Slavery Obscured* p. 140.

406 Barnes, V. "Changes in women's occupations 1775-1830" in Dresser, M (Ed.) *Women and the city: Bristol 1373-2000* (Bristol: Redcliffe Press/The Regional History Centre, University of the West of England, 2016). pp. 70-71; Hutton, *Bristol and its Famous Associations* p. 92. Settlements in Sierra Leone were established in the late 1780s and early 1790s by abolitionists Granville Sharp, John and Thomas Clarkson and others to receive freed African Americans who had fought for the British during the American Revolution.

407 Dresser, *Slavery Obscured* p. 73, 136, 141. Combe's extravagant ways reduced him to poverty; for a £200 per year stipend he wrote political pamphlets for Pitt, before finally writing for *The Times* and later becoming the author of *Dr Syntax*. Hutton, *Bristol and its Famous Associations* pp. 175-176.

408 Aitken, *John Newton,* p. 245.

409 Barnes, "Changes in women's occupations 1775-1830" p. 76.

410 Jones, *Satan's Kingdom* p. iii.

411 Born in Oxford, Jenkinson became First Lord Hawkesbury in 1786 and the Earl of Liverpool in 1796. The family seat was 20 miles north of Bristol in Hawkesbury, Gloucestershire, and his ancestor was sea captain and merchant Anthony Jenkinson. Jenkinson's travels east brought him into contact with Ivan the Terrible and they were recorded by Richard Hakluyt at the end of the sixteenth century.

412 Hochschild, *Bury the Chains* pp. 153-154.

413 Latimer, *Annals of Bristol in the Eighteenth Century* p. 476.

414 Ibid. p. 477.

415 *Records of the Society of Merchant Venturers–Associated Clubs & Societies–West India Association–Administrative–Slave Trade, 1789* BA SMV/8/3/2/5.

416 TNA *Home Office: Domestic Correspondence, George III* HO 42/19 pp. 233-255. This was just after Joseph Priestley's Birmingham home and church had been burnt down. Priestley was a founder of the Unitarian church, a radical and a scientist—he was the first to discover oxygen. He was also one of the 'Lunar Abolitionists' which included Josiah Wedgewood. In 1788 he published *A Sermon on the Subject of the Slave Trade*, where he spoke out against the mental and physical sufferings of enslaved Africans and stressed the role played by slavers in the degradation of women and the separation of their families. Harris, C. *Three Continents, One History: Birmingham, the Transatlantic Slave Trade and the Caribbean* (Birmingham: Afro-Caribbean Millennium Centre, 2008) p. 92.

417 Dresser, *Slavery Obscured* p. 140.

418 *Trans-Atlantic Slave Trade Database* http://www.slavevoyages.org/.

419 Gifford, Z. *Thomas Clarkson and the Campaign Against Slavery,* (London: Anti-Slavery International 1996) p. 28.

420 Hochschild, A. *Bury the Chains* p. 129.

421 Equiano, O. *The Interesting Narrative of the Life of Olaudah Equiano, Or Gustavus Vassa, The African. Written by Himself* (London: Equiano, 1789). One esteemed historian of the Atlantic stated that Equiano's *The Interesting Narrative* was the key book to read when studying the period of the transatlantic slave trade.

422 Cowper, W. *The Negro's Complaint* (1788). The complete poem can be viewed here: https://www.geneseo.edu/~easton/engl313/CowperNC.html.

423 Hochschild, *Bury the Chains* pp. 158-159.

424 For a full extract of the evidence see Dresser and Giles, *Bristol and Transatlantic Slavery* pp. 133-137.

425 Bristol's electorate was relatively large compared to the rest of the country, but, of course, actually only a minority of the population. Fisher, D. R. "Bristol" *The History of Parliament: the House of Commons 1790-1820*, ed. Thorne, R. (London: Boydell & Brewer, 1986). Accessed 2018. http://www.historyofparliamentonline.org/volume/1790-1820/constituencies/bristol.

426 Londoner Tobin was a friend and business partner of John Pinney; the two had worked on the Pinney Plantation in the Caribbean island of Nevis. They both returned to England in the early 1780s and settled in Bristol.

427 Hochschild, *Bury the Chains* p. 162.

428 Dresser and Giles suggest that, as there is no record in St Mary Redcliffe's accounts of payments to bell ringers, this might be a myth. Dresser and Giles, *Bristol and Transatlantic Slavery* p. 95.

429 Walvin, J. *A Short History of Slavery* (London: Penguin Books, 2007) p. 188.

430 Hochschild, *Bury the Chains* p. 112.

431 Latimer, J. *History of the Society of Merchant Venturers of the City of Bristol* (Bristol: J.W. Arrowsmith) p. 186.

432 Best, *The Cradle of Methodism* p. 530.

433 Hannah More's *Village Politics* (1792) was written to counter the influence of Paine's *Rights of Man*.

434 Paine's text sold 50,000 copies in the first two months and 200,000 by the end of the year, eclipsing by orders of magnitude any other popular book in the period. Ball, R. *The guillotine, knitting and terror...So you think you know about the French Revolution* (Bristol: Bristol Radical History Group, 2014). Retrieved from http://www.brh.org.uk/site/articles/guillotine-knitting-terror/.

435 Leifchild, J. *Memoir of the late Rev. Joseph Hughes, A.M.* (London: Thomas Ward and Co. 1835) pp. 129-130. Clarkson's figure has been substantiated by subsequent research. Hochschild, *Bury the Chains*, pp. 192-193.

436 Aitken, *John Newton*, p. 245.

437 Hutton, *Bristol and its Famous Associations*, p. 363.

438 Ball, *The guillotine, knitting and terror...*

439 Gifford, Z. *Thomas Clarkson and the Campaign Against Slavery,* (London: Anti-Slavery International 1996) p. 29.

440 Manson, *"Riot!"* pp. 45-46.

441 Dresser, *Slavery Obscured* p. 134.

442 Manson, *"Riot!"* p. 85.

443 Ibid. pp. 91 and 107.

444 Ibid. p. 117.

445 Ibid. p. 115.

446 Gifford, *Thomas Clarkson and the Campaign Against Slavery*, p. 43.

447 Brierley and Reid, *Go Home and Do the Washing!* p. 53.

448 It is been estimated that black sailors made up to 25 per cent of Royal Navy crews at the end of the Napoleonic Wars (1815). Linebaugh and Rediker, *The Many-Headed Hydra* p. 311.

449 Hochschild, *Bury the Chains* pp. 170-171.

450 It was through Coleridge's friendship with John Pretor Pinney that he met William Wordsworth in Pinney's house in Great George Street, now the Georgian House Museum in Bristol.

451 Stansfield, D. A. *Thomas Beddoes MD 1760–1808: chemist, physician, democrat.* (Dordrecht: D. Reidel, 1984) p. 128.

452 Rodgers, *Ireland, Slavery and Anti-Slavery* pp. 255-256.

453 Hochschild, *Bury the Chains* pp. 281-285.

454 Gifford, *Thomas Clarkson and the Campaign Against Slavery*, p. 42.

455 Greenacre, F. *From Bristol to the Sea–Artists, the Avon Gorge and Bristol Harbour* (Bristol: Redcliffe Press, 2005) p. 33.

456 The Latin term *horresco referens* translates to 'I shudder to relate'. Heath, G. *The History, Antiquities, Survey and Description, of the City and Suburbs of Bristol.* 2nd Edition (Bristol: W. Matthews, 1797) p. 71.

457 Ibid. p. 163.

458 Ibid. p. 168.

459 These words are to be found on the memorial to the suffering of Africans during the transatlantic slave trade in Nantes, France.

460 Hochschild, *Bury the Chains* p. 261.

461 Ibid. p. 259.

462 Ibid. p. 268.

463 Ibid. p. 268.

464 Ibid. pp. 270-275.

465 The Soufriere Foundation "History of Soufriere" http://soufrierefoundation.org/about-soufriere/history (Accessed February 2019).

466 Cox, E. L. "Fedon's Rebellion 1795-96: Causes and Consequences," *The Journal of Negro History* 67, no. 1 (Spring 1982): 7-19.

467 Geggus, D. "Communications: The cost of Pitt's Caribbean Campaigns, 1793-1798" *The Historical Journal*, 26, no. 3 (1983) pp. 702-706.

468 Hochschild, *Bury the Chains* pp. 280-288.

469 Ibid. pp. 286-287.

470 Ball, *The guillotine, knitting and terror...*

471 Fears about the spread of slave insurrections into the newly acquired British possessions encouraged Pitt's government to restrict the import of additional enslaved Africans. Bolton, C. and Fulford, T. (eds.) "The Collected letters of Robert Southey—Part Three: 1804-1809" Romantic Circles. https://romantic-circles.org/editions/southey_letters/Part_Three/HTML/letterEEd.26.899.html.

472 Hochschild, *Bury the Chains* p. 294.

473 Wordsworth, W. *To Toussaint L'Ouverture.* (1807). Retrieved from: https://blogs.brandeis.edu/revolutions/2014/04/14/to-toussaint-louverture-as-an-elegy/.

474 Dresser, *Slavery Obscured* pp. 185 and 187. Bragge changed his name to Bathurst at this juncture.

475 Richardson, *The Bristol Slave Traders* pp. 27-28.

476 Bristol's geography and the tidal range of the city's river limited cargo handling. The introduction of locks and a canal with the creation of the Floating Harbour (1804-1809) enabled goods and merchandise to be handled 24/7 – it greatly increased the size of the docks in the process.

477 Malpass, P. *The Bristol Dock Company, 1803-1848* (Bristol: ALHA Books, 2010) p. 1 and 10.

478 Latimer, J. *The History of the Society of Merchant Venturers in the City of Bristol* p. 236.
479 Hochschild, *Bury the Chains* p. 303.
480 Ibid. p. 303.
481 Gifford, *Thomas Clarkson and the Campaign Against Slavery*, pp. 46-47.
482 Originally a Dutch colony, Demerara was a county of British Guiana, now Guyana, on the northeast coast of South America.
483 Whitting, J. C. *Report on Pill; Ships returning to Bristol after visiting Africa, and the imports they carried.* (1969). BCRL B27997.
484 Hochschild, *Bury the Chains* pp. 312-313.
485 Dresser, *Slavery Obscured* p. 187.
486 Corry, J. and Evans, Rev. J., *History of Bristol*, (Bristol: W. Shepherd, London: Longman and Co. 1816) Appendix No. VIII p. 318.
487 Latimer, *The Annals of Bristol in the Eighteenth Century* p. 455.
488 Bush G. *Bristol and its Municipal Government 1820-51* (Bristol: Bristol Records Society, 1976) p. 34.
489 Dresser, *Slavery Obscured* pp. 196-197.
490 Belchem J. *'Orator' Hunt: Henry Hunt and English Working Class Radicalism* (London: Breviary Stuff, 2012) p. 30.
491 Latimer, J. *The Annals of Bristol in the Nineteenth Century* (Bristol: W. & F. Morgan, 1887) p. 52.

Corruption, Reform and Emancipation (pp. 154-201)

492 Gifford, *Thomas Clarkson and the Campaign Against Slavery*, p. 49.
493 Huzzey, R. "The politics of slave-trade suppression" in *The suppression of the Atlantic slave trade: British policies, practices and representation of naval coercion* Burroughs, R. and Huzzey, R. (Eds.) (Manchester: Manchester University Press, 2018) p. 19.
494 Blackburn, *The American Crucible* p. 230.
495 MacInnes, *Bristol: A Gateway of Empire* pp. 343-344.
496 Thomas Clarkson acted as an advisor for British negotiators at several international peace conferences in the period and "developed a surprisingly good working relationship with the Duke of Wellington". Huzzey, "The politics of slave-trade suppression" pp. 19-20.
497 For example, when the Foreign Secretary reported back to the House of Commons that the Treaty of Paris had allowed France to continue trading slaves for another five years, Wilberforce spoke of it as "a death warrant for thousands". Gifford, *Thomas Clarkson and the Campaign Against Slavery* p. 50.
498 Burroughs, R. "Suppression of the Atlantic slave trade: abolition from ship to shore" in *The suppression of the Atlantic slave trade: British policies, practices and representation of naval coercion.* Burroughs, R. and Huzzey, R. (Eds.) (Manchester: Manchester University Press, 2018) p. 4.
499 This point is important as some British nationalist myth-makers have attempted to conflate the French Revolutionary and Napoleonic wars with Royal Navy actions against the slave trade. This is not only false but contradictory, particularly prior to the abolition Act of 1807. See for example, Jacob Rees-Mogg in BBC News "Blue plaque honours Admiral Benedictus Kelly" 2 October 2016 https://www.bbc.co.uk/news/uk-england-somerset-37529038 (accessed February 2019).
500 Some abolitionists were not in favour of the naval operations as they were pacifists or opposed to overt militaristic tactics, preferring to campaign instead for international treaties.
501 Fryer provides a number of examples of slave-trading activities by the Royal Navy in the eighteenth century in *Staying Power* p. 52.
502 Hochschild, *Bury the Chains* pp. 322-323.
503 Hart, R. *The Abolition of Slavery* (London: Community Education Trust, 1989) p. 32.
504 Hochschild, *Bury the Chains* p. 319. Bussa is memorialised with a massive statue situated on a roundabout just outside of Barbados's capital, Bridgetown. It shows him defiant with a broken chain in each hand, 'Bussa's Statue' is officially known as the 'Emancipation Statue' and was created in 1985 by Barbadian sculptor Karl Broodhagen in honour of the 150th anniversary

of emancipation.

505 Craton, M. "Proto-Peasant Revolts? The Late Slave Rebellions in the British West Indies 1816-1832." *Past & Present*, no. 85 (1979) p. 102.

506 Ibid. p. 105.

507 J. G. Fuller was a donor and subscriber to the Bristol Auxiliary Anti-Slavery Society formed in 1823 and was the printer behind the anti-slavery posters for the 'Slavery Election' of 1830.

508 Nicholls and Taylor, *Bristol Past and Present* Vol III p. 345.

509 Dresser, M., "Daniel, Thomas (1762-1854), merchant." *Oxford Dictionary of National Biography.* Accessed September 2018. http://www.oxforddnb.com/view/10.1093/ref:odnb/9780198614128.001.0001/odnb-9780198614128-e-107411.

510 Bennett, R. J. *Local Business Voice: The History of Chambers of Commerce in Britain, Ireland, and Revolutionary America, 1760-2011,* (Oxford: Oxford University Press, 2012) p. 203.

511 Hart, *The Abolition of the Slave Trade,* p. 27.

512 Ibid. p. 4.

513 *Encyclopedia.com.* (15 November 2018). https://www.encyclopedia.com/history/encyclopedias-almanacs-transcripts-and-maps/amelioration.

514 Hart, *The Abolition of the Slave Trade,* pp. 4, 26-27.

515 Ibid. p. 28.

516 Davis, D. B. "The Emergence of Immediatism in British and American Antislavery Thought." *The Mississippi Valley Historical Review* 49, no. 2 (1962), p. 219.

517 Hochschild, *Bury the Chains* p. 328.

518 Ibid. p. 329.

519 Hart, *The Abolition of Slavery* p. 62.

520 Bryant, J. *Account of an Insurrection of the Negro Slaves in the Colony of Demerara, which Broke Out on the 18th of August, 1823* (Georgetown: A. Stevenson, 1824) p. 66.

521 Hart, *The Abolition of Slavery* p. 62.

522 Hochschild, *Bury the Chains* pp. 330-331.

523 The Golden Grove estate was owned by Bristol born William Hudson Heaven (1800-1883) who received £11,739 in compensation for owning 638 enslaved people after the 1833 Slavery Abolition Act. He purchased Lundy Island in the Bristol Channel for 9,400 guineas in 1834 and built Millcombe House there in 1836. 'William Hudson Heaven', Legacies of British Slave-ownership database, https://www.ucl.ac.uk/lbs/physical/view/-1907012513 [accessed February 2019].

524 Living Easton: Slave Revolts, Rebellions, Revolutions, Rebels, Conspiracies and The Maroon Wars. http://www.cems.uwe.ac.uk/~rstephen/livingeaston/local_history/slavery.html. [Accessed February, 2019]; Brown, P., "Representations of Rebellion: Slavery in Jamaica, 1823-1831" (2014). All Theses. 1984. https://tigerprints.clemson.edu/all_theses/1984 pp. 7-36.

525 Mayer, *All on Fire,* p. 70.

526 Nicholls and Taylor, *Bristol Past and Present* Vol III p. 233.

527 Latimer, *The Annals of Bristol in the Nineteenth Century* p. 88.

528 Jenkins, T. "DAVIS, Richard Hart (1766-1842), of Mortimer House, Clifton, Glos. and 38 Conduit Street, Mdx." in *The History of Parliament: the House of Commons 1820-1832,* ed. Fisher, J. R. (London: Cambridge University Press, 2009). Accessed 2018. http://www.historyofparliamentonline.org/volume/1820-1832/member/davis-richard-1766-1842

529 Dresser, *Slavery Obscured* pp. 201, 204-205.

530 Bush, G. *Bristol and its Municipal Government 1820-1851* Bristol Record Society's Publications Vol. XXIX (Bristol: Bristol Record Society, 1976) pp. 27 and 56-57.

531 Bush, *Bristol and its Municipal Government* p. 40 and 84.

532 Manton, J. *Mary Carpenter and the Children of the Streets,* (London: Heinemann Educational Books Ltd., 1976) p. 42.

533 Dresser, *Slavery Obscured,* p. 206; Latimer, *The Annals of Bristol in the Nineteenth Century* p. 137. The *Bush Tavern* was in Corn Street (opposite the Exchange, now the Bristol Harbour

Hotel), the *White Lion* was in Broad Street (now the Grand Hotel) and the *Rummer Tavern* is in All Saints Lane/High Street.

534 Jenkins, "DAVIS, Richard Hart (1766-1842)…"

535 Marshall, P. *Bristol and the Abolition of Slavery–The Politics of Emancipation*. (Bristol: Bristol Branch of the Historical Association, 1975), p. 11.

536 Dresser, *Slavery Obscured* p. 213.

537 Marshall, *Bristol and the Abolition of Slavery* p. 17.

538 The French Revolution of July 1830 led to the overthrow of Charles X and eventually the Bourbon dynasty.

539 Nicholls and Taylor, *Bristol Past and Present* Vol III p. 323.

540 *Bristol Mercury* 5 October 1830

541 *Bristol Mercury* 26 October, 1830

542 *The Bristolian*, 23 October 1830.

543 *Bristol Mercury* 26 October 1830. Also talking at an anti-slavery meeting on the fateful night of 22nd October was William Wilberforce, just down the road in Bath–as reported in the *Bath Chronicle and Weekly Gazette* of 28 October 1830.

544 In her defence, one of the 'dear sensitive souls', Marianne Schimmelpennick, wrote "…both my cousins and I resolve to leave off sugar, as the only produce of slave labour within our province to discontinue" – obviously not a pipe smoker then. Townsend, T. *Bristol and Clifton Slave Trade Trail* (Wellington: Pixz, 2016) p. 79.

545 *The Anti-Slavery Reporter,* 5 January 1831.

546 *Bristol Mercury*, 16 November 1830.

547 Hart, *The Abolition of Slavery*, p. 28.

548 Gifford, *Thomas Clarkson and the Campaign Against Slavery*, p. 54.

549 Dresser, *Slavery Obscured*, p. 215.

550 Hart, *The Abolition of Slavery*, p. 32.

551 Nicholls and Taylor, *Bristol Past and Present* Vol III p. 324.

552 Ibid. p. 323.

553 Hochschild, *Bury the Chains* p. 331.

554 'Winning' candidate Edward Protheroe junior was presented with a large vase made by Bristol silversmith Charles Taylor "by his Bristol Friends as a tribute of their admiration for his ardent exertions on behalf of Negro Emancipation". *Slavery, Abolition and Emancipation: A Reading List* (Bristol: Bristol Libraries, 2009) p. 32.

555 Jenkins, T. "Bristol" in *The History of Parliament: the House of Commons 1820-1832*, ed. Fisher, D. R. (London: Cambridge University Press, 2009). Accessed 2018. http://www.historyofparliamentonline.org/volume/1820-1832/constituencies/bristol.

556 Nicholls and Taylor, *Bristol Past & Present Vol. 3* pp. 324-325.

557 Ibid. p. 325.

558 Hochschild, *Bury the Chains* p. 337.

559 Wetherell Place in Clifton was named in his honour and a statue to him was erected in 1839 at nearby Meridian Place. Recently restored, the statue now resides under a staircase at the Red Lodge.

560 Yarnspinner V. *Nottingham Rising* (Nottingham: Loaf on a Stick Press, 2014) p. 82.

561 Chilcott, *The History of Bristol*, pp. 68 and 70.

562 Latimer, *The Annals of Bristol in the Nineteenth Century* p. 175. A Whig reformer, Lord Grey became Prime Minister after the fall of the Tory government in November 1830 and presided over the Great Reform Act of 1832.

563 *Bristol Riots, 1831: Report of the Commissioners Appointed Under the Bristol Damages Compensation Act, and Statement of Actions for Damages, and Proceedings Had Therein Under that Act with Their General Results* (Bristol: John Taylor, 1835). Philip Miles's father William, who died in 1803, had been a Jamaican slave factor, plantation owner, sugar refiner and banker. He was Mayor in 1780, chairman of the re-formed West India Association of 1782, warden of the Society of Merchant Venturers in 1789 and an early promoter of the Floating Harbour scheme. Phillip was Miles's second son and became his main heir after the death of his older brother in

1790. He received a £100,000 (equivalent to £128 million in 2016 by GDP per capita conversion) dowry from his father in 1796 on the eve of his wedding and became one of Bristol's two MPs after the election of 1835.

564 Marshall, *Bristol and the Abolition of Slavery* pp. 23-24. Letter writer Pinney's emphasis is in bold.

565 The rebellion of the enslaved in Virginia in August 1831 was known as the 'Nat Turner Revolt' and named after its leader. Although it lasted only a few days, it created widespread fear amongst the white population and led to the formation of militias. The state executed 56 enslaved Africans; a further 120 slaves and free blacks were murdered by the militias.

566 Gaspar, D. B. "Slavery, amelioration, and Sunday markets in Antigua, 1823-1831" *Slavery and Abolition*, 9:1 (1988) pp. 16-19.

567 Hart, R. *Slaves who abolished slavery: Volume 1 Blacks in Bondage* (Jamaica: Institute of Social and Economic Research, University of the West Indies, 1980) p. 223.

568 Hart, *The Abolition of Slavery* pp. 63-64.

569 Hochschild, *Bury the Chains* p. 340. It is interesting to note that the revolt in Jamaica occurred about seven to eight weeks after the end of the reform riots in Bristol. The approximate sailing time from British mainland ports to Jamaica was less than one month, giving time for news from England to arrive and reach the enslaved. A painting by the artist Rachel Hewitt draws reference to the potential connection between the events in Bristol and Jamaica in 1831 and can be viewed here: http://www.brh.org.uk/site/articles/rachel-hewitt/.

570 Hochschild, *Bury the Chains* pp. 339-341. There are life-size sculptures of Sam Sharpe holding a bible and addressing four of his accomplices in Sam Sharpe Square (formerly Charles square), Montego Bay, Jamaica. The memorial was designed by Kay Sullivan and unveiled in 1983.

571 Hutton, *Bristol and its Famous Associations,* p. 369.

572 Coules, *The Trade* p. 191.

573 Hochschild, *Bury the Chains* p. 342.

574 Ibid. p. 345. Catherine Williams and William Black were enslaved Africans.

575 *Poor Man's Guardian,* 25 February 1832.

576 The franchise was extended to males who owned or leased property of significant value.

577 It is estimated that the number of men qualified to vote in Bristol in 1830 was about 7,000. The registered electorate after the Reform Bill of 1832 rose to 10,309. Jenkins, "Bristol" in *The History of Parliament: the House of Commons 1820-1832.*

578 Marshall, *Bristol and the Abolition of Slavery,* p. 26.

579 Jenkins, "Bristol" in *The History of Parliament: the House of Commons 1820-1832.*

580 This was set at six years for agricultural workers (the majority) and four years for all others. Hart, *The Abolition of Slavery* p. 64.

581 Ibid. p. 5.

582 The full title of the 1833 Act was: 'An Act for the Abolition of Slavery throughout the British Colonies; for promoting the Industry of the manumitted Slaves; and for compensating the Persons hitherto entitled to the Services of such Slaves'.

583 This estimate comes from a statement by Sir Hilary Beckles, Vice-Chancellor of The University of the West Indies and Chair of the CARICOM Reparations Commission in February 2018. Caribbean 360. "Slavery Loan Only Fully Repaid by Britain in 2015" http://www.caribbean360. com/news/slavery-loan-fully-repaid-britain-2015 [Accessed 31 December 2018]. A higher estimate of £300 billion was made in an article in *The Guardian* newspaper. Manjapra, K. "When will Britain face up to its crimes against humanity?" *The Guardian* 29 March 2018.

584 *Legacies of British Slave-ownership* https://www.ucl.ac.uk/lbs/. It has been estimated that 30,000 of the slave holders paid compensation 'owned' an average of three enslaved people. McNeil, J. *Scandal! The Slave Profiteers* https://www.brh.org.uk/site/events/scandall-the-slave-profiteers/.

585 HM Treasury Freedom of Information Act 2000: Slavery Abolition Act 1833 (FOI2018/00186) 31 January 2018.

586 *Bristol Mercury* 10 August 1833, *Bath Chronicle* 8 August 1833 and Large, D. *Radicalism in Bristol in the Nineteenth Century* (Bristol: Bristol Record Society, 1981) p. 3 note 2.

587 Hochschild, *Bury the Chains* pp. 347-348.

588 Dryden, J. "Pas de Six Ans!" in *Seven Slaves & Slavery: Trinidad 1777–1838*, A. de Verteuil, (Port of Spain, 1992) pp. 371-379.

589 Blackburn, R. *The Overthrow of Colonial Slavery 1776-1848* (London: Verso, 1988) p. 460.

590 Frucht, R. "Emancipation and Revolt in the West Indies: St. Kitts, 1834" *Science & Society*, Vol. 39, No. 2 (Summer, 1975), pp. 202-203.

591 Ibid. p. 207. Robert Claxton was the son of the Bristol West India merchant of the same name and younger brother of both Christopher Claxton the pro-slavery advocate and organiser and Society of Merchant Venturers Secretary William Claxton.

592 One notable rebel on St Kitts was the maroon Markus who was described thus: "a man named Markus, an African, a most daring and dangerous character, who has been absent three years, and has always been a runaway, goes by the title of King of the Woods, has been condemned for murder, has now a charge of felony . . . hanging over his head, and, as I am credibly informed (only by hearsay evidence, but which I believe), that he has a gang of 30 and upwards under his command in the mountains. His usual haunts are from Stones Fort to Vembell Mountains. He has a musket in his possession and is very skillful in the use thereof. No order may be expected in the country unless he is taken". Quoted from Frucht, "Emancipation and Revolt in the West Indies" p. 211.

593 Ibid. p. 213.

594 Ishmael, O. *The Guyana Story: The End of Slavery* Chapter 44: http://www.guyana.org/features/guyanastory/chapter44.html.

595 A nine-foot-tall memorial to 'captain' Damon was created in bronze by Guyanese sculptor Ivor Thom and unveiled on the 150th Anniversary of Emancipation on 31st July 1988 in Anna Regina on the Essequibo Coast. Ishmael, O. *The Guyana Story: Damon and the Essequibo Rebellion* Chapter 45: http://www.guyana.org/features/guyanastory/chapter45.html.

596 Boa, S. "Experiences of women estate workers during the apprenticeship period in St Vincent, 1834–38: the transition from slavery to freedom" *Women's History Review*, 10:3, (2001) p. 382.

597 Ibid. p. 385.

598 Ibid. p. 394; Anderson, J. and Dunn, R. *Between slavery and freedom: special magistrate John Anderson's journal of St. Vincent during the Apprenticeship*. Philadelphia: University of Pennsylvania Press, 2001 p. 24 note 56.

599 Boa, "Experiences of women estate workers" pp. 396-397.

600 Hart, *The Abolition of Slavery* p. 64.

601 'Company Shops' were part of the 'Truck system' whereby workers were forced or induced to spend their wages in shops owned by their employers. Sometimes they would even be paid in a company currency which could only be exchanged in these shops. The practice was attractive to the owners of business as it allowed them to make profits from both the exploitation of a worker's labour and from their consumption of commodities. In many cases the 'Truck system' was used to entice workers and their families into debt, thereby bonding them to the employer. The system was widespread in Britain in the eighteenth and nineteenth centuries and, despite attempts to outlaw it, continued in some cases into the twentieth.

602 See for example: Port Cities Bristol "Newspaper extract, compensation claims" http://discoveringbristol.org.uk/browse/slavery/newspaper-extract-compensation-claims/ (Accessed 30 December 2018) and Bristol's Free Museums and Historic Houses "Bristol and the Transatlantic Slave Trade: Myths and Truths" https://www.bristolmuseums.org.uk/stories/bristol-transatlantic-slave-trade-myths-truths/ (Accessed 30 December 2018).

603 *Britain's Forgotten Slave Owners* James Van Der Pool (dir.) BBC July 2015.

604 The sole woman was Ann Trotman (née Hamilton) who claimed £3,097 in compensation and was ranked 30 on the list of successful claimants in Bristol. See Appendix 6.

605 For example, the Baillie family were in business with the Ames's who were in turn partners in other enterprises with the Pinney's and the Miles family. Thomas Daniel had been a partner in the Bristol New Bank with the Ames family. Charles Pinney and Jeremiah Ames were brothers-in-law. UCL Legacies of British Slave-ownership database https://www.ucl.ac.uk/lbs/.

606 Little, *The City and County of Bristol* p. 258.

607 Bush, *Bristol and its Municipal Government* pp. 105 and 122-124. Vyvyan Terrace in Clifton

was named in his honour. Ironically Vyvyan became the name of one of the lead characters in the anarchic 1980s TV comedy show *The Young Ones* after one of the script writers wandered past the Terrace looking for inspiration!

608 Marshall, *Bristol and the Abolition of Slavery* pp. 26-27.

609 Chilcott, *History of Bristol*, pp. 337-341. Some of the artwork was from Beckford's folly at Fonthill, the Saloon featured "two handsome china vases, and a circular slab of *verde antique*, mounted on gilt dolphins" and was acquired from the former Jamaican Sugar Baron's estate.

610 Farrell, S. and Fisher, D. R. "MILES, Philip John (1774-1845), of Leigh Court, Abbots Leigh, Som." in *The History of Parliament: the House of Commons 1820-1832*, ed. Fisher, D. R. (London: Cambridge University Press, 2009). Accessed 2017. http://www.historyofparliamentonline. org/volume/1820-1832/member/miles-philip-1774-1845. There's a large stained glass window dedicated to Miles in St Mary Redcliffe church.

611 Bush, *Bristol and its Municipal Government 1820-51* pp. 10 and 23.

612 Burgess, A. *City and Port of Bristol*, (Bristol: W. H. Somerton, Bristol Mercury Office, 1836).

613 Latimer, *The Annals of Bristol in the Nineteenth Century* p. 203.

614 Bush, *Bristol and its Municipal Government 1820–1851* p. 195.

615 Marshall, *Bristol and the Abolition of Slavery*, p. 27.

616 Vaughn, A. *Isambard Kingdom Brunel*, (London: John Murray (Publishers) Ltd. 1991) p. 44.

617 *Bristol Mercury* 4 April 1868.

618 Bush, *Bristol and its Municipal Government 1820–1851* p. 136.

619 Farr, G. *The SS Great Western, the first Atlantic Liner*, (Bristol: Branch of the Historical Association the University, Bristol. 1988), pp. 3-4 and 11.

620 Clifton Suspension Bridge "Our Heroes" https://www.cliftonbridge.org.uk/visit/history/whos-who.

621 In 1840, of the 923 listed workers, 609 were 'girls' (under 18 years), 113 'boys' (under 18 years), 17 women and 184 men. Richardson, M. *The Maltreated and the Malcontents*. Bristol Radical Pamphleteer #37 (Bristol: Bristol Radical History Group, 2016) pp. 9-10 and 20-21.

622 See entries for '*Thomas Daniel*', '*George Gibbs*', '*Richard Bright*', '*Philip John Miles*', '*Philip William Skynner Miles*', '*Edward Protheroe (senior)*', '*John Cave of Brentry*', '*Stephen Cave*', *Thomas Kington the younger*', '*Peter Baillie*', '*Evan Baillie*', '*James Evan Baillie*', 'and '*Hugh Duncan Baillie*' in the *Legacies of British Slave-ownership database* https://www.ucl.ac.uk/lbs/.

623 McGrath, P. *The Merchant Venturers of Bristol* (Bristol: The Society of Merchant Venturers of the City of Bristol, 1975) p. 293.

624 Stone, G. F. *Bristol: as it was and as it is.* (Bristol: Walter Reid, 1909) p. 14.

625 Little, *The City and County of Bristol* p. 167.

626 McGrath, *The Merchant Venturers of Bristol* p. 262.

627 BA *Records of the Society of Merchant Venturers–Associated Clubs & Societies—West India Association—Letters–Letters to Claxton and Daniel (1847-49)* SMV/8/3/3/10.

628 Hart, *The Abolition of Slavery* pp. 42-43.

629 Freeman, A. B. *Bristol Worthies and notable residents in the district.* 2nd series (Bristol: Burleigh Press, 1909) p. 28.

630 Bush, *Bristol and its Municipal Government 1820 – 1851*, p. 25.

631 Thomas Daniel & Co. in Liquidation Concession Ref. 972.981 Barbados Museum & Historical Society.

The Battle Cry of Freedom (pp. 202-237)

632 McFerran, A. *Elizabeth Blackwell First Woman Doctor*, (New York: Grosset & Dunlap, 1966) pp. 18-21.

633 Wilson, D. C. *Lone Woman—The Story of Elizabeth Blackwell, The First Woman Doctor* (London: Hodder & Stoughton Ltd., 1970) p. 48.

634 McFerran, *Elizabeth Blackwell First Woman Doctor*, pp. 22-23.

635 James, W. *Memoir of John Bishop Estlin*, (London: Charles Green, Hackney. 1855) p. 13.

636 Coules, *The Trade* p. 191.

637 Latimer, *Annals of the Nineteenth Century* p. 188.

638 Stott A., *Hannah More—the first Victorian,* (New York: Oxford University Press, 2003) pp. 330-331.

639 Mayer, *All on Fire* p. 586.

640 Gifford, *Thomas Clarkson and the Campaign Against Abolition,* p. 57.

641 Mayer, *All on Fire* pp. 155 and 164. Unlike Wilberforce however, Garrison was outside of government and in this sense was more akin to campaigner Thomas Clarkson.

642 Wilson, *Lone Woman,* p. 47. The Georgia legislature had offered a $5,000 reward to anyone who could arrest Garrison and bring him to the state to be tried for seditious libel. Mayer, *All on Fire* pp. 122-123.

643 Stange, D. C. *British Unitarians against American Slavery 1833-1865* (Cranbury, N. J. & London: Associated University Presses, 1998) p. 85.

644 Manton, *Mary Carpenter and the Children of the Streets,* p. 76.

645 Stange, *British Unitarians against American Slavery 1833-1865,* p. 224.

646 Mayer, *All on Fire,* pp. 168 and 208-209.

647 Emden, P. H. *Quakers in Commerce—A Record of Business Achievement* (London: Sampson Low, Marston & Co., Ltd. 1939) pp. 77-78.

648 Sturge, J. and Harvey, T. *The West Indies in 1837,* (London: Hamilton, Adams & Co., 1838). Appendix Section XIII. p. xci.

649 Of course, these practices were commonplace in prisons in Victorian Britain; penal treadmills had been invented in 1818 but weren't finally abolished until the Prison Act of 1902. Treadmills were introduced into the British Caribbean after the Abolition of Slavery Act of 1833, specifically for the 'disciplining' of 'apprentices'. Hart, *The Abolition of Slavery,* p. 11.

650 Sturge, J. and Harvey, T. *The West Indies in 1837,* Appendix Section XIII. p. xciv.

651 Slavery Abolition Act 1833.

652 Wright, M. *Elizabeth Blackwell of Bristol, The First Woman Doctor* (Bristol: Bristol Branch of the Historical Association, 1995) pp. 6-7.

653 Hochschild, *Bury the Chains* pp. 348-349. By referring to "aged 276 years" Knibb was locating the start of England's colonial slavery to Sir John Hawkins' first slaving voyage to Africa.

654 Hochschild, *Bury the Chains* pp. 348-349 and 358.

655 Gifford, *Thomas Clarkson and the Campaign Against Slavery,* p. 56.

656 Fenton, L. *'I Was Transformed' Frederick Douglass: An American Slave in Victorian Britain* (Stroud: Amberley Publishing, 2018) pp. 33-34.

657 Schama, *Power of Art* pp. 286-287.

658 Ibid. p. 295. Blackburn, *The Overthrow of Colonial Slavery 1776-1848* p. 468. The Bostonians felt aggrieved at their purchase initially because the picture lacked its celebrated purple colour - made famous by the painting's first owner, John Ruskin. He had eulogised so much over the original artwork that he coined the phrase 'purple prose' – it had subsequently been cleaned off by Ruskin and his dad by mistake...

659 Dresser, *Slavery Obscured* p. 3.

660 Stange, *British Unitarians against American Slavery 1833-1865,* p. 61.

661 Manton *Mary Carpenter and the Children of the Streets,* p. 76.

662 Fenton, *'I Was Transformed'* p. 147.

663 Carpenter objected strongly to the term 'ragged schools' (made popular in the public press) and thought it an insulting name, preferring to call them 'free schools'. Manton, *Mary Carpenter and the Children of the Streets,* p. 84.

664 Stange, *British Unitarians against American Slavery 1833-1865.* p. 84.

665 Nicholls and Taylor, *Bristol Past and Present* Vol III p. 345.

666 Fenton, *'I Was Transformed'* pp. 7 and 142.

667 Ibid. p. 189.

668 Gifford, *Thomas Clarkson and the Campaign Against Slavery,* p. 58.

669 Stange, *British Unitarians against American Slavery 1833-1865,* p. 85.

670 Fenton, *'I Was Transformed'* p. 147.

671 Ibid. pp. 147-149.

672 Manton, *Mary Carpenter and the Children of the Streets*, p. 77.

673 Fenton, *'I Was Transformed'* p. 166.

674 Ibid. p. 188.

675 Stange, *British Unitarians against American Slavery 1833-1865*, pp. 84-85.

676 *Bristol Mercury* 3 April 1847. C. J. Thomas was the brother of fellow Unitarian Herbert Thomas of the soap-making firm and was Bristol's Mayor from 1874-1875.

677 Fenton, *'I Was Transformed'* pp. 183-184.

678 Manton, *Mary Carpenter and the Children of the Streets*, p. 78.

679 Blackburn, *The Overthrow of Colonial Slavery* pp. 494-501.

680 This was not his original surname; he took the name Wells Brown in recognition of a Quaker who helped him during his escape from slavery.

681 The 'International Peace Congress' was a series of international meetings of representatives from peace societies from throughout the world held in various places in Europe from 1843 to 1853. The Congress met in Paris in August 1849.

682 *Bristol Mercury* 13 April 1850.

683 *Bristol Mercury* 20 April 1850.

684 This verse is from the abolitionist song *Fling out the Anti-Slavery Flag* (sung to the tune of *Auld Lang Syne*) which appeared in Brown's *The Anti-Slavery Harp; A Collection of Songs for Anti-Slavery Meetings* (Boston: Bela Marsh, 1848).

685 Mary Carpenter's *Poetical Extract* notebook contains a treasure trove of entries from American anti-slavery activists, including William Lloyd Garrison, Samuel J May, Caroline Weston, Sarah Parker Remond and William Craft, who wrote in Mary's book in 1682: "I shall always remember my visits to Bristol and the deep interest you have always taken in the cause of the oppressed" Bristol Archives *Records of Mary Carpenter and the Red Lodge Reformatory–Mary Carpenter's Poetical Extract Book, March 1836 to July 1875 containing extracts by a number of prominent abolitionists and reformers* Ref: 12693/20.

686 Like William Wells Brown, Pennington took his name from a Quaker, in this case Isaac Penington, who was an influential writer of the sect in seventeenth century England.

687 *Bristol Mercury* 19 October 1850.

688 The short-lived anti-slavery 'Free Soilers' party had been created to try and stop newly acquired US territories from becoming slave States.

689 Mayer, *All on Fire*, p. 408.

690 *Bristol Mercury* 5 April 1851. This article states that the canvas was 2,000 feet long, which may be a typographical error.

691 *Bristol Mercury* 12 April 1851.

692 *Bath Chronicle* 22 May 1851.

693 Even the *Bristol Mercury* was openly criticising the organisation in articles, see for example 30 August 1851.

694 Brown, W. W. *The American Fugitive in Europe: Sketches of Places and People Abroad*. (Boston: John P. Jewett and Company, 1855) pp. 32, 160-161, 304.

695 *Bath Chronicle* 3 September 1863

696 Stange, *British Unitarians against American Slavery 1833-1865*, pp. 128-129.

697 Huzzey, "The politics of slave-trade suppression" p. 36.

698 It is estimated that in 1870 only 10 percent of Africa was under direct European control. By 1914 it had increased to 90 percent. For 'bridgeheads' see Darwin, J. "Imperialism and the Victorians: the dynamics of territorial expansion." *The English Historical Review* 112, no. 447 (1997): 614-642.

699 Eltis quoted in Huzzey, "The politics of slave-trade suppression" p. 43.

700 Burroughs, "Suppression of the Atlantic slave trade" p. 8.

701 Fenton, *I was Transformed*, p. 210.

702 James, *Memoir of John Bishop Estlin*, pp. 16-17.

703 Baily was responsible for the statues of Nelson in Trafalgar Square and Earl Grey in Newcastle

704 Hanham, J. and Martin, M. "Women in Bristol 1835-1914" in Dresser, M. (Ed.) *Women and the City: Bristol 1373-2000* (Bristol: Redcliffe/Regional History Centre UWE, 2016) pp. 97-98 and 102.

705 McFerran, *Elizabeth Blackwell First Woman Doctor*, p. 149.

706 Ibid. p. 149.

707 Wright, M. *Elizabeth Blackwell of Bristol*, p. 14. Blackwell had always opposed separate education for women and men arguing that women's education would be perceived as inferior. The continuing problem women had to get a medical education at all made her change her mind.

708 Mayer, *All on Fire* p. XIII. Radical abolitionist John Brown led a raid on the United States arsenal at Harpers Ferry, Virginia in an unsuccessful attempt to initiate an armed revolt of the enslaved. It is widely accepted that this incident hastened the start of the American Civil War.

709 Alford, B. W. E. *W. D. & H. O. Wills and the development of the U.K. tobacco industry 1786-1965* (London: Methuen 1973) pp. 115-116.

710 Richardson, *The Maltreated and the Malcontents* pp. 58-61.

711 Atterton, G. *Cotton Threads–the History of the Great Western Cotton Factory* (Bristol: Barton Hill History Group, 2015) pp. 19-20.

712 Ball, R., Parkin, D. and Mills, S. *100 Fishponds Road: Life and Death in a Victorian Workhouse*. Bristol Radical Pamphleteer #34 2nd edt. (Bristol: Bristol Radical History Group, 2016) pp. 46-48; Richardson, *The Maltreated and the Malcontents* p. 61.

713 Mayer, *All on Fire*, p. 541.

714 Richardson, *The Maltreated and the Malcontents* pp. 59-60.

715 Mayer, *All on Fire*, p. 197.

716 Richardson, *The Maltreated and the Malcontents* p. 60 and n. 179. For more on the interesting figure of Emma Martin see Taylor, B. 2004 "Martin [née Bullock], Emma (1811/12–1851), socialist and freethinker." *Oxford Dictionary of National Biography*.

717 Hanham, J. and Martin, M. "Women in Bristol 1835-1914" in Dresser, M. (Ed.) *Women and the City: Bristol 1373-2000* pp. 97-98.

718 Linebaugh and Rediker, *The Many Headed Hydra*, p. 290.

719 Manton, *Mary Carpenter and the Children of the Streets*, pp. 220-221.

720 Ibid. p. 240.

721 Woolfe, G. "No slavery after WW2" *Bristol Post*, 31 December 2018.

722 Manton, *Mary Carpenter and the Children of the Streets*, p. 77.

723 Stange, *British Unitarians against American Slavery 1833-1865*, p. 129.

724 Mayer, *All on Fire*, p. 423.

725 Murphy, B. and Thorne, R. "Hobhouse, Benjamin (1757-1831) – Member Biography" *The History of Parliament: the House of Commons 1790-1820*, ed. Thorne, R. (London: Boydell & Brewer, 1986). Accessed 2019.

726 Wilkins, *Ecclesiastical History of Westbury-on-Trym*, pp. 27-28.

727 Hochschild, *Bury the Chains* p. 314.

728 National Westminster Bank, *Three Banks in Bristol* pp. 2-3.

729 Walvin, J. "Slavery and the Building of Britain", *BBC History*, Accessed March 2018. http://www.bbc.co.uk/history/british/abolition/building_britain_gallery_02.shtml; Martin, S. "How African slaves created a prosperous new Britain", *The Voice*, 23 August 2011. http://www.voice-online.co.uk/article/how-african-slaves-created-a-prosperous-new-britain.

The Cult of Colston (pp. 238-254)

730 Tovey, S. G. *Colston, the Philanthropist: Memorials of his life and deeds* (Bristol: T. D. Taylor, 1863) p. 49.

731 Morgan, S. "Memory and the merchants: Commemoration and civic identity". *International Journal of Heritage Studies*. 4, no. 2 (1998) p. 107.

732 Ibid. pp. 105-106.

733 Jordan, S. *The development and implementation of authority in a regional capital: A study of Bristol's elites, 1835-1939* (Unpublished PhD Thesis, University of West of England, 1999) p. 299.

734 Wilkins, *Edward Colston Supplement*, p. 31. According to the legend Colston had chiselled on his tomb he had given away over £70,000 during his lifetime (it should be noted not just to Bristol but also London and Manchester). This equates conservatively to £167 million (by GDP per capita conversion) in 2016, based upon his death in 1721. Using a similar comparison Reynolds donated over £201 million (by GDP per capita).

735 Jordan, *The development and implementation of authority in a regional capital* p. 297.

736 Ibid. p. 297.

737 Ibid. p. 323.

738 Jordan demonstrates that prior to WW1 over 80 per cent of Dolphin, Anchor and Grateful presidents could be linked to at least one of sixteen other 'elite' organisations examined in his study. Ibid. p. 295.

739 Ibid. pp. 301-302.

740 Ibid. p. 302.

741 Ibid. pp. 310-311.

742 Ibid. p. 311.

743 Marshall, E. *In Colston's Days: A Story of Old Bristol* (London: Seeley and Co., 1901) p. x. The writer of this piece acquired a copy of this book which has a paper label at the front that bears the legend 'North St. [Bedminster, Bristol] Wesleyan Sunday School Loan Library (1901).'

744 Hutton, *Bristol and its Famous Associations* p. 197.

745 Dresser, *Slavery Obscured* p. 3.

746 This story turned out to be true at least in part. In the early 2000s *The Bristolian* broadsheet published a story about the 'hair and nails' which was roundly dismissed by several commentators. In 2016 the Countering Colston group (CC) noticed an extract from an essay in the CGS newsletter by a pupil who had been on a school trip to Merchants' Hall and had been "disgusted" on seeing the relics. *Colston's Chronicle* "Heritage Day" Newsletter of CGS Edition XXXI Summer 2012 p. 4. In 2017 CC received a photograph of the hair and nails in a cabinet in Merchant's Hall taken during a civic dinner. When questioned on Charter Day in 2017, representatives from the Society of Merchant Venturers at first denied the relics were held in Merchants' Hall but later admitted they were, claiming that they "probably weren't Colston's".

747 This story reappeared in a letter from persistent religious defender of Colston in the *Bristol Post*: Whittern, D. "There's just no evidence to stack up" *Bristol Post: Your Say* 24 October 2017.

748 Taylor, J. "Ancient Bristol—Historical Sketch" in *Bristol and its Environs: Historical, Descriptive & Scientific* (London: Houlston, Bristol: J. Wright, 1875) p. 50.

749 Foyle, *Bristol, Pevsner Architectural Guides* p. 121.

750 According to George Stone "A vast amount of controversy had been caused by the extravagance of the Ecclesiastical Commissioners in their erection and adornment of the residence for the Bishop at Stapleton, and when, after being tenantless for a long while, it was purchased by the Merchant Venturers for the new Colston School, the £12,000 paid for it represented only half its cost. The removal of the school was the theme for much discussion. The change was declared to be contrary to the intentions of the founder. The matter subsequently drifted into the law court, and a petition was presented against the removal, but the Master of the Rolls, on February 24th, 1859, declined to accede to its prayer. On 21st October 1861 the change took place, and a local chronicler writing about it said, 'the school left our city in an undemonstrative, almost imperceptible manner.'" Stone, *Bristol: as it was and as it is* p. 172.

751 Hudleston, *How to see Bristol*, p. 30.

752 *The City and County of Bristol the Capital of the West: The Official Handbook of the Corporation of Bristol*, (Cheltenham and London: Ed. J. Burrow & Co., c.1962/3) p. 67.

753 All seven founders of the Colston Hall were Bristol Worthies with mostly Liberal tendencies. You can't help but wonder what their views would be today if the name given to their benevolence was proving to be so divisive—especially the two sons of Joseph Storrs Fry, eminent anti-slavery campaigner that he was and the Thomas brothers. Mathew, M. *1869 Trade Directory for Bristol*.

754 The Canynges Society was first formed in 1848 in order to raise funds to restore St Mary Redcliffe Church and re-build the spire. It was disbanded in 1873 and revived in 1927 to facilitate

more work. It's still going to this day.

755 Latimer, *The Annals of Bristol in the Nineteenth Century* p. 378.

756 Cobb, P. C. *The Stained Glass of St Mary Redcliffe, Bristol* Transcript of the Bristol and Gloucestershire Archaeological Society CXII (1994) pp. 150-152.

757 Smith, M. Q. *The Stained Glass of Bristol Cathedral* (Bristol: Redcliffe Press, 1983) p. 84.

758 Rogan, J. *Bristol Cathedral: History and Architecture* (Stroud: Tempus, 2000) p. 13 and 118.

759 "Dean of Bristol considers 'slavery' window removal" *BBC News* 23 February 2017. Accessed March 2018. http://www.bbc.co.uk/news/uk-england-bristol-39063133; Grimshaw, E. "Stained Glass Window has Colston Link" *Bristol Post* 23 February 2017.

760 Rebuilt in 1976 it was soon noticed that the building at the north end of the Square had an early eighteenth century bust of Edward Colston. The bust was replaced by a replica and the original placed within Bristol City Museum.

761 Morgan, "Memory and the merchants" p. 106.

762 Merritt, D. *Sculpture in Bristol* pp. 30-31.

763 Wilkins, *Edward Colston,* p. 90.

764 Smith, M. Q. *The Stained Glass of Bristol Cathedral.* (Bristol: Redcliffe Press, 1983) p. 86.

765 Dunn, S. *Colston Girls' School: The First Hundred Years* (Bristol: Redcliffe, 1991) pp. 4-5.

766 Ibid. pp. 5-6.

767 Clarke, *The Society of Merchant Venturers* pp. 51-53.

768 The 'Colston Nominees' were originally chosen by Edward Colston but became a self-selecting organisation after his death. Dunn, *Colston Girls' School* p. 12.

769 Ibid. pp. 14-26.

770 Ibid. pp. 154-156.

771 Yong, M. "Colston's Primary School makes decision on removing controversial slave trader's name" *Bristol Post* 1 December 2017. Accessed March 2018. https://www.bristolpost.co.uk/news/bristol-news/colstons-primary-school-makes-decision-864514.

772 Yong, M. "This is why Colston's Girls' School will not be removing the slave trader's name" *Bristol Post* November 2, 2017. Accessed March 2018. https://www.bristolpost.co.uk/news/bristol-news/colstons-girls-school-not-removing-717476.

773 Yong, M. "Why Colston's Girls' School does not want to change its name" *Bristol Post* November 2, 2017. Accessed March 2018. https://www.bristolpost.co.uk/news/bristol-news/colstons-girls-school-not-want-717435.

774 For example, in 2008 the Society of Merchant Venturers educational arm took over Withywood School in south Bristol and renamed it the 'Merchants' Academy'.

775 The latter actually converted to a state-funded Academy in September 2008 after financial difficulties. Colston Primary School was assumed by many to be part of CGS but in fact has always been a state school with no direct connections to its namesake.

776 Charles, G. W. "The Merchant Venturers' Technical College, Bristol" *The Vocational Aspect of Secondary and Further Education,* 3 No. 6, (1951) pp. 87-88.

777 This organisation later became known as the 'Colston Research Society'. From 1908 to 1948 it applied its resources in grants towards specific research projects in various departments of Bristol University. The Society has been supporting symposia since 1948. http://www.bristol.ac.uk/pace/committees/colston-research/.

778 Churchill, L. "Bristol University makes decision over renaming Wills Memorial Building after slavery debate" *Bristol Post* 4 July 2017. Accessed March 2018. https://www.bristolpost.co.uk/news/bristol-news/bristol-university-makes-decision-over-163397.

779 Churchill, L. "Call to rename University of Bristol's Wills Memorial Building because of slavery links" *Bristol Post* 29 March 2017. Accessed March 2018. https://www.bristolpost.co.uk/news/bristol-news/call-rename-university-bristols-wills-15176.

780 Churchill "Bristol University makes decision over renaming".

781 Major, S. D. *New Illustrated Handbook to Bristol, Clifton, and Neighbourhood* (Bristol: W. Mack, 1872) p. 205.

Dissent and Protest (pp. 255-285)

782 Garrard, *Edward Colston, The Philanthropist, His Life and Times* p. 435.

783 *Bristol Mercury* 16 July 1894

784 *From apprentices to the elderly* p. 9.

785 *Bristol Mercury* 14 November 1895.

786 Ibid.

787 *Bristol Mercury* 13 November 1895.

788 Morgan, "Memory and the merchants" p. 106.

789 Latimer, J. *The Annals of Bristol in the Nineteenth Century (concluded) 1887-1900* (Bristol: William George's Sons, 1902) p. 46.

790 *Arrowsmith's: Dictionary of Bristol* (Bristol: J. W. Arrowsmith, 1906) p. 113.

791 Dunn, *Colston's Girls' School* p. 53.

792 Cotton workers from the Great Western Cotton Factory along with gas workers, miners, dockers and confectionary workers were all involved in long and bitter strikes in the period. For detailed accounts of these events see Backwith, D. et al., *Strikers, Hobblers, Conchies & Reds: A Radical History of Bristol, 1880-1939* (London: Breviary Stuff, 2014).

793 Jordan, *The development and implementation of authority in a regional capital* pp. 326-32. The day after addressing the Anchor Society dinner on 'Colston Day' 13th November 1909, Winston Churchill and his wife Clementine were met on the platform at Temple Meads Railway Station by ardent Suffragette Theresa Garnett. Winston Churchill, a self-proclaimed opponent of votes for women, was attacked by Garnett with a 'dog-whip' who shouted, "Take that, you brute, for the women of England!" Garnett was arrested on the spot and imprisoned where she promptly went on hunger strike and then endured force feeding. Brierley and Reid, *Go Home and Do the Washing!* p. 150 and 153. There was a re-enactment of this event by Bristol Radical History Group in 2009: https://www.brh.org.uk/site/events/suffragette/.

794 Wilkins, *Edward Colston.*

795 Coates, R. *Wilkins of Westbury & Redland: the life and writings of Rev Dr Henry John Wilkins (1865-1941)* (Bristol: ALHA Books No. 24, 2017) p. 14-15.

796 Ibid. p. 15.

797 These included St Wulfstan and the later abolitionists Hannah More and Mary Carpenter.

798 Wilkins, *Edward Colston Supplement* p. 6. Coates also quotes a letter Wilkins wrote to the *Western Daily Press* in 1922 proposing a general celebration of benefactors 'Commemoration day for Bristol'–not just Colston. Coates, *Wilkins of Westbury & Redland* p. 34.

799 Dresser, M. "Remembering Slavery and Abolition in Bristol" *Slavery & Abolition*, 30, no. 2, (2009) p. 227.

800 Steen, M. *The Sun is My Undoing* (Collins: London, 1941). There's a widely held belief in Bristol that the fictional Flood family was based on the Smyth family of Ashton Court.

801 Dresser, "Remembering Slavery and Abolition in Bristol" pp. 227-228.

802 MacInnes, *Bristol: A Gateway of Empire.*

803 MacInnes, *Bristol: A Gateway of Empire* p. 179 and *Bristol and the Slave Trade* p. 8. In the former MacInnes states that "William Colston...became a member of the Royal African Company in 1680". This is clearly an error as it was Edward that is being referred to.

804 MacInnes, *Bristol and the Slave Trade* p. 9.

805 See for example Appendix 5 in Pettigrew, *Freedom's Debt* pp. 240-246.

806 Neptune, "There were two sides to Mr Colston" *Bristol Evening Post* 30 October 1961.

807 For the successful campaign against the colour bar on Bristol buses which momentarily united African-Caribbean workers, radical students and other civil rights activists see Dresser, M. *Black and White on the Buses: The 1963 Colour Bar Dispute in Bristol* (London: Bookmarks, 2013).

808 Robinson, *A Darker History of Bristol* p. 7.

809 Ibid. pp. 60-61.

810 Ibid. p. 78.

811 Foot, David *Famous Bristolians* (Bristol: Redcliffe Press, 1979).

812 See for examples, Marshall, *Bristol and the Abolition of Slavery* (1975); Richardson, *The Bristol Slave Traders: A collective portrait* (1985) and the introductions to the four volumes published by the Bristol Record Society and authored by Richardson, *Bristol, Africa and the Eighteenth-Century Slave Trade to America* (1986-1996).

813 Mahtowin, "First Nations protest celebration of genocide" *Workers World* 10 July 1997.

814 *Bristol Evening Post* 31 July 1995.

815 Ian Bone went on to form the popular anti-corruption scandal sheet *The Bristolian* which remains in print in 2020. Other organisations involved in the protest included the squatting group *Bristol Housing Action Movement* and members of the east Bristol sports club the *Easton Cowboys*. The scale of the protest and the size of the police operation were reflected by the fact that nearly 50 people were arrested. *Western Daily Press* 11 September 1995.

816 *Bristol Evening Post* 9 August 1995.

817 Atkinson, D. and Laurier, E. "A Sanitised City? Social Exclusion at Bristol's 1996 International Festival of the Sea" *Geoforum* 29, no. 2 (1998) p. 199.

818 Criticism was proffered at the time that there was hardly any mention of slavery but this wasn't entirely accurate. Artist Annie Lovejoy was commissioned to contribute her 'Stirring at the International Festival of the Sea' installation artwork: "Lovejoy, a Bristol artist, placed 40,000 sugar packets in cafes and bars within the perimeter fence of the festival boundary. The triangle and circle refer to the 'triangular trade' and the 'Great Circuit' of the slave trade. A postcard showed the sites where the sugar packets were placed". Dresser and Giles, *Bristol and Transatlantic Slavery*, Exhibit 177.

819 For example Charles St John Hartnell, a prominent member of the Society of Merchant Venturers' inner circle, was a director of the company that ran the festival. Cookson, R. Who are the Merchant Venturers? *Venue*, n.d. Accessed March 2018. http://www.public-interest.co.uk/aseye/merchant.htm; "The Bristol International Festival of the Sea (1996) Limited", Companies House, Accessed March 2018. https://beta.companieshouse.gov.uk/company/02860010/officers.

820 Atkinson and Laurier, "A Sanitised City?" p. 199.

821 Ibid. p. 203.

822 Mahtowin, "First Nations protest celebration of genocide" *Workers World* 10 July 1997.

823 It is interesting to note that in most histories of 'Cabot 500' and the *Matthew* the protests in Bristol and Canada have been written out.

824 Wilkins, E. "Graffiti attack revives Bristol slavery row." *The Times* 29 January 1998.

825 The exhibition was visited by 160,000 people.

826 Dresser, "Remembering Slavery and Abolition in Bristol" p. 229.

827 Dresser and Giles, *Bristol and Transatlantic Slavery* p. 57.

828 Onions, I. "Slave Bridge Attack; New name a snub to city benefactor" *Bristol Post*, 17 November 1998. The benefactor in question was John James (1906-1996).

829 It is interesting to note that since 1965, to reflect decolonization and a changing world, the SPG has renamed itself a few times. The organisation is still at work today.

830 The legal reason for announcing a 'statement of regret' rather than an apology is that the former is not an admission of guilt or responsibility. This protected the British state from claims for reparation or compensation for slavery.

831 *The Observer* 26 November 2006.

832 *Bristol Evening Post* 28 November 2006.

833 Dresser, "Remembering Slavery and Abolition in Bristol" pp. 230-231 and 235. The British Empire and Commonwealth Museum opened in 2002 at Temple Meads as a privately funded institution charging admission to visitors. It closed in 2008 after the management claimed it was moving to London, something which failed to happen. In 2011, the director of the museum was dismissed from his post after a police investigation into "unauthorised disposal of museum objects".

834 *Commemorating the abolition of the Slave Trade: Consortium Of Black Groups (COBG)*

Position Statement & Recommendations (2006). The reference to the 'Merchants Quarter' was a controversy over the naming a new shopping centre in Bristol in 2006. Many people found 'Merchants Quarter' offensive with its connections to Bristol's history of slave trading. The name was dropped after complaints and the shopping centre was renamed 'Cabot Circus'. Saville, R. "Bristol shuns slave trade name" *The Telegraph* April 21, 2006.

835 The debate was chaired by the philosopher A.C. Grayling and included the historian Hugh Thomas, Ekow Eshun, the artistic director of the Institute of Contemporary Arts in London, and Isabel Hilton, a *Guardian* columnist. Hall, A. "City agonises over slavery apology" *The Guardian* 7 May 2006.

836 *Bristol Radical History Group Proposal: The 200th anniversary of the abolition of the slave trade*, 12 December 2006.

837 Blackburn, R. "Imperial Margarine" *New Left Review* 35 (2005) p. 128.

838 "Slavery - The Hidden History", Bristol Radical History Group, accessed March 2018. https://www.brh.org.uk/site/event-series/slavery-the-hidden-history-slavery-the-hidden-history/.

839 Dresser, "Remembering Slavery and Abolition in Bristol" p. 231.

840 Ibid. p. 234.

841 Email to authors. Martin, R. 23 July 2017.

842 Dresser, "Remembering Slavery and Abolition in Bristol" p. 238, Fig. 6.

843 Ibid. p. 237.

844 BBC Bristol "Abolition". 26 March 2007. Accessed March 2018. http://www.bbc.co.uk/bristol/content/articles/2007/03/26/abolition_debate_feature.shtml.

845 Dresser, "Remembering Slavery and Abolition in Bristol" p. 233, Fig. 3. There is a great deal of cynicism about 'statements of regret' as legally they are not 'apologies' which may entail an admission of guilt and thus potentially reparation.

846 Bristol Radical History Group "Cry Freedom, Cry Seven Stars" Accessed March 2018. https://www.brh.org.uk/site/events/cry-freedom-cry-seven-stars/.

847 Steeds, M. *Cry Freedom, Cry Seven Stars: Thomas Clarkson In Bristol, 1787*. Bristol Radical Pamphleteer #1, 2nd edition (Bristol: Bristol Radical History Group, 2010). Other donors included Trade Unions and the Lipman-Miliband Trust.

848 It wasn't until the 1920s that St Wulfstan received any recognition in Bristol. A stained-glass window was erected at Holy Trinity Church, Westbury-on-Trym. This depicted a group of significant historic Westbury figures—including St Wulfstan–in memory of Sec. Lt. Henry William Knowlsom Williams who was killed during WWI. This ecclesiastical memorial is the only known recognition of St Wulfstan currently in Bristol.

849 Richardson, *The Bristol Slave Traders* p. 1.

850 *Nantes Memorial to the Abolition of Slavery* Visitors pamphlet (Nantes: 2015).

851 Public Enquiry "Bishop Michael Hill: Merchant Venturer Edward Colston profiting from slave trade is 'speculation'". Filmed [November 2014]. YouTube video, 04:25. Posted [November 2014] https://www.youtube.com/watch?v=tNHBdpvGYHc.

852 "Bristol bishop says slave trader remarks 'misinterpreted'" BBC News Bristol 12 November 2014. Accessed March 2018. http://www.bbc.co.uk/news/uk-england-bristol-30016789; Brown, C. "Bishop defends views on slave trader" *B24/7* 12 November 2014. Accessed March 2018. https://www.bristol247.com/news-and-features/news/bristol-bishop-defends-views-on-slave-trader/.

853 "Slavery protest spun by Colston's school and media" *The Bristolian* n.d. Accessed March 2018. https://thebristolian.net/tag/colston-schools-commemoration-day/.

854 The text of the leaflets for adults and children can be found here: "Colston and slavery still obscured?" *The Bristolian*. n.d. Accessed March 2018. https://thebristolian.net/2015/11/20/colston-and-slavery-still-obscured/. The sources for the leaflet can be found here: "Colston and slavery still obscured?" Bristol Radical History Group. n.d. Accessed March 2018. https://www.brh.org.uk/site/articles/colston-and-slavery-still-obscured/.

855 Perry, A. Letter to parents. Colston Girls School. 13 November 2015.

856 De Bruxelles, S. "Protesters target girls over school's links to slavery" *The Times* 17 November 2015; *Daily Mail* "Schoolgirls face 'slave' protest: Pupils warned about wearing uniforms in public

after protesters target them over link to 17th-century slave trader" 17 November 2015; Francis, W. "Pupils told 'don't wear uniform' for fear of backlash" *The Sun* 17 November 2015; Yong, M. "Pupils at girls' school warned not to engage over slave trade roots" *Bristol Post* 17 November 2015.

857 Countering Colston: Minutes to *Colston School Meeting 17/12/15.*

858 Countering Colston: Minutes to *Meeting between 'Colston Protestors' and representatives of Bristol Cathedral, Bristol Cathedral, 8 December 2015 2.30pm*; Perry, A. Letter to parents. Colston Girls School. 13 November 2015.

859 *Countering Colston* https://counteringcolston.wordpress.com/.

860 Letter to CC from ARE Brown, Chair of Trustees, CGS. 19 September 2016.

861 Letter to CC from Dr David Hoyle, Dean of Bristol, Bristol Cathedral, 2 September 2016. It is interesting to note the reference to the quotation from Colston's will and the foundation of the CGS in relation to an "accurate account of his life and legacy". There was never any direct reference to a 'Girls' School' in Colston's will as CGS was created 170 years later.

862 (Sir) Jimmy Saville (OBE) was a well-known television and radio personality who helped raise over £40 million in charitable donations. Described as a 'prodigious philanthropist', he was accused after his death of being a prolific sex offender, responsible for hundreds of cases of rape and sexual assault involving both adults and minors.

863 Edward Colston's birthday was originally on November 2nd but due to the change from the Julian to Gregorian calendars in 1752 it was revised to November 13th.

864 *Countering Colston* carousel images 273, 275, 276, 279, 280 and 281. Accessed March 2018. https://counteringcolston.wordpress.com/who-was-edward-colston-2/#jp-carousel-273.

865 Churchill, L. "Colston call: Renewed plea to rename venue" *Bristol Post* 9 February 2017, p. 31.

866 Yong, M., Cork, T. and Davies, N. "Colston Hall to be renamed for 2020 relaunch". *Bristol Post* 26 April 2017. Accessed March 2018. https://www.bristolpost.co.uk/news/bristol-news/colston-hall-renamed-2020-relaunch-36108.

867 Yong, M. "Colston Hall name change was a 'moral decision' not a financial one, as bosses gear up for backlash". *Bristol Post* 27 April 2017. Accessed March 2018. https://www.bristolpost.co.uk/news/bristol-news/colston-hall-name-change-moral-37171.

868 Pennock, L. "Comment: 'Renaming Colston Hall is an opportunity to rediscover the hidden history of Bristol'" *Bristol Post* 6 March 2017. Accessed March 2018. https://www.bristolpost.co.uk/news/news-opinion/comment-renaming-colston-hall-opportunity-6353.

869 Pennock, L. "Prominent Tory: Renaming Bristol's Colston Hall 'panders to tiny minority'" *Bristol Post* 28 February 2017. Accessed March 2018. https://www.bristolpost.co.uk/news/bristol-news/prominent-tory-renaming-bristols-colston-4259.

870 Pennock, "Comment: 'Renaming Colston Hall'".

871 Yong et al. "Colston Hall to be renamed for 2020 relaunch".

872 Yong, "Colston Hall name change was a 'moral decision'". One mischievous commentator asked if Eddy was boycotting the Hall "because he will only go to venues that are named after slave-traders?". They went on to point out to Eddy that "Bristol is not named after a slave trader, so please try and boycott the whole city". "Colston Hall Name Change—Hally McHallface?" *The Bristolian*, n.d. Accessed March 2018. https://thebristolian.net/2017/05/03/colston-hall-name-change-hally-mchallface/.

873 See *Bristol Post* letters 28 September, 4 October, 24 October and our response on 6 November 2017.

874 Heaven, W. "Must Edward Colston fall? Bristol's struggle with the complicated legacy of a slaver". *The Spectator* 22 July 2017. Accessed March 2018. https://www.spectator.co.uk/2017/07/must-edward-colston-fall/.

875 *The Community of Saint Stephen's: Annual Report & Accounts 2016*. Accessed March 2018. http://www.saint-stephens.com/pcc-annual-report p. 5.

876 "Colston Day cancellation shocker" *The Bristolian*, n.d. Accessed March 2018. https://thebristolian.net/2017/11/14/colston-day-cancellation-shocker/.

877 Cork, T. "Bristol church refuses to host most important thanksgiving service to honour slave trader Edward Colston for the first time in almost 300 years" *Bristol Post* 15 November 2017. Accessed March 2018. https://www.bristolpost.co.uk/news/bristol-news/bristol-church-refuses-host-most-782798.

878 Cork, T. "Colston's Girls' School Commemoration Day will not mention Edward Colston–but will remember slavery" *Bristol Post* 16 October 2017. Accessed March 2018. https://www.bristolpost.co.uk/news/bristol-news/colstons-girls-school-commemoration-day-640090.

879 Heaven, W. "For his links to slavery, Edward Colston has become he-who-must-not-be-named". *The Spectator* 23 October 2017. Accessed March 2018. https://blogs.spectator.co.uk/2017/10/for-his-links-to-slavery-edward-colston-has-become-he-who-must-not-be-named/.

880 Cork, T. "Buns, sermons and slave songs–how slave trader Edward Colston was awkwardly commemorated on Anti-Slavery Day" *Bristol Post* 20 October 2017. Accessed March 2018. https://www.bristolpost.co.uk/news/bristol-news/buns-sermons-slave-songs-how-652628.

881 The Head teacher explained the new house names in the school newsletter "They are named after George Müller (who was famous for setting up orphanages in Bristol which helped more than 10,000 children), Eric Liddell (who was the Scottish 400m Olympic champion who was featured in the film 'Chariots of Fire'), Olaudah Equiano (who published his autobiography in 1789 and played a major role in the anti-slavery movement), Rosalind Franklin (who took the key X ray crystallography photo that established the structure of DNA) and Katherine Johnson (who worked for NASA as a mathematician and who was one of the people featured in the recent film 'Hidden Figures')". "House Names" *St Mary Redcliffe & Temple School Newsletter* (January 2019).

Conclusion (pp. 286-292)

882 Hochschild, *Bury the Chains* pp. 343-344.
883 Lane, M. *Running!* (London: Macmillan, 1977).

Picture Notes and Credits

Covers and Frontispiece

Front cover—Rysbrack's recumbent Colston tomb (in All Saints' Church, Corn Street) with Saint Wulfstan depicted in a detail from the Goodman Window in Worcester Cathedral. The photograph of the tomb is from *Bristol and its Famous Associations* by S. Hutton (Bristol: Arrowsmith 1907) p387. For more details about the Goodman Window see https://aclerkofoxford.blogspot.com/2013/01/wulfstans-worcester.html

Back cover—"Colston Tower at night glowering down on Pero's Bridge". BRHG Archive.

Frontispiece—Richard Hart unveiling the Seven Stars plaque. BRHG archive.

Introduction

Colston, Cabot and Brunel—BRHG Archive. Edward Colston by John Cassidy, 1895, The Centre. Isambard Kingdom Brunel by John Doublebay, 1982, Temple Back East. John Cabot by Charles Wheeler, 1952, College Green. Cabot's statue is officially titled An Elizabethan Mariner; for details about the claim that it is a statue of Cabot see the Wikipedia page on John Cabot footnote 62, and the Royal Academy of Arts 1952 exhibition catalogue can be found at www.royalacademy.org.uk/art-artists/exhibition-catalogue/ra-sec-vol184-1952, look for item 1423.

Saint Wulfstan

Wulfstan's Worcester—*(Some Chapters on the) Ecclesiastical History of Westbury-on-Trym* by H. Wilkind (Bristol: J. W. Arrowsmith 1909) between pp10 and 11.

Bristol Castle keep—Appears in the border of James Millerd's *Exact Delineation of the Famous Citty of Bristoll and the suburbs thereof*, the map is dated 1671, printed with the border in 1673. See museums.bristol.gov.uk/narratives.php?irn=8787 for more details.

King John's tomb—Photograph by Dun.can on flikr.com. CC Attribution 2.0.

The Carmelite Priory

Map of medieval priories—*Bristol Past and Present. Vol. I* by J. F. Nicholls and J. Taylor (Bristol: J. W. Arrowsmith 1882) p.129.

Ricart's map detail—*The Maire of Bristowe is Kalendar* by Robert Ricart, circa 1479. Reprinted 1872 (London: Camden Society 1872) available on Archive.org. The original 1479 edition is in Bristol Archives.

Sebastian Cabot—*John and Sebastian Cabot. Biographical Notice with Documents* by Francesco Tarducci, translated from Italian by Henry F Brownson (Detroit: H. F. Brownson 1893), frontispiece. Available on Archive.org.

Bishop John Hooper burnt at the stake—Original source unknown.

The Great House

Queen Elizabeth in Bristol—*Bristol Past and Present. Vol. I* by J. F. Nicholls and J. Taylor (Bristol: J. W. Arrowsmith 1882) p. 255.

The Red Lodge— *Bristol Past and Present. Vol. I* by J. F. Nicholls and J. Taylor (Bristol: J. W. Arrowsmith 1882) p. 259.

Robert Thorne's map of 1527—*Divers Voyages Touching the Discoverie of America and the Ilands Adjacent unto the Same, Made First of All by Our Englishmen and Afterwards by the Frenchmen and Britons: With Two Mappes Annexed Hereunto* Richard Hakluyt, 1582. A reprint by the Hakluyt Society, 1859 is on Archive.org.

The Great House—Appears in the border of James Millerd's *Exact Delineation of the Famous Citty of Bristoll and the suburbs thereof,* the map is dated 1671, printed with the border in 1673. See museums.bristol.gov.uk/narratives.php?irn=8787 for more details.

Robert Aldworth's tomb—*How to see Bristol, A Complete and Well Illustrated Guide to the City of Bristol* by C. R. Hudleston (Bristol: J. W. Arrowsmith 1931).

Dorothy Hazard—*Bristol Past and Present. Vol. I* by J. F. Nicholls and J. Taylor (Bristol: J. W. Arrowsmith 1882) p. 91.

James Naylor punished—*James Nailor Quaker set 2 howers on the Pillory at Westminster, whiped by the Hang man to the old Exchange London, Som dayes after, Stood too howers more on the Pillory at the Exchange, and there had his Tongue Bored throug with a hot Iron, & Stigmatized in the Forehead with the Letter: B: Decem: 17 anno Dom: 1656:* by Richard Gaywood (1644 – 1677).

Edward Colston

Royal African Company badge—The original is in the British Museum.

St Peter's Hospital— *How to see Bristol, A Complete and Well Illustrated Guide to the City of Bristol* by C. R. Hudleston (Bristol: J. W. Arrowsmith 1931). Available on Archive.org.

Badge of the Society for the Propagation of the Gospel in Foreign Parts—*An account of the Society for Propagating the Gospel in Foreign Parts, established by the Royal Charter of King William III. With their proceedings and success, and hopes of continual progress under the most happy reign of her most excellent majesty Queen Anne* by Joseph Downing (printer) (London: Joseph Downing 1706), frontispiece. Available on Archive.org.

Detail of Millerd's map—James Millerd's *Exact Delineation of the Famous Citty of Bristoll and the suburbs thereof,* dated 1671, printed with the border in 1673. See museums.bristol.gov.uk/narratives.php?irn=8787 for more details.

Mr Colston's Settlements—*Copies of Mr Colston's Settlements,* Bristol Archives BRO 09478. Reproduced courtesy of Bristol Archives.

Betty's Hope plantation—Photograph © Mark Steeds, 2018.

Bishop Robinson's runic inscription—*How to see Bristol, A Complete and Well Illustrated Guide to the City of Bristol* by C. R. Hudleston (Bristol: J. W. Arrowsmith 1931) p. 114. Available on Archive.org.

The Asiento trade agreement—Title page of the of the English translation of the Asiento, 1713. Available on Wikicommons.

Edward Colston and the South Sea documents—Bristol Archives BRO 42198/6/1. Reproduced courtesy of Bristol Archives.

Slavery, Rebellion and Abolition

Nanny of the Maroons—*The Abolition of Slavery* by Richard Hart (London: Community Education Trust 1989).

Prince Klaas—Photograph © Mark Steeds, 2018.

Silas Told—*Industry and Idleness, Plate 11; The Idle 'Prentice Executed at Tyburn*, 1774 by William Hogarth (1697 - 1764). Available on Wikicommons.

Fort James—*Fort James, Accra*, Engraved by Thomas Medland (1765-1833) after Nicholas Pocock (1740 - 1821) (Bunney & Gold, 1799). From Mark Steeds' collection.

Amistad revolt—*A history of the Amistad captives: being a circumstantial account of the capture of the Spanish schooner Amistad by the Africans on board, their voyage and capture near Long Island, New York, with biographical sketches of each of the surviving Africans: also, an account of the trials had on their case, before the district and circuit courts of the United States for the district of Connecticut* by John W Barber, (New Haven: E.L. & J.W. Barber, 1840), frontispiece. Available on Archive.org.

Merchant and enslaved African woman—*Histoire philosophique et politique des établissemens et du commerce des Européens dans les deux Indes* by Guillaume Thomas Raynal, (The Hague: Gosse & Sons), frontispiece engraved by Nicolas De Launay (1739 - 1792). Available Archive. org (note illustrations vary considerably between editions).

Merchants' Hall—*The History and Antiquities of the City of Bristol* by William Barrett (Bristol: William Pine 1789), pull-out leaf. Reproduced courtesy of Bristol Central Library.

Thomas Clarkson—Charles Turner (1773-1857), after Alfred Edward Chalon (1780-1860), published 1828.

John Wesley addressing the Mayor—*John Wesley Preaching before the Mayor and Corporation of Bristol*, 1788 by William Holt Yates Titcomb (1858 - 1930). Reproduced courtesy of Bristol Museums and Art Gallery.

Romantics triptych—*Samuel Taylor Coleridge*, 1804 by James Northcote (1746–1831), the original is in Dove Cottage and The Wordsworth Museum. *Ann Yearsley, the Bristol Milk Woman and Poetess* by Wilson Lowry (1762–1824) engraving published 1787. *Robert Southey*, 1800 by John James Masquerier (1778–1855).

Toussaint L'Ouverture—*An historical account of the black empire of Hayti: comprehending a view of the principal transactions in the revolution of Saint Domingo; with its antient and modern state* by Marcus Rainsford (London: James Cundee 1805), frontispiece engraved by John Barlow (1759/60 - 1810 or later) from a drawing by Marcus Rainsford. Available on Archive.org.

The Exchange in Corn Street—Cigarette card in Mark Steeds' collection.

White Lion Inn—Broad Street showing the White Hart Hotel, before 1865, Bristol Pictorial Survey, Bristol Central Reference Library 627/L93.11. Reproduced courtesy of Bristol Central Library.

Corruption, Reform and Emancipation

West India Association meeting notice—Bristol Central Reference Library # AN 2712804 0 (M0005920AN). Reproduced courtesy of Bristol Central Library.

Sam Sharpe—*The Abolition of Slavery* by Richard Hart (London: Community Education Trust 1989) p. 29.

Co-joined uprisings in Bristol and Jamaica—Reproduced with kind permission of the artist Rachel Hewitt.

Jamaican schoolroom at the time of the Emancipation—*The Commemorative Wreath: The commemoration of the extinction of negro slavery in the British dominions* (London: Edmund Fry 1835), frontispiece engraved by J Crosland.

Jamaican treadmill—*An interior view of a Jamaica house of correction* (London: Central Emancipation Committee, 1838).

SS Demerara—"Demerara Ashore in the Avon 1851", *A Short History of the Port of Bristol* by Charles Wells (Bristol: J W Arrowsmith 1902) p. 102. Available on Archive.org.

Thomas Daniel—Published E Mitchell print seller Bristol. Bristol Central Reference Library Thomas Daniel Archive #69. Reproduced courtesy of Bristol Central Library.

The Battle Cry Freedom

Thomas Clarkson addressing the London International Slavery Meeting—*The Anti-Slavery Society Convention*, 1840 by Benjamin Robert Haydon (1786 – 1846). The original is in the National Portrait Gallery.

Bristol Blind Asylum—*The Bristol asylum or school of industry for the Blind* drawn by S.C. Jones, T. Rickman published Day & Haghe. Wellcome Collection.

Mary Carpenter—*Bristol Past and Present. Vol. 3* by J.F. Nicholls and J. Taylor (Bristol: J. W. Arrowsmith, 1882) p. 280.

Frederick Douglass—Adapted from a BRHG event flyer, 2018. The original flyer can be seen at brh.org.uk/site/events/the-lion-of-the-occasion-frederick-douglass-in-bristol/.

Anti-Slavery flag—*The anti-slavery harp: a collection of songs for anti-slavery meetings* by William Wells Brown (Boston: B. Marsh 1849), inside back-cover. Available on Archive.org.

William Wells Brown—*Narrative of William W. Brown, a fugitive slave* by William Wells Brown (Boston: Anti-slavery Office 1847), frontispiece. Available on Archive.org.

Ellen Craft—"Mary Carpenter's Poetical Extract Book" Bristol Archives 12693/20. Reproduced courtesy of Bristol Archives.

Old Dominion—Atlas Civil War Cards 10.10 Blockade Running Ship *Old Dominion*.

Miles bank note—*A History of Banking in Bristol from 1750 to 1899* by Charles Henry Cave (Bristol: W Croft Hemmans 1899). Reproduced courtesy of Bristol Central Library.

The Cult of Colston

Colston's old school—*Colston's School, Bristol* engraved by John McGahey, drawn by G. Price. Wellcome Collection.

New Colston Hall—By Samuel Loxton (1857 - 1922) in *Bristol: As it was and as it is. A record of fifty years of progress* G. F. Stone (Bristol: Walter Reid, 1909) p. 202.

Colston Window—Photograph © Jacek Wojnarowski.

The Bristol Magpie cartoon—*Bristol Magpie* November 15, 1906 pp. 8-9. Reproduced courtesy of Bristol Central Library.

Rocque's map—*Bristol: As it was and as it is. A record of fifty years of progress* G. F. Stone (Bristol: Walter Reid, 1909) p. 214.

Colston Hall and Tower—BRHG Archive.

Bristol University arms and logo—Reproduced as "fair dealings" Copyright, Designs and Patents Act 1988 Section 29(1).

Dissent and Protest

Colston statue and panels—BRHG Archive.

Book cover—*Shocking History of Bristol* by Derek Robinson (Abson Books, 1973).

Replica of the *Matthew*—BRHG Archive.

Codrington College—"Church History Exhibitions B.4236" Bristol Central Reference Library Reproduced courtesy of Bristol Central Library.

BRHG poster—A BRHG poster for Slavery – The Hidden History in 2007. The engraving of Leonard Parkinson is from *Proceedings of the governor and Assembly of Jamaica, in regard to the Maroon negroes: published by order of the Assembly. To which is prefixed, An introductory account, containing, observations on the disposition, character, manners, and habits of life, of the Maroons, and a detail of the origin, progress, and termination of the late war between those people and the white inhabitants* (London: John Stockdale 1796), frontispiece engraved by Abraham Raimbach (1776 – 1843); there is a copy on Archive.org.

150th anniversary pop-up banner—The banner was produced by Countering Colston in 2017 to mark the 150th anniversary of Colston Hall. The design mimicked the official art work for the commemoration. The picture is from the BRHG Archive.

Colour Plates

Colston's coat of arms—The original is in The Red Lodge Museum, Bristol. Photograph © Mark Steeds, 2018.

Florence Smyth—*Daughter of Thomas and Florence Smyth of Ashton Court, with her Black Page* by Gilbert Jackson (c.1595/1600 – after 1648). Reproduced courtesy of Bristol Museums and Art Gallery. The portrait hangs in the Red Lodge, Bristol.

Colston on his deathbed—*The Death of Edward Colston* by Richard Jeffreys Lewis (1822/1823 – 1883). Reproduced courtesy of Bristol Museums and Art Gallery.

Wills 'Three Castles' cigarette—From Mark Steeds' collection.

Sold Down the River—*Sold Down the River*, 1999 by Tony Forbes (1964-). The original is in M Shed, Bristol. Reproduced courtesy of Bristol Museums and Art Gallery.

Bristol ablaze 1831—*The City of Bristol As it appeared generally on Sunday night (time from 6 to 12 o'clock) 30th Octbr 1831. When the New Gaol, the Toll Houses, the Bishops Palace, two sides of Queen Square, including the Mansion House, Custom House, Excise Office Warehouses with various other Buildings & other property to the Amount of upwards of One Hundred Thousand Pounds Sterling was totally Destroyed. From a Scetch Taken From Brandon Hill* by C H Walters (London: John Bysh).

Bibliography

Books, Journals and Articles

A new and general biographical dictionary; containing an historical and critical account of the lives and writings of the most eminent persons in every nation; Particularly The British And Irish; From the earliest Accounts of time to the present period. Wherein Their remarkable Actions and Sufferings, Their Virtues, Parts, and Learning, Are Accurately Displayed. With a Catalogue of their Literary Productions. London: W. Strahan et al., 1784.

An Account of the Proceedings of the Great Western Railway Company: With extracts from the evidence in support of the bill before the committee of the House of Commons in the session of 1834. London: Smith & Ebbs, 1834.

Aitken, J. *John Newton—from Disgrace to Amazing Grace.* London: Continuum, 2000.

Alford, B. W. E. *W.D. & H. O. Wills and the development of the U.K. tobacco industry 1786-1965* London: Methuen, 1973.

Anderson, J. and Dunn, R. *Between slavery and freedom: special magistrate John Anderson's journal of St. Vincent during the Apprenticeship* Philadelphia: University of Pennsylvania Press, 2001.

Arrowsmith's: Dictionary of Bristol (Bristol: J. W. Arrowsmith, 1906).

Atkinson, D. and Laurier, E. "A Sanitised City? Social Exclusion at Bristol's 1996 International Festival of the Sea" *Geoforum* 29, no. 2 (1998): 199- 206.

Atterton, G. *Cotton Threads–The History of the Great Western Cotton Factory* Bristol: Barton Hill History Group, 2015.

Backwith, D., Ball, R., Hunt, S. and Richardson, M. *Strikers, Hobblers, Conchies and Reds: A Radical History of Bristol, 1880-1939.* London: Breviary Stuff, 2014.

Ball, R., Parkin, D. and Mills, S. *100 Fishponds Road: Life and Death in a Victorian Workhouse* Bristol Radical Pamphleteer #34 2nd edt. Bristol: Bristol Radical History Group, 2016.

Ball, R. *The guillotine, knitting and terror...So you think you know about the French Revolution* Bristol: Bristol Radical History Group, 2014. Retrieved from http://www.brh.org.uk/site/articles/guillotine-knitting-terror/.

Ball, R. Edward Colston Research Paper #1: *Calculating the number of enslaved Africans transported by the Royal African Company during Edward Colston's involvement (1680-92)* Bristol: Bristol Radical History Group, 2017. Retrieved from http://www.brh.org.uk/site articles/edward-colston-research-paper-1/.

Ball, R. Edward Colston Research Paper #2: *The Royal African Company and Edward Colston (1680-92).* Bristol: Bristol Radical History Group, 2017. Retrieved from http://www.brh.org

uk/site/articles/edward-colston-research-paper-2/.

Barker, P. and Guy, C. (Eds.) *St Wulfstan 1008 – 1095 His Life and Times*. Revised edition. Worcester: Worcester Cathedral, 2008.

Barrett, W. *The History and Antiquities of the City of Bristol*. Bristol: William Pine, 1789.

Belchem J. *'Orator' Hunt: Henry Hunt and English Working Class Radicalism*. London: Breviary Stuff, 2012.

Benezet, A. *Some Historical Account of Guinea...with an Inquiry Into the Rise and Progress of the Slave Trade...: Also a Republication of the Sentiments of Several Authors...Particularly an Extract of a Treatise Written by Granville Sharpe*. London: W. Owen, E. and C. Dilly, 1772.

Bennett, R. J. *Local Business Voice: The History of Chambers of Commerce in Britain, Ireland, and Revolutionary America, 1760-2011*, Oxford: Oxford University Press, 2012.

Behrendt, S. D., Eltis, D. and Richardson, D., "The Costs of Coercion: African Agency in the Pre-Modern Atlantic World". *The Economic History Review*, 54 (2001): 454-476.

Best, G. M. *The Cradle of Methodism 1739 – 2017* Bristol: New Room Publications, 2017.

Best, G. M. *In Their Words, the Story of Early Methodism* Bristol: New Room Publications, 2018.

Bettey, J. H. *Bristol Observed: Visitors' Impressions of the City from Domesday to the Blitz*. Bristol: Redcliffe Press, 1986.

Bettey, J. H. "Feuding Gentry and an Affray on College Green, Bristol, in 1579" *Transactions of the Bristol and Gloucestershire Archaeological Society* 122 (2004): 153-159.

Blackburn, R. *The Overthrow of Colonial Slavery 1776-1848*. London: Verso, 1988.

Blackburn, R. *The Making of New World Slavery: From the Baroque to the Modern 1492-1800*. London: Verso, 1998.

Blackburn, R. "Imperial Margarine" *New Left Review* 35 (2005): 124-136.

Blackburn, R. *The American Crucible: Slavery, Emancipation and Human Rights*. London: Verso, 2011.

Boa, S. "Experiences of women estate workers during the apprenticeship period in St Vincent, 1834–38: the transition from slavery to freedom" *Women's History Review*, 10:3, (2001): 381-408.

Bradley, J., Dyer, D., Lalla, R. and Beeson, A. *Slavery, Abolition and Emancipation: A Reading List*. Bristol: Bristol Libraries, 2009.

Breward, M. "Crewing the Slave Trade: The Bristol Ships' Muster Rolls, 1790-1795" in Poole, S. (Ed.) *A City Built Upon the Water—Maritime Bristol 1750-1900*. Bristol: Redcliffe/Regional History Centre UWE, 2013.

Brierley, L. and Reid, H. *Go Home and Do the Washing! Three Centuries of Pioneering Bristol Women*. Bristol: Broadcast Books, 2000.

Bristol Riots, 1831: Report of the Commissioners Appointed Under the Bristol Damages Compensation Act, and Statement of Actions for Damages, and Proceedings Had Therein Under that Act with Their General Results. Bristol: John Taylor, 1835.

Brown, C. "Bishop defends views on slave trader" *B24/7* 12 November 2014. Accessed March 2018. https://www.bristol247.com/news-and-features/news/bristol-bishop-defends-views-on-slave-trader/

Brown, H. and Harris, P. J. *Bristol, England*. Bristol: Burleigh Press, 1971.

Brown, P., "Representations of Rebellion: Slavery in Jamaica, 1823-1831" (2014). All Theses. 1984. https://tigerprints.clemson.edu/all_theses/1984

Brown, W. W. *The Anti-Slavery Harp; A Collection of Songs for Anti-Slavery Meetings*. Boston: Bela Marsh, 1848.

Brown, W. W. *The American Fugitive in Europe: Sketches of Places and People Abroad*. Boston: John P. Jewett and Company, 1855.

Bryant, J. *Account of an Insurrection of the Negro Slaves in the Colony of Demerara, which Broke Out on the 18th of August, 1823*. Georgetown: A. Stevenson, 1824.

Bush G. *Bristol and its Municipal Government 1820-51* Bristol: Bristol Records Society, 1976.

Burgess, A. *City and Port of Bristol*. Bristol: Somerton W. H. printer Bristol Mercury Office, 1836.

Burke, E. "Sketch of the Negro code" in *The Works of the Right Honourable Edmund Burke, Vol. 5.* New York: Eastburn, Kirk and Co. and West and Richardson, and Oliver C. Greenleaf, 1813.

Burroughs, E. A. *Bristol Cathedral—Its History, Architecture, Associations and Mission.* Bristol: Partridge and Love Ltd, 1924.

Burroughs, R. "Suppression of the Atlantic slave trade: abolition from ship to shore" in *The suppression of the Atlantic slave trade: British policies, practices and representation of naval coercion.* Burroughs, R. and Huzzey, R. (Eds.) Manchester: Manchester University Press, 2018.

Buchholdt, M. "The Wider Family of Colston." *The Bristol Templar,* (1992).

Button, A. *Bristol's White Slave Trade: Indentured and Enforced Labour In The 17th Century.* Bristol Radical Pamphleteer #13. Bristol: Bristol Radical History Group, 2010.

Caffentzis, G. *John Locke: The Philosopher of Primitive Accumulation.* Bristol Radical Pamphleteer #5. Bristol: Bristol Radical History Group, 2008.

Charles, G. W. "The Merchant Venturers' Technical College, Bristol" *The Vocational Aspect of Secondary and Further Education,* 3 No. 6, (1951): 86-89.

Chilcott, J. *Chilcott's descriptive history of Bristol, ancient and modern: or, A guide to Bristol, Clifton, & the Hotwell: including an account of the Bristol riots: with topographical notices of the neighbouring villages, etc.* 3rd ed., improved. Bristol: J. Chilcott, 1835.

Churchill, L. "Colston call Renewed plea to rename venue" *Bristol Post* 9 February 2017.

Clark, W. E., *Josiah Tucker, Economist: A Study in the History of Economics* (New York: Columbia University Press, 1903).

Clarke, C. C. *The Society of Merchant Venturers of Bristol—by Charles Cyril Clarke (Master 1920-21) being a Lecture given at the Royal Colonial Institute, Bristol, on Jan 2nd, 1922.* Bristol: J. W. Arrowsmith, 1922.

Clarkson, T. *An Essay on the Slavery and Commerce of the Human Species, Particularly the African, Translated from a Latin Dissertation, Which Was Honoured With the First Prize in the University of Cambridge, for the Year 1785, With Additions.* London: J. Phillips, 1786. Accessed 2018. http://www.gutenberg.org/ebooks/10611.

Clarkson, T. *The history of the rise, progress, and accomplishment of the abolition of the African slave-trade, by the British Parliament. Vol. I.* New York: John S. Taylor, 1836.

Clarkson, T. *The history of the rise, progress, and accomplishment of the abolition of the African slave-trade, by the British Parliament. Vol. II.* London: Longman, Hurst, Rees and Orme, 1808.

Coates, R. *Wilkins of Westbury & Redland: the life and writings of Rev Dr Henry John Wilkins (1865-1941).* Bristol: ALHA Books No. 24, 2017.

Cobb, P. C. *The Stained Glass of St Mary Redcliffe, Bristol* Transcript of the Bristol and Gloucestershire Archaeological Society CXII (1994), 143-166.

Colston's Chronicle "Heritage Day" Newsletter of CGS Edition XXXI Summer 2012.

Cookson, R. Who are the Merchant Venturers? *Venue,* n.d. Accessed March 2018. http://www.public-interest.co.uk/aseye/merchant.htm.

Cork, T. "Colston's Girls' School Commemoration Day will not mention Edward Colston–but will remember slavery" *Bristol Post* 16 October 2017. Accessed March 2018. https://www.bristolpost.co.uk/news/bristol-news/colstons-girls-school-commemoration-day-640090

Cork, T. "Buns, sermons and slave songs–how slave trader Edward Colston was awkwardly commemorated on Anti-Slavery Day" *Bristol Post* 20 October 2017. Accessed March 2018. https://www.bristolpost.co.uk/news/bristol-news/buns-sermons-slave-songs-how-652628.

Cork, T. "Bristol church refuses to host most important thanksgiving service to honour slave trader Edward Colston for the first time in almost 300 years" *Bristol Post* 15 November 2017. Accessed March 2018. https://www.bristolpost.co.uk/news/bristol-news/bristol-church-refuses-host-most-782798

Corporation of Bristol, *Bristol England—The Official Handbook of the Corporation of Bristol 1962-63.* Bristol: Corporation of Bristol, 1963.

Corry, J. and Evans, Rev. J., *History of Bristol,* Bristol: W. Shepherd, London: Longman and Co 1816.

Coules, V. *The Trade: Bristol and the Transatlantic Slave Trade.* Edinburgh: Birlinn, 2007.

Cowper, W. *The Negro's Complaint.* 1788.

Cox, E. L. "Fedon's Rebellion 1795-96: Causes and Consequences," *The Journal of Negro History* 67, no. 1 (Spring 1982): 7-19.

Craton, M. "Proto-Peasant Revolts? The Late Slave Rebellions in the British West Indies 1816-1832." *Past & Present*, no. 85 (1979): 99-125.

Daily Mail "Schoolgirls face 'slave' protest: Pupils warned about wearing uniforms in public after protesters target them over link to 17th-century slave trader" 17 November 2015.

Darwin, J. "Imperialism and the Victorians: the dynamics of territorial expansion." *The English Historical Review* 112, no. 447 (1997): 614-642.

Davies, K. G. *The Royal African Company.* London: Longmans, Green & Co., 1957.

Davis, D. B. *The Problem of Slavery in Western Culture.* New York: Oxford University Press, 1966.

Davis, D. B. "The Emergence of Immediatism in British and American Antislavery Thought." *The Mississippi Valley Historical Review* 49, no. 2 (1962), p. 219.

De Bruxelles, S. "Protesters target girls over school's links to slavery" *The Times* 17 November 2015.

Dresser, M. *Black and White on the Buses: The 1963 Colour Bar Dispute in Bristol* London: Bookmarks, 2013.

Dresser, M. *Slavery Obscured: The Social History of the Slave Trade in Bristol.* Bristol: Redcliffe Press, 2007.

Dresser, M. "Remembering Slavery and Abolition in Bristol" *Slavery & Abolition*, 30, no. 2, (2009): 223-246.

Dresser, M. (Ed.) *Women and the City: Bristol 1373-2000.* Bristol: Redcliffe/Regional History Centre UWE, 2016.

Dresser, M. "Daniel, Thomas (1762–1854), merchant." *Oxford Dictionary of National Biography.* 2016. Accessed July 2018. http://www.oxforddnb.com.ezproxy.sussex.ac.uk/view/10.1093/ref:odnb/9780198614128.001.0001/odnb-9780198614128-e-107411

Dresser, M. and Fleming, P. *Bristol: Ethnic Minorities and the City 1000 – 2001,* London: Phillimore, 2007.

Dresser, M. and Giles, S. (Eds.) *Bristol and Transatlantic Slavery* (Catalogue of the exhibition 'A Respectable Trade? Bristol and Transatlantic Slavery'–1999). Bristol: Bristol Museum and Art Gallery, 2000.

Drummond, M. M. "LAROCHE, James (1734-1804), of Over, nr. Bristol, Glos." In *The History of Parliament: the House of Commons 1754-1790,* ed. Namier, L. and Brooke J., London: Boydell and Brewer, 1964. Accessed 2019. https://www.historyofparliamentonline.org/volume/1754-1790/member/laroche-james-1734-1804

Dryden, J. "Pas de Six Ans!" in *Seven Slaves & Slavery: Trinidad 1777–1838,* A. de Verteuil, Port of Spain: 1992.

Dunn, S. *Colston Girls' School: The First Hundred Years.* Bristol: Redcliffe, 1991.

Eason, H. *Bristol's Historic Inns.* Bristol: Redcliffe Press 1982.

Eltis, D. "The Volume and African Origins of the British Slave Trade before 1714." *Cahiers d'études Africaines,* Vol. 35, no. 138-139 (1995): 617-627.

Emden, P. H. *Quakers in Commerce—A Record of Business Achievement* London: Sampson Low, Marston & Co., Ltd. 1939.

English, C. "Guy, John (c.1575 – 1628), colonial governor." *Oxford Dictionary of National Biography.* https://doi.org/10.1093/ref:odnb/11799. Accessed July 2018.

Equiano, O. *The Interesting Narrative of the Life of Olaudah Equiano, Or Gustavus Vassa, The African. Written by himself.* London: Equiano, 1789. http://www.gutenberg.org/files/15399/15399-h/15399-h.htm. Accessed 2018.

Evans, J. *A Chronological Outline of the History of Bristol, and the Stranger's Guide Through its Streets and Neighbourhood.* Bristol: Printed at the Office of the late 'Bristol Observer', 1824.

Farr, G. *The SS Great Western, the first Atlantic Liner,* Bristol: Branch of the Historical Association the University, Bristol. Third Printing 1988.

Farr, J. "Locke, Natural Law, and New World Slavery." *Political Theory* Vol. 36, no. 4 (2008): 495-522.

Farrell, S. and Fisher, D. R. "MILES, Philip John (1774-1845), of Leigh Court, Abbots Leigh, Som." in *The History of Parliament: the House of Commons 1820-1832*, ed. Fisher, D. R. London: Cambridge University Press, 2009. http://www.historyofparliamentonline.org/volume/1820-1832/member/miles-philip-1774-1845 Accessed 2017.

Fenton, L. *'I Was Transformed' Frederick Douglass: An American Slave in Victorian Britain* Stroud: Amberley Publishing, 2018.

Fisher, D. R. "Bristol" *The History of Parliament: the House of Commons 1790-1820*, ed. Thorne, R. London: Boydell & Brewer, 1986. Accessed 2018. http://www.historyofparliamentonline.org/volume/1790-1820/constituencies/bristol

Fleming, P. and Costello, K. *(Discovering) Cabot's Bristol*. Bristol: Redcliffe Press, 1998.

Foot, D. *Famous Bristolians*. Bristol: Redcliffe Press, 1979.

Foyle, A. *Bristol, Pevsner Architectural Guides*. New Haven & London: Yale University Press, 2004.

Francis, W. "Pupils told 'don't wear uniform' for fear of backlash" *The Sun* 17 November 2015.

Freeman, A. B. *Bristol Worthies and notable residents in the district*. 1st series. Bristol: Burleigh Press, 1907.

Freeman, A. B. *Bristol Worthies and notable residents in the district*. 2nd series. Bristol: Burleigh Press, 1909.

From apprentices to the elderly: Celebrating 250 years of the Grateful Society. Bristol: Grateful Society, 2008.

Frucht, R. "Emancipation and Revolt in the West Indies: St. Kitts, 1834" *Science & Society*, Vol. 39, No. 2 (Summer, 1975).

Fryer, P. *Staying Power—The History of Black People in Britain*. London: Pluto Press, 1984.

Garrard, T. *Edward Colston, The Philanthropist, His Life and Times*. Bristol: J. Chilcott, 1852.

Gaspar, D. B. "Slavery, amelioration, and Sunday markets in Antigua, 1823-1831" *Slavery and Abolition*, 9:1 (1988) 1-28.

Geggus, D. "Communications: The cost of Pitt's Caribbean Campaigns, 1793 – 1798" *The Historical Journal*, 26, no. 3 (1983) 699-706.

Gifford, Z. *Thomas Clarkson and the Campaign Against Slavery*, London: Anti-Slavery International, 1996.

Grimshaw, E. "Stained Glass Window has Colston Link" *Bristol Post* 23 February 2017.

Greenacre, F. *From Bristol to the Sea–Artists, the Avon Gorge and Bristol Harbour*. Bristol: Redcliffe Press, 2005.

Griffiths, K. and Steeds, M. *Pirates and Privateers out of Bristol*. Bristol: Fiducia Press, 2010.

Hague, W. *William Pitt the Younger*. London: HarperCollins, 2004.

Hall, A. "City agonises over slavery apology" *The Guardian* 7 May 2006.

Hall, I. V. *A history of the sugar trade in England with special attention to the sugar trade of Bristol*. Unpublished MA thesis, University of Bristol, 1925.

Hanham, A. A. "Bristol" in *The History of Parliament: The House of Commons 1690-1715*, eds Hayton, D., Cruickshanks, E. and Handley, S. London: Boydell and Brewer, 2002. Accessed 2018. https://www.historyofparliamentonline.org/volume/1690-1715/constituencies/bristol

Hanham, A. A. "COLSTON, Edward II (1636-1721), of Mortlake, Surr." in *The History of Parliament: The House of Commons 1690-1715*, eds. Hayton, D., Cruickshanks, E. and Handley S. London: Boydell and Brewer, 2002. Accessed 2017. http://www.historyofparliamentonline org/volume/1690-1715/member/colston-edward-ii-1636-1721

Hanham, A. A. "DAINES, Sir William (1647-1724), of St. Leonard's, Bristol" in *The History of Parliament: The House of Commons 1690-1715*, eds. Hayton, D., Cruickshanks, E. and Handley S. London: Boydell and Brewer, 2002. Accessed 2017. http://www.historyofparliamentonline org/volume/1690-1715/member/daines-sir-william-1647-1724

Hanham, A. A. "EDWARDS, Thomas (c.1673-by 1743), of the Middle Temple and Filkin

Hall, Oxon." in *The History of Parliament: The House of Commons 1690-1715*, eds. Hayton, D., Cruickshanks, E. and Handley, S. London: Boydell and Brewer, 2002. Accessed 2018. http://www.historyofparliamentonline.org/volume/1690-1715/member/edwards-thomas-1673-1743

Hanham, J. and Martin, M. "Women in Bristol 1835-1914" in Dresser, M. (Ed.) *Women and the City: Bristol 1373-2000* Bristol: Redcliffe/Regional History Centre UWE, 2016.

Harris, C. *Three Continents, One History: Birmingham, the Transatlantic Slave Trade and the Caribbean* (Birmingham: Afro-Caribbean Millennium Centre, 2008).

Hart, R. *From Occupation to Independence: A Short History of the Peoples of the English-speaking Caribbean*. London: Pluto Press, 1998.

Hart, R. *The Abolition of Slavery* London: Community Education Trust, 1989.

Hayton, D. W. Appendix XXVI: Contemporary lists of Members. Published in The History of Parliament: the House of Commons 1690-1715, ed. D. Hayton, E. Cruickshanks, S. Handley, 2002.

Hawkesbury Local History Society *Hawkesbury Chronicles 972-1899AD*. Hawkesbury: Hawkesbury Local History Society, 2008.

Heath, G. *The History, Antiquities, Survey and Description, Of the City and Suburbs of Bristol.* 2nd Edition. Bristol: W. Matthews, 1797.

Heaven, W. "Must Edward Colston fall? Bristol's struggle with the complicated legacy of a slaver". *The Spectator* 22 July 2017. Accessed March 2018. https://www.spectator.co.uk/2017/07/must-edward-colston-fall/

Heaven, W. "For his links to slavery, Edward Colston has become he-who-must-not-be-named". *The Spectator* 23 October 2017. Accessed March 2018. https://blogs.spectator.co.uk/2017/10/for-his-links-to-slavery-edward-colston-has-become-he-who-must-not-be-named/

Hochschild, A. *Bury the Chains: The British Struggle to Abolish Slavery*. London: Macmillan, 2005.

Horne, G. *The Counter-Revolution of 1776: Slave resistance and the origins of the United States of America*. New York: NYU Press, 2014.

Hudleston, C. R. *How to see Bristol, A Complete and Well Illustrated Guide to the City of Bristol.* Bristol: J. W. Arrowsmith, 1931.

Hunt, T. "A jewel of democracy", *The Guardian*, 26 October 2007. https://www.theguardian.com/world/2007/oct/26/humanrights.past

Hutton, S. *Bristol and its Famous Associations*. Bristol: J. W. Arrowsmith, 1907.

Huzzey, R. "The politics of slave-trade suppression" in *The suppression of the Atlantic slave trade: British policies, practices and representation of naval coercion*. Burroughs, R. and Huzzey, R. (Eds.) Manchester: Manchester University Press, 2018.

Jackson, M. *Let This Voice Be Heard: Anthony Benezet. Father of Atlantic Abolitionism.* Pennsylvania: Penn Press, 2009.

James, C. L. R. *The Black Jacobins*, London: Penguin, 2001.

James, W. *Memoir of John Bishop Estlin*, London: Charles Green, Hackney. 1855.

Jenkins, T. "DAVIS, Richard Hart (1766-1842), of Mortimer House, Clifton, Glos. and 38 Conduit Street, Mdx." in *The History of Parliament: the House of Commons 1820-1832*, ed. Fisher, J. R. London: Cambridge University Press, 2009. Accessed 2018. http://www.historyofparliamentonline.org/volume/1820-1832/member/davis-richard-1766-1842

Jenkins, T. "Bristol" in *The History of Parliament: the House of Commons 1820-1832*, ed. Fisher, D. R. London: Cambridge University Press, 2009. Accessed 2018. http://www.historyofparliamentonline.org/volume/1820-1832/constituencies/bristol

Jenks, L. H. *The Origin of the South Sea Company 1710–1714*. Unpublished M.A. Thesis University of Kansas, 1914.

Jones, P. *Satan's Kingdom: Bristol and the Transatlantic Slave Trade*. Bristol: Past and Present Press, 2007.

Jordan, S. *The development and implementation of authority in a regional capital: a study of Bristol's elites, 1835-1939*. Unpublished PhD Thesis, University of West of England, 1999.

Kupperman, K. O. "Errand to the Indies: Puritan Colonization from Providence Island through the Western Design." *The William and Mary Quarterly* 45, no. 1 (1988): 70-99.

Kupperman, K. O. *Providence Island, 1630-1641: the other Puritan colony.* London: Cambridge University Press, 1995.

Kurlansky, M. *Cod: A Biography of the Fish That Changed the World.* London: Vintage, 1999.

Lamoine, G. *Bristol Gaol Delivery Fiats 1741-1799.* Bristol: Bristol Record Society, 1989.

Lane, M. *Running!* London: Macmillan, 1977.

Large, D. *Radicalism in Bristol in the Nineteenth Century.* Bristol: Bristol Record Society, 1981.

Latimer, J. *The Annals of Bristol in the Nineteenth Century.* Bristol: W. & F. Morgan, 1887.

Latimer, J. *The Annals of Bristol in the Eighteenth Century.* Bristol: W. & F. Morgan, 1898.

Latimer, J. *The Annals of Bristol in the Seventeenth Century.* Bristol: William George's Sons, 1900.

Latimer, J. *The Annals of Bristol in the Nineteenth Century (concluded) 1887-1900.* Bristol: William George's Sons, 1902.

Latimer, J. *The History of the Society of Merchant Venturers of the City of Bristol.* Bristol: J. W. Arrowsmith, 1903.

Laurence, A. "The Emergence of a Private Clientele for Banks in the Early Eighteenth Century: Hoare's Bank and Some Women Customers" *The Economic History Review,* New Series, 61, no. 3 (August, 2008): 565-586.

Lea, R. S. "EDWARDS, Thomas (?1673-1743), of the Middle Temple, London, and Filkins Hall, Oxon." in *The History of Parliament: The House of Commons 1715-1754,* ed. Sedgwick, R. R. London: Boydell and Brewer, 1970. Accessed 2017. http://www.historyofparliamentonline.org/volume/1715-1754/member/edwards-thomas-1673-1743

Leifchild, J. *Memoir of the late Rev. Joseph Hughes, A.M.* London: Thomas Ward and Co. 1835.

Little, B. *The City and County of Bristol -A Study of Atlantic Civilisation.* Republished Wakefield: S. R. Publishers Limited, 1967. First published Birmingham and London: T. Werner Laurie Limited, 1954.

Linebaugh, P. and Rediker, M. *The Many-Headed Hydra: Sailors, slaves, commoners, and the hidden history of the revolutionary Atlantic.* London: Verso, 2000.

Lowther Clarke, W. K. *A History of the S.P.C.K.* London: SPCK, 1959.

McCartney, M. Virginia's First Africans. In *Encyclopedia Virginia.* (accessed 23 December 2018) http://www.EncyclopediaVirginia.org/Virginia_s_First_Africans.

MacInnes, C. M. *Bristol and the Slave Trade.* Bristol: Bristol Branch of the Historical Association, 1963.

MacInnes, C. M. *Bristol: A Gateway of Empire.* Newton Abbot: David & Charles (Holdings), 1968.

Major, S. D. *New Illustrated Handbook to Bristol, Clifton, and Neighbourhood.* Bristol: W. Mack, 1872.

Malpass, P. *The Bristol Dock Company, 1803-1848.* Bristol: ALHA Books, 2010.

Manson, M. *"Riot!" The Bristol Bridge Massacre of 1793.* Bristol: Bristol Books, 2013. First published 1997.

Manton, J. *Mary Carpenter and the Children of the Streets,* London: Heinemann Educational Books Ltd., 1976.

Marshall, E. *In Colston's Days: A Story of Old Bristol.* London: Seeley and Co., 1901. First published 1883.

Marshall, P. *Bristol and the Abolition of Slavery—The Politics of Emancipation.* Bristol: Bristol Branch of the Historical Association, 1975.

Mathew, M. *1869 Trade Directory for Bristol*

Matthews, S. "DAINES, Sir William (c.1656-1724), of Bristol, Glos" in *The History of Parliament. The House of Commons 1715-1754,* ed. Sedgwick, R. London: Boydell and Brewer, 1970. Accessed 2017. http://www.historyofparliamentonline.org/volume/1715-1754/member daines-sir-william-1656-1724

Mayer, H. *All on Fire—William Lloyd Garrison and the Abolition of Slavery.* New York: St. Martin's Press, 1998.

McFerran, A. *Elizabeth Blackwell First Woman Doctor,* New York: Grosset & Dunlap, 1966.

McGrath, P. *The Merchant Venturers of Bristol.* Bristol: The Society of Merchant Venturers of the City of Bristol, 1975.

McNeill, J. *The Life and Family of William Penn.* Bristol Radical Pamphleteer #18. Bristol: Bristol Radical History Group, 2012.

Merritt, D. *Sculpture in Bristol.* Bristol: Redcliffe Press, 2002.

Mills, S. *A Barbarous and Ungovernable People!* Bristol Radical Pamphleteer #11. Bristol: Bristol Radical History Group, 2009.

Mintz, S. W. *Sweetness and Power: The place of sugar in modern history.* New York: Viking Penguin, 1985.

Morgan, K. *Edward Colston and Bristol.* Bristol: Bristol Branch of the Historical Association, 1999.

Morgan, S. "Memory and the merchants: Commemoration and civic identity". *International Journal of Heritage Studies.* 4, no. 2 (1998): 103-113.

Nantes Memorial to the Abolition of Slavery Visitors pamphlet (Nantes: 2015).

National Westminster Bank *Three Banks in Bristol: The National Westminster Bank in Corn Street 1750-1980.* National Westminster Bank Stationery and Purchasing Department, n.d.

Nicholls, J. F. and Taylor, J. *Bristol Past and Present.* Vol. I, II and III. Bristol: J. W. Arrowsmith, 1882.

Nicholls, J. F. and Taylor, J. (and other authors) *Bristol and its Environs.* London: Houlston and Sons; Bristol: J. Wright & Co. 1875.

Patterson, O. "Slavery and slave revolts: A socio-historical analysis of the First Maroon War Jamaica, 1655-1740." *Social and Economic Studies* Vol. 19, No. 3, (1970): 289-325.

Parker, M. *The Sugar Barons: Family, Corruption, Empire and War* London: Hutchinson, 2011.

Peile, J. H. F. (Trans.) *William of Malmesbury's Life of Saint Wulfstan: Bishop of Worcester* (Original version, 1934). Burnham-on-Sea: Llanerch Press, 1996.

Pelteret, D. A. E. *Slavery in Early Medieval England: From the Reign of Alfred until the Twelfth Century.* Suffolk: Boydell and Brewer, 2001.

Pennock, L. "Comment: 'Renaming Colston Hall is an opportunity to rediscover the hidden history of Bristol'" *Bristol Post* 6 March 2017. Accessed March 2018. https://www.bristolpost.co.uk/news/news-opinion/comment-renaming-colston-hall-opportunity-6353.

Pennock, L. "Prominent Tory: Renaming Bristol's Colston Hall 'panders to tiny minority'" *Bristol Post* 28 February 2017. Accessed March 2018. https://www.bristolpost.co.uk/news/bristol-news/prominent-tory-renaming-bristols-colston-4259.

Pettigrew, W. A. "Free to Enslave: Politics and the Escalation of Britain's Transatlantic Slave Trade, 1688-1714" *The William and Mary Quarterly,* Third Series, Vol. 64, No. 1, (2007): 3-38.

Pettigrew, W. A. *Freedom's Debt: The Royal African Company and the politics of the Atlantic Slave Trade, 1672-1752.* Chapel Hill: University of North Carolina, 2013.

Poole, S. "'Till our liberties be secure': popular sovereignty and public space in Bristol, 1780-1850" *Urban History,* 26, No. 1 (1999): 40-54.

Poole, S. and Rogers, N. *Bristol from Below: Law, Authority and Protest in a Georgian City.* Woodbridge: Boydell & Brewer, 2017.

Porter, R. "The Crispe Family and the African Trade in the Seventeenth Century." *The Journal of African History* 9, no. 1 (1968): 57-77.

Portman, D. "A business history of the Clifton Suspension Bridge." *Construction History* 18 (2002): 3-20.

Rediker, M. *The Slave Ship: A Human History.* London: John Murray, 2007.

Richardson, D. *The Bristol Slave Traders: A collective portrait.* Bristol: Bristol Branch of the Historical Association, 1985.

Richardson, D. *Bristol, Africa and the Eighteenth-Century Slave Trade to America Vol. 1 The Years of Expansion 1698-1729.* Bristol: The Bristol Record Society, 1986.

Richardson, D. *Bristol, Africa and the Eighteenth-Century Slave Trade to America Vol. 2 The Years of Ascendency 1730-1745*. Bristol: The Bristol Record Society, 1987.

Richardson, D. *Bristol, Africa and the Eighteenth-Century Slave Trade to America Vol. 3 The Years of Decline 1746-1769*. Bristol: The Bristol Record Society, 1991.

Richardson, D. *Bristol, Africa and the Eighteenth-Century Slave Trade to America Vol. 4 The Final Years 1770-1807*. Bristol: The Bristol Record Society, 1996.

Richardson, M. *The Maltreated and the Malcontents*. Bristol Radical Pamphleteer #37. Bristol: Bristol Radical History Group, 2016.

Robinson, D. *A Darker History of Bristol*. Bristol: Countryside Books, 2005. First published as *A Shocking History of Bristol*. London: Abson Books, 1973.

Rodgers, N. *Ireland, Slavery and Anti-Slavery: 1612-1865*. London: Palgrave Macmillan, 2007.

Rogan, J. *Bristol Cathedral: History & Architecture*. Stroud: Tempus, 2000.

Sacks, D. H. *The Widening Gate–Bristol and the Atlantic Economy, 1450-1700*. Berkley: University of California Press, 1991.

Saville, R. "Bristol shuns slave trade name" *The Telegraph* 21 April 2006.

Schama, S. *Simon Schama's Power of Art*. London: BBC Books, 2006.

Scott, W. R. "The Constitution and Finance of the Royal African Company of England from Its Foundation Till 1720." *The American Historical Review* 8, no. 2 (1903): 241-259.

Sedgwick, R. R. "Bristol" in *The History of Parliament: the House of Commons 1715-1754*. ed. Sedgwick, R. R. London: Boydell and Brewer, 1970. Accessed 2018. http://www.historyofparliamentonline.org/volume/1715-1754/constituencies/bristol

Sharp, G. *A Representation of the Injustice and Dangerous Tendency of Tolerating Slavery*. Cambridge: Cambridge University Press, 2014.

Simpson, W. and McNeill, J. *Nicotiana Brittanica: The Cotswolds' Illicit Tobacco Cultivation in the 17th Century*. Bristol Radical Pamphleteer #9. Bristol: Bristol Radical History Group, 2009.

Sloane, H. *A Voyage to the Islands Madera, Barbados, Nieves, S. Christophers and Jamaica with the Natural History of the Herbs and Trees, Four-footed Beasts, Fishes, Birds, Insects, Reptiles, Etc., of the Last of Those Islands... Illustrated with the Figures of the Things Describd... by Hans Sloane...* Vols. I and II. London: Benjamin Motte, 1707, 1725.

Sluiter, E. "New Light on the '20 and Odd Negroes' Arriving in Virginia, August, 1619," *William and Mary Quarterly*, 54 (1997): 396-98.

Smith, M. Q. *The Stained Glass of Bristol Cathedral*. Bristol: Redcliffe Press, 1983.

Stange, D. C. *British Unitarians against American Slavery 1833-1865* Cranbury, N. J. & London: Associated University Presses, 1998.

Stansfield, D. A. *Thomas Beddoes MD 1760–1808: chemist, physician, democrat*. Dordrecht: D. Reidel, 1984.

Steeds, M. *Cry Freedom, Cry Seven Stars: Thomas Clarkson In Bristol, 1787*. Bristol Radical Pamphleteer #1, 2nd edition. Bristol: Bristol Radical History Group, 2010.

Steen, M. *The Sun is My Undoing*. Collins: London, 1941.

Stone, G. F. *Bristol: As it was and as it is. A record of fifty years of progress*. Bristol: Walter Reid, 1909.

Stott, A. *Hannah More—The First Victorian*. New York: Oxford University Press, 2003.

Sturge, J. & Harvey, T. *The West Indies in 1837; Being the Journal of a Visit to Antigua, Montserrat Dominica, St. Lucia, Barbados, and Jamaica; undertaken for the purpose of ascertaining the actual condition of the negro population of those islands*. London: Hamilton, Adams & Co. 1838.

Taylor, B. 2004 "Martin [née Bullock], Emma (1811/12–1851), socialist and freethinker." *Oxford Dictionary of National Biography*.

Taylor, E. R. *If we must die: Shipboard insurrections in the era of the Atlantic slave trade* Baton Rouge: Louisiana State University Press, 2006.

Taylor, J. "Ancient Bristol—Historical Sketch" in *Bristol and its Environs: Historical, Descriptive e Scientific* London: Houlston, Bristol: J. Wright, 1875.

The City and County of Bristol the Capital of the West: The Official Handbook of the Corporation o

Bristol, Cheltenham and London: Ed. J. Burrow & Co., c.1962/3.

The Community of Saint Stephen's: Annual Report & Accounts 2016. Accessed March 2018. http://www.saint-stephens.com/pcc-annual-report

Thomas, H. *The Slave Trade: The Story of the Atlantic Slave Trade, 1440-1870.* London: Picador, 1997.

Thomas, P. D. G. "BRICKDALE, Matthew (1735-1831), of Clifton, Glos. and Taunton, Som." in *The History of Parliament: The House of Commons 1754-1790*, ed. L. Namier, J. Brooke, London: Boydell and Brewer, 1964. Accessed 2018. http://historyofparliamentonline.org/volume/1754-1790/member/brickdale-matthew-1735-1831

Told, S. *The Life of Silas Told Written by Himself With a Note to the Serious Reader by John Wesley*, 1786.

Tovey, S. G. *Colston, the Philanthropist: Memorials of his life and deeds.* Bristol: T. D. Taylor, 1863.

Townsend, T. *Bristol and Clifton Slave Trade Trail* (Wellington: Pixz, 2016).

Vaughn, A. *Isambard Kingdom Brunel; Engineering knight-errant*, London: John Murray (Publishers) Ltd. 1991.

Walvin, J. *A Short History of Slavery* London: Penguin Books, 2007.

Weare, G. E. *A Collectanea Relating to the Bristol Friars Minors (Gray Friars) and Their Convent: Together with a Concise History of the Dissolution of the Houses of the Four Orders of Mendicant Friars in Bristol.* Bristol: W. Bennett, 1893.

Wesley, J. *Thoughts upon Slavery.* London: R. Hawes, 1774.

Wilkins, E. "Graffiti attack revives Bristol slavery row." *The Times* 29 January 1998.

Wilkins, H. J. (*Some Chapters on the) Ecclesiastical History of Westbury-on-Trym.* Bristol: Arrowsmith, 1909.

Wilkins, H. J. *Edward Colston (1636-1721 A.D.), A Chronological Account of His Life and Work Together with an Account of the Colston Societies and Memorials in Bristol.* Bristol: Arrowsmith, 1920.

Wilkins, H. J. *Edward Colston (1636-1721 A.D.), Supplement to a Chronological Account of His Life and Work Together with an Account of the Colston Societies and Memorials in Bristol.* Bristol: Arrowsmith, 1925.

Williams, Mary E. *Civic Treasures of Bristol.* City Archivist 1984.

Wilson, D. C. *Lone Woman—The Story of Elizabeth Blackwell, The First Woman Doctor.* London: Hodder & Stoughton Ltd., 1970.

Wilson, E. G. *The Clarksons of Wisbech and the Abolition of the Slave Trade.* Wisbech: Wisbech Society, 1992.

Wordsworth, W. *To Toussaint L'Ouverture.* 1807. Retrieved from: https://blogs.brandeis.edu/revolutions/2014/04/14/to-toussaint-louverture-as-an-elegy/

Wright, M. *Elizabeth Blackwell of Bristol, the First Woman Doctor.* Bristol: Bristol Branch of the Historical Association, 1995.

Yarnspinner V. *Nottingham Rising.* Nottingham: Loaf on a Stick Press, 2014.

Yong, M. Cork, T. and Davies, N. "Colston Hall to be renamed for 2020 relaunch". *Bristol Post* 26 April 2017. Accessed March 2018. https://www.bristolpost.co.uk/news/bristol-news/colston-hall-renamed-2020-relaunch-36108

Yong, M. "Colston Hall name change was a 'moral decision' not a financial one, as bosses gear up for backlash". *Bristol Post* 27 April 2017. Accessed March 2018. https://www.bristolpost.co.uk/news/bristol-news/colston-hall-name-change-moral-37171.

Archives and libraries

Barbados Museum & Historical Society
Thomas Daniel & Co. in Liquidation Concession Ref. 972.981
Bristol Archives
Records of the Society of Merchant Venturers–Associated Clubs & Societies—West India Association—Administrative Ref. SMV/8/3/2-3
Records of All Saints' Church Lands Charity–Historical material–Edward Colston memoranda (1715-1716) Ref. 42198/6/1
Records of Mary Carpenter and the Red Lodge Reformatory–Mary Carpenter's Poetical Extract Book, March 1836 to July 1875 containing extracts by a number of prominent abolitionists and reformers Ref. 12693/20
Bristol Central Reference Library
Whitting, J. C. Report on Pill; Ships returning to Bristol after visiting Africa, and the imports they carried (1969) Ref. B27997.
The National Archives
The Royal African Company Trades for Commodities along the West African Coast [Transcript] (1672) CO 268/1.
Home Office: Domestic Correspondence, George III HO 42/19
Hoare & Co Bank Archive
Account of Colston, Edward Esq (1703-1724): Customer ledger/folio nos: 5/347, 6/91+315, 7/139+362, 8/384, 10/162, 11/359, 13/97, 14/241, 15/340, 16/320, 17/369, 18/289, 19/167, 20/206, F/294+314+369+418, Exors: G/23+110.

Newspapers, periodicals, newsletters and broadsheets

Colston's Chronicle (Newsletter of CGS)
Redcliffe & Temple School Newsletter
The Anti-Slavery Reporter
The Bath Chronicle
The Bristol Mercury
The Bristol (Evening) Post
The Bristolian
The Daily Mail
The Observer
The Poor Man's Guardian
The Spectator
The Sun
The Telegraph
The Times
The Voice
Workers World

Reports and documents

Brown, A. R. E. (Chair of Trustees, Colston Girls School) *Letter to Countering Colston* 19 September 2016.
Commemorating the abolition of the Slave Trade: Consortium Of Black Groups (COBG) Position Statement & Recommendations (2006)
Countering Colston: Minutes to Colston School Meeting, 17 December 2015.
Countering Colston: Minutes to Meeting between 'Colston Protestors' and representatives of Bristol Cathedral, Bristol Cathedral, 8 December 2015, 2.30pm.
HM Treasury Freedom of Information Act 2000: Slavery Abolition Act 1833 (FOI2018/00186) 31 January 2018.
Hoyle, D. (Dean of Bristol, Bristol Cathedral) *Letter to Countering Colston* 2 September 2016.
Perry, A. *Letter to parents.* Colston Girls School. 13 November 2015.
The Community of Saint Stephen's: Annual Report & Accounts 2016.

TV and videos

Britain's Forgotten Slave Owners James Van Der Pool (dir.) BBC July 2015
Public Enquiry "Bishop Michael Hill: Merchant Venturer Edward Colston profiting from slave trade is 'speculation'". Filmed [November 2014]. YouTube video, 04:25. Posted [November 2014] https://www.youtube.com/watch?v=tNHBdpvGYHc.

Websites

BBC History http://www.bbc.co.uk/history/
BBC News http://www.bbc.co.uk/news/
Bristol Past http://www.buildinghistory.org/bristol/
Bristol Radical History Group https://www.brh.org.uk/site/
British Tars: 1740-1790 https://www.britishtars.com/
Christ's Hospital School https://www.christs-hospital.org.uk/
Clifton Suspension Bridge https://www.cliftonbridge.org.uk/
Colston Research Society http://www.bristol.ac.uk/pace/committees/colston-research/
Companies House https://beta.companieshouse.gov.uk/
Countering Colston https://counteringcolston.wordpress.com/
Encyclopedia.com https://www.encyclopedia.com/
Encyclopedia Virginia http://www.EncyclopediaVirginia.org/
Grace's Guide to British Industrial History https://www.gracesguide.co.uk/
Legacies of British Slave-ownership https://www.ucl.ac.uk/lbs/
Living Easton http://www.cems.uwe.ac.uk/~rstephen/livingeaston/index.html
Map your Bristol https://www.mapyourbristol.org.uk/
MeasuringWorth https://www.measuringworth.com/
Nonesuch Expeditions http://www.nonesuchexpeditions.com/index.htm
Romantic Circles https://romantic-circles.org/
Slave Revolt in Jamaica, 1760-1761: A Cartographic Narrative http://revolt.axismaps.com/
Society for Promoting Christian Knowledge http://spckpublishing.co.uk/
The Abolition Project http://abolition.e2bn.org/slavery_40.html
The Bristolian https://thebristolian.net/
The History of Parliament http://www.historyofparliamentonline.org/
The Society of Merchant Venturers https://www.merchantventurers.com/
The Soufriere Foundation http://soufrierefoundation.org/
Trans-Atlantic Slave Trade Database http://www.slavevoyages.org/
Wikipedia: Mortlake https://en.wikipedia.org/wiki/Mortlake

Names Index

Places Index

General Index

417

Elizabeth Heyrick (1769-1831).